MW01052939

THE DISCIPLES

THE DISCIPLES
A Struggle for Reformation

D. DUANE CUMMINS

CHALICE
PRESS

ST. LOUIS, MISSOURI

Copyright © 2009 by D. Duane Cummins

All rights reserved. For permission to reuse content, please contact Copyright Clearance Center, 222 Rosewood Drive, Danvers, MA 01923, (978) 750-8400, www.copyright.com.

Bible quotations, unless otherwise noted, are from the *New Revised Standard Version Bible,* copyright 1989, Division of Christian Education of the National Council of the Churches of Christ in the United States of America. Used by permission. All rights reserved.

Those quotations marked RSV are from the *Revised Standard Version of the Bible,* copyright 1952, [2nd edition, 1971] by the Division of Christian Education of the National Council of the Churches of Christ in the United States of America. Used by permission. All rights reserved.

Cover and interior design: Elizabeth Wright

Visit Chalice Press on the World Wide Web at
www.chalicepress.com

10 9 8 7 6 5 4 3 2 1   09 10 11 12 13 14

Library of Congress Cataloging–in–Publication Data

Cummins, D. Duane.

The Disciples : a struggle for reformation / by D. Duane Cummins.

   p. cm.

Includes bibliographical references (p.   ) and index.

ISBN 978-0-8272-0637-3 – ISBN 978-0-8272-0636-6 (leather ultra ed.)

1. Christian Church (Disciples of Christ)–History. I. Title.

BX7315.C86 2009

286.6'3–dc22   2009017915

Printed in the United States of America

Contents

Acknowledgments

The research and writing of this history was made possible through financial support from the Disciples of Christ Historical Society, for which I will remain eternally grateful. Glenn Carson, president of the historical society, has been especially gracious and helpful in bringing this project to fruition.

Particular appreciation must also be expressed to the Christian Board of Publication, the editing staff who gave the manuscript its final editorial review, and to president and publisher Russ White for his professional assistance in the publication of this work. The vision of CBP for the educational value of such a book for Disciples is genuinely and warmly acknowledged.

The first five chapters of this volume are drawn from a massive quantity of secondary sources. To the authors of those volumes I owe a huge debt of gratitude. Their individual works, carefully researched and thoughtfully written, provided an extraordinarily rich collection of resources from which those five chapters emerged and on which they were built. Because most histories of the Disciples end at the time of restructure, secondary literature is sparse on the forty-year period from 1968 to 2008. Most of the research for the final three chapters, out of necessity, was conducted through primary sources and from personal interviews. Major assistance with this research came from the Disciples of Christ Historical Society, repository for most of the primary sources. Assistance was also provided by the Campbell Archives at Bethany College and its exceptionally capable archivist, Jeanne Cobb, for whom I express warm appreciation. A special word of gratitude is also expressed to Howard E. Bowers, editor of the Year Book and Directory in Indianapolis, for his prompt and thorough assistance with the statistical research that appears throughout this volume. Credit for photographs in this volume must be given to Ian S. Davidson and his excellent personal Campbell Heritage collection, the Campbell Archives at Bethany College, the photographic archives of the Disciples of Christ Historical Society, and the Communications office archives of the Disciples general offices in Indianapolis.

The staff of the historical society—Sara Harwell, vice president; Mac Ice, director of public services; Sharmon Hartson and Elaine Philpott, curators; Marlene Patterson, operations manager; and Jean Arnold in financial services—were extremely helpful, understanding, and encouraging in locating materials and supporting the work and purpose of this writing. My abiding appreciation to them is hereby sincerely and gratefully acknowledged.

Many persons generously consented to be interviewed for this work, including the following general ministers and presidents: Sharon Watkins, Richard Hamm, John Humbert, Kenneth Teegarden, and Dale Fiers–the latter two for their recent biographies. The insights provided by all of them were absolutely invaluable.

I am especially grateful to a group of scholars and friends who read select portions and in some cases all of the manuscript prior to its completion, helping me avoid historical errors and contributing exceptionally helpful emendations. These include Huberto Pimentel, David Vargas, Geunhee Yu, and Timothy James, who kindly reviewed the sections on cultural expressions; Robert Welsh, who reviewed the section on Christian unity; and Newell Williams, Lester McAllister, Robert Friedly, Peter Morgan, Larry Steinmetz, Pablo Jiménez, and Glenn Carson, who thoroughly and thoughtfully read the entire manuscript and graciously shared sage advice– all of which strengthened the work. My gratitude for their professionalism runs exceedingly deep. Any errors in the manuscript are totally my own.

Most especially, I express abiding love and affectionate appreciation to my wife Suzi for her patience, interest, and sustaining support for this work. Without her warm companionship, personal charm, and cheerful spirit, this work would likely never have been started, much less completed.

D. Duane Cummins
November 22, 2008

Preface

*Whenever the history of this effort at reformation shall have been
faithfully written, it will appear, we think, bright as the sun, that our
career has been marked with a spirit of forbearance, moderation, a
love for union, with an unequivocal desire for preserving the integrity,
harmony and cooperation of all those who teach one Lord, one faith one
immersion.*

ALEXANDER CAMPBELL, 1840[1]

A small gathering of people, about sixty or seventy, from various
denominations assembled under an oak near the Lower Buffalo in the
far western reaches of Virginia. Around the Lord's table, spread there
in the woods, the little circle of neighbors received the loaf and the cup,
covenanting with each other to follow the truth wherever it might lead.
An unknown twenty-three-year-old immigrant preacher named Alexander
Campbell, not yet ordained and just entering his third month of marriage,
delivered the sermon. They called themselves Brush Run, a congregation
barely nine months removed from the day of its founding.

The young preacher chose for his text the words of the old Arab prophet
Bildad in Job 8:7: *Though your beginning was small, your latter days will be very
great.*[2] He opened his sermon with the words:

> We commence our career as a church under the banner of "The
> Bible, the whole bible, and nothing but the Bible," as the standard
> of our religious faith and practice… Our inferences and opinions
> are our own… Christians are the sons of liberty–the Lord's free
> men. The right to choose and to refuse the opinions of men is the
> essence of liberty… We are a weak band, a humble beginning; but
> so much the better. So were they of Galilee…and such were the
> founders of this great nation.[3]

From the perspective of long years, Alexander Campbell later recalled
raising two questions in his long-ago sermon: *Who are we? For what are we
here convened?*[4]

Those two questions were destined to beleaguer the tiny community
of faith congregated on that distant summer day; two questions destined to
torment their leaders, their progeny, and several generations of historians
who attempted to tell the story of their journey through the next two
hundred years. Was this small, obscure band of Christians a movement, a
sect, a church, a cult, a society, an association, or a denomination? Were

they reformers, restorationists, responsible pilgrims, wayfaring strangers, or simply a rebellious, dissenting fringe? They would be known by all of those names and more; and their identity would be the subject of endless debate, ultimately becoming acrimonious.[5]

What terms did the founders use to define their movement? Barton Stone, who led his Kentucky Christians into union with Campbell's Disciples in 1832, thereby creating the Stone-Campbell Movement, used the phrase "Reformation Movement" in his *History of the Christian Church in the West,* written in 1827. He did not portray his work as "restoration," nor did he ever use the term "Restoration Movement." He affirmed that he had no intention of starting another "church," asserting that when he and his colleagues left the synod in Kentucky, they "withdrew from the judicatories with which we stood connected, and *not* from the church." Stone considered his ministry a reformation *within* the church. In his autobiography, published twenty years later, he wrote of the brief life of the Springfield Presbytery, "From this period I date the commencement of that *reformation* which has progressed to this day." Stone further affirmed that it was a *reformation* for Christian unity.[6]

When Thomas Campbell authored the *Declaration and Address* in 1809, he declared, "This society, by no means considers itself a church, nor does it at all assume to itself the powers peculiar to such; members do not consider themselves a church—but voluntary advocates for church *reformation.*" He proclaimed in the *Declaration and Address,* "The church of Christ upon earth is essentially, intentionally and constitutionally one," placing unmistakable emphasis upon "unity," *not* on restoration. His son, Alexander Campbell—the pivotal leader of the Movement—authored numerous articles for the *Christian Baptist* and *The Millennial Harbinger* on the subject of *reformation.* Eva Jean Wrather noted, "While others sidestepped the problem of unity, Campbell believed no movement could be vital that did not have as its basic motive union of all Christians—one body visible and invisible." In her view, the Movement was a reformation focused on Christian unity. Campbell almost always called his work a reformation based upon *Catholic principles.* By using the term "catholic," he meant all-embracing, all-inclusive, all-encompassing, and broad-based. His work was predicated on catholic principles *within* the church, where he pled for unity on catholic grounds, but not as a separate Church. In an 1835 article on "Reformation and Restoration," Campbell made the terms mean the same thing. The New Testament church, Campbell believed, offered a means of reforming the church toward union on a common ground.[7]

Among the several professional historians who have spoken to this question is Leroy Garrett in his 1994 revised edition of *The Stone-Campbell Movement*—a title deliberately chosen to counter the frequent use of "reformation" or "restoration" (although he added the subtitle *The Story of the American Restoration Movement*). When either the term "reformation" or "restoration" appears in the title of a Disciples history book, it normally discloses the author's broad interpretation of the Movement: *Reformation*–emphasizing inclusiveness, liberty, unity, and toleration; *Restoration*–emphasizing exclusiveness, restrictions, independence, and disquisitions over minutiae of the "ancient order." J. H. Garrison, for example, entitled his 1901 essay collection on Disciples history *The Reformation of the Nineteenth Century*. He clearly interpreted the Movement as a reformation.[8]

Winfred E. Garrison and Alfred DeGroot, who wrote their history of the Disciples in 1945, generally avoided use of either term, preferring instead to call their work *The Disciples of Christ: A History*. Regarding the terms "reformation" or "restoration" Garrison and DeGroot reflected Campbell's view:

> All churches claim to perpetuate what is essential in the primitive church, and all reformers claim to restore it. There has never been any other formula of reformation. The distinction sometimes made between "reformation" and "restoration" has no historical foundation.

Instead of presenting the Movement as either a reform or restoration,. Garrison (1874–1969), holder of the first Ph.D. ever awarded in church history in the United States, and nearly four decades after his death still respected as the dean of all Disciples historians, analyzed the fundamental tension between liberty and union within the Movement along with the social process of revising and adapting its traditions to changing environments. Lester McAllister and William E. Tucker also avoided use of "reformation" or "restoration" in the title of their 1975 history, choosing instead *Journey in Faith*. In telling the Movement's story, the terms "reform" and "restoration" were used sparingly by McAllister and Tucker.[9]

All authors, however, used the term "movement," defined by Robert Fife as "a community of understanding and concern that exists and serves *within* the Church, and for its edification." Fife noted that persons are not baptized into a movement, nor do they commune as members of a movement. A movement, he says, "defines its distinctiveness in terms other than the church, and yet in a way that relates to a church." Using Fife's definition, Leroy Garrett contended the early pioneers "saw their efforts as a *movement within the church at large*."[10]

Clark Gilpin noted the writing of Disciples history by professional historians did not begin until the early twentieth century. During the mid-to-late-nineteenth century scholarly ministers and editors–including Robert Richardson, William T. Moore, and James H. Garrison–wrote the histories. Among those early writers, William T. Moore provided the first comprehensive history of Disciples, written to commemorate the centennial of *The Declaration and Address* in 1909. Like other authors, he called it a *movement* rather than a *church* or a *denomination*. The aim of the Movement, he wrote, was to reform all denominations through a plea for Christian union. Yet, he inserted on the title page, "This is an account of an effort to *restore*," and then routinely referred to the Disciples as a "restoration movement" throughout his narrative.[11]

James Deforest Murch titled his 1962 publication *Christians Only: A History of the Restoration Movement,* the orthodox angle of vision for nearly all Churches of Christ and Christian Churches–Churches of Christ historians, including Earl West, Homer Hailey, Henry Webb, and James B. North. The title used by Richard Hughes in his 1990 history, *Reviving the Ancient Faith,* offers a slightly more subtle characterization, although the subject heading "Restoration Ideal" occupied the largest space in the index. Hughes claimed denominational histories of the Movement are biased, treating the Churches of Christ as a footnote, a splinter, a stepchild, or a spin-off of the Disciples. Hughes believed the reverse was actually true because, in his opinion, the Churches of Christ were the ones who remained true to the founding principle of restoration.[12]

Robert Richardson, an eyewitness to many of the most important moments in the story as well as a personal friend to several Disciples founders, authored the baseline studies *Memoirs of Alexander Campbell* and *The Principles and Objects of the Reformation, urged by A. Campbell* as well as a long series of articles in *The Millennial Harbinger* entitled "The Reformation." He repeatedly used phrases such as, "the cause of *reformation*," "the *reformatory* movement," "the story of *reformation*," and "scattering the seeds of *reformation* in the West." Richardson used the term "reformation" almost exclusively in the *Memoirs,* while the term "restoration" rarely appears. Walter Scott, on the other hand, was the founding father most closely associated with restoration of the ancient gospel. Yet, even he referred to Alexander Campbell as the leader of the "famous *reformation.*"[13]

Because of the catholic principles driving their ideal of Christian unity, the Campbells and Stone resented the Movement being labeled a sect or sectarian, regarding itself as the only true body of Christ possessing exclusive truth. Nor did they consider themselves a separate denomination, but rather merely a segment of the universal body of Christ. They were not a sect, not a church, not a cult, not a denomination, not wayfaring dissenters. This telling of the story will refer to the founders as responsible pilgrims, early pioneers of an intended *reformation movement within the church,* advocating the principles of liberty, toleration, and Christian unity, while taking the Bible as their only rule of faith and seeking unity upon that common ground. It was an intended *reformation* within the church, born of the love of union. Their journey of reform would be arduous and long. In reply to frequent suggestions that he write a history of the "Reformation," Alexander Campbell responded in 1833:

> Let us first see a reformation in fact–a reformation in sentiment, in practice–a reformation in faith and manners, before we talk of

writing a history of it... All that could now be written, would be rather the history of *a struggle for reformation.*[14]

One hundred fifty years later, descendants of those founding pilgrims on the distant edge of the American nation had become a church, a denomination of international stature, the Christian Church (Disciples of Christ), known in a larger context as part of the Stone-Campbell Movement. Their beginning was humble; their struggle continuous; but their latter days would contain greatness. This is their story—a storyline of struggle covering more than two centuries. It is an unfinished story, and therefore visible to us in limited perspective, because it cannot be seen as a whole. We do not know how the struggle will end nor are we able to see the present in its fullness because of our own fleeting roles in the story. But from the vantage point of our limited perspective, the part of the story we do know can be told.

In this particular telling the beginning is set in the eighteenth-century Enlightenment and the First Great Awakening to familiarize the reader with the contours of the larger setting. The middle period of the Disciples struggle for reformation is presented in the sociocultural context of the nineteenth-century Second and Third Great Awakenings, the age of Romanticism, and Jacksonian Democracy, from which the Disciples Reformation Movement is inseparable, with a lesser emphasis on the setting of the Westward Movement of the Frontier so ably provided by W. E. Garrison in his several comprehensive Disciples histories. And the story of the twentieth century is written around the central feature—or historical hinge—"restructure," beginning with the decades of unfolding events leading to restructure, and concluding with the emerging effects of restructure during the decades that followed.

Restructure deliberately receives detailed treatment in this narrative because it has not been previously integrated into or made an integral part of the larger picture in the writing of Disciples' comprehensive histories; and there has not been a significant educational effort to assist the membership in understanding the full meaning of *restructure, church,* and *covenant.* Some do *not* understand the meaning of those terms. Many *do* understand, intellectually, but have neither accepted nor internalized them. Hence, I offer a conscious effort in this writing to present the meaning of restructure, with the hope of revitalizing our unique "community in covenant" through the talents, vision, and creative perspective of a New Age generation of readers as they continue the "struggle for reformation" in the new millennium—a struggle born of a love for Christian unity.

CHAPTER I

Roots

European Background

We are grateful to all who have labored in the cause of the emancipation of the human mind from the shackles of kingcraft and priest-craft… We are mindful of our immediate benefactors, [and] we are not to forget the praises due to those who have long since died and whose victories were more efficient and salutary…than those achieved by the sword or the cannon.

ALEXANDER CAMPBELL
Debate with Robert Owen, 1829[1]

The Disciples story offers several points from which to begin the telling. One option is antiquity, the age of the New Testament in Palestine when the scriptures say we were "first called Christians at Antioch" (Acts 8:26). Others who tell the story begin with the forerunners of the Protestant Reformation in the twelfth to fifteenth centuries: Peter Waldo (1140–1218), John Wycliffe (1330–1384) and Jan Hus (1370–1415). These anti-ecclesiastical agitators challenged the authority of the church, sought to restore Christianity to a perceived pristine simplicity, and struggled for the individual right to appeal to scripture they held to be superior to dogma. These reformers were hanged, burned, or branded heretics. This Medieval period of Christian history, maintained Ronald Osborn, is often treated, inaccurately, as an "irrelevant appendix." He believed that we have allowed Disciples history to become much too entwined with the Reformation and the Enlightenment.

More often, Disciples historians have chosen the sixteenth century Protestant Reformation as the point of beginning. The Reformation was a complex of many separate independent movements against Medieval Catholicism led by extraordinarily talented religious figures such as Martin Luther (1483–1546), Ulrich Zwingli (1484–1531), John Calvin (1509–1564), and John Knox (1514–1572), all of whom believed unyieldingly in the freedom of individual conscience. As did their forerunners, they revolted against dogmas and corrupt clergy. They sought to free the church from priestly bondage and to return the church to its early state, as well as restore the primitive gospel. They advocated the priesthood of all believers, scripture as superior to churchly tradition, and faith over works. It was the intent of these Protestant leaders to reform the church, not splinter it, yet a fractured Christendom resulted.[2]

Still others begin the story with religious reform movements in Colonial and Revolutionary North America; while some root the story in a few religious philosophers whose ideas fashioned the Disciples theological heritage. The history of Disciples has many potential points from which to begin the telling: classical history, the late Middle Ages, the Reformation, Colonial North America, or with a few renowned theologians.

The point of beginning for *this* history will be the eighteenth-century European Enlightenment and Religious Awakening. Choosing this point of beginning does not devalue the seventeen centuries of Christian history preceding the Enlightenment and Awakening; it builds upon them. It is a point in time that establishes historical bearings for the story. The four primary founders of the Christian Church (Disciples of Christ)–Thomas Campbell (b. 1763), Barton Stone (b. 1772), Alexander Campbell (b. 1788), and Walter Scott (b. 1796)–and four secondary founders–James O'Kelly (b. 1735), Elias Smith (b. 1769), Rice Haggard (b. 1769), and Abner Jones (b. 1772)–were all born during the eighteenth-century European Enlightenment that spanned the period from the English Revolution in 1688 to the French Revolution in 1789–94, and the great Religious Awakening dating from the 1730s to the 1780s. Three of the founders were born in Northern Ireland, one in Scotland, the remainder in colonial North America. All were children of the Enlightenment and the Awakening–captives and descendants of the ideas championed by both movements.

One of the most decisive shifts in the history of ideas in modern times occurred during this era. Historian Jay Winik suggested, "The final area of exploration and settlement in the eighteenth century was not geographic… but philosophical and political." Traditional structures of authority, scientific thought, and belief were refuted. The Enlightenment introduced a powerful set of ideas–*equality, democracy, and universality.* The weight of those ideas effectively challenged and ultimately toppled the conventional rationale for monarchy, aristocracy, slavery, ecclesial authority, dominance of man over woman, and theology's control of education and learning. The Religious

Awakening, countering the rationalist Enlightenment, reintroduced the concepts of *scriptural revelation, spiritual experience, and divine inspiration.* Founders of the Disciples Movement discovered the dynamic and substance of their ideas rooted in the inevitable conjunction of these two large-scale historical forces–Enlightenment and Religious Awakening, intellect and emotion, head and heart. Garry Wills contended the struggle between these forces–necessary, inescapable, unending–is the history of Christianity in the United States.

European civilization in the eighteenth century is often called the "Age of Reason," the era of "Rationalism." Immanuel Kant (1724–1804), author of the famed *Critique on Pure Reason* (1781), said of the Enlightenment, "It was Humankinds' final coming of age," an undermining of the Medieval worldview, an emancipation of human consciousness through knowledge, education, and science from the shackles of ignorance, superstition, and theological dogma. It was an intellectual liberation. The great thinkers of this age, known internationally as *philosophes,* came from all the major nations of Europe: from Scandinavia to Sicily; from Spain to Russia. John Locke, Isaac Newton, Francois Voltaire, Henri Rousseau, David Hume, Edward Gibbon, Denis Diderot, Charles Louis Montesquieu, Immanuel Kant, Adam Smith, and Benjamin Franklin are but a small representative fraction of an enormous galaxy. They generated an immense store of new knowledge about government, society and human nature.

Particular mention should be made of John Locke (1632–1704) because of his enduring influence upon Disciples founders. Locke, a faithful Anglican and graduate of Oxford, was a towering philosopher of the Enlightenment who spoke in the characteristic voice of the eighteenth century: "a belief in reason happily espoused to common sense." He authored several masterpieces: on religious liberty,–*Letter concerning Toleration,* 1689; on political liberty,–*Second Treatise of Government,* 1689; and on intellectual liberty,–*An Essay Concerning Human Understanding,* 1689, his greatest intellectual achievement. Thomas Campbell, who studied Locke during his student years at the University of Glasgow, introduced Locke's writings to his son, Alexander, when he reached the age of sixteen. Alexander found in Locke his surest touchstone, the philosophical argument for those ideas of religious liberty with which he would later challenge religious leadership in America. The steady theme of Locke's works was the value and freedom of the individual. He is credited with laying the foundation for Western democracy. Locke argued that no one has the right to impose belief upon another; and he was among the first to call for religious toleration, to define the church as a voluntary society, and to claim that faith was an intellectual act. In later years, Thomas Campbell wrote the *Declaration and Address,* a document owing a heavy debt to John Locke. Alexander Campbell called Locke "The Christian Philosopher," and included him among his personal trinity of intellectual heroes–Locke, Newton, and Bacon. Some claimed that traveling evangelists in nineteenth-century America, including Walter Scott, carried three publications in their saddlebags–the Bible, a hymnal, and Locke's *Second Treatise of Government*. One Disciples historian remarked, "John Locke is to classic Disciple theology as Aristotle is to Thomas Aquinas."[3]

The *philosophes* developed a body of progressive and liberal ideas with the objective of analyzing and changing the world. These ideas included a scientific understanding of man as a social being; cosmopolitanism (placing the interests of humankind above country); rights for women; freedom of thought and toleration; growth in humanitarian sentiment; and the idea that every person possessed free will, as contrasted with being thought of as a programmed machine. Isaiah Berlin, widely respected as one of the leading liberal philosophers of the twentieth century, observed: "The eighteenth century is perhaps the last period in the history of Western Europe when human omniscience [all-knowing, all-wise] was thought to be an attainable goal." And the Enlightenment historian, Peter Gay, described the century as a time that saw a "recovery of nerve," humanity regaining a sense of trust in its own power.[4]

While the *philosophes* disagreed with each other on many things, they were all in accord on the principle of individual freedom and liberty. Voltaire–poet, dramatist, essayist, historian, novelist, and philosopher known for his power of ridicule and as an unsparing enemy of institutional Christianity–was the most famous individual of the century. It is said he accomplished for the human mind what Newton accomplished for nature. He was a relentless advocate for human rights and an uncompromising critic of religious intolerance and persecution. Will Durant once wrote, "When we cease to honor Voltaire we shall be unworthy of freedom"; and the Danish scholar, Georg Brandes, added, "Voltaire summarizes a century." It is both noteworthy and ironic that a few decades after Voltaire's 1794 death, Alexander Campbell, a Christian scholar, would find himself characterized as "the Voltaire of the Ohio Valley." Alexander Campbell scorned the comparison, yet Eva Jean Wrather wrote, "The philosopher of Ferny and the theologian on the Buffaloe were both children of the Enlightenment. Voltaire writing for the court of Louis XV annihilated with a keen thrust of the rapier. Campbell writing for the American Frontier, laid about him with the broad sword. Both weapons were effective."[5]

Prime targets of Enlightenment intellectuals were the church and theology. One of their chief objectives was to emancipate people from the tyranny of the Church. Voltaire, especially critical of priests, constantly railed against them and the Pope. Writing about the wars of religion, the burning of heretics, and the execution of witches, he claimed organized Christianity was a fraud. Edward Gibbon, who during those same years authored the *Decline and Fall of the Roman Empire,* maintained Christianity and barbarians destroyed civilization, ushering in a period of darkness. As for religion in the Roman Empire, Gibbon added, "The people believed it true; the philosophers thought it false; the rulers knew it was useful." In their views of Christianity, Voltaire and Gibbon were typical of many Enlightenment leaders.[6]

The age is now viewed as a great cultural and religious divide. With the Enlightenment came the demise of magic, astrology, the occult, and waning belief in literal heaven and hell. In their place came the sciences: the natural science of Newton, the social science of Voltaire, the political science of David Hume, and the economic science of Adam Smith–to name only a few. All were aimed at a scientific understanding of human behavior. It has been written, "The pervasive and continuing conflict between religion and science…became a living drama in the eighteenth century, which has resulted in the secularism of our times." The credibility of religion was challenged by these sciences. Educated classes in Europe and America lost faith in the theology that had guided Western thought for fifteen centuries; and the church began to lose control over schools, universities, and learning in general, a fact characterized by cultural historians as "the virtual end of ecclesiastical control of intellectual life." For 1500 years the clergy had commanded the means of disseminating information–churches, pulpits, universities, and schools. But the Enlightenment launched a secularization of European thought, producing a secular intelligentsia powerful enough to challenge the clergy. Religion began to lose the support of learning and science. One of the most radical features of the Enlightenment was the break from a biblical framework for understanding humankind and society, always rooted in theology and preached from the pulpit. The Enlightenment ushered onto the world stage urban, industrial societies, driven by scientific advancement. It changed the way people thought, the way cultures worked. Isaiah Berlin captured this change by quoting a line of poetry from Alexander Pope:

> Nature and Nature's Laws lay hid in Night:
> God said, Let Newton be! And all was Light.[7]

Religious low tide is almost always followed by a wave of renewal. During the early eighteenth century, both the British Empire and Colonial North America witnessed a serious religious decline. The rationalist Enlightenment attack on Christianity coupled with English industrial development had created what some called a spiritual wasteland. It was said that fewer than six members of the House of Commons in England attended church. Some Anglican clergy, smitten by the new rationalism and finding their inspiration in science, tended to ignore the traditional foundation of Christian faith: scriptural revelation and spiritual experience. Moreover, industrial growth created population centers at a rate faster than the established church was staffing parishes. Churches also ignored the common people: the young, the poor, town workers, tradesmen, artisans, and the uneducated—who were expected to defer to learned authorities. But religion began to contest these conditions by using evangelical revivals to generate a popular spiritual renewal.[8]

Defenders of Christianity appeared during the fourth decade of the eighteenth century and beyond, devoting themselves to the rehabilitation of Christian faith and life. Among them were the brothers Wesley, John (1703–1791) and Charles (1707–1788), along with George Whitefield (1714–1770). In 1729, the Wesleys, later joined by Whitefield and twelve of their classmates at Oxford, founded a movement within the Anglican Church. Their detractors called them "Methodists" because of their commitment to "practice Christianity with methodical thoroughness." They spoke to the emotions of believers, emphasizing the process of conversion, thereby giving sinners eternal salvation.

John Wesley, son, grandson, and great-grandson of Anglican ministers, believed the God of rationalists was cold and distant. In his view, true religion went beyond the reach of rationalism, seeking direct contact with the Holy Spirit. He believed in divine inspiration, supernatural mysteries, witchcraft, ghosts, demons, angels, miracles (especially healing), and heartfelt worship. Wesley appealed to the emotions of fear and hope, rather than reason. People, it was claimed, were moved to hysteria when they heard his sermons as he traveled through England and Wales. He trained many obscure, unordained, itinerant lay preachers of modest learning, without fixed parishes or pulpits, to carry the message of the Gospel to the working classes across England, Scotland, Wales, and Ireland, preparing them for the revivalist visits of Wesley and Whitefield. Being of the same social class as their listeners and using common speech, the lay preachers were quite successful. Wesley traveled 4,000 miles per year for forty years by horseback, coach, boat, and afoot to the far corners of England, preaching in churchyards, inns, streets, parks, fields, ships, coaches, and prisons. The great success of Methodism was in converting the poor with a message that was evangelical, a counterattack on nationalism.[9]

In 1736, John and his brother Charles sailed to North America, and to the southern colony of Georgia, where they began to remake the evangelical revival into an inter-colonial phenomenon. John preached in Savannah while Charles ministered on St. Simons Island. This itinerant venture met opposition. Following multiple appearances before local grand juries, the Wesleys left Georgia in 1738.

The year they departed, George Whitefield arrived, the first of his seven voyages to the colonies. Son of a Gloucester innkeeper and graduate of Oxford where he experienced a personal religious awakening, he was at odds with the dominant rationalism of the Church of England and not pleased with the ministerial assignments the church was giving him. He decided to defy the tightly organized Anglican parish system and preach directly to the lay masses, a frontal challenge to the authority of the priests.

By going straight to the people, Whitefield snubbed established authority, hierarchy, and social tradition. He began by preaching to coal miners in an open field near Bristol, England. An accomplished orator, he, like Wesley, appealed to the people's fears and hopes. Wherever he spoke, large crowds gathered. Also like the Wesleys, he made England, Scotland, Wales, Ireland, and America his parish, speaking in all manner of locations. His preaching stimulated the eighteenth-century Protestant revival in both England and America.[10]

Whitefield's 1738 trip to Georgia ignited the inter-colonial phase of the Great Awakening. His raw charismatic preaching focused on sin, the terror of hell, and the irresistability of grace. When preaching, he ranted and raved, made dramatic gestures and danced around the pulpit. The following year he returned to America, landing in Philadelphia and, after a month of preaching there, worked his way south to Savannah. Word of his success reached Jonathan Edwards in Northampton, Massachusetts, who, upon learning that the evangelist was planning a visit to Boston in 1740, invited him to Northampton. Whitfield, who spoke in seven colonies during his 1740 tour and addressed at least half the population in those colonies, accepted the invitation. He was a shrewd entrepreneur, a master promoter, the first to apply modern commercial techniques to religious purposes, using advanced publicity to build his celebrity, and employing networks of correspondents to report the news of his successes in handbills and newspapers. Whitefield was a case study in the commercialization of religion. In September, he arrived in Boston, where he preached for four weeks–normally for forty hours per week, plus three sermons on Sunday, to reportedly massive crowds before traveling on to Northampton. There he was warmly received, and a mutual admiration developed between him and the entire Edwards family. After Northampton, he traveled north to Maine and from there to points south. Although New England Anglican churches closed their doors to him, Whitefield rode 800 miles in 73 days and preached 130 sermons. His seven voyages to America, covering the seaboard from Maine to Georgia over a period of three decades, changed the American colonies. George Marsden describes him as the first American "star," providing the American colonies with their first inter-colonial cultural event. It spawned the first vague outline of a common American cultural identity. Some suggest that Whitefield's brand of evangelical religion also helped inspire a democratic, social, and political ideology.[11]

However, Jonathan Edwards was the most important religious figure in the history of New England–some say, in the history of America. A graduate of Yale, an orthodox Calvinist, and a rigorous intellectual authoritarian, he was also an extremely caring person of immense integrity. He followed his grandfather, Solomon Stoddard–the "Pope of New England"–as the pastor of Northampton in 1729. Perry Miller, the historian of Puritanism, treated Edwards, who was thoroughly immersed in Locke and Newton, as an Enlightenment thinker. Edwards embraced the use of reason as an expression of faith. "The real life of Jonathan Edwards," said Miller, "was the life of his mind." But more recent historians place him in the theological world of the evangelical revival. In fact, he was equally a man of the Enlightenment *and* the Awakening. Edwards, more than Whitefield, it is claimed, gave the eighteenth-century religious revival its theology. In his Northampton congregation, Edwards was preaching a series of sermons on justification by faith when he noticed an emotional change in his parishioners that he interpreted as a "religious rapture," a sign of the approaching millennium. He recorded the experience in a 1737 publication, *A Faithful Narration of the Surprising Work of God in the Conversion of Many Hundred Souls in Northampton.* Edwards' work was immediately reprinted in London and Edinburgh, where it became both a sensation and an instant classic, the standard for judging other similar events on both sides of the Atlantic. John Wesley read it in 1738 while walking from London to Oxford and adopted it as the template for his work. Whitefield read Edwards' book when he first arrived in Savannah in 1738. It was Edwards who sparked the religious awakening in New England in 1734, three years prior to Wesley's arrival in Georgia, and four years before Whitefield arrived. And it was Edwards's writing that inspired both Wesley and Whitefield to careers as itinerant evangelists.[12]

Tragedy struck at the peak of the Northampton religious zeal in 1735 when Edwards' uncle, Joseph Hawley, a respected and wealthy Northampton merchant, committed suicide as result of psychological despair over Edwards' relentless exhortations on sin and hell. Something of a suicide craze followed in the community, and the people's confidence in their new spirituality quickly cooled. Not a single addition came into the congregation for four years. Then George Whitefield arrived and religious enthusiasm was once again rekindled in Northampton—so much so that Edwards, after Whitefield's departure, delivered a series of sermons warning the congregation not to be deceived by spiritual excesses and enthusiasms. Although he deplored its excesses, he continued to support the Awakening. Edwards correctly saw himself as part of an international Reformed Evangelical Movement, and he is considered pivotal to the emergence of international evangelicalism in the eighteenth century. He inaugurated the idea of revival that became the pattern for evangelism for the next two centuries, and his theological thought is held to be the most enduring result of the eighteenth–century religious revival.

Edwards lived at the scene of conflict among three civilizations—the British Protestant, the French Roman Catholic, and the Native American—each fiercely struggling to control North America. It has been said the Spanish came to the Americas for "gold, God, and glory," the French for "fish, fur, and faith," and the English for "land, land, and land." It has also been written that Spanish civilization *crushed* the Indian; French civilization *embraced and cherished* the Indian; while English civilization *scorned and neglected* the Indian. Edwards' biographers noted that he gave much of his time and writing to concerns about Roman Catholicism and the Indians, their respective places in God's plans, and their places in the context of the history of his time. Evangelists expended much energy in the 1740s attempting to convert the Narragansett, the Mohegan, and the Pequot. After leaving Northampton and before becoming president of Princeton, Edwards spent nearly a decade as a missionary teaching among the Indians near Stockbridge in western Massachusetts. There, in the quiet reaches of the wilderness, he wrote three of his greatest works—*The Nature of True Virtue, Original Sin,* and *Freedom of the Will.* It is claimed that passages from these works on the beauty of holiness are the finest in American literature.[13]

For many decades, historians have referred to the religious phenomena of the eighteenth century as "The Great Awakening." Certain modern scholarship questions the use of this term, pointing out that instead of one Great Awakening sweeping through the colonies, there were many heterogeneous, widely scattered local awakenings spread over thirty years. There is a huge gap between what actually occurred at the meetings and how they were reported and interpreted. The correspondents and promoters who gave accounts of the events tended to enhance their descriptions of the spiritual enthusiasms, the numbers of converts, and the attendance at the revivals in order to rebut the threat posed by religion grounded in reason. Historian Frank Lambert claims the concept of a "Great Awakening" is an invention of eighteenth-century revivalist clergy, but an invention that was very effective. The actual term, "Great Awakening," was not used for another one hundred years. Passions ran strong both for and against the eighteenth-century revivals. Those who favored the revivals were called "New Lights." Those who opposed were "Old Lights." Even Edwards described it as a cultural war between rationalists and evangelicals—revivalists versus anti-revivalists. The revivalists and itinerant ministers, such as George Whitefield and the many untrained lay ministers (often called obnoxious and mindless troublemakers), preaching where they had not been invited, alarmed and alienated many. They left in their wake angry ministers, divided congregations, divided towns, and sharpened sectarian antagonisms. Lay itinerants planted many new congregations, founded new sects, and brought people into the church, and thereby had a more lasting and significant effect than the "grand itinerants."[14]

The Awakening may be described as (a) a stage in the development of Protestant theological tradition; and as (b) the foundation for the development of evangelicalism—the formation of its core commitments, its ethos and beliefs. Nathan Hatch and Gordon Wood, two American historians, offer insightful observations on the impact of evangelicalism in eighteenth-century Colonial America. Hatch declared, "The right to think for oneself became the hallmark of popular Christianity"; and

Wood added, "Emotion-soaked religious seekings acquired a validity they had not earlier possessed... Thousands of common people were cut loose from all sorts of traditional bonds and found themselves freer, more independent, more unconstrained than ever before in their history." This powerful *democratic, evangelical* impulse in American religious life was a product of the Enlightenment and the Awakening—a product of Voltaire and Edwards, of Newton and Whitefield, of Locke and Wesley. Only about 25 percent of the clergy in New England ever participated in a revival. It was rooted more firmly in the South, preparing the soil for the Stone-Campbell Movement that emerged there half a century later. A second revivalistic Awakening would occur during the early nineteenth century, largely in Kentucky, Tennessee, and adjacent states. It would furnish the setting for the Christian and Disciples Movements, particularly Barton W. Stone. "New Light" Samuel Davies, a disciple of Edwards and president of Princeton, trained David Caldwell and other "New Lights" or revivalists. David Caldwell, in turn, became mentor to Barton Stone during his student days in North Carolina. From the Enlightenment, the Campbells would bring a rationalist heritage and an irrevocable commitment to individual freedom to the Movement, a commonsense religion both reasonable and practical; and from the evangelical revival (Great Awakening), Stone would bring the dimension of spiritual revelation to the Movement. The heritage of the Christian Church (Disciples of Christ) was rooted in and shaped by the crosswinds of *equality, democracy, universality* and *divine inspiration, scriptural revelation, spiritual experience*; rationalism and evangelicalism; the Enlightenment and the Great Religious Awakening—producing a religious faith embraced by both the intellect and the heart.[15]

A final piece of European heritage crucial to the founding and formation of the Disciples Movement is the genealogy of two ideas—*Christian Unity* and *Restoration*. The history of Christianity brims with numerous efforts to unite Christendom. Despite the fact that Christianity is intrinsically ecumenical in character, it has suffered repeated fragmentation born of differing understandings of faith and traditions, including human creeds. In 1054 the patriarch of the Greek Orthodox Church excommunicated the pope, and the pope then excommunicated the patriarch, creating a split that has never been reconciled. The Protestant Reformation of the sixteenth century opened another saga in the history of Christianity's divisions. Instead of one Protestant Church emerging from the Reformation, several churches appeared, including most prominently Lutheran, Baptist, Presbyterian, Anglican, and Congregational. And of course there was the Colonial era cold war between Protestants and Catholics. George Marsden noted that the "British colonies were Protestant outposts in a predominantly Catholic hemisphere."

The stage was set for a period of bitter religious strife in the seventeenth century, and it seemed that Protestantism might well destroy itself by dividing and subdividing into a multiplicity of religious sects. Church-to-church attempts at unity simply did not exist. Ecumenical witness during that century came instead from individuals. Among that band of courageous voices, almost none of whom are recognized or remembered by the Church today, were Rupertus Meldenius (1582–1651), a Lutheran theologian who, in his effort to develop a formula combining diversity and unity, authored the classic slogan: "In essentials unity; in nonessentials liberty; in all things, charity." Hugo Grotius (1583–1645) lent his great intellect to an attempt at union between Roman Catholics and Protestants. Gottfried Leibniz (1646–1716) worked tirelessly toward reconciliation between Lutheran and Reformed communions. John Dury (1596–1680), through extensive travel, attempted to unite all Protestants by abolishing sectarian names and creeds, and establishing national churches. William Wake (1657–1737) tried to create a basis for union between Rome and the Church of England. And Richard Baxter (1615–1691), a Scotsman, was the chief voice in the effort to bring harmony to the Church of Scotland and the Church of England. Baxter said that unity and concord are the Church's beauty. There were other equally obscure prophets: George Calixtus (1586–1656), who claimed only heresy could break fellowship; Philipp Melanchthon (1497–1560), who advocated compromise on nonessentials; Martin Bucer (1491–1551) and Johannes Coccejus (1603–1669). These were figures of large soul and wide spiritual vision, but the issues of doctrine and polity always overpowered the lonely voices advocating union. Their impression on the religious world was faint, and they failed to launch any lasting movement toward Christian unity.[16]

One of the main reasons the church could not unite was the church's political attachment to the government of its own country: the Church of Scotland, Church of England, Church of Sweden, Church of the Netherlands, and the Church at Geneva. Unity within each country was compulsory, rather than voluntary, although in the eighteenth century this theory of compulsory unity would break down under the rise of civil liberty. Reinforcing their contentment with separation was the fact that they were products of separate reform movements; and the forces of division were much too strong for the disconnected ecumenical voices to overcome. For the most part, those voices fell silent during the eighteenth century and were largely forgotten. Sectarianism became an accepted way of life for Protestantism.[17]

Restoring the New Testament church was the second major idea driving the Disciples Movement. Across the centuries, it seemed that all reforming churches desired to restore primitive Christianity. Each was convinced its doctrine and polity were sanctioned by the New Testament. Independents, Baptists, and Congregationalists were all equally sure. Luther, Zwingli, and Calvin all made their appeal directly from Scripture. The Russian Orthodox asserted they alone "preserved the picture of Christ." Lutherans believed, "The Lutheran Church is the old original church." And the Presbyterians claimed, "The Presbyterian Church comes nearest to the apostolic model."

Meanwhile, John Wesley wrote, "The Methodists follow the Scriptures and the primitive church." W. E. Garrison, reflecting on the multitudes of sects and denominations claiming to restore and preserve primitive Christianity, remarked:

> These preservers and restorers of the primitive had very different ideas as to what was essential in the primitive and how it should be restored. Some of them must have been wrong, and all of them may have been. The point is that none of them undertook to improve upon original Christianity: all would preserve or restore.[18]

During the eighteenth century there emerged in the British Isles a substantial number of small independent sects that took up the cause of "restoration." They sought more literal ways of returning to the practices, worship, and organization of the New Testament Church. From their perspective, worship had become too formal, clergy too professional, creeds too complicated. They wanted their congregations to be completely independent and they held absolutely no expectation of unity. One calculation estimates forty such groups sprang up across Great Britain. But they were scarcely noticed by the larger Protestant bodies.

Disciples claimed some connection with John Glas (1695–1773), a Presbyterian minister–graduate of St. Andrews, ordained at Dundee, a man of vigorous and humane mind–who founded one of these small groups. He was suspended from the Church of Scotland in 1728 and formally deposed in 1730 for advocating against a national church, due to his belief that the church was purely a spiritual community. He also believed in weekly communion, strict conformity to primitive Christianity, a literal approach to scripture, infant baptism, and foot washing. He contended that accumulation of wealth was unscriptural and that each congregation was independent, governed by lay elders. This small, independent group, which had almost no influence on the Church of Scotland, became known as Glasites. Robert Sandeman (1718–1771), graduate of the University of Edinburgh and married to the daughter of John Glas, gave up his weaving business in 1741 to devote his time fully to being an elder of the Glasite church. He became the theological leader of the movement, ultimately settling in Danbury, Connecticut, and founding a congregation in 1765, seven years before the birth of Barton W. Stone. Some have considered this little congregation in Danbury the first Disciples congregation. Sandeman believed that faith came first through human reason and believing the evidence. Change of heart, resulting from faith, came later. He also believed in the independence of the local congregation and in primitive Christianity regarding ordinances, worship, and organization.

Minor reformers of interest to Disciples were Robert Haldane (1764–1842) and his brother James (1768–1851), wealthy laymen who disliked formalism while believing in baptism by immersion, congregational independence, weekly observance of the Lord's supper, foot washing, and restoration of the primitive Church. They devoted their considerable fortunes to an attempted reformation of the church, the organization of Sunday schools, and missionary efforts. They withdrew from the Church of Scotland in 1799 to organize their own independent churches—one in Glasgow and one in Edinburgh. The Haldanes constructed churches, chapels, and institutions of education, but their major contribution was the founding in 1798 of the *Society for the Propagation of the Gospel at Home* for Wesley-Whitefield style evangelizing. That same year, Thomas Campbell and his associates in Northern Ireland formed *The Evangelical Society of Ulster,* based on the Haldanian model.[19]

Alexander Campbell would occasionally be asked about his Glasite, Sandemanian, or Haldanean heritage, and if Disciples should be characterized as an offshoot. While acknowledging a debt, Campbell strongly resisted these claims.

> While I acknowledge myself a debtor to Glas, Sandeman…as much as to Luther, Calvin and John Wesley; I candidly and unequivocally avow that I do not believe that any one of them had clear and consistent views of the Christian religion as a whole…
>
> As to Haldane, I am less indebted to him than to most of the others.[20]

Pressed again by a critic who charged, "Mr. Campbell's views are not new, at least, not many of them—Sandeman, Glass [*sic*], the Haldanes, were master spirits upon this system many years ago," Campbell retorted, "To call me a Sandemanian, a Haldanian, a Glasite—you might as well nickname me a Gnostic. I do most unequivocally and sincerely renounce each and every one of these systems. Anyone that is well read in those systems must know that the *Christian Baptist* advocates a cause, and an order of things which not one of them embraced."[21]

The Campbells combined the well-known philosophy of restoring the principles of the New Testament with the neglected and disregarded ideal of union that would become the bedrock of the Movement. This twofold plea of restoring the ancient order and pursuing Christian unity became a profound paradox, at once both inclusive and exclusive, a paradox that Disciples Reformers would never be able to reconcile and one that would fracture the Movement. But together, these two ideas gave the Movement its theological and ideological DNA.

The American Setting–1800

*The favorable opportunity which Divine Providence has put into [our]
hands in this happy country...a country happily exempted from the
baneful influence of a civil establishment of any form of Christianity–
from under the direct influence of the anti-Christian hierarchy...still
more happy will it be for us if we duly esteem and improve those great
advantages for high and valuable ends. Can the Lord expect or require,
any thing less, from a people in such unhampered circumstances, from
a people so liberally furnished with all means and mercies, than a
thorough reformation in all things civil and religious.*

THOMAS CAMPBELL
Declaration and Address, 1809

The United States in 1800 offered a strikingly favorable environment
for religious reform. It was created by intent to be religiously neutral with
no official connection to a church or other religious institution–the first
government in the world established not on the authority of religion but
on the foundation of human reason. James Madison, along with most of
the early leaders, believed the nation was founded neither as Christian nor
secular...but upon religious liberty. Thomas Campbell had been in America
only two years when, in 1809, he wrote the *Declaration and Address,* but he
had been there long enough to recognize the assimilation of the European
Enlightenment and Great Awakening into the social, cultural, and political
setting and the promise it held for his proposed religious reforms.

In the novel environment of religious freedom, Thomas Campbell
envisioned a new approach for the Christian message. The most auspicious
characteristic of American society for religious reformers during the opening
years of the nineteenth century was a developing constitutional democracy
in tension with the theology of John Calvin. The new American government
democratized the politics of the people, who in turn democratized heaven
and democratized ministry. The old Calvinist view of a select few predestined
for heaven was challenged. Anyone could attain it. Likewise, belief in the
"priesthood of all believers" was liberated by the disestablishment of state
religion. Anyone could preach.

Among characteristics of the United States populace attractive to
reformers were a rich intellectual legacy of Enlightenment ideas, political
freedom, a representative government based upon popular sovereignty,
equality of all citizens, a secular state unaffiliated with any official religion, a
nation not weighed down by encrusted traditions or embedded institutions;
and a nation of physical and economic assets expanding its territorial
reach. Encouraging forces of change gathering strength at the time
included the old adversary of the Enlightenment, religious revivalism–an
evangelical enthusiasm sparked by yet another Awakening and called

by some the golden age of democratic evangelism; the formation and growth of a new religious institution called the "voluntary association" for missionary, reform, and benevolent purposes; the appearance of religious seminaries; the establishment of city Bible societies and local Sunday school societies; a burst of humanitarian reform and moral crusades (e.g., temperance, abolition of slavery); and, most profound of all, an extensive democratization of society, crucial to understanding the eruption of popular religious movements in early nineteenth century America rebelling against Calvinism and authoritarian forms of social hierarchy. The Enlightenment and the Awakening provoked this singular and befitting constellation of conditions. Historian Gordon Wood described early nineteenth-century America as the "most egalitarian, most materialistic and most evangelical Christian society in western history."[22]

Freedom of religion existed in America as never before in Christendom. No church in the United States held legal advantage or preeminence. They were supported by voluntary gifts rather than taxation, thereby releasing powerful religious energies. All persons were free to practice and promote the religion of their choice, or no religion at all. This new and vigorously practiced personal liberty was rooted in the Bill of Rights, particularly the First Amendment: "Congress shall make no law respecting an establishment of religion or prohibiting the free exercise thereof."

Although the words "church" and "state" do not appear in the text, the amendment effectively separated the two—despite the fact it had been designed to protect states rights from federal intrusion. As recently as the close of the American Revolution, eleven of the thirteen states had religious qualifications for office holding; four states barred non-Christians and non-Protestants from holding office; and at least six states had government-supported churches—Massachusetts being the last to separate church and state in 1833. But with the coming of the Constitution and the Bill of Rights, government (state and federal) was displaced as a source of religious authority by voluntary support that fostered a new understanding about the relationship of religion to government and society. Several of the founding fathers saw religion as divisive and tribal. They believed regional rivalries were heightened by religious conflicts that in turn threatened national unity. It followed, in their thinking, that government should distance itself from direct religious interests. The result of the First Amendment, in the words of sociologist Roger Finke, was "religious deregulation." It was James Madison who noted church and state "when married bring out the worst in each other."[23]

Religious populism provided the fertile ground from which new religious movements sprouted, soon drawing the church into the mainstream of popular culture. Church historian Nathan Hatch concluded that during the early decades of nineteenth-century America, Christianity became a liberating force, according people the right to think, act, and experiment for themselves. The intent of the activists, who were themselves sparingly educated, was to be all-inclusive in their appeal without regard for a person's social standing. Their message, however, was pitched to the unschooled. Common, ordinary people, therefore, became the leaders of the new religious movements and builders of denominations. According to Hatch, the result was a "delineation of the fault line of class within American Christianity." Through this evangelistic process, religious authority was refashioned on the foundation of popular democracy.[24]

American Christianity became a mass enterprise. By one measurement there were 1,800 ministers in America in 1775; by 1845 there were 40,000, and the number of denominations had doubled. Between 1780 and 1820, 10,000 new church buildings were constructed; between 1820 and 1860, 40,000 were constructed. Growth by denomination is illustrated in the following chart.

Denomination	Congregations 1780	Congregations 1820	Congregations 1860
Methodists	50	2,700	20,000
Baptists	400	2,700	12,150
Presbyterians	500	1,700	6,400
Lutherans	225	1,700	2,100
Congregationalists	750	1,100	2,200
Episcopalians	400	600	2,100
U.S. Population	4 M	10 M	31 M

The shift from government to voluntary support energized denominational expansion and integrated denominations into the mass culture.[25]

The America of 1800, in which the Disciples Movement was about to make its appearance, was only four years removed from the presidency of George Washington and one year from his death. It had just experienced a momentous national election in which Thomas Jefferson, a deist, became president—a new president, a new party, a new government. The city of Washington was not much more than a village with a scattering of wooden cabins and a few brick houses surrounding a swamp. Only one wing of the capital was ready for occupancy, and the capital dome stood open. Only three cities had populations of 25,000 or more. Sixteen states composed the nation, with only 10 percent of the population living west of the Alleghenies. Wealth, industry, and culture were concentrated in the tidewater extending from Boston to Charleston, but the time has actually been described as one of cultural decline, contrasted with the previous American century that is considered an era of brilliant creativity. The Scottish Enlightenment philosophy of "Common Sense" rose to prominence in national thought by the early nineteenth century and maintained its hold on the American intellect until at least the Civil War. Deeply rooted in agrarian economy, nine-tenths of the nation's population was involved in agriculture. Sparked by the 1803 Louisiana Purchase, which doubled the size of the country, the nation began its move westward, propelled by a sense of "Manifest Destiny." Symbolic of the westward expansion was the new state of Ohio. By 1820 it had a population of 230,000; ten years later its population exceeded 900,000, swelled by people who had exchanged the rule of seaboard aristocracy for the popular freedom of the frontier. They managed their affairs by appeal to the majority and established the principles of popular will and local self-government. Disciples were destined to follow the westward migration, especially its faith in the democratic ideal. Under these social, cultural, religious, and political conditions the early Disciples began their struggle for reformation, a struggle to facilitate the *union* of all Christians.[26]

American Prologue

The man who appears in any public service and is faithful to his trust, will have a double character; by the unjust and them who judge from the testimony of such, he will be considered a disturber of the peace, as turning the world upside down, and stirring up the people to revolt; but by the well informed lovers of truth, he will be considered a light to them who otherwise would sit in darkness.

ELIAS SMITH
Herald of Gospel Liberty, 1808[27]

During the opening years of the nineteenth century, new religious movements appeared almost annually and in all sections of the country. The separation of church and state, the right of free choice available to individuals, a continuing revival movement growing out of a new Awakening, an enormous population of unchurched that could be freely evangelized, a populist hostility to creeds and clergy, and the growing tension between Calvinism and democracy—all combined to cause an unprecedented rise of new religious movements. At least two of these movements identified themselves as "Christian" movements, manifesting the clash between the old Calvinism and the new democratic individualism. Calvinism's belief in human depravity contradicted the new faith in human reason; its belief in foreordination and eternal punishment contradicted the new humanitarian ideas of justice; and its belief in dogmatic theology contradicted the new assertion of the right of private judgment.

The first of these "Christian" movements arose among the Methodists. Francis Asbury (1745–1816), a simple, unlearned man, came to the American colonies in 1771 with the assigned responsibility of establishing and overseeing the growing network of Methodist circuit riders serving the

Wesleyan societies. But on Christmas day 1784 the Methodists became a church, adopting the name *Methodist Episcopal Church*. From that date Methodist ministers were at last able to offer the sacraments, perform weddings, baptize, ordain, and conduct funerals. Under the leadership of Thomas Coke (1747–1814), Asbury was ordained and appointed superintendent, then quickly named the first bishop of the new church. One of Asbury's tasks was assigning ministers to districts. He took easily to the exercise of power; in fact, he was attracted to the whole concept of centralized authority. Contemporaries described him as a person of indomitable will who was autocratic and domineering but also as a person who had the heart of a shepherd. He regularly rode the circuit, making forty trips by horseback over the Appalachians in every season, incurring every imaginable kind of injury and disease. Beguiled by the lure of power, he expanded the authority of his ministry of episcopacy by not allowing his circuit riders, often called "Asbury's Ironsides," the right to appeal their district assignments. This new restriction stirred resentment among several of the ministers—in particular James O'Kelly (1734–1826), who was provoked by this new restriction to challenge Asbury's autocratic rule.[28]

Virginia, North Carolina, and Ireland all profess to be the birthplace of James O'Kelly. No one knows with certainty, but most scholars agree with O'Kelly's earliest biographer that he was born in Ireland, October of 1734 or 1735, and migrated to America about 1760. His ancestry was filled with priests, preachers, and church builders. It is known that he settled in Surry County, Virginia, moved to North Carolina where he served in the colonial militia during the American Revolution, was married to Elizabeth Meeks, and was an accomplished violinist. His conversion occurred at about age forty, a conversion that came, according to his own words, by gradual "illuminations of the spirit." He "consigned his fiddle to the flame," joined the Methodist circuit riders who licensed him to preach in January 1775, and was ordained on Christmas eve 1784 by Thomas Coke when the Wesleyan Societies became a church. All reports confirm that he was a powerful preacher. His biographer, W.E. MacClenny, noted Thomas Jefferson arranged for O'Kelly to preach in the hall of United States House of Representatives. At the conclusion of the sermon, Jefferson reportedly commented, "In my opinion James O'Kelly is one of the greatest preachers living."[29]

At the 1792 General Conference of the Methodist Episcopal Church held at Otterbein's Church in Baltimore, James O'Kelly—assigned to the Guilford, Mecklenburg district of North Carolina—introduced a resolution requesting the right of ministers to appeal their appointments.

> After the bishop appoints the preachers at Conference to their several circuits, if any one thinks himself injured by the appoint-ment, he shall have the liberty to appeal to the Conference and

state his objection, and if the Conference approve his objection, the bishop shall appoint him to another circuit.

Asbury saw his authority directly challenged, outmaneuvered his opponents, and defeated O'Kelly's resolution. O'Kelly thereupon resolved to separate from the eight-year-old church, and, on December 25, 1793, in Manakintown, Virginia, established the *Republican Methodist Church*. It is estimated that thirteen to nineteen ministers and about one thousand parishioners joined O'Kelly in this venture. Methodist historians refer to this event variously as the "Republican Methodist Succession," the " O'Kelly Secession," or the "O'Kelly Schism," while other church historians refer to it as the southern phase of the "Christian Connection."[30]

Rice Haggard (1769–1819), a friend and companion of James O'Kelly, was born in Virginia and was a neighbor of Thomas Jefferson. He was well educated for his time, ordained at age twenty-two by Francis Asbury, served as one of "Asbury's Ironsides," then joined with O'Kelly in protest against Asbury, as well as in the subsequent separation and founding of the Republican Methodist Church. Haggard recommended that the new church be renamed "Christian." His recommendation, "henceforth and forever the followers of Christ be known as Christians simply," was placed before a meeting of the Republican Methodists in Surry County, Virginia, and was unanimously approved August 4, 1794, thereby forming the Christian Church. Shortly, O'Kelly, Haggard, and other leaders of this group developed a set of guiding tenets–"Cardinal Principles of the Christian Church." This set of principles, reflecting the ideals of the Enlightenment and the Awakening, predated the Stone-Campbell Movement by at least a decade.

1. The Lord Jesus Christ is the only Head of the Church.
2. The name Christian to the exclusion of all party and sectarian names.
3. The Holy Bible our only creed, and a sufficient rule of faith and purpose.
4. Christian character, the only test of church fellowship and membership.
5. The right of private judgment, and the liberty of conscience, the privilege and duty of all.
6. The union of all Christians to the end that the world may believe.[31]

When those principles were written, Barton Stone was a twenty-four-year-old Presbyterian clergyman in Kentucky about to receive pastoral appointment at Cane Ridge, and Alexander Campbell was a seven-year-old schoolboy in Ireland. Leroy Garrett observed these principles were stated "more effectively and concisely than either the *Last Will and Testament of the Springfield Presbytery* or the *Declaration and Address*." He also applauded their "disarming brevity." Disciples scholars have not often mentioned this set of early "Principles," yet the content advocates freedom of individual judgment, the centrality of the Scriptures, and are based on Christian unity, not on restoration. James O'Kelly later authored a forty-point plan for the union of all Protestant bodies, published numerous pamphlets, and traveled regularly to the congregations. The old hero of the Asbury protest died in Chatham County, North Carolina, October 16, 1826, at the grand age of ninety-two.[32]

Rice Haggard, later ministering in Kentucky, was with Barton Stone in 1804 prior to the disbanding of the Springfield Presbytery. In that year Haggard authored and published a treatise entitled *Address to the Different Religious Societies on the sacred import of the Christian Name*. The thirty-one–page booklet–theologically substantive, thoughtfully written–artfully advocated the use of the Christian name. By Barton Stone's own account, the "Address" had a direct influence on Stone's churches in Kentucky. They too adopted the name "Christian." Haggard cited extensive scriptural references throughout the "Address"; he included a lengthy history of the evils of "partyism" and divisions caused by the endless variety of denominational names; and he concluded with a plan for healing a divided church:

1. We are to worship one God.
2. Acknowledge one Savior, Jesus Christ.
3. Let the Bible be the one and only confession of faith.
4. Let us have one form of discipline and government, the New Testament, which is the constitution of the Christian Church.
5. Let all Christians consider themselves members one of another–with Christ Himself as the head.
6. All Christians ought to be members of one church; there is one foundation which is Christ; the name of this body originates from its head which makes it the Christian Church.
7. Let us all profess one religion. If that be the religion of Jesus Christ, then let it be called by his name.
8. Let none be received as members of the church but such as are made alive in Christ, for the Lord's temple is a spiritual house.

Haggard's Plan of Unity was strikingly similar to the "Principles" developed by James O'Kelly; and equally similar to the Christian unity thoughts of Barton Stone and to the thoughts Thomas Campbell would later record in the *Declaration and Address*. Haggard died unexpectedly in 1819, at age fifty, before the Stone-Campbell Movement gained momentum.[33]

The second of the "Christian" movements arose among the Baptists in the hills of New England. Freewill Baptists, Unitarians, and Universalists were rebelling against orthodox Calvinism. One of their leaders, Elias Smith (1769–1846), was evocatively depicted by Nathan Hatch with the words, "There were few characters in Jeffersonian America more inherently interesting than Elias Smith." Reformer, preacher, journalist, herbal physician, songwriter–Smith was born in the coastal town of Lyme, Connecticut. He grew up in the 1780s under frontier conditions on a crude farm near Woodstock, Vermont. During his youth, Smith developed a strong dislike of almost everything ecclesiastical. These feelings likely began with his tortured baptismal experience at age eight. Resisting baptism, Smith attempted to bolt from the church when he learned he was to be baptized, only to be roughly seized by an elder and his father. His hands and feet were tied and he was carried to the baptismal font where he was sprinkled against his willful protest. At age sixteen he experienced a frightening conversion. While walking on a log and carrying another log on his shoulder, he slipped, fell, and was pinned, remaining for a time unconscious. Interpreting this as a conversion, he preached his first sermon in 1790 at age twenty-one, became an itinerant evangelist, and was ordained by Baptists in 1792. He soon found himself at odds with Baptist Calvinism and established an independent congregation in Portsmouth, New Hampshire, in 1802. Smith advocated a profound simplification of the gospel, abandoning all creeds but the Bible, freedom of individual choice in governance and worship, and elimination of sprinkling as a form of baptism. He was an ardent Jeffersonian Republican with an egalitarian passion, always linking the New Testament and the Declaration of Independence in his sermons. Smith–with the able assistance of his closest colleague, Abner Jones (1772–1841), described as less gifted but emotionally more stable than Smith–established at least fourteen Christian Churches across New England. Smith, while twice defecting to the Universalists, traveled into New York, Pennsylvania, and as far west as Ohio preaching, singing, and distributing pamphlets. In 1811 he traveled to Virginia in hopes of uniting with the O'Kelly Christians. They agreed to an informal common fellowship and an expression of hope for cooperation, but not union. And in 1818 he published the first known hymnal by an American Christian Church movement.[34]

Abner Jones, also a creature of the New England hinterland, was born in Royalton, Massachusetts. He too spent his childhood in Vermont, was baptized in 1793, and one week later went to visit Elias Smith. Like Smith he believed religious liberty was a birthright and no one should be subservient to ecclesiastical authority. Together, Smith and Jones formed the "Christian Conference," an attempt to bring some connection to the New England churches.

In 1805 Smith began publishing a quarterly periodical entitled *The Christian's Magazine* that contained scathing attacks on the clergy and creeds. On September 1, 1808, he commenced the publication of a weekly newspaper, *The Herald of Gospel Liberty*. Smith promoted it as the first religious newspaper in the United States, although three evangelical periodicals already existed in the Northeast.

A religious newspaper is almost a new thing under the sun; I know not but this is the first ever published to the world. The design of this paper is to shew [*sic*] [that] liberty belongs to men as it respects their duty to God and each other.

Elias Smith is usually considered the founder of religious journalism in America. The publication of his newspaper, although under different names and forms, has continued to this day. In the first issue he reprinted Stone's *Last Will and Testament of the Springfield Presbytery*; he also reprinted Haggard's *Address on the Christian Name;* and, later, O'Kelly's forty-point *Plan of Union.* Smith's *Herald* provided a means through which the diverse Christian groups could talk to one another across regions. Mutual acquaintance was limited among the Smith-Jones Christians, the O'Kelly-Haggard Christians and the Stone Christians, but there was an historic affinity and they were obviously aware of each other. In this, the *Herald* played a significant role. At their peak, the O'Kelly and Smith Christians reached a combined membership of about 20,000. Most of the O'Kelly churches, and many of the Smith churches–though not a unity movement–eventually united in the Christian Connection that later united with the Congregationalists to form the Congregational Christian Churches, which later still united with the German and Reformed to become the United Church of Christ.[35]

Some scholars refer to the O'Kelly Movement as an important parallel movement to the Stone-Campbell reformation. It was more. The O'Kelly Christians were the first in time, the first to develop a set of principles for reformation, the first to produce an ecumenical document, and the first to set forth the name "Christian." They were trailblazing forbearers, ahead of the reformation curve that would reach its fruition with the Campbells and Stone. The Smith Christians major contribution was in the field of religious journalism, promoting the principles of the Christian Church and offering a means of fraternal communication. They also contributed three prominent female itinerant evangelists, all former Freewill Baptists, to the Second Great Awakening–Nancy Towle, Clarissa Danforth, and Harriett Livermore. Both groups sought simplicity and intelligibility against an older theology. Both groups affirmed the right of private judgment against the old belief in dogmatic creeds. Both groups deserve recognition for their contributions and for laying a large part of the foundation on which their spiritual descendants, Stone and Campbell, would later build the Disciples reformation.

> The legacy of the Christian movement is riddled with irony. Instead of taking America by storm, the Christian Connection under Smith and O'Kelly vanished into insignificance, while the Disciples of Christ under Stone and Campbell grew into a major denomination only by practicing the kind of organization the reformers had once hoped to stamp out.[36]

CHAPTER II

Barton Warren Stone

The Early Years

The man who honestly…points the way of reformation must certainly be engaged in a work pleasing to God. This is our design, and to accomplish this desirable end shall our best exertions be enlisted and engaged. We feel…an ardent desire for the restoration and glory of the ancient religion of Christ–the religion of love, peace and union on earth.

BARTON WARREN STONE
The Christian Messenger, *1826*[1]

Third in time among the "Christian" movements, but more important and more complex than the earlier two, came the "Christian" movement born of southern revivalism and western Presbyterians. One of the founding fathers of the Christian Church (Disciples of Christ), Barton Warren Stone (1772–1844), gave leadership to the movement. Being called a founding father is a recent promotion for Stone. A shift in Disciples historiography near the middle of the twentieth century lifted Stone from relative obscurity to founding status. Earlier historians characterized Stone as merely a harbinger, a tributary movement to the Campbell mainstream, a "John the Baptist" for the more celebrated ministry of Alexander Campbell. Current scholarship has elevated the Stone Movement to a position alongside the Campbell Movement, even co-titling the Movement with his name in front of Campbell's. One historian suggested this historical revival of Stone transformed him from "precursor to Icon." Other recent scholars caution against reading modern ecumenism into Stone's thought, thereby according him more credit than he is due in carrying the mantle of unity for Disciples.

Some argue that unity was the primary thrust of his ministry; others say it was freedom and liberty–independence from all structures. Clearly, Barton Stone is an enigma, and today's historians are not in agreement on the magnitude or lack thereof of his impact on the formation of the Christian Church (Disciples of Christ). In this writing, however, he is identified as one of the four founders, although neither primary nor foremost as either a founder or advocate of Christian unity.[2]

Barton Stone could claim heritage as a fifth-generation American. His great-great-great-grandfather, Captain William Stone (1603–1695), emigrated from London to Virginia in 1633. Within fifteen years he had become the first Protestant governor of the Catholic Province of Maryland. Dismissed from the post by Oliver Cromwell, he subsequently led a loyalist protest and was condemned to death, only to be later pardoned and rewarded with an estate grant of five thousand acres on the Potomac, which he named the "Manor of Avon." From his maternal lineage, Barton Stone descended from Richard Warren, a Puritan adventurer on the Mayflower. An early ancestor in this lineage, Col. Humphrey Warren, commander of a county "Regiment of Foot," settled in Maryland on the ancestral plantation, "Frailty," the birthplace of Stone's maternal grandfather, Barton Warren.

The birth of Barton Stone occurred on Christmas Eve 1772 near Port Tobacco, the county seat of Charles County in Southern Maryland. His father, John Stone, a tidewater planter, raised "kite-foot" tobacco, owned sixteen slaves, and identified with the upper middle class. Barton Stone's second cousin, Thomas Stone, a signer of the Declaration of Independence, owned a large nearby plantation. Across the Potomac from the Stones' stood the home of George Washington. Barton Stone was only three when his father died. Four years later his mother, Mary Warren Stone, moved her family and slaves to Pittsylvania County in western Virginia near the North Carolina border. His older siblings, thought to be half-brothers from his father's previous marriage, "shouldered their firelocks and marched away to the tented fields" to fight in the American Revolution. His young mind permanently imprinted by the revolutionary experience, Barton Stone wrote: "From my earliest recollection I drank deeply into the spirit of liberty… I could not hear the name British or Tories without feeling a rush of blood." Surging through the bloodline of Barton Stone were the spirit of protest, the spirit of independence, and the spirit of liberty.[3]

"From the time I was able to read I took great delight in books," Stone recalled in his autobiography. His early schooling began soon after the family arrival in Pittsylvania County. Stone believed the schoolmaster, influenced by the educational conventions of the day, to be a "tyrant" because of his use of corporal punishment. After a few days he transferred to another school where the teacher, Robert Somerhays, possessed a more irenic temperament. He studied with Somerhays four or five years with negligible attainment in reading, writing, and arithmetic, but Somerhays pronounced Stone a finished scholar. Although Stone loved books, he read little beyond the Bible in school. Surprisingly, someone in Pittsylvania County owned a novel by London playwright Henry Fielding, *The History of Tom Jones,* and at least two novels by Tobias Smollett, the *Adventures of Roderic Random* and the *Adventures of Peregrine Pickle.* Barton Stone called them "trash" and claimed to have read them only because nothing else was available.[4]

Stone came into his inheritance at age seventeen and decided to invest it in a liberal education, "thus qualifying myself as a barrister." On February 1, 1790, he entered the Academy at Guilford, North Carolina, thirty miles southwest of his Pittsylvania home, a "New Light" Presbyterian school under the tutelage of sixty-five-year-old David Caldwell (1725–1821). A 1761 graduate of Princeton, native of Lancaster County, Pennsylvania, and an ordained minister, Caldwell served two nearby Presbyterian parishes. He founded the Academy around 1770, a two-story log house annually enrolling fifty to sixty students, and remained its sole teacher. The little log college in the Carolina wilderness graduated five governors and fifty Presbyterian ministers serving North Carolina congregations. Here, in a stronghold of Presbyterianism hospitable to revivalism, Stone pursued a classical course of studies in Latin, Greek, mathematics, and natural philosophy taught from a syllabus of lectures prepared by Dr. John Witherspoon at Princeton. Stone completed the course of study at the Guilford Academy between 1790 and 1793, abandoned his intention to study law, and decided to become a minister. Caldwell, to whom Stone once referred as "father," was the caring and experienced friend and mentor who guided Stone through his Guilford years and the angst of a career change.[5]

Conversion, Early Ministry, and the Cane Ridge Communion

In the commencement of the present century, the more pious…agreed to meet often in prayer to God to revive religion… The humble Christians prayed fervently and sang the praises of God with warm devotion. Their prayers reached the ears of the Lord; he answered by fire; for he poured out his spirit in a way almost miraculous. This powerful work was first experienced…in [Kentucky] among Presbyterians in the summer of 1800.

BARTON STONE
The Christian Messenger, *1827*[6]

While an infant, Stone was christened into the Church of England. Following the Revolution, when Virginia abolished financial support for the church, Anglican ministers departed for England. In his boyhood, Stone heard primarily Methodist and Baptist ministers in the backwoods of Pittsylvania County. Baptists called Methodists "locusts of the Apocalypse" and the Methodists responded in kind. For a time, young Stone vacillated between the two, but, soon discouraged, quit praying and became a youth of the world. Then he entered the Guilford Academy, where he encountered a great religious enthusiasm among the students. James McGready (1763–1817), "M'Grady" as Peter Cartwright wrote it, offering a clue to its pronunciation, a Presbyterian evangelist and eventual architect of the Second Great Awakening of the early nineteenth century, had accepted pastorates at Haw River and Stoney Creek in Guilford County in 1789 and soon converted at least thirty students. At first Stone thought of transferring to Hampden-Sydney College to escape the religious upheaval, unaware a student awakening was at work in that college as well. But he decided to ignore the religious excitement and continue his studies at Guilford. At length, his roommate, Ben McReynolds, invited him to hear James McGready preach. Stone, stirred by the appeal, wrote that his "mind was chained" by McGready. He found himself in the throes of conversion, "tossed on the waves of uncertainty"—should he relinquish his plans for a career in law and consign his life to religion, or must he be damned? In February 1791 he heard McGready again, fell into despair without the resolve to continue seeking conversion. Despondent, he went home for a time, but returned to Guilford Academy and soon heard a young minister at Alamance in Guilford County, William Hodge, preach on the subject "God is Love." Like McGready, Hodge would become a leader of the Second Great Awakening. Afterward, Stone walked into the woods with his Bible, prayed and read for a long time, then joined the Presbyterian Church and yielded his life to ministry. His personal conversion struggle ended, and Caldwell's Academy had become the center of development for several leaders of the coming Second Awakening.[7]

As candidates for ministry in the spring of 1793, Stone along with two of his Guilford classmates were subject to theological trials by the Orange Presbytery. Each was given a subject to prepare–in Stone's case, the mystery of the Trinity. He felt lost because he had not read any book on theology other than the Bible. The Presbytery recommended a classical treatment of the Trinity by Herman Witsuis, but it only confused him: "It was idolatry to worship more Gods than one, and yet equal worship must be given to the Father, the son and the Holy Ghost." William Hodge gave Stone a copy of *Glories of Christ,* written by Isaac Watts (widely known for his hymns), a book Stone more easily understood: "three principles of action but only one God." Six months later Stone came before the Presbytery where the venerable old Scot, Henry Patillo (1726–1801), administered the examinations. Patillo, aged seventy, a "New Light" Presbyterian educated by Samuel Davies (1723–1761)–fourth President of Princeton and leader of the earlier Great Awakening in Virginia–accepted Watts' interpretation. His questions of Stone were brief and tactful. Stone passed, but the experience caused him to waver briefly from the ministry due to his intellectual "embarrassment with abstruse doctrines." Stone traveled to Oglethorpe County, Georgia, to live with his brother Matthew for a time. In January 1795 he became a teacher of languages at the newly established Succoth Academy, a Methodist institution in Wilkes County. Hope Hull, founder of the Academy, was present two years earlier at the famed Baltimore conference where James O'Kelly withdrew from the Methodists. Hull, although a sympathizer with James O'Kelly's attempts to democratize ecclesial structures, did not join the O'Kelly schism. Through Hull's arrangements in 1795, Stone traveled with him to meet Francis Asbury. Stone also became acquainted with a local minister, John Springer, whose sermons, friendship, and counsel rekindled an irresistible pull toward ministry. In the spring of 1796, after one year at Succoth, Stone returned to the Orange Presbytery to receive his license to preach. Patillo commissioned him for a missionary tour in the lower coastal counties of North Carolina. With that charge, his formal ministry began.[8]

Finding few Presbyterians in the coastal counties, Stone rode westward to Wythe and Montgomery counties in Virginia where he preached in several congregations until July 1796. It became clear to him that Presbyterians were migrating west to the Cumberland region of Tennessee. Afoot and by horseback, Stone made his way through the lands of the Cherokee to Nashville, population 346, a community he described as "a poor little village hardly worth notice." Arriving at Shiloh church near Nashville he found two Guilford Academy classmates and friends, William McGee and John Anderson. Stone and Anderson traveled and preached in settlements throughout the Cumberland Plateau, particularly Davidson and Sumner counties.

McGee and Anderson persuaded Stone to go to the growing Presbyterian settlements near Lexington, Kentucky, a state only four years old. In the winter of 1796 Stone began his Kentucky ministry at Concord and Cane Ridge near Lexington, succeeding Robert Finley who had been dismissed in October. While itinerant ministry in North Carolina and Virginia had been less than successful, Stone found his niche as a preacher in Kentucky. Within a few months fifty people had joined the congregation at Concord and thirty had taken membership at Cane Ridge. Barton Stone, the twenty-four-year-old licentiate, only ten months after being licensed, agreed to become their permanent pastor. He accepted the formal call through the Transylvania Presbytery in the spring of 1798 and was ordained at Cane Ridge by the Presbytery on October 4, 1798. The key question at his ordination centered upon the requirement he adhere to the Westminster Confession, to which he claimed to have responded, "I do, so far as I see it consistent with the word of God." This claim appears to be at variance with the memories of his colleagues who were present. Several biographers conclude his theological struggle with Calvinism remained unresolved, although some maintain Stone never abandoned his southern Calvinist piety.[9]

Two major events occurred in the life of the twenty-eight--year-old Barton Stone in 1801; the first was his marriage to the seventeen-year-old Elizabeth or "Eliza" Campbell on July 2. She was one of four daughters of prominent parents in Greenville, Kentucky. Stone traveled two hundred miles in six days for the wedding, then returned with his bride to the 100-acre farm he purchased for $500 in 1799, about five miles east of Cane Ridge on Hingston Fork. Stone barely mentions Elizabeth in his autobiography, saying simply she was "pious and much engaged in religion," and "intelligent and cheerful; nothing could depress her." Elizabeth bore him four daughters and a son, Barton Warren Stone Jr., who died shortly after his birth in 1809. Elizabeth died in May 1810.[10]

The legendary Cane Ridge "Communion," more often called "revival," was the second major 1801 event in Stone's life. Taking place in August of that year, it is characterized by Paul Conkin as the "American Pentecost," a "small landmark in the history of Christianity," and described by Sydney Ahlstrom as a "landmark in the history of revivalism" and a "watershed in American Church history." Perry Miller labeled it a "religious revolution," and Peter Cartwright wrote, "Since the day of Pentecost there was hardly ever a greater revival of religion than at Cane Ridge." Part of the Second Great Awakening, also called the Great Western Revival (1797–1805), the Cane Ridge event echoed the old Scottish religious festivals of the seventeenth and eighteenth centuries: "Communion Seasons" celebrating the Lord's supper. A few historians have accurately interpreted the era of great revivals in America as a grand display of the old Scottish "Sacramental Occasions," manifested in American religious life, mostly east of the Appalachians. Others have mistakenly called all revivals the "Frontierization" or "Americanization" of

American Christianity. The revivals were less exceptionally American than the term implies. In old Scotland, these immense festal communions were as much a routine part of the summer calendar as they were spontaneous awakenings. Eucharistic festivals, powerful displays of religious fervor, were important popular events central to Scottish Presbyterian culture. Lasting three days or more, they involved outdoor preaching, throngs of people numbering into the thousands, emotional outbursts of the spirit (fainting, weeping, swooning, and praying), multiple communion tables with successive servings, and multiple ministers preaching. The famous sacramental meeting near Glasgow at Cambuslang, Scotland, in August 1742 attracted 30,000 persons–nearly sixty years before Cane Ridge in Kentucky. These sacramental meetings, or "Holy Fairs" as the poet Robert Burns called them, were an appendage of transplanted Presbyterianism in America, with one festival recorded in New England as early as 1724. They were an established and distinguishing feature of Presbyterian evangelical life in eighteenth-century America.[11]

The principal field for this new wave of religious revivals, or sacramental occasions, encompassed Tennessee and Kentucky, initially centered on the Kentucky-Tennessee border in Logan County, often called the cradle or birthplace of the Great Western Revival. After receiving a threatening letter written in blood and finding his pulpit burned by the opposition he aroused, James McGready left North Carolina in 1796 and moved to Logan County. McGready, known as one of the "Sons of Thunder," had participated in several "Sacramental Occasions" during his Pennsylvania years before moving to North Carolina. In Logan County, which he described as a place of "universal deadness and stupidity," McGready became pastor of three new congregations, Red River, Muddy River, and Gasper River. During the summers of 1798 and 1799 he held small sacramental meetings in each of those congregations and each congregation experienced an "awakening."[12]

In June 1800 McGready held a second sacramental meeting, part ritual, part revival, at Red River attended by 1,000 persons. Among the preachers assisting him were William Hodge and William McGee, both friends of Stone. The next month a similar meeting was held at Gasper River attracting people from as far as 100 miles away. They parked their wagons and camped on the grounds, giving Gasper River the honor of claiming to have been the first "Camp Meeting." Those who attended were focused more on "revival than on 'sacrament.'" Eight more meetings were held that summer, the largest at Shiloh Church in Sumner County, Tennessee, where William Hodge succeeded William McGee as pastor. Due to his mother's death, Stone was in Virginia during this time but learned of the growing crescendo of "awakenings" on his return to Kentucky. Curious, Stone traveled 200 miles to attend another Logan County camp meeting at Red River led by McGready in May of 1801. Stone recounted the behavior of the people:

The scene to me was new, and passing strange. It baffled description. Many, very many fell down, as men slain in battle, and continued for hours together in an apparently breathless and motionless state– sometimes for a few moments reviving, and exhibiting symptoms of life by a deep groan, or piercing shriek, or by a prayer for mercy most fervently uttered. After lying thus for hours, they obtained deliverance... They would rise shouting deliverance, and then would address the surrounding multitude in language truly eloquent and impressive. With astonishment did I hear men, women and children declaring...the glorious mysteries of the gospel. Their appeals were solemn, heart-penetrating, bold and free.

Although he described some of what he saw as "fanaticism," he found himself convinced of its genuineness, so inexplicable that it must be the work of God. He concluded God spoke to people who read or heard the Gospel, *transforming their inner will.* Stone became something of an advance agent for the religious excitement, contributing to its spread from community to community throughout the Bluegrass Country. At the May 1801 Red River meeting led by McGready, fifteen-year-old Peter Cartwright converted. He would later become one of the most famous Methodist circuit riders and evangelists in the nineteenth century.[13]

On the first Sunday in June, Stone conducted a sacramental meeting at his own Concord congregation. Between 5,000 and 6,000 persons attended. It continued for five days, with seven Presbyterian ministers and one Methodist minister participating. In Late June, meetings were held at both Lexington and Indian Creek concurrently on the same Sunday. At Indian Creek 10,000 gathered, and Stone was one of the preachers. Near the end of June, Stone began to publicize a sacramental meeting to be conducted at Cane Ridge on the first weekend in August.

Historians generally agree the Cane Ridge communion should be dated August 6–11. People began to arrive on Friday, August 6. By Saturday it was estimated that 125 to 148 wagons were on the grounds, covering an area the size of four city blocks. Stone observed, "The roads were literally crowded with wagons, carriages, horsemen and footmen moving to the camp." Estimates of the number who came range from 10,000 to 30,000 persons. By all measurements it was a mammoth meeting, with a likely attendance in the range of 12,000 to 20,000 and resulting in an estimated 300 to 1,000 conversions, the high water mark of the revival phenomena in Kentucky. Between eighteen and forty ministers participated (Presbyterian, Methodist, and Baptist), with five to seven persons preaching simultaneously from wagon boxes, stumps, tree trunks, and makeshift platforms. Among the conspicuous preachers were Presbyterians Richard McNemar, Robert Marshall, Matthew Houston, John Lyle, Barton Stone–and Methodists

William Burke, Benjamin Lakin, and Samuel Hitt. Hallmarks of the traditional Presbyterian "Communion Occasion" were evident. The action sermon, the communion tables, the successive servings, the large number of ministers all suggest Scottish tradition, an underpinning of Scottish Presbyterian ritual.[14]

Some thought the extravagant behavior of the people bizarre, even outrageous, while others saw it as the direct action of the Holy Spirit. Called everything from "exercises" to "convulsive paroxysms" to "religious ecstasy," the bodily manifestations of the Spirit included falling, jerking, dancing, barking, laughing, and singing. Stone did not condemn these exercises; neither did he participate in them. But he preached to and prayed with the gatherings and found himself swayed by the religious culture he witnessed. With a sympathetic pen he provided graphic descriptions:

Falling Exercise: The subject of this exercise would, generally, with a piercing scream, fall like a log on the floor, earth or mud, and appear as dead… after awhile they rose and spoke of the love of God and the glory of the gospel.

Jerking Exercise: The subject of the jerks would be affected in some one member of the body, and sometimes in the whole system. When the head alone was affected, it would be jerked backward and forward, or from side to side, so quickly that the features of the face could not be distinguished.

Dancing Exercise: The subject, after jerking awhile, began to dance and then the jerks would cease. Such dancing was indeed heavenly to the spectators. There was nothing in it calculated to excite levity in the beholders.

Barking Exercise: A person affected with jerks, especially in his head, would often make a grunt, or bark, if you please, from the suddenness of the jerk.

Laughing Exercise: The subject appeared rapturously solemn, and his laughter excited solemnity in saints and sinners. It was a loud hearty laughter; it excited laughter in none else.

In Stone's judgment the behavior did not discredit Cane Ridge:

That there were many eccentricities, and much fanaticism in this excitement, was acknowledged by its warmest advocates; indeed it would have been a wonder if such things had not appeared in the circumstances of that time. Yet the good effects are seen and acknowledged in every neighborhood, and among the different sects…it promoted unity…

Some viewed Cane Ridge as a turning point in theology, heralding the way for evangelical, ecumenical, and eucharistic forces. For others, the excesses of the revival were deeply disturbing, generating bitter controversies and schisms.[15]

Following Cane Ridge, the "sacramental occasions" or "revivals" spread rapidly for a short time into Tennessee, to Georgia in the south and across the Ohio River north into the Western Reserve and Pennsylvania. Camp meetings occurred in October 1801 at Hawfields, North Carolina; in April 1802 at Lancaster, South Carolina; and in September 1803 near Baltimore, Maryland; each attracting between 3,000 and 8,000 persons. But in 1803 the excitement began to decline. Soon evangelical revivalism began to displace "Communion Seasons," and would become a persistent part of American society throughout the nineteenth century, with periodic outbursts and lulls. A lull came, for example, with the War of 1812, but renewal quickly followed. Revivals stimulated membership gains, strengthened the moral character of some communities, and created a form of religious assembly, the camp meeting revival, that became a staple of American religious development in the West.

The ecumenical character of the Awakening surfaced as one of its important contributions. Stone saw how the revival had generated a harmonious association and a reduction of denominational differences among various denominational participants during the frontier meetings. His idea of Christian unity, claim some scholars, had its genesis in the revival experiences; born of evangelistic enthusiasm, it sparked an attitude of openness, a vision of a unified church based on a spontaneous, free fellowship. Stone noted: "Wherever this revival is going...there Christians lose sight of their creeds, confessions...and flock together as members of one body, knit by one spirit."

Some historians claim that as result of the Cane Ridge experience, Christian unity became a guiding tenet of Stone's future ministry. William G. West offered a supporting view of this theory.

> The Great Revival was intoxicating wine to the ignorant masses; a stumbling block to the orderly Presbyterians; foolishness to the upper strata of Kentuckians; hysteria to contemporary and present-day rationalists; but to Stone, it may be likened to the release of another kind of atomic energy, disintegrating the bonds of creedal orthodoxy, and holding the promise that a new Christian order might unite the churches on the Bible... The revival had opened to [Stone] the doors of a new idea... If men of many denominations can be united in a revival, there is no reason why they should not be united all of the time.[16]

Most authorities, however, claim that Stone was a millennialist who thought Christ's earthly reign of peace and justice was near but that it could not begin until Christianity cleansed itself of "the spirit of party" and "national attachments." He advocated "mutual forbearance, less disputation and that all heartily unite with Christian brethren of every name" as a means of preparing for the millennium, not ecumenical partnership.

Formation and Dissolution of the Springfield Presbytery

We, the above named witnesses of the Last Will and Testament of the Springfield Presbytery, knowing that there will be many conjectures respecting the causes which have occasioned the dissolution of that body, think proper to testify, that from its first existence it was knit together in love, lived in peace and concord, and died a voluntary and happy death.

RICHARD MCNEMAR
Last Will and Testament of the Springfield Presbytery,
June 28, 1804

Controversy erupted within three months after the dust settled from the last wagon departing the Cane Ridge campground. Three elders in the Cabin Creek congregation accused their pastor, Richard McNemar (1770–1839), of holding "dangerous and pernicious" ideas "hostile to the standards of the Presbyterian Church." The Presbytery took no action; but McNemar moved to Turtle Creek, Ohio, in 1802. Six months later seven Ohio congregations asked that he be reexamined. The Washington Presbytery ruled the request out of order, so the congregations appealed to the Lexington, Kentucky, Synod. In September 1803 the newly created Lexington Synod charged him with heresy and censored the Washington Presbytery for allowing persons to preach who held "Methodist" doctrines. The "anti-revivalist" Presbyterians disapproved of the disorderly exercises of the participants at Cane Ridge. Even more, they disapproved of the ministers preaching that Christ died for all instead of the elect.[17]

At the Synod meeting of September 1803 the members were in the midst of preparing a resolution to formally try McNemar when five ministers (Robert Marshall, John Dunlavy, Richard McNemar, Barton Stone, and John Thompson) suddenly entered the meeting and presented a statement read by Robert Marshall. McNemar, Dunlavy, and Thompson were former members of Stone's Cane Ridge congregation; McNemar had served as an elder and committed his life to ministry at Cane Ridge. Signed by all five dissenting ministers, the statement protested the proceedings of the Synod and announced their withdrawal from its jurisdiction. The document proclaimed the right to interpret the scriptures without threat or reprimand and then closed with the statement, "We bid you adieu until, through the providence of God it seems good to your rev. body to adopt a more liberal plan, respecting human Creeds and Confessions." It was the Movement's first declaration of freedom. Having "no desire to separate from the communion," they constituted themselves as a separate presbytery with the intent to remain Presbyterian. A committee of three, appointed by the Synod to talk with the dissenters, attempted to bring them back into the fold. The revivalist faction offered to answer questions and to return if they were constituted into one presbytery; but the Synod rejected this offer by a vote of twelve to seven. The five were suspended and their pulpits declared vacant.[18]

The tragedy of Presbyterianism at that time was its inability to reconcile diverse attitudes. They treated the actions of minor, obscure clerics as subversive acts. Presbyterians could have made the wiser choice of concession, but chose harsher, repressive measures. The loose alliance of dissenters could have been satisfied at relatively small cost. Instead, complaints grew into demands, overriding compromise and even partial reform. The only solution was to break away. The five wanted to remain Presbyterian, and would not have chosen independence if diversity had been allowed.

Immediately following their expulsion (two weeks after Lewis and Clark embarked upon their famous expedition to the Trans-Missouri West) the five men created the Springfield Presbytery, September 12, 1803, at Springfield, Ohio, near Cincinnati. It was never formally organized. There were no officers, no churches and no structure. Basically it consisted of a group of five ministers with the common purpose of reform. It should be noted to withdraw and to continue as Presbyterians was not a totally unprecedented act. It happened many times in Scotland. The "Seceder" church, for example, to which both Thomas and Alexander Campbell originally belonged, resulted from such a withdrawal. The difference could be found in McNemar's attack on and rejection of creeds. The five dissenters claimed the Bible alone would be their guide. They renounced the rule of creeds that denied people the right to examine doctrines by scripture and prove them to be wrong.

The five did two things. First, on January 31, 1804, they issued a three-part, 100-page Apology [justification] entitled An Abstract of an Apology for Renouncing the Jurisdiction of the Synod of Kentucky, Being a Compendious View of the Gospel and a Few Remarks on the confession of Faith; part one written by Robert Marshall, part two written by Barton Stone, and part three written by John Thompson. The second part, authored by Stone, stated their position on important theological matters: opposition to all confessions and creeds; Christ died for all; faith is belief of testimony; and the gospel is the only rule of faith. This second part also contained one of the fundamental ideas of the Reformation Movement–unity, achieved through rejection of creeds.

> The Christian church has long been divided into many different sects. Each has a creed, confession of faith or brief statement of doctrine... The people have no privilege to examine it by scripture and prove it to be wrong... If any should do this he is cast out as a heretic... Is it not better to clear away all the rubbish of human opinion and build the church on the rock of ages?... Creeds split

the church... Christians would be united if human creeds were laid aside...

There was nothing in the lengthy document regarding *restoration*. In the minds of several scholars, the *Apology* is at least as important, if not more so, as the *Last Will and Testament*. The brief, nine-month life of the Springfield Presbytery was a transition stage and is best described as anti-Calvinist, anti-creedal, and anti-institutional, the emphasis being freedom and liberty with an occasional reference to unity. Soon after the *Apology* was signed, Stone went to his congregations at Concord and Cane Ridge to explain that he could no longer be their minister. He had agreed by virtue of signing the *Apology* to shed sectarianism and the party spirit, and therefore could not pastor a Presbyterian congregation. Stone tore up his contract and absolved the congregations of paying his salary.

It soon became clear, however, if they were going to be independent, a presbytery would not be necessary. The second action of the five revivalists dissolved the Springfield Presbytery. When the group convened for a meeting at Cane Ridge in June 1804, Richard McNemar surprised them by arriving with a document he had written proposing dissolution. It was entitled *The Last Will and Testament of the Springfield Presbytery*. After debating the proposal for several days, the group unanimously agreed. Robert Marshall, John Dunlavy, Richard McNemar, Barton Stone, John Thompson, and David Purviance—a neighbor of Stone and elder at Cane Ridge—signed it on June 28.[19]

The Last Will and Testament of the Springfield Presbytery has been described as "whimsically phrased," "delightfully ironical," and as a "sorry attempt at wit." Newell Williams calls it a "Presbyterian document with a heavy dose of millennial enthusiasm." In any case it is considered a founding document in Disciples history. It opened with the great unity principle, cited by those scholars who make the case for Stone as an advocate for unity: "We will that this body die, be dissolved, and sink into union with the Body of Christ at large; for there is but one body, and one spirit, even as we are called in one hope of our calling."

Selected excerpts from the 800-word document are offered here to provide the flavor of its intent to protect congregational polity, to promote freedom and liberty, to anticipate the millennium, and to accept the Bible as the rule of faith. While "unity" was not a prominent feature of the *Last Will* as written by McNemar, Stone scholars contend it was prominent in the thought of Barton Stone as a means to the millenium.

We will that our name of distinction, with its Reverend title, be forgotten.

We will that our power of making laws for the government of the church, and executing them by delegated authority, forever cease.

We will that the Church of Christ resume her native right of internal government.

We will that each particular church, as a body…choose her own preacher and support him by a free will offering, without a written call.

We will that the people henceforth take the Bible as the only sure guide to heaven.

We will that preachers and people, cultivate a spirit of mutual forbearance; pray more and dispute less. Behold the signs of the times–look up, and confidently expect that redemption draweth nigh.

We will that our weak brethren, who may have been wishing to make the Presbytery of Springfield their king…betake themselves to the Rock of Ages, and follow Jesus.

Finally we will, that all our sister bodies read their Bibles carefully, that they may see their fate…and prepare for death before it is too late.

The withdrawing ministers appended a "Witnesses' Address" to the *Last Will.* They urged the world to contemplate the "beautiful simplicity of Christian Church government stript [*sic*] of human inventions," and they "cheerfully consented to retire from the din and fury of conflicting parties." The purpose, now, of the departing ministers would be to "heartily unite with our Christian brethren of every name," and though the Presbytery was dead they would "yet live and speak in the land of gospel liberty."[20]

What to call themselves appeared as an immediate problem for the signers. Among the names offered by their enemies were "New Lights," "Stonites," "Trash Trap," "Disorganizers" and "Agents of Hell." Barton Stone identified the term "Christian" with the Reformation Movement. Rice Haggard, however, recommended the name in an April 1804 sermon on Acts 11:26 at Bethel. Stone also published and circulated the "Address" Haggard delivered some years before on the subject. No author's name appears on the version printed in 1804, only the following statement:

Some may, perhaps be anxious to know who the author of the following pages is, his name, and to what denomination he belongs. Let it suffice to say, that he considers himself connected with no party, nor wishes to be known by the name of any–he feels himself united to that one body of which Christ is the head, and all his people fellow members.

Surprisingly, four of the six signers defected. McNemar and Dunlavy, brothers-in-law, were attracted to and joined the Shaker movement in 1805. In Stone's words they were "carried away with that miserable delusion."

Marshall and Thompson ultimately broke with the Movement and returned to Presbyterianism in 1811. Stone, alone, remained faithful to the Movement. By attrition or default, he is therefore referred to as a founder of the Christian Church. Stone lamented the departure of his friends, noting late in his career, "Of all the five of us that left the Presbytery, I only was left."[21]

Information is sparse on Stone from 1803 to the 1820s, a period when he was earning a living as a farmer and school teacher while attempting to serve the new Movement, which was under constant attack. On October 31, 1811, Stone married the nineteen-year-old Celia Wilson Bowen, a cousin of his first wife, Elizabeth. She birthed four sons and two daughters. The year after their wedding, Stone sold his beloved Cane Ridge farm and moved to Tennessee, but in 1814 returned to Kentucky. He taught English, Latin, and Greek; became principal of Rittenhouse Academy in Georgetown; and learned Hebrew from a Prussian doctor—all the while continuing to preach at a newly founded congregation in Georgetown. In June 1807 a parishioner requested of Stone baptism by immersion. After a long conference with several ministers in the new Movement, Stone agreed and baptized several members, including David Purviance. Stone, subsequently immersed, remained flexible on the subject and is regarded by some as the one who began the practice of open membership, accepting into membership those who had not been immersed.[22]

Certain scholars believe the loss of the defectors actually freed the Movement from a fanatical fringe. In any case, after their departure, the Movement grew rapidly. By 1810 there were fifteen Christian congregations, but no organization, no control or coordination of congregations, no blueprint or prospectus for a movement. On August 8, 1810, exactly nine years after Cane Ridge, and after several fellowship conferences during which the subject of baptism became the center of discussion, a conference of the fifteen churches convened at Bethel, where a formally reached agreement loosely united them as a group. By the time Barton Stone first met Alexander Campbell in 1824, the Stone Movement had grown to 300 congregations with 15,000 members. The meeting with Campbell would open a new chapter in the life of Stone's Movement, indeed in the history of the Disciples.

> Nothing worthy of particular note occurred till the period when Alexander Campbell, of Virginia, appeared… When he came into Kentucky, I heard him often in public and in private. I was pleased with his manner and matter. I saw no distinctive feature between the doctrine he preached and that which we preached for many years. I will not say there are no faults in Brother Campbell; but that there are fewer, perhaps, in him than any man I know on earth… I am constrained, and willingly constrained, to acknowledge him the greatest promoter of this reformation of any man living.[23]

CHAPTER III

Thomas and Alexander Campbell

Thomas Campbell: A Profile

That it is the grand design, and native tendency, of our holy religion, to reconcile and unite men to God, and to each other, in truth and love, to the glory of God, and their own present and eternal good, will not, we presume, be denied, by any of the genuine subjects of Christianity… In so far as this holy unity and unanimity in faith and love is attained; in the same degree is the glory of God and the happiness of men promoted and secured.

THOMAS CAMPBELL
Declaration and Address, 1809

Thomas Campbell is distinguished as a principal founding father of the nineteenth-century Disciples Movement in America. According to genealogists the family descended from Highlander stock, the Clan Campbell of Argyle Shire in western Scotland. Thomas, Scottish by lineage and education, was born February 1, 1763, near Newry in County Down, Ireland. His father, Archibald Campbell, a crusty, fearless old soldier, fought in the British army during the French and Indian War with General James Wolfe on the Plains of Abraham at the battle of Quebec. Archibald–eccentric, genial, energetic, irascible, quick tempered–returned to Ireland after the war, married Alice McNally, joined the Anglican Church, and settled permanently near Newry. Thomas, the eldest of four sons (Thomas, James, Archibald, and Enos) and four daughters (the girls all dying in infancy), grew to manhood in Newry. Recent scholarship suggests Thomas received his grandfather's name, Thomas Campbell (1680–1787) of Dyerlake Wood in County Down. Grandfather Thomas, husband of Alice

38

McIvor, lived to the grand old age of 107. Beyond grandfather Thomas, there is lack of agreement among genealogists on the family lineage. It is believed, however, the Campbell ancestors migrated from Scotland in the late seventeenth or early eighteenth centuries, as part of the British effort to colonize Northern Ireland. It is known Grandfather Thomas migrated from Argyle Shire, Scotland, to County Down, Ireland, in 1710.[1]

Archibald provided each of his four sons a solid English classical education at a military regimental school near Newry. The curriculum consisted of English grammar and reading, Latin and Greek, writing and arithmetic. Thomas, an irenic, deeply spiritual person of gentle disposition, quiet manner, genial Irish warmth, and quick intelligence, found deeper satisfaction with the rigid Anti-burgher, Seceder Presbyterians than with his father's Anglican church. He experienced a spiritual conversion during his youth, interpreting it as a call to ministry. But his father did not initially support either the choice of career or choice of church, so Thomas departed County Down for the poverty-stricken province of Cannaught in western Ireland, where he successfully established a school. Before long, his father summoned him home, and the obedient Thomas returned to teach in the hamlet of Sheepbridge. Brother James joined him as a teacher at Sheepbridge while brothers Archibald and Enos opened an academy in Newry.[2]

At Sheepbridge, a friend and neighbor of the Campbells, John Kinley (or M'Kinley), a Seceder Presbyterian of prominence and means, saw in the twenty-year-old Thomas the talent and promise for ministry. Kinley offered to finance the young man's preparation for ministry, if his father approved. Archibald grudgingly consented. Thomas, like most Ulster Scots of his time who sought education, sailed across the North Channel to attend one of Scotland's five famous centers of learning, the 330-year-old University of Glasgow. Scotland was still in a cultural golden age of intellectual, literary, scientific, and artistic achievement, an extraordinary outburst of intellectual activity, a brilliant intellectual awakening known as the *Scottish Enlightenment.* Leaders of this Enlightenment included Adam Smith, David Hume, Thomas Reid, Adam Ferguson, William Robertson, James Watt, James Hutton, Alexander Carlyle, and a score of others. They created the basic ideals of modernity. Known as *literati,* they carried a fundamental belief in the importance of reason, and an uncompromising opposition to imposed, repressive orthodoxy. They also believed a free, open, sophisticated culture was compatible with a solid, moral, and religious foundation. Scottish ministers were educated in Scottish universities, in urban centers, learning through rational inquiry as the only effective approach to the study of theology. One of the *literati,* Alexander Carlyle, an ordained minister, wrote of the effect of studying for ministry at a university:

> A new school was formed in the western provinces of Scotland
> where the clergy, till that period, were narrow and bigoted...

Professors opened and enlarged the minds of the students which soon gave them a turn for free inquiry, the result of which was candour [*sic*] and liberality of sentiment.[3]

Schooled in this educational environment, Thomas Campbell received a ministerial education of greater depth and range than any of the other founders of the Disciples Movement. On the basis of existing information, it appears he attended the University of Glasgow from 1783 to 1786. At the time of his arrival the university had recently acquired an astronomical observatory, a scientific laboratory, and a natural history museum. Scientific study became a prominent part of the curriculum, particularly the study of Newton and Bacon. Among his professors were the highly respected John Young, who taught Greek; and the philosophically inclined George Jardine, who taught logic and Latin. Young's teaching methods included weekly essays and oral examinations, all designed to enhance the ability to think. Commonsense philosophy, one of the underlying educational principles of the university, originated with the famous Glasgow professor Thomas Reid (1710–1796), whose landmark work *Intellectual Powers* received wide recognition following its 1785 publication during Thomas Campbell's Glasgow years. The commonsense philosophy supported Christian faith against the skepticism of philosophers such as David Hume (1711–1776). All Glasgow students were immersed in this philosophy. Thomas also attended medical lectures because students for ministry were required to have this knowledge to serve the poor in their parish who could not afford medical care. He completed his studies with honors at the university in 1786.[4]

The following year Thomas entered a theological school, Divinity Hall at Whitburn, maintained by the Anti-burgher church, midway between Glasgow and Edinburgh. Highly esteemed Archibald Bruce (d. 1816), pastor of the Whitburn church, managed Divinity Hall and became mentor to Thomas Campbell. The course of study leading to licensing and eventual ordination consisted of five annual sessions of eight weeks each. Annual enrollment ranged between twenty and thirty students. Thomas completed this work in 1791, earning classification as a probationer. By age twenty-eight, his calm tenacity of purpose resulted in the completion of a rich and thorough preparation for ministry.

During the forty-four-week period away from Scotland each year, Thomas taught school in the village of Ballymena, County Antrim, in Northern Ireland. It is believed during his first teaching term at Ballymena he met Jane Corneigle (1763–1835), likely an Irish corruption of the French name Corneille. Of Huguenot ancestry, she inherited an intrepid spirit and intellectual independence. People described her as beautiful, dignified, of fine complexion, dark hair, and modest disposition. Her ancestors, who were farmers and school builders, settled on the fertile shores of Lough Neagh in County Antrim. Thomas and Jane, both twenty-four, were married in June 1787 and set up their home with Jane's mother in Ballymena. On September 12, 1788, their first son, Alexander, was born.[5]

In 1791 Thomas moved his family to Sheepbridge and then to Market Hill in County Armagh, where he taught school in addition to preaching in Seceder congregations. During the early 1790s, daughters Dorothea and Nancy were added to the Campbell family. A call came in 1798 to pastor a recently established church at Ahorey near Rich Hill, about thirty-five miles southwest of Belfast. Ahorey, where Thomas served nine years, offered a period of relative permanency to the Campbells. Parishioners considered Thomas a faithful, diligent, fair-minded pastor; popular, intelligent, caring, and exhibiting a pattern of good works. His prayers were described as eloquent, solemn, fervent, and sincere; his sermons engaged the attention of the audience. Alexander Campbell said of his father's ministry at Ahorey, "He was the most earnest, indefatigable and devoted minister in the Presbytery and Synod to which he belonged." Family spiritual development and educational instruction occurred daily, in the morning and evening. Campbell was a sound Calvinist who disagreed with very little in the Westminster Confession of Faith. He took special care to regularly examine his own spiritual development.[6]

Thomas, an Old Light, Anti-burgher, Seceder Presbyterian (a name he thought ludicrous), and a student of Locke's *Letters Concerning Toleration,* believed firmly in the freedom of choice for individuals and the toleration of opinions. Northern Ireland, however, a country of stark certainties and violent passions, had a pronounced sectarian spirit. Seceders left the Presbyterian Church to preserve the right to choose their own minister. Anti-burghers did not require their burgesses to take an oath supporting the Church of Scotland. And the Old Light, New Light controversy broke over an obscure point in church-state relations regarding the power of civil magistrates in religion. Thomas concluded these divisions were trivial. In 1804, the year Barton Stone and his colleagues dissolved the Springfield Presbytery, Thomas Campbell appeared before the Synod in Belfast, Ireland, *proposing church union.* He addressed the "evil nature and tendencies of our unhappy division" and proposed union between the Burgher and Anti-burgher factions, explaining that being divided was "inconsistent with the genius and spirit of the Christian religion which has union, unity and communion in faith, hope and love for its grand object upon earth." Thomas Campbell, elected moderator by the Irish ministers in 1805, traveled to Scotland in a frustrating effort to argue the matter of union before the higher court. He presented the case in Glasgow, where it was reported, "he out-argued them, but they out-voted him." Although the effort failed, fifteen years later a similar effort succeeded.[7]

Four more children were added to the family between 1800 and 1806: Jane, Thomas, Archibald, and Alicia. A family of three sons and four daughters was difficult to support on his meager salary of £30 to £50 per year. Finding it necessary to supplement the family income he opened an academy in Rich Hill, two miles from Ahorey. Alexander assisted him as an instructor in the school. The twin burdens of teaching and preaching took a toll on the forty-five-year-old Thomas' health, and friends suggested he take a sea voyage, perhaps a visit to America. Many of his Ahorey friends had migrated to America or were in the process of doing so due to the cauldron of religious violence between Protestants and Catholics in Ireland, the lack of economic prospects for the middle class, and the growing hostilities between tenants and landlords. Partly due to ill health, partly due to the desire to find improved opportunities for his family, Thomas ultimately agreed to visit America. If conditions were good, he would send for the family to join him; if not, he would return. Leaving his eighteen-year-old son Alexander in charge of the Rich Hill Academy, Thomas set sail from Londonderry, April 8, 1807, on the ship *Brutus*. Hanna Acheson, a young lady from his Ahorey congregation who wished to join her family who had previously migrated to Washington County, Pennsylvania, accompanied him under his escort.[8]

On May 13, 1807, the *Brutus* arrived in Philadelphia. By coincidence, the Anti-burgher Associate Synod of North America was in session at Philadelphia when Thomas entered port and it cordially welcomed him. Within five days, and at his request, the Synod assigned Thomas to the Chartiers Presbytery in Southwestern Pennsylvania. Many of his Ahorey friends, including the Achesons, had settled near the community of Washington, 350 miles distant. The steady stream of Presbyterian immigrants to Pennsylvania caused some to call the state "American Ulster." Within weeks the James Foster and Thomas Hodgens families arrived from Ahorey and settled on farms in the Washington vicinity. Less than three months after leaving Ahorey, Campbell was preaching to a circuit of communities on the Pennsylvania frontier among persons who knew his worth.

Thomas Campbell, probably one of the best-educated ministers on the Pennsylvania frontier, soon found himself in conflict with less intellectually refined Presbyterians who were threatened by his scholarship, leadership, and popularity. His tolerant, nonsectarian, liberal nature was incompatible with the intolerant conservatism of the Chartiers Presbytery clergy. Among its restrictions was the prohibition of sharing communion with others. Campbell's sense of fraternity for all Christians always led him to relax the rigidity of divisive rules.

The Chartiers Presbytery requested Campbell to preside at a "Sacramental Occasion" in the community of Cannamaugh on the Allegheny River in Indiana County, north of Pittsburgh. It is a familiar story, first told by Robert Richardson, Alexander Campbell's biographer. Many were in attendance who belonged to other branches of the Presbyterian family and who had not participated in the Lord's supper for a long time. Thomas Campbell, who never "fenced" the communion table, declared in his preparation sermon a personal lament for the existing divisions, and permitted, as Anti-burghers were accustomed to doing in both Scotland and Ireland, those present who felt prepared and without respect to their Presbyterian connection to enjoy the benefits of communion. The story spread, growing into a legend, that the invitation had been extended to everyone.

Presbytery leadership failed to grasp that Campbell was not merely a sentimental unionist, but a serious theological thinker whose ideas were governed by well-considered convictions that happened to challenge selected doctrines of his Church. In October the Presbytery investigated Campbell on charges brought by a John Anderson—irascible by nature with pinched theological views—who had not been present in Cannamaugh, but based his charges on hearsay. Campbell protested, to no avail. In January a set of seven charges were brought against Campbell, to which he responded in writing with erudition and sincerity. But his answers were used as cause for his censure and indefinite suspension for "teaching opinions inconsistent with Seceder testimony."[9]

In May, Campbell appealed to the Synod in Philadelphia. Numerous petitions submitted by loyal parishioners rallying to his defense supported his appeal. The Synod reversed the suspension, rebuked the conduct of Anderson and ruled the Presbytery proceedings out of order. But it also rebuked and admonished Campbell for his unorthodox views. Campbell, indignant over its action, in a moment of petulance withdrew from the Synod, but quickly recanted. The rankled Chartiers Presbytery, despite lifting Campbell's suspension, refused to give him any preaching assignments. On September 13, 1808, he submitted a letter refusing the authority of the Presbytery and the Synod, and officially withdrew from their jurisdiction. This action, marking formal separation, resulted in his immediate suspension. Once again, as in the case of Barton Stone and his colleagues, the nineteenth-century Presbyterian inability to reconcile diverse attitudes, their treatment of clerics with alternate views as subversives, and their choice of repression over compromise left no choice but to break away. In his letter of withdrawal to the Synod, Campbell expressed his pain:

> It is with sincere reluctance…that I find myself duty bound to refuse submission to their decision as unjust and partial; and also finally to decline their authority, while they continue thus to overlook the grievous and flagrant mal-administration of the Presbytery of Chartiers. I hereby decline all ministerial connection with the Associate Synod of North America… The corruptions of [Chartiers] Presbytery now become the corruptions of the whole Synod.[10]

The Declaration and Address

From the series of events which have taken place in the churches for many years past, especially in this Western country, as well as from what we know in general of the present state of things in the Christian world, we are persuaded that it is high time for us not only to think, but also to act, for ourselves; to see with our own eyes, and to take all our measures directly and immediately from the divine standard; to this alone we feel ourselves Divinely bound to be conformed, as by this alone we must be judged.

THOMAS CAMPBELL
Declaration and Address, 1809

Following his suspension, Thomas Campbell continued preaching uninterrupted for nearly a year around Washington, Pennsylvania, in the houses and barns of his old Ahorey friends. He enjoyed great personal popularity throughout Washington and Allegheny Counties, where many were dissatisfied with the divided church and were therefore persuaded by his pleas for union, cooperation, and Christian liberality. The need grew to form a society in order to give more "definiteness to the movement." A large group gathered at the farm home of Abraham Altars near Washington, Pennsylvania, in the summer of 1809 to explore ways in which they might organize. Campbell addressed the group, closing his remarks with a proposed guiding principle: *Where the scriptures speak, we speak; where the scriptures are silent, we are silent.* The principle, immediately adopted, resonated with the people. On August 17, 1809, at a second meeting held near the headwaters of the Buffalo, the *Christian Association of Washington* was organized and named. These immigrant, frontier folk had no intention of founding a church. They called it an association, not a church, organized as voluntary advocates of *church reformation,* an independent society working for reform *through* and *within* the churches. At their August meeting, they decided to build a log structure on the nearby Sinclair farm to house their future meetings and double as a schoolhouse. More important, they appointed a standing committee of twenty-one to develop a statement of purpose. Thomas Campbell agreed to draft a proposal. Living in a room above the kitchen in the farm home of a Dr. Welch, Campbell spent an entire week closeted in that attic researching and writing a proposed draft. Finally, on September 7, 1809, when the group gathered at the farm home of Jacob Donaldson, Campbell presented his completed draft of a fifty-six-page document entitled *The Declaration and Address of the Christian Association of Washington.* It received unanimous approval. Thomas Campbell and his friend of long years from Ireland, Thomas Acheson, affixed their signatures to make it official.[11]

With its simple and honest words this unpretentious document presented itself as a remarkable achievement, considered by the more progressive and inclusive the most important writing to emerge from the early history of Disciples. *The Declaration and Address* has been defined as a "charter of unity for the church"; a "charter of liberty for free Christians everywhere"; the "charter document of the Stone-Campbell Movement"; "the Magna Charta of the Movement"; the "Founding document of Disciples"; a "seminal document in the history of American ecumenism"; one of the "great documents in American church history"; a "classic of Christian Literature"; the "design for the movement"; a "prospectus for reformation"; a "great milestone on the path of Christian Unity in America"; and "one of the immortal documents of religious history." Disciples view the document as the true beginning point of their history, celebrating their centennial in 1909, and their bicentennial in 2009. The *Last Will and Testament* of 1804 provided neither a prospectus nor a design for the reformation. It is widely believed that without *The Declaration and Address* there would not have been a Disciples Movement. Charles Louis Loos, a contemporary religious pioneer and colleague of the Campbells, accurately observed: "The inceptive thought and first scheme of this extraordinary Movement had their origin with Thomas Campbell." It is a document, said one historian, which belonged to the future—and was a century ahead of its time.[12]

The *Declaration and Address* is structured around four divisions: (a) a three-page Declaration containing four principles and nine articles forming the Christian Association of Washington; (b) an eighteen-page Address containing thirteen propositions universalizing the purpose of unity; (c) a thirty-one page Appendix responding to anticipated objections; and (d) a Postscript proposing the publication of a magazine. After opening with a daring pronouncement of independence, "We are persuaded that it is high time for us not only to think, but to act for ourselves…," four guiding principles appear in the introduction:

1. Every person has the right of private judgment.
2. The Scriptures will be the sole authority; no human creeds or inventions.
3. The sectarian spirit is evil; bitter jarrings and janglings of party spirit, clashing human opinions should be at rest; restore unity and peace.
4. The Bible alone for our rule; the Holy Spirit for our teacher of truth; and Christ alone as our salvation.

These defining principles, nearly identical to the James O'Kelly cardinal principles written fifteen years before, are followed by nine resolutions serving as a constitution for the Christian Association of Washington to carry out the purpose of "promoting evangelical Christianity." A standing committee of twenty-one, to be chosen annually, was to guide the work of the association, which met biannually in May and November. Volunteer offerings were to be used to support the ministers and the missionaries. One resolution stated their expectation of forming similar associations to assist in promoting the reformation.

The Christian Association of Washington, founded as a voluntary, parachurch, missionary society, promoted simple evangelical Christianity. The model for the Christian Association of Washington is taken from the evangelical missionary and Bible societies that first arose in Ireland and England in the 1790s. Thomas Campbell, one of the founders of the Evangelical Society of Ulster in 1798, rose to a position of leadership at that time, but was ultimately challenged by the Presbyterian Synod and withdrew from the Society. The *Address and Constitution of the Evangelical Society of Ulster,* along with the *Plan of Society* for the London Missionary Society founded in 1795, served as archetypes for the structure of the *Declaration and Address.*[13]

Campbell, hopeful about the potential for growth as he created this document, chose as its philosophical base John Locke's Enlightenment doctrine of universal reason. He expected the association to become a potent instrument of reformation. But, as Disciples historian Lester McAllister insightfully noted, it was extremely difficult to belong to such an association and maintain membership in a denominational church. The hopes of the association were not realized. No ministers joined, no missionaries were sent out, and no additional associations were formed.

The Address is a tract, or platform, for what Thomas Campbell called the "sacred cause of Christian Unity." W. E. Garrison wrote of the Address, "Few more logical or more impassioned appeals for that cause have ever been written." The theme of unity consumes the first ten and final five pages of the Address. Between those two sections are three pages containing thirteen propositions for achieving unity. Scholars consider this the heart of the Address, particularly significant in light of subsequent developments. First among those propositions is the most quoted, most influential, and most famous statement ever written in the history of the Movement. It became the Disciples theology of church–namely, the church is one. The thirteen propositions, written to clear away the "rubbish of the ages," are consolidated and condensed into the ten summary statements below. In substance, the final twelve propositions merely expand upon the first.

1. The Church of Christ upon earth is essentially, intentionally and constitutionally one.
2. Congregations, necessarily separate, ought to be in close fellowship with one another. There should be no schisms, no uncharitable divisions among them.
3. The New Testament is a perfect constitution for the worship, discipline and government of the Church.
4. Human authority can not make new laws for the Church where the Scriptures are silent.
5. Doctrinal exhibitions must not be made terms of communion, because they are the product of human invention.

6. Realization of the need of salvation, faith in Christ as Savior, and obedience to him are all that is essential to membership in the Church.
7. Love each other as brothers and be united as children of one family.
8. Division among Christians is a horrid evil. Destroys the visible unity of the Body of Christ.
9. For the perfection of the Church, receive those who profess faith in Christ, ministers teach only what is revealed, and divine ordinances be observe after the example of the primitive church.
10. Direct attention to first principles; remove the rubbish of the ages.[14]

Campbell saw the divisions in the body of Christ as primarily doctrinal, whereas most modern scholars interpret those divisions as primarily socioeconomic. His emphasis upon Christian unity was in part a reflection of the growing importance of inter-denominational cooperation in the Second Great Awakening. The First Awakening had confronted a complacent church, appealing to individuals outside the church, in a struggle against eighteenth-century Enlightenment rationalism. Although the First Awakening concerns persisted, the Second Awakening, beginning in 1800 with its communal appeal, was more an internal experience. It was not an exclusive effort to convert the heathen. Its voice was addressed more to those already in the church. Denominations thought they must unite through evangelism to save humankind, and they consequently organized evangelistic societies that were ecumenical in character. Thomas Campbell was influenced by this trend, indeed one of its leaders in Ireland. His Address explains how families of faith can unite in the common cause of evangelizing, thereby making evangelism both a source for, as well as a vehicle to achieve, unity in the church.

The free-flowing style of the Appendix contrasted with the well-structured earlier sections, and was apparently added to assure readers that no campaign to proselytize members would occur. It also made the lengthy case that opposition to creeds did not make the association "latitudinarian" (too liberal with too much latitude to espouse flabby doctrine and teachings). Campbell advised the association to allow gracious and charitable diversity, and to avoid easy orthodoxy supported by creeds. As a thorough student of Enlightenment commonsense philosophy, he believed Christian unity hinged on universal consensus, not ecclesiastically engineered orthodoxy. Universal consensus, he believed, could be achieved through the common sense of Christians.

The foundation of Campbell's hope for union, and the breadth of his tolerance for divergent opinions, claimed W. E. Garrison, found its finest expression in these words from the Address:

> It is, to us, a pleasing consideration that all the churches of Christ, which mutually acknowledge each other as such, are not only agreed in the great doctrines of faith and holiness; but are also materially

agreed, as to the positive ordinances of Gospel institutions; so that our differences, at most, are about the things in which the kingdom of God does not consist, that is, about matters of private opinion, or human invention. What a pity, that the kingdom of God should be divided about such things![15]

The Postscript, written several months after the first printing, suggested a monthly magazine, titled the *Christian Monitor,* would be published to expose anti-Christian corruptions. It would begin when 500 subscribers were secured. Few subscribers were secured and the project did not materialize. Neither the rich expressiveness nor precise principles of the *Declaration and Address* generated a supportive response beyond the group of immigrant founders. Having not achieved any of its stated objectives, the existence of the Christian Association of Washington lasted for less than two years. But the life of the *Declaration and Address* had barely begun.

Alexander Campbell: A Profile

I dare not be a party man because Christ has…commanded us to keep the unity of the spirit; to be of one mind and one judgment; God loves his children more than our creeds; all "parties" oppose reformation; I speak not against any denomination—but against all… I fight for the faith once delivered to the saints.

ALEXANDER CAMPBELL
Comments following a sermon, 1811[16]

During the printing of the *Declaration and Address* by William Sample in his Washington, Pennsylvania, newspaper office, Thomas Campbell received word his family had safely arrived in New York City, had proceeded on to Philadelphia, and departed there by wagon toward Washington. Eager to see his wife and children, Thomas rode to meet them. On an ancient Indian trading path—variously known as Pennsylvania State Road, Forbes Road, the Old Glad Road, or Turkey Trot Road, a short distance east of the Chestnut Ridge summit, the Campbell family reunited—October 19, 1809. In the wagon were Jane Campbell, her four daughters, and three sons. The eldest was Alexander, who passed his twenty-first birthday during the fifty-four-day voyage from Grennock, Scotland, to New York. Together, the family descended the western slope of Chestnut Ridge, crossed the Monongahela on the Williamsport ferry and made their way home to Washington, Pennsylvania. Every mile found them sharing a new episode from the drama of their lives during the two-year separation.

Alexander Campbell would become the pivotal founder and leader of the Reformation Movement. The American portion of his life's journey opened that October, a journey that had begun in the quiet village of Ballymena, county Antrim, Ireland, in the parish of Broughshane, September 12, 1788. While still an infant, he moved with his family to County Armagh, settling first at Market Hill, then Rich Hill. The picturesque countryside surrounding these villages–meadows, hills, stonewalls, small neighboring farmsteads, lakes–a region described as one of the most beautiful in Ireland, provided the setting for his youth. His earliest education came principally from the elementary school in Market Hill. At age ten or eleven his father dispatched him to Newry to study in the academy of his uncles, Archibald and Enos. Soon he returned home to study under his father's watchful tutelage in the hope of taming his lively temperament. By his own recollection he was a reluctant student:

> I then regarded my father as a severe and strict master, and rather envied my schoolmates who had more indulgent parents… When I was a boy I sometimes played truant… I would sometimes write off my lessons on a slip of paper, cut according to the dimensions of my book, and with this before me I was enabled to translate with some degree of fluency…

He also recalled "the double portion of the rod I used to receive for such a trick."[17]

For a few years, full of the energy of youth, Alexander worked on his father's farm with the laborers, where he evolved into a virile young man. He loved the freedom of outdoor life, especially hunting, fishing, and swimming. But around the age of fourteen he became his father's son. His intellectual talents emerged and he expressed the desire to become one of the best scholars in the kingdom. Thomas taught him the English classics–Shakespeare, Milton, Pope, Samuel Johnson–as well as French, Latin, and Greek classics, including Homer, Horace, and *Aesop's Fables*. He especially liked Gray's *Elegy* and actually memorized Milton's entire *Paradise Lost*. On his sixteenth birthday his father introduced him to the writings of John Locke–*Letters of Toleration* and *Essay on Human Understanding*–whose ideas of civil and religious liberty left a lasting impression on young Alexander. Thomas Campbell wanted his son to be well educated, and worked tirelessly to perfect his knowledge for eventual attendance at the University of Glasgow. But with the increased size of the family (seven children) prospects of attending the university seemed a far reach.[18]

Intense religious study was integral to the Campbell home experience. Indeed, it was a required part of Thomas's ministry. One of the several Synod demands upon its ministers was to "worship God in his family by singing, reading and prayer morning and evening; that he should instruct them at least once a week in religion; remember the Lord's Day to keep it holy; and shall himself maintain a conversation becoming the gospel."

Thomas was faithful to every requirement. Each member of the Campbell family was expected to memorize a passage of scripture daily and to recite it at evening worship. On the Lord's Day they were expected, upon their return home from worship, to remember the chapter, verse, and meaning of the scripture and tell something of the minister's sermon. Through these family practices Alexander became an accomplished student of the scriptures. He also experienced internal tension regarding his own salvation.

> From the time I could read the scriptures, I became convinced that Jesus was the Son of God. I was also fully persuaded that I was a sinner... This caused me great distress of soul... Finally after many strugglings, I was enabled to put my trust in the Saviour, and to feel my reliance on him as the Saviour of sinners.

But after reading Locke, he came to the conclusion that *simple trust in Christ was all sufficient.* Only then did he find peace of mind and become a communicant in his father's church at Ahorey. Aware of his father's wish that he become a minister, Alexander shifted a portion of his educational regimen to theological reading and ecclesiastical history.[19]

His father and his mother, both of whom he idolized, were the prime molders of his character. Thomas was an inseparable companion and inspiration to Alexander through personal example. About his father he wrote:

> In the Christian ministry, or out of it, I knew no man that so uniformly, so undeviatingly, practiced what he taught... His family discipline was the most perfect I ever witnessed. He always honored his own word. What he promised, he performed.

And of his mother, he added:

> She...possessed a mental independence which I have rarely seen equaled and certainly never surpassed by any woman... Greatly devoted to her children, and especially to their proper training for public usefulness, and for their own individual and social enjoyment, she was indefatigable in her labors of love, and in her attention to their physical, intellectual, moral and religious development.

It has been written of the Campbell home that it was a house of prayer, a house of hope, a house of happiness, and–it should be added–a house of learning.[20]

When his father immigrated to America, Alexander shouldered the management of the Rich Hill Academy, and, along with his mother, the care of the family. To generate additional income for them he served as a private tutor to the children of a William Richardson and taught occasionally at his Uncle Archibald's academy in Newry. All the while he remained relentless in his passion for self-education. He took seriously, too, the words of a letter his father wrote to the family on the day of his embarkation: "Live to God; be devoted to him in heart and in all your undertakings. Be a sincere Christian…believe the promises of the gospel…read it, study it, pray over it, embrace it as your heritage." Alexander copied the entire letter into his personal or "commonplace" notebook, alongside the quotations he kept from his expanded range of reading.[21]

In March of 1808 word came from Thomas urging his family to join him in America. As they were making preparations for the voyage, smallpox struck the family, delaying their departure until autumn. They made their way to Londonderry in September, as the *Hibernia* captained by Jacob Jumer was scheduled to sail on September 28. Unfavorable winds delayed the departure until October 1, and then again until October 7. Finally the ship weighed anchor, fired its ten-cannon announcement of departure, and sailed from Lough Foyle. A few leagues out of the harbor it was caught in a severe storm tore its hull on a rock and began to sink. Two other ships caught in the same storm, sunk losing all passengers. During the height of the storm, while clinging to a broken mast of their wrecked ship, Alexander promised that if his life should be spared he would spend it in ministry. The storm eased, Alexander helped get his family safely to shore, then returned to salvage their possessions, particularly the casks containing his father's books. Too late in the season to attempt another Atlantic crossing, the family decided to winter in Glasgow where Alexander could enroll at the university.[22]

On November 8, 1808, one month almost to the day after the shipwreck, Alexander matriculated at the University of Glasgow. The six-month education he received there supplemented the excellent home schooling he had received from his father. The Glasgow experience, although brief, deepened his familiarity with the main currents of English thought and placed him at the center of a religious reform movement that, according to Robert Richardson, instilled in young Campbell the "first impulse toward a career of religious reformation." Among his professors were George Jardine and John Young, both of whom had taught his father twenty-five years earlier. He also attended the popular natural science lectures of Dr. Andrew Ure. His first class, French, began at 6:00 a.m.; then Greek at 7:00 a.m.; and Latin from 8:00 to 10:00 a.m. In the afternoon he studied advanced Greek with John Young, followed by the class Logic and Rhetoric taught by George Jardine. With resolute industry he spent substantial time in the university's 20,000-volume library. His personal notebooks were filled with lecture notes, translations, and quotations from which it is easily discerned that Jonathan Edwards, described by Campbell as the "greatest theologian ever produced in America," became his favorite theological author. At the annual distribution of prizes in the spring, Alexander received recognition in Logic "For the best Specimens of Analysis and Composition on Subjects of Reasoning and Taste."[23]

Outside the walls of the university Campbell quickly developed a friendship with Greville Ewing, pastor of the Haldanian tabernacle in Glasgow, former head of a Haldane seminary, and personal friend of James Haldane. Among other things, the Haldanians advocated substituting the Bible for human creeds, congregational self-governance, weekly communion, and baptism by immersion. Ewing assisted Alexander, who was a frequent guest for dinner and tea, in finding a place for the family to live in Glasgow. Through Ewing, Campbell came in contact with many Glasgow civic and religious leaders. An eager student, he regularly engaged them in religious conversation, especially on the issues of reconciling Calvinism with independent church government, reconciling the notion of absolute truth of the gospels with individual opinion, and reconciling Enlightenment toleration with religious conviction—issues he would neither fully resolve then nor later during his leadership years in an American religious movement. Referring to the variety of religious views swirling about him, challenging his thought and adding to his growing dissatisfaction with the Seceder Presbyterian Church, Alexander said, "Whenever I saw a pretty feather in any bird, I plucked it out, and plumed myself with it, until I became so speckled that not a single species would own me." By the time of the semiannual communion season of the Seceder Church, he had passed his examination and received the metallic token necessary for communion. On Sacrament Day in April, 1,809 communicants were approved to receive the Lord's supper in shifts at nine tables. Near the end of the line, when his turn came, Alexander took his seat at a table, dropped the communion token upon the plate, but *refused the sacrament,* thereby breaking with his religious past. Richardson remarked of the moment, it was "a token not of communion but of separation"; and Leroy Garrett observed, "[The] ring of the token announced the beginning of the reformation he would soon launch in the new world." Others would draw a more lofty parallel between the ring of Campbell's token and the ring of Luther's hammer nailing the ninety-five theses to the cathedral door in Wittenburg.[24]

June and July were spent preparing for their voyage to America on the *Latonia,* captained by Thomas McCray and scheduled to depart the port of Grennock on August 1. Delayed until August 5 by headwinds and a fleet of warships on its way to fight Napoleon, the *Latonia* finally sailed down the Firth of Clyde and into the Atlantic. On Friday, September 29, fifty-eight days out of Grennock, the *Latonia* cast anchor in the harbor of New York. Both Thomas and Alexander were now in America, set free from their religious past, and primed to launch a religious reformation in America.

Brush Run: The Birth of a Church

I labor to see sectarianism abolished and all Christians of every name united upon the one foundation upon which the apostolic church was founded...

ALEXANDER CAMPBELL
Christian Baptist, *1826*[25]

Reunited, the Campbell family settled in Washington, Pennsylvania, an 1809 frontier community of about 175 scattered homes. The town, spread over a hilltop amid the handsome landscape of the valley of Chartiers Creek, held many reminders of their former home in Rich Hill, Ireland, especially its scenery and old Ahorey friends.

Upon his arrival, Alexander began reading the proof sheets of the *Declaration and Address* as quickly as they came off press. Intellectually prepared to appreciate its clear and noble principles, he found in its pages purpose, direction, and a cause. At once he resolved to devote his life to the promotion of its principles and informed his father of his intent to prepare himself as an advocate for the proposed reformation. Thomas, obviously delighted, advised his son to "retire to your chamber, take up the Divine Book and make it the subject of study for at least six months." Toward that end Alexander spent his first American winter and spring in "examination of the scriptures, ecclesiastical history, systems of divinity, and all the Protestant platforms of church union, communion and co-operation." Under his father's direction, he established a systematic daily routine: one hour of Greek, one hour of Latin, one-half hour of Hebrew, two hours for study of biblical commentaries and the scriptures in their original language, and three to four hours reading church history.[26]

Thomas first asked Alexander to preach on July 15, 1810. Neither licensed nor ordained, and having withdrawn from the Anti-burgher Presbyterians in Glasgow, Alexander did not hold membership in any church. But his sermon was a critical and popular success. He spoke like a seasoned veteran, not a novice; he spoke with careful, logical analysis, with thorough research and preparation, and proceeded to deliver 106 sermons during the next twelve months, mostly in small gatherings.

Meanwhile, it became evident to Thomas the cause so eloquently articulated in the *Declaration and Address* was neither widely accepted nor progressing. He decided to apply to a Synod of the Presbyterian Church in the United States in Pittsburgh for reinstatement as a minister, believing this would relieve the anxiety of Association members who were trying to maintain memberships in their respective congregations. The Synod rejected his application, claiming Thomas had encouraged his son to preach without authorization, opposed creeds, exhibited ambivalence toward

infant baptism, advocated the union of all Christians, and further criticized
Campbell's Movement as "destructive of the whole interest of Religion."

At the semiannual meeting of the Christian Association of Washington,
November 1, 1810, Alexander spoke to the gathering in his father's defense,
delivering with unusual maturity a spirited rebuttal in which he noted (a)
they considered lay preaching as authorized, and recognized no distinction
between clergy and laity; (b) each congregation was independent; (c)
infant baptism was a human tradition, not scriptural; (d) they anticipated
the Association becoming a church; and (e) a church without creeds was
the chief object of their proposed reformation. Alexander became much
admired and acclaimed for the vigorous manner in which he championed
the cause of his father. Neither father nor son ever forgot the rejection by
the Synod. The rejection, in fact, became the catalyst for establishing a
new church. Once again, a Presbyterian hierarchy proved incapable of
compromise with those they thought to be theologically subversive, leaving
no alternative but to break away.[27]

The Christian Association of Washington–at the next semiannual
meeting, May 4, 1811–constituted itself as a church. It became a separate
entity, one small country congregation committed to the autonomy of
the local congregation without ecclesiastical sanction from a bishop,
presbytery, or conference. The Association elected Thomas Campbell as
elder; Alexander Campbell as preacher; and four deacons: James Foster,
William Gilcrist, George Sharp, and John Dawson. An uncharted brook
provided the name by which the congregation is known in history–"Brush
Run Church." The *Declaration and Address* provided its guiding principles.
Reformation would no longer be attempted from *inside* the church; it would
come from the *outside,* from a new Movement. The following day, May 5,
thirty pilgrims joined in celebrating the Lord's supper under an oak tree
on a distant hillside in the western Appalachians, a sacramental moment
marking the adoption of the Haldanian practice of weekly communion,
and marking these pilgrims as people of the table.[28]

Arrangements were made for the construction of a meetinghouse on
the farm of William Gilcrist near the junction of Brush Run Creek and
Buffalo Creek. On June 16, 1811, the first service was held in the new but
uncompleted building. Twenty-two-year-old Alexander, delivered the first
sermon. The young minister chose for his text the words of the old Arab
prophet Bildad in Job 8:7–*Though your beginning was small, your latter days
will be very great.* Campbell opened his sermon with the words:

> We commence our career as a church under the banner of "The
> Bible, the whole Bible, and nothing but the Bible," as the standard
> of our religious faith and practice… Our inferences and opinions
> are our own… Christians are the sons of liberty, the Lord's free
> men. The right to choose and to refuse the opinions of men is the

essence of liberty… We are a weak band, a humble beginning; but so were they of Galilee…

John Boyd built the 18' x 36' clapboard structure, but did not receive the final payment of $98.00 until 1814. Alexander Campbell was ordained in this modest structure on January 1, 1812, with Thomas Campbell officiating as senior minister and assisted by the four deacons. The building was used for worship until 1828, when it was removed to West Middleton, Pennsylvania, where it became successively a blacksmith shop, post office, and finally a stable.[29]

Baptism by immersion became the second major theological benchmark (following the adoption of weekly communion) in the development of Brush Run Church. The impact of that decision proved profound. While in Glasgow, Alexander learned the Haldanes and Sandemanians baptized by immersion. He apparently gave the subject little thought at the time. But it became a serious issue for him three years later when his first child, Jane, was born, a year after Alexander married Margaret Brown, daughter of Thomas Campbell's friend John Brown. In the fall of 1810 Thomas loaned some books to John Brown, a prosperous carpenter and millwright, as well as successful farmer, a man of independent thought and unyielding integrity. Thomas requested Alexander take the books to the Brown residence and Alexander soon found himself smitten with Brown's attractive eighteen-year-old daughter, Margaret–slender, graceful, engaging, dark hair, energetic. By the end of the year she had agreed to become his wife, and they were married on March 12, 1811, in the parlor of the Brown home. The Browns were members of the Presbyterian Church in West Liberty; their pastor, the Rev. Mr. Hughes, performed the ceremony. The couple moved in with the Browns, and Alexander assisted with the management of the farm. One year later, March 13, 1812, their daughter Jane was born, named for Alexander's mother. Suddenly, the subject of baptism, particularly infant baptism, gained immediate importance.[30]

Engaging in an intense study of the subject, Alexander gathered all the books on baptism he could find. He concluded infant baptism to be a human invention, not scriptural, and therefore not authorized in the scriptures. Sprinkling of infants, in his view, did not constitute baptism. The Greek word for baptism, by his interpretation, meant immersion. Baptism, Campbell further concluded, should follow a confession of faith and should be confined to believers only; therefore, Alexander himself should be baptized. On June 12, 1812, Alexander and Margaret, his sister Dorothea, his parents Thomas and Jane, and three other Brush Run members were immersed in Buffalo Creek by a Baptist preacher, Elder Mathias Luce. Seven hours of preaching by Thomas and Alexander explaining baptism followed their immersion. Thirteen other members were baptized the next Lord's Day, and soon all who were members had been immersed. Alexander later observed:

> This...was the first community in the country that was immersed
> into that primitive, simple, and most significant confession of faith
> in the divine person and mission of the Lord Jesus Christ, without
> being brought before a church to answer doctrinal questions.

The adoption of immersion by the reformers brought a radical change to
the principles for union as stated by Thomas Campbell in the *Declaration and
Address*. The form of baptism could no longer be viewed as a human opinion
to be tolerated for the sake of union; immersion had become essential, a
perceived New Testament practice, and churches needed to be persuaded
to accept this "ordinance" that only Baptists believed was mandated by the
New Testament. While this requirement set them further apart from their
Presbyterian heritage and placed a barrier between the reformers and nearly
all other churches, it created a mutually reinforcing relationship with the
Baptists. In the autumn of 1813 Brush Run Church received an invitation
to membership from the Redstone Baptist Association. It accepted on its
own terms outlined in a lengthy document including the provision: "We
should be allowed to teach and preach whatever we learned from the Holy
Scriptures, regardless of any human creed."

A tense and uneasy relationship continued with the Baptists for
seventeen years. The Brush Run folk were not Baptists in either doctrine or
practice. By W. E. Garrison's evaluation, "they did not regard themselves
as merged indistinguishably in the Baptist denomination, and their sense
of special mission did not diminish."[31]

Scholars believe the decision to immerse was the moment leadership
shifted within the Movement from Thomas to Alexander. The son had led
the way in researching the question of baptism and urging immersion. The
father had followed. Robert Richardson was first to detect the change:

> From this hour the positions of father and son were reversed, and
> each tacitly occupied the position allotted to him. Alexander became
> the master-spirit, and to him the eyes of all were now directed. As
> before, it was still a constant and affectionate co-operation.[32]

Thomas soon migrated to Cambridge, Ohio. In 1815 he moved to
Pittsburgh where he opened a school that also became a church. He taught
for a time at the Burlington Academy in Newport, Kentucky, but returned
to Washington County, Pennsylvania in 1819. He made frequent preaching
tours throughout Western Pennsylvania and the Western Reserve of Ohio.
His biographer said he became "an able assistant" and counselor to his
gifted son. Alexander continued to manage his father-in-law's farm, lead the
Brush Run congregation, and preach in several Baptist congregations.

On August 30, 1816, at the Redstone Association meeting, when
a speaker unexpectedly cancelled because of illness, Alexander was
reluctantly invited to preach. He delivered perhaps his most famous and
influential sermon, entitled "Sermon on the Law," based on Romans 8:3.

God, he said, was a covenant maker. God dealt with humankind: through a succession of covenants. The Old Testament and the New Testament were not, claimed Campbell, a single covenant; and the New Testament was not an extension of the Old. The coming of Christ introduced a whole new covenant. The Old Testament tells of a covenant of law with Hebrew and Jewish institutions, including a specific nation. The New Testament tells of a new covenant in Christ with terms for the whole human race. The Old Testament was a covenant under law; the New, a covenant under grace; the Old, the law of Moses; the New, faith in Christ. He reminded his listeners that Jesus said, "Teach disciples all *I* have commanded," not what Moses commanded. He asked his listeners if they were disciples of Moses or disciples of Christ.[33] Campbell later said the "Sermon on the Law" began a seven-year war.

Although they respected the brilliance of his learning, many members of the thirty-three Baptist congregations in the Association viewed him as a person with dangerous views and regularly charged him with heresy. The printed sermon received an immediate censure from the Redstone Association. Thomas' little Pittsburgh congregation applied for membership in the Redstone Association at the same 1816 meeting; it was rejected.[34]

The Campbell Movement experienced little progress during its first eight or nine years. For Alexander, however, these were years of financial and intellectual preparation. When it was proposed that a colony be established in Zanesville, Ohio, John Brown reacted to the potential departure of his daughter, Margaret, by deeding his farm to Alexander. The Campbells stayed in Virginia. Brown's generous act provided Alexander with financial security for the remainder of his life. He expanded his land holdings near Buffalo Creek to 2,000 acres and added land through speculation in both Ohio and Illinois. These were years of intense study as well: on baptism, on ecclesiastical history, on biblical interpretation, on unity and cooperation. All prepared him for the coming reformation.

A transformational event thrust Alexander Campbell into regional prominence. John Walker, a Seceder Presbyterian in Mt. Pleasant, Ohio, challenged the Baptists to a debate on baptism. While the Baptists considered Campbell theologically suspect, they believed him to be solid on baptism and urged him to represent them in the debate. Reluctantly he agreed. The date was June 19–20, 1820, and the place was Mt. Pleasant, Ohio. Walker, defending infant baptism, used the standard argument of infant circumcision as the seal of the Jewish covenant and infant baptism as the seal of the Christian covenant, a historic continuity. Campbell called it a fictitious analogy and added that if Presbyterians really believed it, only boys could be baptized.

Drawing from his "Sermon on the Law, " Campbell presented the Christian covenant as a new covenant with a new law. He argued that the parties involved (other than God) and the terms of agreement changed between Sinai and the present. The Old Testament command to be circumcised he defined as a directive for the racial descendants of Abraham; the New Testament command to be baptized he defined as a directive for those who had faith in Christ, those who were *believers.* Under the New Testament covenant, Christians had been liberated from the Mosaic Law and from Judaism. Alexander Campbell triumphed in the debate. Even the Presbyterians thought Walker had performed poorly. Printed copies went through two quick printings, the first, 1,000 copies; the second, 3,000 copies. The debate brought popular notice to Campbell, even a degree of fame throughout the Ohio valley. Through this debate Campbell found he had natural ability as a debater. He also discovered the power of the printed page and the vast numbers of persons it could reach. Baptists were thrilled with his victory, but concerned they had paid too high a price by providing a platform for him to further expound the content of his "Sermon on the Law," giving momentum and encouragement to his reform movement.[35]

At the close of the Walker debate, Campbell declared his readiness to meet any minister from any denomination in debate on the subject of infant sprinkling. Three years later the Reverend W. L. MacCalla, a Presbyterian minister in Bracken County, Kentucky, accepted Campbell's challenge. They set the date of October 15–22 for the debate, and chose Washington, Kentucky, as the site. In August Campbell learned that the old guard (orthodox Baptists of the Redstone Association) had drawn up a "bill of heresies" against his "Sermon on the Law" with the intent to excommunicate him at the September Association meeting. Campbell cleverly secured letters of dismissal for himself and thirty-one members of the Brush Run Church for the purpose of establishing a church in Wellsburg, Virginia. The new church was immediately and cordially received into the new Mahoning Association of Baptist Churches across the river in Ohio. When the Redstone Association meeting convened in September, critics attempted to excommunicate Campbell, but were surprised to learn that he was not a member of Brush Run, not a member of any church in the Association, and therefore not a member of the Association. They could do nothing. Campbell had completely outmaneuvered them.

MacCalla opened the Kentucky debate on infant baptism the same way as Walker, with the favorite argument of basing infant baptism on the continuity of the Jewish and Christian covenants with the analogy of baptism and circumcision. "Baptism was substituted for circumcision," claimed MacCalla. "It was attached to the same covenant, and is now a sign and seal of the covenant with Abraham." As in the Walker debate, Campbell responded with much of his "Sermon on the Law," shattering MacCalla's thesis and claiming that infant sprinkling was a human tradition. In the previous debate, Campbell had focused on subjects (believers) and means (immersion), but with MacCalla he moved the argument to another level, the remission of sins, the "washing of regeneration," the washing away of believers' personal sins. The purpose of the ordinance was for the forgiveness of sins, argued Campbell. He quoted the scripture, "Repent and be baptized," which he contended meant *believer's* baptism. The sacrament demanded personal choice, personal belief, and personal responsibility. How could such a rite be administered to infants? He argued further that this is not a "water salvation." The blood of Christ *really* cleanses us, said Campbell, and the water of baptism *formally* washes away our sins. He introduced the Greek word *baptizein,* meaning burial and implying immersion as the form of baptism. Once again, Campbell was victorious and sparked much popular acclaim throughout Kentucky, Tennessee, and Ohio. It moved Campbell to proclaim: "This is one of the best means of propagating the truth… We are fully persuaded that a week's debating is worth a year's preaching for the purpose of disseminating truth."[36]

Twenty years later, November 1843, in his longest and last debate, Campbell engaged another Presbyterian minister, Nathan L. Rice, on the same subject–baptism. Earlier, in January 1837, Campbell gained significant public recognition through the medium of debate when he defended Protestantism in a debate with the Archbishop of Cincinnati, John B. Purcell. At the conclusion of the Purcell debate, however, Campbell distanced himself from anti-Catholic activity.

Christian Baptist

The Christian Baptist shall espouse the cause of no religious sect, excepting that ancient sect called "Christians first at Antioch." Its sole object shall be the eviction of truth and the exposing of error in doctrine and practice.

ALEXANDER CAMPBELL
Christian Baptist, *1823*[37]

Campbell noted the brisk sales of the printed versions of his debates, leading him to speculate he could reach more people through print than through preaching. Fourteen years earlier Thomas Campbell's *Declaration and Address* included in the postscript a proposal to publish a magazine with definitive purpose: "a periodical publication for the express purpose of detecting and exposing the various anti-Christian enormities and corruptions which infect the Christian church."

Alexander decided to implement his father's recommendation. He purchased type and a press, constructed a building near the river on his farm to house the printing operation, and issued a prospectus. On August 3, 1823, a twenty-four-page monthly, named *Christian Baptist,* made its appearance. It would prove to be a highly controversial piece, described favorably by Moses Lard as "the masterpiece of [Campbell's] life. In polish and completeness of thought, it cannot be pronounced equal to some volumes of his *Harbinger*, but in originality and utility he has written nothing to excel it." Isaac Errett considered it a "model of polemical theology, unexcelled in completeness of information, ripeness of judgment, strength of argument; seldom is such playfulness of wit and keenness of satire joined with such gentlemanly dignity and logical power." And a contemporary historian noted, "No periodical has created so profound a sensation in modern times." But there was an equal amount of opinion of a quite different sort. One Baptist historian, in his *A History of the Baptists in the Middle States,* denounced Campbell by declaring, "No polemical literature in the country…has equaled *Christian Baptist* in sarcasm, bitterness, and unrelenting severity of attack. The violence of his language is so absurd that one is at a loss to know how so sane-minded a man could have used it, or why it was not received as the ravings of a madman." And a writer for the *Presbyterian Review* exceeded the Baptist virulence by describing Campbell's periodical: "*The Christian Baptist* abounded with vulgar phrase, coarse invectives, clap-trap appeals to current prejudices, low witticisms, bitter raillery, haughty defiance intermingled occasionally with histrionic buffoonery, sarcastic jibes, unsparing vituperations and low-lived jests."[38]

Campbell believed a bold shock was required to arouse the people and exorcise the ecclesiastical system. The Christian community, in his view, needed to be jolted, so he adopted a lively, sarcastic, iconoclastic style tinged with rhetorical exaggeration, paradox, playful irony, and satire. He knew it would compel attention, even if it did not generate popular approval. He was an artist at satire, a quite useful quality in debate, but not so useful as an instrument of reconciliation. Eight years later, reflecting on his early *Christian Baptist* writings, Campbell said he had viewed the Christian community as having lost its health, a community in need of a desperate remedy. The first volume of *Christian Baptist,* he admitted, was "the most uncharitable, the most severe, sarcastic and ironical I ever wrote." He portrayed it as an experiment to determine if the church could be moved to feel its ailment. Campbell recognized, however, that his penchant for satire sometimes carried him into extreme expressions. He confided in a letter to his friend Spencer Clack:

> My writings, I have learned from many sources, sometimes possess an asperity which is not at all indicative of my temperament of mind. I am, perhaps, in this sort of paradox– constitutionally mild and charitable; but, as a writer, tart and severe.

To another correspondent he confessed:

> In a controversy so long and diversified, and with such a host as have opposed our progress, it would have been super-human and beyond the good fortune of erring mortals, not to have spoken

or written something which ought not to have seen the light. We plead no exemption from the common lot of fallible man;...had we now again to run the same race, we would avoid some hills and swamps, some narrow passes, and some winding labyrinths, which have impeded our progress.[39]

With an unsparing pen he fearlessly launched a controversial attack upon three traditional ecclesial themes–*creeds, societies,* and *clergy*–themes that came under repeated criticism in the pages of *the Christian Baptist* throughout its seven-year history. Following the lead of the *Declaration and Address,* Alexander Campbell denounced creeds. He depicted them as "commandments of men," "human inventions," "philosophical speculations," symptoms of adherence to a sect or denomination. He viewed them as products of philosophers and enthusiastic preachers, often resulting in the laity being treated as heathen, when in fact they were entitled to the rights and privileges of Christ's church. Creeds, he asserted, arose from sectarian constitutions. They spawned ignorance and superstition; they set friend against friend and relative against relative. Unification and purification of the faith, declared Campbell, were achieved by embracing the scriptures, not creeds, and by returning to the original gospel.

> The only bond of union among them was faith in him and submission to his will. No subscription to abstract propositions framed by synods; no decrees of councils sanctioned by kings; no rules of practice commanded by ecclesiastical courts were imposed upon them as terms of admission into this holy brotherhood.

The church, declared Campbell, was founded on Christ, not a creed. Faith was belief in Christ, not belief in doctrinal creeds. No clergyman, he argued, had the right to decree church laws simply by individual will.[40]

In like manner Campbell expressed his opposition to societies and organizations. Unauthorized by scripture, he pronounced societies human creations, exalting the inventions of humans above the wisdom of God. He believed ecclesiastical structures–synods, conferences, societies, presbyteries, and assemblies–were perverted for denominational aggrandizement rather than established for service to God or humanity. The New Testament church, he said, "was not fractured into missionary societies, Bible societies, educational societies; nor did they dream of organizing such." He argued further that no council, ecclesiastical court, or synod should have administrative control over a congregation. Again he recommended the study of the scriptures, claiming the New Testament church free from intrusion of organizations such as synods, societies, conferences, and presbyteries. "In their church capacity alone they moved," he concluded.[41]

Campbell's criticism of the clergy provoked the most outrage. He thought clergy had become pretentious, proud, and worldly, as reflected in their professional mannerisms and array of titles: Pope, reverend, doctor of divinity, cardinal, archbishop, metropolitan, diocesan bishop, rector, dean, priest, arch deacon, presiding elder, ruling elder, circuit preacher, local preacher, licentiate, abbot, monk, friar, etc., an array that led Campbell to brand them the "Kingdom of the Clergy." He was concerned that ministers and their sermons had usurped the place of God in worship. His two most famous articles on clergy were the "Third Epistle of Peter" (July 1825), and "The Parable of the Iron Bedstead" (October 1826). In his judgment a sharp distinction had developed over the centuries between a growing hierarchy of clergy on the one hand and the laity on the other, with the laity becoming servile and the clergy becoming lords of the church. Campbell objected to the exclusive right of clergy to interpret scriptures, a circumstance he called "clerical ascendancy over the human mind." Clergy, he charged, took knowledge from the people and kept them in ignorance. Campbell argued for a simple church structure of elders and deacons, and he denied distinction between laity and clergy: "We wish, cordially wish, to take the New Testament out of the abuses of the clergy and put it into the hands of the people."[42]

A series of articles written by Campbell under the title "Restoration of the Ancient Order of Things" appeared from February 1825 to September 1829 in thirty-two installments. The basic theme of these essays was the *necessity for union of all Christians*–not a mere federation, but a corporate, organic unity in one body. In these essays he talked far more about the early church than about the union of Christians, because he believed in the catholic simplicity of the New Testament. The apostolic church, from Campbell's perspective, presented the perfect model for union. His purpose was to build unity on purely catholic and apostolic principles, a concept from which he did not waver throughout his entire career. For Campbell, to be catholic was to be apostolic. Understanding the apostolic church was indispensable to his concept of Christian union.

The subjects he addressed in the "Ancient Order" series–faith, sacrament, ministry, worship, discipline–were the main issues addressed in the twentieth century by the "Faith and Order" Movement of the World Council of Churches. He appealed to the churches of his day to reform by substituting the apostolic order for their denominational particularities. Campbell objected to treating the New Testament like a Leviticus manual because he was *not* a legalistic restorationist. He did not view the scriptures as a "rigid primitivist pattern"; rather, he urged openness to the fresh revelation to be derived from studying the Word, what is known today as historical-critical method. "Open the New Testament," he said, "as if mortal man had never seen it before." Campbell described the church as a community of divine grace, "God's revelation in history." Jesus served humankind in body, and then gave to his disciples a body, the church, that they too might serve the world. The New Testament, said Campbell, grieved at the very idea of division of the body of Christ, describing it as a virtual rending of his body. Failure of the modern church to work for unity, said Campbell, is unthinkable.

Unity in Campbell's mind could be achieved through a *common faith, common sacraments, common ministry,* and a *common mode of worship.* Persuaded the church had forgotten the meaning of the two great sacraments of unity, the two central redemptive rites, baptism and the Lord's supper, Campbell's reformation purpose was to help the church relearn, to recover the nature and design of those ordinances. He would later write, "All the wisdom, power, love, mercy, compassion, or grace of God, is in the ordinances." He named preaching, immersion, the Lord's Day, reading the Bible, and the Lord's supper among other sacred ordinances, but the two primary ordinances were immersion and the Lord's supper. Later still he would avow:

> The current reformation, if conspicuous now or hereafter for anything, must be so because of the conspicuity it gives the Bible and its ordinances as the indispensable moral means of spiritual life and health. [The] distinguishing characteristic is, a restoration of the ordinances…to their place and power.

Initially, Campbell said the belief of one fact only is all that was required for salvation: "The belief of this one fact, and submission to one institution expressive of it, is all that is required for admission into the church…that Jesus the Nazarene is the Messiah—the one institution is baptism." Roland Bainton observed that had Campbell stopped there he might have had a basis for a very large union, but he began to narrow the range with absolutes—e.g., adult baptism by immersion, weekly observance of communion—that cut off the possibility of union with almost everyone. These restrictive principles became essentials in the Movement's thought, for both salvation and unity.[43]

Controversies over the content of *Christian Baptist* set in place conflicting mind-sets, laying the groundwork for division within the Movement. Certain Churches of Christ scholars, represented here through the writings of James North and Earl West, generally contend that "restoration" was a mind-set for restoring and maintaining the primitive, one true and perfect church—a prized, if radically sectarian ideal. In their worldview, restoration, or "primitivism" as they liked to call it, was unsuited for Christian unity. Union and restoration, they suggest, were mutually exclusive. For restoration advocates the concept of union was essentially nonexistent. Their object was "not to be united with other Christians, but to be right." Ecumenism was unthinkable to the one true church. They consistently refer to the Movement as the "Restoration Movement." The objective: restore the church, not unify Christendom. As J. W. McGarvey would later write, "Truth first, union afterward; and union only in the truth." Some believed there were *two* Alexander Campbells, and that a single Alexander Campbell was a myth; the "*Christian Baptist* Campbell" decisively shaped their beliefs. Claiming that a new Campbell emerged as the years passed, they saw Churches of Christ as heirs of the spirit and outlook of the *Christian Baptist* Campbell.[44]

Disciples of Christ historian Eva Jean Wrather, offered an alternative perspective. In her view the two Campbells theory was a myth; there was only *one* Campbell, consistent in his thought on toleration, cooperation, and unity, neither sectarian nor primitivist. Ms. Wrather, a lifelong Campbell scholar, declared:

> There is a common fallacy about Campbell. It is often said there are really two Campbells. He is spoken of as if there was the destructive iconoclast of the *Christian Baptist*; then there was the other man, the conservative master-builder of the *Millennial Harbinger* years–a sort of schizophrenic personality. Nothing is really further from the truth.[45]

From beginning to end Campbell's writings reveal him to be an advocate of church union and cooperation. He did not write wiser or stronger statements on the subject of union than those he prepared as editor of *Christian Baptist.* Among those statements he said:

> [The] plan of making our own nest and fluttering over our own brood, and confining all goodness and grace to our noble selves and to the "elect few" who are like us, is the quintessence of sublimated Pharisaism.

Wrather believed the greatest challenge to Campbell was the "misguided Restorers of the Ancient Order," who perverted and exaggerated the cardinal principles of the Movement. She referred to them as "minor spirits trying to ape the *Christian Baptist* without perceiving its underlying concept, small men seeking to cut Alexander Campbell's ideas down to their own stature." Wrather continued with a withering summation:

> These pure "restorers of ancient order" pressed their claims with arrogant self-assurance and condescending pity for all those who did not share their ideas of interpreting the Scriptures. Only those who accepted their version of the "ancient order" were of God's elect; they did not perceive that a narrow, simple creed and form might be as deadening as a complex creed and form, never perceiving that the sterility lay not in the elaborateness of its form but in its rigidity, in the veneration with which it was held and in the purposes for which it was practiced. The less learned these legalistic restorers, the more certain they were of their complete understanding of all God's purposes and designs. Theirs was the arrogance of ignorance. Restorers were busy erecting new restrictions, setting themselves up

as a model of the "true church" while damning all who disagreed with them, never perceiving that sectarianism was not so much a matter of dogma as of temperament, was not so much in the nature of the thing believed as in the nature of the person believing. They exalted themselves as sole arbiters of God's word. They identified their own opinions with the mind of God. Clearly, Campbell's early iconoclasm reaped an ugly harvest at the hands of the ignorant and bigoted self-righteous. Some of Campbell's finest concepts, [inclusiveness, unity, toleration] penetrating the inner philosophy of religion were ignored, while his more barren concepts were reiterated ad nauseam. Those unable to penetrate the rich inner core of Campbell's spirit had simply grasped the externals easiest to comprehend and trumpeted them as divine will. Thus, while one group was seeking to expand the broad principles of the Reform Movement into a world movement for federation and toleration, the other group was threatening to make the Disciples into a narrow, jangling sect which had lost all broad ideals in petty disquisitions over minutia of the "ancient order."

By the 1830s, Campbell realized that the little handful of reformers who had so hopefully established a church at Brush Run in 1811 were actually evolving into two divergent movements. Congregations of Reformers were known above all else for their fierce spirit of independence—an attitude Campbell knew had been created by his own writings. He was anxious they not carry this position to extreme. Sensing that the appeal to "ancient order" could be a boomerang in the hands of extremists, he cautioned the Reformers in the October 3, 1831, issue of *The Millennial Harbinger*:

> The New Testament furnished the principals which call forth our energies, but [does not] furnish us with a list of all the crimes to be avoided and all the virtues to be practiced in the ever changing habits, circumstances and relations of society…
>
> Some weak but honest minds are for converting the New Testament into a ritual, expecting to find a code of laws concerning everything about economy and co-operation as if these were parts of Christian faith and morals… Some have even thought it a sin to enumerate the names of the members of one congregation because David was punished for enumerating Israel and Judah… Such eccentricities of mind resemble the conduct of a man who, because his father was drowned, would not pass a shallow ford, and another who, because he had been burned when a child, would never approach a fire to warm by it.

Campbell turned to the New Testament church (rarely using the term "primitive") to reduce the essentials for unity to simple terms, while recommending liberty of opinion for nonessentials and to focus the church on its sources, to cleanse itself from the silt of time, and to stand on the personality and ideals of Christ. He was convinced the autonomy of a local congregation and its union in one body were complimentary, not contradictory.

Both the *Declaration and Address* and the *Christian Baptist* argued that church government was rooted in two sources of authority: the New Testament and human reason. Campbell believed in reason, tempered with common sense. And believing in humanity's ability to *think,* he did not presuppose some final truth for all time and he did not intend his theology to be a test of church membership. As a Scottish pragmatist he understood reality as always in the making. However fixed reality might seem, humanity still had the liberty to modify it, thereby assuring that part of any reality would come from the future. His writings on the clergy were regularly misunderstood as well. Steering a middle way between clerical despotism and anarchical equality, he focused on abuses, directing his attacks toward the methods and systems of clergy, rather than the ministers themselves, including himself and his father. Eva Jean Wrather said it best, "He was not so much anti-clerical as non-sacerdotal."

Recent scholarship has produced another view of young Campbell. This interpretation holds that a tension had always existed in Campbell's thought between restoration and unity. He attempted to construct an ecclesiastical plan from two intellectual traditions, restoration and unity. As time passed, Campbell grew disillusioned with those in the Movement who turned the meaning of restoration in the direction of sectarian conformity. He saw how narrow and oppressive the restoration ideal had become in the hands of some. Campbell did not seek rigid uniformity, but rather unity through the restoration of a few essentials while extending liberty on nonessentials. But the Movement faltered on the definition, or lack thereof, of essentials. By seeking unity through the restoration of the apostolic church, Campbell caused the question of essentials and nonessentials to become controversial. It became the fundamental source of theological tension forever troubling the Movement. This view contends there was only one Campbell, never static, always willing to learn, always maturing, always growing in thought and experience, and who consequently changed with the passage of years. During the 1840s, Campbell himself affirmed this view when he remarked to his *Harbinger* readers:

> It is always more or less detrimental to the ascertainment of truth to allow our previous conclusions to assume the position of fixed and fundamental truth to which nothing is to be at any time added either in correction or enlargement. On the contrary, we ought rather to act under the conviction that we may be wiser today than yesterday.

In his long quest for unity, he moved away from restoration as the means of its achievement. But he never lost his passion for unity, nor did he ever abandon the quest.

Still another view suggested that beyond unity or restoration, Campbell's ultimate concern centered upon Christ's millennium on earth. Unity would be the means to the millennial dream, and restoration the means to unity. In this view it is deemed significant that Campbell did not name his second periodical the *Unity Harbinger* or the *Restoration Harbinger.* Making clear his major concern, he named it *The Millennial Harbinger.*[46]

The *Christian Baptist* years constituted a crucial period in Campbell's life, and what he wrote during those years was often misunderstood by later historians, thereby contributing to a depreciation of Campbell's contribution to American religious history and his role as a reformer. Although he was a profound scholar, he did not win much praise from scholars in his day; rather, he was often branded an enemy. Later generations of readers did not always perceive the fine distinctions so apparent to Campbell. The very qualities that made the little magazine so widely read also contributed to misunderstanding. William K. Pendleton commented on this matter in *The Millennial Harbinger* in 1866 shortly after Campbell's death.

> There is a class among us, who have a sort of bibliolatry toward the *Christian Baptist,* and, as is usual in such cases, they imagine that it has uttered many oracles, which upon a more careful study it will be found are not to be discovered on its pages.[47]

Campbell and Stone Compared

Your talents and learning we have highly respected; your course we have generally approved; your religious views in many points accord with our own; and to one point we have hoped we both were directing our efforts, which point is, to unite the flock of Christ scattered in the dark and cloudy day.

LETTER FROM STONE TO CAMPBELL
Christian Baptist, 1827

The first meeting between Alexander Campbell and Barton Stone occurred November 6, 1824, in Georgetown, Kentucky. Campbell, on a preaching tour of Kentucky, received an invitation from Stone to speak in his Georgetown congregation and to lodge in his home. Campbell accepted. Robert Richardson reported the two formed "a warm, personal acquaintance." A mutual friend observed they held high esteem for each other "as advocates of the same great principles." And Stone wrote of their conversation, "Our views were one."[48]

Indeed, this historic meeting, the first of many between the two founders, did serve to reveal a number of similarities and points of agreement. Both were religious reformers and ordained ministers with Presbyterian backgrounds; both passionately advocated Christian unity; both supported open and democratic processes in congregational governance, free from ecclesiastical control; both rejected creeds as tests of membership; both were editors (Campbell only beginning, Stone about to begin); both repudiated infant baptism and both were immersed (although Stone did not believe "immersion" should be a test of church membership, while Campbell initially believed it should, until 1837 when he stated otherwise); both, believing Christ died for all, rejected the Calvinistic emphasis on limited atonement and predestination; and both held that Christ was the basis and object of faith.[49]

But there were several differences, revealing that their views were not "one." Stone practiced open communion for all believers, while Campbell believed only the immersed should be admitted to the Lord's table. Campbell's Reformers took communion weekly. Stone's Christians did so less frequently, but in 1830 Stone adopted Campbell's position. Campbell's intellectual and concrete approach to unity contrasted with Stone's ethereal plea for unity, based on the Holy Spirit. Stone believed ordained ministers were required to decide on the ordination of an individual and made a distinction between elders and clergy; Campbell believed the vote of a congregation sufficient for ordination and made no distinction between elders and clergy. Campbell, a product of Enlightenment rationalism, believed persons acquired faith by reason, by an intellectual process, and a rational acceptance of biblical testimony. Stone, a product of the First and Second Great Awakenings, emerged from enthusiastic camp meeting Christianity often using the "mourning bench" or "anxious seat" that repentant sinners could come to as they sought salvation. Campbell was a postmillennialist (Christ would reign on earth 1,000 years before the judgment); Stone was a premillennialist (Christ would come in judgment prior to his 1,000-year reign); Campbell was extroverted, aggressive, self-reliant, a dominating personality; Stone's demeanor was self-effacing, gracious, modest, irenic, melancholic, and polite. Campbell enjoyed confrontation; Stone was forbearing. Campbell enjoyed debates; Stone disliked them and declined every opportunity to do so. In later years, Stone withdrew from all civil and governmental participation; Campbell interacted with the likes of Presidents Madison, Monroe, Buchanan, and with many public officials including John Marshall, James Garfield, Jefferson Davis, John C. Calhoun, Henry Clay, and Daniel Webster—many of whom were guests in his home. Finally, Stone believed the Movement should be called "Christians," a name divinely appointed (Acts 11:26) and universal in character. Campbell, however, strongly advocated the name "Disciples," a more ancient New Testament term, the name most often used by the Apostles. It was more distinctive, more humble, and more scriptural; plus, it identified the faithful as learners and followers. Furthermore, he believed the name "Christians" had been given in derision by ancient Romans and not divinely given at all. He also believed that the term Christian more properly belonged to the whole body of Christ, rather than be associated with a group's sectarian peculiarities. Campbell and Stone were never able to resolve the issue. Both names were and are still used to identify the Movement. Throughout the nineteenth century the names "Christian Church," "Disciples of Christ," and "Church of Christ" were used interchangeably.

Despite their differences, the two men forged a warm friendship and mutual respect that made eventual union of many of their separate congregations possible. Their similarities outweighed their differences, allowing the Disciples (Reformers) and Christians to work their way toward unity.

For both men, the years immediately following their 1824 Georgetown meeting were frenzied. Stone launched his periodical, *The Christian Messenger,* in November 1826. Within three months he began publishing a yearlong series entitled "History of the Christian Church in the West." Following quickly came a second series, "An Humble Address to the various Denominations of Christians in America," advocating union based on the scripture, "Love one another," with a design he described as a "religion of love, peace and union of God's family on earth." In September 1832 Stone published an article in *The Christian Messenger* entitled "An Address to the Churches of Christ" in which he urged forbearance to "our [Campbell & Stone] opinions," particularly the meaning of baptism; and in which he recorded his most famous statement on the subject of Christian unity: "Let the unity of Christians be our polar star. To this let our eyes be continually turned, and to this let our united efforts be directed."[50]

Out of his long-standing opposition to slavery, Stone became a strong supporter of the American Colonial Society, with the purpose of creating a colonial home for freed slaves in Liberia. He led an effort to petition Congress on this subject. A little more than a decade later, after having endorsed the immediate abolition of slavery, he became disillusioned with politics and advocated withdrawal on the part of citizens from participation in civil government, a notion he carried to the extent of nonresistance and ultimately to pacifism in wartime.

While Stone was launching *The Christian Messenger,* Campbell simultaneously wrote over a five-year period the series "The Ancient Order of Things" and the "Ancient Gospel." Early in 1825 he began another series on the "History of the English Bible," commenting, "It is a remarkable coincidence in the history of all the noted reformers that they all gave a translation of the Scriptures in the vernacular tongue of the people whom they labored to reform." In July he published a prospectus for a new translation of the New Testament. He used translations made fifty years earlier by three

Scottish clergymen (two Presbyterians, one Congregationalist)–George Campbell (Gospels), James Macknight (Epistles), Philip Doddridge (Acts and Revelation). For the basic Greek text, he used the 1805 edition produced by J. J. Greisbach, considered by scholars the finest of its time. To these basic sources Campbell added a historical and critical preface to each book, an appendix, 100 pages of notes, and filled in with passages from numerous other translations, particularly from the one by Charles Thompson printed in Philadelphia, 1808. He always disliked the division of the Bible into chapters and verses, and structured his version into "thought" sections with paragraphs. "Thy," "thou," and "thine" were removed; "Holy Spirit" replaced "Holy Ghost;" the word "church" does not appear; the word "bankers" was substituted for "exchangers"; but most controversial was his substitution of the word "immerse" for "baptize" throughout the New Testament. Campbell maintained in light of the constantly changing living language and expansion of scholarship, a new translation was needed for the sake of simplicity and clarity.[51]

He did not intend to be original. Rather, he gleaned from many different translations he thought expressed the ideas most clearly for the common reader. Presbyterians and Baptists were equally outraged, especially with the word "immerse." But modern scholars such as Luther Weigle of Yale, who chaired the committee that produced the Revised Standard Version in the 1950s, believed Campbell understood the principles of interpretation and translation, used excellent Greek, and further noted there was a "large degree of likeness between Campbell's translation and the Revised Standard Version of our own day." Campbell titled the new translation *The Sacred Writings of the Apostles and Evangelists of Jesus Christ, commonly styled the New Testament* and issued a printing of 2,000 copies on April 19, 1826. The names George Campbell, James Macknight, and Philip Doddridge appear on the title page, but Alexander Campbell's name is cited simply as "printer." It went through six subsequent, profitable editions, but its circulation appears to have been mostly with Reformers or Disciples congregations. He declined a seventh edition, due to his involvement with the American Bible Union as one of forty scholars selected to produce a new revision of the scriptures in 1854. By the late 1800s Campbell's New Testament had fallen out of use, displaced by later translations.

In the midst of translating the New Testament, his wife, suffering from tuberculosis, steadily failed. On October 22, 1827, came the terrible personal loss of his beloved Margaret. They carried her to the little cemetery beyond the orchard, where Campbell would eventually bury ten of his fourteen children. In the autumn of 1827 he found himself a widower with five daughters. He would never thereafter be a stranger to grief. The following year, as Margaret had insisted before her death, he married her good friend Selina Bakewell on July 31, 1828, a union that would last until his death nearly forty years later. Selina–tall, slender, raven hair, becomingly educated, determined–was twenty-five years old; Campbell, thirty-nine.

Campbell, the "religious reformer," soon engaged in the most celebrated of his several debates, this one with the internationally renowned British utopian "social reformer" and pioneer in cooperative movements, Robert Owen. The debate occurred in Cincinnati April 13–23, 1829, little more than a month after the presidential inauguration of Andrew Jackson. It generated the greatest publicity Campbell ever enjoyed, enlarging his provincial reputation to national stature and prestige, and greatly advancing his religious reform. Founder of the "Village of Co-operation" at New Harmony, Indiana, Owen prepared to prove that "the principles of all religions are erroneous," founded on ignorance and fear, and their origin a fable; Campbell prepared to defend religion, something he had done in the early issues of *Christian Baptist* in his "Six Letters to a Skeptic." When the event began, before an audience of 1,200 from many states, Owen actually refused to debate by simply ignoring everything Campbell said. Impervious to argument Owen simply read over and over his twelve points from a prepared manuscript on man in infancy. One historian judged the closing words of Campbell's opening address to be among the most impressive in the history of the Movement.

> It is not the ordinary affairs of this life, the fleeting and transitory concerns of today or tomorrow; it is not whether we shall live all freemen or die all slaves; it is not the momentary affairs of empire, or the evanescent charms of dominion–nay, indeed all these are but the toys of childhood, the sportive excursion of youthful fancy, contrasted with the question, What is man? Whence came he? Whither does he go?

Near the end of the debate, when it became clear that Owen had nothing more to say, he turned the floor to Campbell, who followed with a substantive twelve-hour speech on the evidences of Christianity and a critical attack on Owens' system. Among the visitors in the audience was a tourist from England, Mrs. Trollope, mother of the novelist Anthony Trollope. She was a careful observer of the proceedings and soon published a book on her American travels entitled, *Domestic Manners of the Americans.* She devoted four pages to the Campbell-Owen debate, noting that Owen entrenched himself behind his twelve laws and she wondered, "How he can have dreamed that they could be twisted into a refutation of the Christian religion, is a mystery which I never expect to understand." Of Campbell she wrote, "He quizzed Mr. Owen unmercifully; pinched him here for his parallelograms; hit him there for his human perfectibility, and kept the whole audience in a roar of laughter… Mr. Campbell's watch was the only one which reminded us that we had listened to him for half an hour; he sat down with the universal admiration of his audience." At the close of the debate, the *Cincinnati Chronicle and Literary Gazette* noted that the supporters of Robert Owen "appeared to be sadly disappointed," but of Campbell the paper added:

> He is undoubtedly a man of fine talents, and equally fine attainments. With an acute, vigorous mind, quick perceptions, and rapid powers of combination, he has sorely puzzled his antagonist, and at the same time both delighted and instructed his audience by his masterly defense of the truth, divine origin, and inestimable importance of Christianity.[52]

Shortly after he returned home from the debate, Campbell entered the political arena by winning election as a delegate from Brooke County to the 1829 Virginia Constitutional Convention in Richmond. Although criticized for this worldly work, he served anyway, becoming a prominent participant in the debates. On the afternoon of October 4, after a thirteen-day journey, Campbell arrived and took his seat in the Hall of Delegates. Seated around him were two ex-Presidents of the United States, James Madison and James Monroe; the Chief Justice of the Supreme Court, John Marshall; the Governor of the State, William B. Giles; a former Governor of the State, James Pleasants; the two United States Senators, John Tyler (who would become president of the United States) and Littleton Tazewell; and eleven members of the House of Representatives. Others would distinguish themselves as future judges, governors, ambassadors, and congressmen. Amid this group was only one preacher, Alexander Campbell, most often identified at the convention as the "Reverend Gentleman from Brooke." W. E. Garrison commented:

> Campbell crossed swords with them all. Reading those speeches today in the printed minutes of the convention and ignoring, if one can, the names and reputations of the speakers, one would say that, for argument and eloquence and for understanding of the principles of a democratic society, the victory lay clearly with the young preacher from the far northwestern corner of the state. But the others had the votes.[53]

Campbell stood out for his acumen and oratory, even in the illustrious company of more conservative elder statesmen. He represented a new generation of leaders, a generation whose views were in the minority on every issue. He helped lead the fight to democratize the government of Virginia by addressing the convention on abolition of the Virginia county court system, human rights, extension of suffrage to majority rule, and general public education. Campbell returned from the convention a confirmed advocate for the common (public) schools. In *The Millennial Harbinger,* public education is second only to peace among the issues he presented. On the question of representation on the basis of majority rule of free white population or on the basis of rule by the propertied minority (slaves: 400,000 in the East, 50,000 in the West, hence the advocacy for slavery in the East), Campbell favored majority rule of the white population and reasoned before the convention:

> The gentleman starts with the postulate, that there are two sorts of majorities: of numbers and interest; in plain English, of men and money. I do not well understand, why he ought not to have added, also, majorities of talent, physical strength, scientific skill and general literature. These are all more valuable than money and as useful to the State. A Robert Fulton, a General Jackson, a Joseph Lancaster, a Benjamin Franklin are as useful to the state as a whole district of mere slave-holders. Now, all the logic, metaphysics and rhetoric of this Assembly must be put to requisition to show why a citizen, having a hundred negroes, should have ten times more power than a Joseph Lancaster or a Robert Fulton with only a house and a garden.

After several weeks of debate, Campbell delivered his final remarks on this question arguing that general suffrage was "in the spirit of the age." He spoke to those present as men "who feel the current of the time." There was "one august tribunal to which time will make us all do homage–the tribunal of public opinion." And public opinion in "no less than half the States in this Union" already decided to disregard the property qualification for electors. Then he closed:

> When we disenfranchise one class of men, or deprive them of their political and natural rights, to secure any property or privilege we possess, we endanger that very property and those very privileges, more…than we protect them… It is in the nature of man to hate, and to attempt to impair and destroy, that which is held at his expense and which degrades him in his own estimation. For the safety, then, and the preservation of those very interests, I would conceive this extension of the Right of Suffrage indispensable.

Campbell lost decisively on this issue, and on every measure he supported. But some of his views were later assimilated in the constitution of 1852.[54]

One historian included Campbell among the "most notable and distinguished members" at the Convention. Another, John P. Little, writing for the *Southern Literary Messenger,* described Campbell as "an intellect"–"a cool and cautious Scotsman, thoroughly imbued with, and active in carrying out the most enthusiastic ideas"–"an enthusiasm accompanied by the firm decision of character, instinctive wisdom, honorable fairness of conduct, [and] abiding sense of religious truth." Hugh Blair Grigsby, a young elected delegate to the Convention who later wrote a history of the experience, observed of Campbell, "he was a fine scholar…his pleasing address and social feelings rendered him very acceptable. As a controversialist he had some great qualities; he was bold, subtle, indefatigable, and as insensible to attack as if he were sheathed in the hide of a rhinoceros. With the exception of Col. Bierne, he was, I think, the only foreign born citizen in the body." Campbell preached regularly in the Richmond churches during his time at the Convention, and former President Madison heard him often. Of Campbell, Madison said, "he was the ablest and most original expounder of the Scriptures I have ever heard."

Disciples and Christians: The Joining of Congregations

We are happy to announce to our brethren, and to the world the union of Christians in fact in our country. A few months ago the Reformers and the Christians in Georgetown, agreed to meet and worship together. We soon found that we were indeed in the same spirit, on the same foundation, the New Testament… We saw no reason why we should not be the same family. A great many…of both descriptions, assembled together, worshipped together in one spirit, and with one accord.

BARTON W. STONE & JOHN T. JOHNSON
The Christian Messenger 1832[55]

The achievement of union grew out of the process of separation. In fact, separation and union began simultaneously and continued during a span of five years. In 1826 Campbell had written, "I and the church with which I am connected are in 'full communion' with the Mahoning Baptist Association, Ohio." By 1831 he wrote, "We cannot fight under Baptist colors." Campbell's essays in *Christian Baptist* during the 1820s agitated the Baptists as well as other denominations. Baptists grew to believe they had enjoyed peace and harmony before Alexander Campbell entered their midst and wanted to be rid of him. They agreed with him on believers' baptism and on the New Testament as a basis of faith. But they did *not* agree on union, the value of associations, their name, or the role of the ordained in baptism and communion. Within the Baptist fold Campbell's followers were known variously as Reformers, New Testament Baptists, Reforming Baptists, and Campbellites. By whatever name, they were growing faster than the Baptists, a fact that alarmed the Baptist old guard.[56]

Baptists began to exclude numerous Reform congregations from their associations, but some were converting on their own from Baptist to Reformer. Several individual Reform converts had become effective evangelists. "Raccoon" John Smith (1784–1868), for example, converted because of censure by the Baptists for reading Campbell's New Testament. Plainspoken and dynamic, he became a highly successful evangelist for the Reformers. Every major history of the Movement quotes his famous statement, "I have *baptized* 700 sinners and *capsized* 1,500 Baptists." In Nashville, Philip S. Fall (1798–1890) left the Baptist church in 1827 to establish a new Reform congregation, later named Vine Street Christian Church. Fall–refined in manner, eloquent in speech, a man of reason, dignified without presumption, affable without familiarity–became one of Alexander Campbell's closest friends.[57]

In 1826, the Redstone Baptist Association established a pattern that would continue when a minority of ten orthodox congregations expelled a majority of thirteen Reform congregations from their association. It happened repeatedly. By 1830 all the associations in Kentucky had taken a stand against the Reformers. In 1832, when the Dover Association in Virginia took action to "separate all persons from their communion who were promoting controversy and discord under the name Reformers," Campbell wrote in *The Harbinger,* "The Rubicon is passed." But the watershed event occurred in August 1830, when the Mahoning Baptist Association–the center of Reformer activity–officially disbanded. Walter Scott pushed for the resolution to dissolve the association. It passed unanimously, and thereafter the "Campbellites" and "Scotties" were called *Disciples of Christ.*[58]

Not until 1905 did tradition begin including Walter Scott–sensitive, poetically eloquent, idealist, intelligent, endowed with a musical voice, vivid imagination, lively wit and fiery zeal–among the founders of the Disciples Movement. Scott was born in Moffatt, Scotland, October 31, 1796, the sixth of ten children, and the son of strict Presbyterian parents, John and Mary Innes Scott, his father a celebrated music teacher and a man of considerable culture. Walter became the most accomplished flutist in Edinburgh, and an excellent vocalist. At age sixteen Walter entered the University of Edinburgh with the intent of fulfilling the wishes of his parents for him to become a minister. He graduated in 1818 credentialed as a minister and teacher. At the invitation of his uncle he sailed to New York after graduation where he taught English, Latin, and Greek in a school at Jamaica, Long Island. One year later, May 1819, he traveled westward to Pittsburgh, joining with George Forrester, a clergyman who ministered to a small Haldanian congregation while serving as headmaster of a school. In 1820, Forrester accidentally drowned, causing Scott to become director of the school and pastor of the congregation, and to inherit Forrester's religious library. Scott left Pittsburgh for about a year, but the parents of his finest, most promising student, Robert Richardson, wrote urging his return by offering a private school with generous compensation. During Scott's year of absence Robert Richardson studied with Thomas Campbell, who also had a school in Pittsburgh.[59]

In 1821–22, Scott met Alexander Campbell, who visited his father regularly in Pittsburgh. It was a social gathering in the Richardson home. Both Thomas and Alexander were guests; Walter Scott was present; and so was the youthful Robert Richardson. Richardson knew both men well, and saw in them an interesting contrast:

> In Mr. Campbell the understanding predominated, in Mr. Scott the feelings; and, if the former excelled in imagination, the latter was superior in brilliancy of fancy. If the tendency of one was to generalize, to take wide and extended views and to group a multitude of particulars under a single head or principle, that of the other was to analyze, to divide subjects into their particulars and consider their details... In a word, in almost all of those qualities of mind and character, which might be regarded differential or distinctive, they were singularly fitted to supply each others wants and to form a rare and delightful companionship.

By 1826 Scott was married, teaching school in Steubenville, Ohio, and had begun work with Campbell's Reformers. He attended the 1826 meeting of the Mahoning Baptist Association; and again in 1827. Upon Alexander Campbell's recommendation, the Association employed Walter Scott as Evangelist to serve in Ohio. Building on Acts 2:38, Scott created a theologically simple five-point evangelistic formula for salvation: faith, repentance, baptism, remission of sins, and gift of the Holy Spirit. It appealed to the populace with stunning success. He called it the "Five Finger Exercise." This was Walter Scott's great contribution to the Movement, transforming the intellectual insights of Alexander Campbell into the practice of a new evangelism. William Amend was Scott's first convert, November 18, 1827, at New Lisbon, Ohio. After three years in the Western Reserve Scott had converted 3,000 persons who were not members of any church, in addition to the transfer of thousands of Baptists. The combination of Scott's evangelistic success coupled with Campbell's articles in *Christian Baptist* generated substantial opposition to Reformers and especially toward Alexander Campbell. Although each side blamed the other, actions of both Baptists and Reformers contributed to the separation: Baptists excluding both congregations and individuals on the one hand; and Campbell's inflammatory articles coupled with the Reformers' proselytizing on the other. The dissolution of the Mahoning Baptist Association, orchestrated by Scott, constituted a mutual withdrawal, Baptists from Reformers, Reformers from Baptists. Campbell maintained, "Nothing in their system or ours compelled separation," and when Jacob Creath was asked why Disciples left the Baptists, he responded, "for the same reason that Jonah left the ship, when the sailors pitched him head foremost into the sea, and said he could not stay in the ship." By 1833 the separation was complete. Dwight Stevenson provides a generous description of Scott's role:

> Scott...by the genius of his analytic mind and his infectious enthusiasm, had completed the creation of the Disciples, given them an

evangelistic method, separated them beyond all return from the Baptists, and set them on their independent course.[60]

A moment of significant change came in 1830. In addition to the dissolution of the Mahoning Association, Campbell discontinued the publication of the *Christian Baptist* and introduced a new magazine, *The Millennial Harbinger,* representing a change of tactics and tone, but not a change in principles or doctrine. Born for a special moment in history, the *Christian Baptist,* in Campbell's judgment, had outlived its usefulness. *The Millennial Harbinger* heralded a new era of constructive reform. The first issue appeared January 4, with a declaration in the prospectus, "This work shall be devoted to the destruction of Sectarianism." Its purpose also included restoring ordinances and the organization of the apostolic church; and its tone regarding extra congregational organizations would be far more conciliatory than *Christian Baptist.* Despite the twenty-eight periodicals birthed by the Reform Movement during the 1830s and 1840s, W. E. Garrison characterized *The Millennial Harbinger* as the backbone of Disciples periodical literature for a generation and more. One of those twenty-eight periodicals, added to the *Messenger* and the *Harbinger,* was Walter Scott's new publication, *The Evangelist,* begun in 1832. He wrote of the apostolic church, the "restored gospel," baptism, and church union, as well as popularizing the term "restoration," with its unfortunate connotation of sectarian legalism. Throughout the remainder of his career, Scott–a passionate zealot, jealous of priority, inclined toward irritability, dogmatic, legalistic–felt the Movement did not adequately credit his evangelistic role in nurturing the Disciples (Reformers) toward union with the Christians. As much as Campbell loved Walter Scott, Scott became a sore trial. Preeminently suited by talents for the earlier work of the Reformation Movement, Scott was by no means well fitted for the work of organization of an established communion.[61]

The conflict between Baptists and Reformers attracted Barton Stone's attention. He saw in the impending separation the possibility of unity. In September 1829, Stone inserted in *The Christian Messenger* a brief three-paragraph statement urging union: "New Testament reformers among the Baptists have generally acted the part which we approve… In fact, *if there is a difference between us, we know it not.* We have nothing in us to prevent a union; and if they have nothing in them in opposition to it, we are in spirit one." Stone was clearly the initiator. Between September 1830 and December 1831, he and Campbell exchanged at least seven articles on the subject in the *Messenger* and the *Harbinger.* Most were cordial; some were heated. Near the end of November 1830 Stone received a letter from a parishioner in Ohio, stating, "I believe the Christians and the Reformers would unite in many places were it not for the preachers." One year later a letter arrived from a member in Indiana, reflecting a spontaneous impulse toward unity arising among the people and urging, "We hope the dispute between you and Brother Campbell about names will forever cease, and that you go on united." In 1831 Campbell published a statement in the *Harbinger* indicating, with reservations, the path toward union was not totally blocked:

> We might be honored much by a union formal and public, with a society so large and so respectable as the Christian denomination. We have very high respect for [Barton Stone] and the brethren who are with him. Many of them with whom we are acquainted we love as brethren; *and we can, in all good conscience, unite with them, in spirit and form, in public or in private, in all acts of social worship.*

Although citing their differences, Stone confessed, "I have sincerely wished that the Christians and Reformers, who are united in spirit, should also be united in form."[62]

Stone thought progress toward union slight, although he found encouragement through his friend and neighbor John T. Johnson (1788–1856). Johnson, a lawyer who became a Disciples minister in 1831, had served in the Kentucky legislature and as a representative to Congress. His brother Richard, a United States Senator, would be elected Vice President with President Martin Van Buren. Johnson's Disciples congregation and Stone's Christian congregation began worshiping together in Georgetown. Both agreed they should be one. A four-day conference of nearby Christians and Disciples was planned to begin in Georgetown on Christmas Day 1831. John T. Johnson and "Raccoon" John Smith were the central figures for the occasion. A larger joint meeting followed at Hill Street Christian Church in Lexington on January 1, 1832. Stone and Smith were the chief spokesmen for their respective groups. John Smith, an architect of the approaching union, addressed all those gathered:

> While there is but one faith, there may be ten thousand opinions; and hence if Christians are ever to be one, they must be one in faith, and not in opinions. Let us, then, my brethren, be no longer Campbellites or Stoneites, New lights or Old Lights, or any other kind of lights, but let us all come to the Bible alone, as the only book in the world that can give us all the Light we need.

At the conclusion of Smith's remarks, Stone extended his hand. A handshake sealed the union. There were no agencies, no societies to be merged; no legislative body to approve or disapprove, no negotiated agreement with terms and conditions. John Williams, biographer of "Raccoon" John Smith, recorded simply:

> It was now proposed that all who felt willing to unite on these principles, should express that willingness by giving one another the hand of fellowship; and elders and teachers hastened forward, and joined their hands and hearts in joyful accord. A song arose,

and brethren and sisters, with many tearful greetings, ratified and confirmed the union.

And he insisted further that neither group was surrendering to the other:

> It was an equal and mutual pledge… The brethren of Stone did not join Alexander Campbell as their leader, nor did the brethren of Campbell join Barton W. Stone as their leader; but each, having already taken Jesus the Christ as their only leader…became one body.[63]

The union–a small, local event, little more than an expression of hope–was a turning point in the history of the Reformation Movement. In time approximately 200 congregations containing between 12,000 and 15,000 Disciples members (Scotties and Campbellites) and an estimated 10,000 Christians (Stonites) ultimately united. Several Stone congregations did, however, refuse to do so. Walter Scott's effective work in the Western Reserve had numerically positioned Campbell to unite with Stone. John Smith and John Rogers were appointed to ride throughout the country, visiting and uniting the congregations, a ministry that required three years. The Movement became an independent religious body, a church. Alexander Campbell, concerned about Stone's view of atonement, ordination, and admission to the Lord's table, did not attend the 1832 meeting, but he did, with hesitancy, express hope for success of the Union. Stone saw it as a triumph. "This union," he reflected, "I view as the noblest act of my life." And in the next issue of *the Messenger* he joyfully announced, "The spirit of union is spreading like fire in dry stubble."[64]

CHAPTER IV

Revivalism, Evangelicalism, and the Disciples Reform Movement

Effects on Membership–
Growth and Expansion

Disciples have rapidly increased in number, not by these accessions from the Baptists so much as by a general diffusion of their principles amongst all parties, and especially by an almost unprecedented success in the conversion of those who had not, as yet, embraced any of the religious systems of the day. Many have come over from the Presbyterians; some from the Episcopalians and from the Lutherans; but more, both of preachers and people, from the Methodists.

Robert Richardson
The Millennial Harbinger, 1854[1]

Not all of Stone's Christians participated in the joining of their congregations with Campbell's Reform congregations. In fact, most Ohio Christians, including Stone's close friend David Purviance, rejected the union because they perceived Disciples (or Alexander Campbell) as "spiritless" and as too rigid on the issues of baptism and communion and did not wish to follow "the watery way to Campbellism." A decade after the union, Barton Stone expressed sadness over the opposition to union: "I never dreamed, but that my brethren everywhere would rejoice at such an event, so congenial with our first principals. But alas, I am disappointed." Congregations in Tennessee, Kentucky, Ohio, Indiana, and Illinois were generally able to find common ground, but the implacable wall of opposition to union was in the East where the older liberalisms—Christian Connection and Unitarians—were there before Disciples

What then did those who supported the union believe to be the unifying elements of doctrine in 1832? What message would be most effective? What did the people most want to hear? What were Disciples evangelists advocating that resulted in such phenomenal church growth over the ensuing decades? What techniques most readily promoted membership growth? And what elements in the sociocultural and political environment of the country contributed to the size and pace of Disciples unprecedented expansion?

The evangelism of Walter Scott coupled with the separation from the Baptists formed a benchmark in the history of the Disciples Reformation Movement. An internal shift of emphasis surfaced within the Movement after 1830, a shift from the development of ideas to the development of organization, a shift from a small movement of intellectual activity to a growing independent religious institution spread over an expanding geography, a shift from an intellectual movement to a church.

Although other shifts would occur as the decades passed, core beliefs of the newly united Disciples and Christians were largely in place by 1830 and included at least these nine essentials:

1. Centrality of the Bible: beliefs and practices based upon scripture; faith based on credible New Testament witness to the divinity of Jesus.
2. Autonomy and self-sufficiency of congregations: democratically governed congregations without interference from higher ecclesial structures.
3. Lay ministry: laity and clergy were generally viewed with little distinction: clergy were not placed above the laity, nor set apart by the title of reverend.
4. Believer's baptism by immersion for remission of sins (Acts 2:38).
5. The prominence of weekly communion in worship.
6. Simplicity of worship.
7. Complete atonement; Christ died for all.
8. Passionate advocacy of Christian unity.
9. Strong opposition to creeds; rejected Puritan adulation of the Old Testament; the church stood on the authority of Jesus and the New Testament.

It has been said Disciples did not fit any broad category—Wesleyan, Lutheran, Reformed, Presbyterian, Baptist, Brethren, or Catholic—but they shared similarities with nearly all of them, while positioning themselves almost alone among Protestants on the question of weekly communion. Disciples were described as "unique in their simple, historically oriented conception of faith." Two decades later Robert Richardson summarized Disciples principles in a little book entitled *The Principles and Objects of the Religious Reformation urged by A. Campbell and Others.* He named three principles: first, distinction between *faith* and *opinion*–to find the solid core of "common Christianity," allowing each person the right of personal opinion but not the right to make those opinions tests of religious fellowship; second, Christian faith is *personal,* not *doctrinal*–faith in the *person* of Jesus Christ, not in abstract doctrines, a *direct relation* and *personal fellowship* with Christ; and third, *Christian Union,* a *catholicity* of spirit as distinguished from *uniformity.* And from these principles, wrote Richardson, stemmed several "objects" including baptism by immersion, weekly communion, and autonomy of the congregations. With this theology, the Disciples Reformation Movement equipped itself for the work of the nineteenth century.[2]

The years between the point of union in 1832 and the end of the nineteenth century were the most active and successful for membership growth in Disciples history. Disciples and Christians, however, differed on the issue of evangelism. Campbell did not develop a method of evangelism, leaving that task to Walter Scott. However, he did think revivalism was unscriptural at best and fanatical at worst, calling it the "fanaticism of this age," although he approved Scott's ever so slightly more rational "five finger exercise." The genesis of Stone's Christians, on the other hand, is traced to revivalism, placing emphasis on emotional conversion. Although there were differences, no real conflict appears to have developed between Disciples and Christians regarding their programs of evangelism–most likely because both were successful.[3]

Evangelists by the score from Protestant denominations traveled the countryside. From 1832 to 1854 the population of the United States increased by 88 percent, while the number of evangelical clergy increased 175 percent. Between 1820 and 1860 a total of 40,000 new church buildings were constructed in the United States–an average of 1,000 per year. Disciples evangelists formed an eclectic assortment including farmers, teachers, blacksmiths, artisans, merchants, ministers, and a few lawyers. Traveling by horseback, wagon, and afoot, they first preached the gospel across the rural frontier in homes, barns, open fields, and country schoolhouses, fulfilling the crucial role of planting congregations wherever they went. Their method was emotional, an appeal to "feeling." One Disciples evangelist noted:

> In my speech I kept steadily in mind a plain, honest boy of sixteen.
> I knew if he had no great cultivated mind to comprehend the
> subtleties of Christianity, he had an anxious yearning heart to feel
> its blessed provisions. To this I trusted largely.

The names of most Disciples evangelists, numbering in the hundreds, have been lost to history. A few are known to us, among them: William Kinkaid (b. 1783), John Secrest (b. 1795), Samuel (Uncle Sam) Rogers (1789–1877), Chester Bullard (1809–1893), Elijah Goodwin (1807–1879), James Mathes (1808–1892), Abigail Roberts (1791–1841), Clara Babcock (1850–1924), Sadie McCoy Crank (1863–1948), Pardee Butler (1816–1888),

Knowles Shaw [the singing evangelist who composed "Bringing in the Sheaves"] (1834–1878), James Updike (1850–1907), Benjamin Franklin (1812–1878), Thomas M. Allen (1797–1871), Tolbert Fanning (1810–1874), "Raccoon" John Smith (1784–1868), John Rogers (1800–1867), John T. Johnson (1788–1856), and, of course, the most celebrated evangelist in the Movement, Walter Scott (1796–1861). Benjamin Franklin was highly influential. His volume of sermons, the *Gospel Preacher,* published in 1869, went through thirty-one editions, was one of the Disciples' most popular pieces of literature, and served as a primer for hundreds of untrained young preachers in several frontier denominations.[4]

The Second Great Awakening was more successful in the small towns, where the majority of the population lived, rather than either the city or rural stretches. Cities at first resisted the work of evangelists, so this determined band of preachers turned their efforts toward Western towns in the 1840s and 1850s. The century-long migration from the country to urban centers had begun, making cities the spearheads of frontier settlement and the vital centers of the nation. Between 1820 and 1850, due to transportation improvements coupled with the growth of commerce, manufacturing, and industry, Pittsburgh, for example, had grown from 7,000 to 46,000; Cincinnati from 9,000 to 115,000. But Disciples from the beginning had an aversion to cities, especially Eastern cities, an aversion clearly expressed by Alexander Campbell: "Cities generally are the great radiating centers of crime. They are fountains of iniquity… Their tendencies are to corruption… Their history is the history of the perfection of human infamy."

Disciples were more in the mold of what historian Henry Adams characterized as the "primitiveness and parochialism" of much of American life in the 1800s, a society whose diverse character was more evident than its unity. Disciples developed strength in several small Midwestern and Western county seat towns, but due to their long-held distaste for cities they remained largely a small-town Movement. In 1890 only 6 percent of Disciples membership (compared with 12 to 50 percent in other denominations) resided in communities of 25,000 or more; and as late as 1917 approximately 82 percent of Disciples congregations and 50 percent of the membership were in towns of 2,500 or less, evidence of a failure to develop an urban strategy. Despite this aversion, many evangelists followed the population and began preaching in courthouses, parks, and railroad stations. While Campbell supplied the doctrinal base and exegetical principles for the new church, the itinerant evangelists were the primary suppliers of members. Campbell did not consider himself an evangelist: "When I make a tour," he said, "it is more to disseminate the general principles of reformation than to proclaim the ancient gospel for the purpose of converting sinners to God." Nonetheless he was, in the words of Louis Cochran, the "showpiece of the Movement." His name was famous and he attracted a large audience wherever he spoke.[5]

At the time of union, the combined membership of Reformers and Christians was approximately 22,000. By 1860, prior to the outbreak of the Civil War, the total membership had grown to 192,323, a ninefold increase due to the intensive labor of itinerant evangelists. In the seven states composing the lower South (Alabama, Florida, Georgia, Louisiana, Mississippi, South Carolina, and Texas), the membership in 1860 totaled 9,408; in the middle South (Arkansas, North Carolina, Tennessee, and Virginia), the total was, 17,042; in the border South (Delaware, Kentucky, Maryland, and Missouri), the membership totaled 65,000; in the Midwest (Illinois, Iowa, Indiana, and Ohio), the total was: 75,000; in the Northeast (Connecticut, Maine, Massachusetts, New Hampshire, New Jersey, New York, Rhode Island, and Vermont), a more modest membership totaled 6,800; the upper Midwest (Michigan, Minnesota) reported a sparse total of 1,080; and the far western territories, along with the states of California, Kansas, and Oregon, reported a token membership of 300. The Disciples of Christ Movement in 1860 found its center in the Midwest and Border States. The expansion continued unabated after the Civil War. From 1860 to 1875 the membership more than doubled, reaching 400,000. And in the next quarter century the church nearly tripled in size, totaling 1,120,000 by 1900, making it one of the largest religious groups in the United States. From the 1832 joining of Disciples and Christians, the history of the Movement advanced through seven decades of remarkable growth and expansion in the sociocultural context of the Second and Third Awakenings, the political context of Jacksonian Democracy and the Civil War, the physical context of an advancing frontier environment, and in the context of a new worldview–the Age of Romanticism.[6]

Early twentieth-century Disciples historians emphasized the *physical* environment of the frontier in analyzing the nature and growth of the Movement. W. E. Garrison called Disciples the "Christian expression of American Frontier Society," and opened his 1931 history of Disciples, *Religion Follows the Frontier,* with the statement:

> It was along the advancing frontier, as it was moving from western Pennsylvania to Missouri, and among the pioneers who had but lately crossed the Alleghenies into the old Northwest Territory or into Kentucky, that the movement of the Disciples had its origin.

He proceeded to present the genesis of the Movement as a phenomenon of the frontier and within the framework of Frederick Jackson Turner's frontier thesis. While this view helped Disciples understand their Reformation Movement and influenced the writing of several subsequent histories, it resulted in insufficient attention to other elements of the *social* environment provided by other large sociological swings in the culture within which pioneer Disciples found themselves. Disciples were shaped at least as much by these forces as they were by their frontier physical environment and by their Jacksonian political heritage.

Romanticism, a new worldview dating from the late eighteenth century, extended through much of the nineteenth. The Age of Romanticism is known variously as the counter-Enlightenment, successor to the Age of Reason, a resistance to the Enlightenment, and a reaction against the use of rationalist and scientific principles to reorganize knowledge and society. Romanticism modified the Enlightenment. Romanticism's emphasis upon intuition and imagination bespoke "a way of feeling," rather than reasoning; a preoccupation with the life of the spirit and a great turning toward emotionalism. Isaiah Berlin referred to the Age of Romanticism as the "greatest single shift in the consciousness of the West that has occurred in the nineteenth and twentieth centuries." Among the fathers of this movement were Johann Herder and Giambattista Vico. They believed human beings were possessors of souls with spiritual needs. In their view, rationalism blocked human sentiment. The rationalist work of Locke and Newton, they claimed, held little concept of what moved human beings. It had petrified the human spirit by reducing reality to mathematical pieces. God, they argued, was not a mathematician, but a poet; mathematics, from their perspective, was a *method* and not a body of truths.

In music it was the age of Chopin, Mendelssohn, Beethoven, and Wagner; the world of art was marked by the lyrical paintings of J.M.W. Turner, George Innes, Thomas Cole, John James Audubon, and George Caleb Bingham. In politics the watchword was nationalism; in religion this era sparked a celebration of human goodness and divinity, expressed by the Transcendental Movement through Ralph Waldo Emerson and Henry David Thoreau. In literature it was the era of William Wordsworth, Johann Wolfgang Goethe, William Butler Yeats, Sir Walter Scott, Thomas Carlyle, Washington Irving, Henry David Thoreau, Walt Whitman, Herman Melville, Samuel Coleridge, and William Blake, who wrote the famous lines:

A Robin Red breast in a Cage
Puts all Heaven in a Rage,…

…the cage being the Enlightenment in which he and others like him believed they were suffocating. It is difficult to envision a more welcoming environment for the emotion of revivalism and millenarian creeds, the subordination of reason and intellect to intuition and uncritical faith. The new Age of Romanticism thought universal laws, absolute principles, final truths, eternal models, and the tendency of rationalism to generalize obliterated differences and uniqueness in cultures. The age was attracted to religious and political *irrationalism*–faith over reason, insight over logic, and political imagination over the application of traditional principles.

Romanticism's appreciation for the past also sparked early signs of a return to high churchmanship—gothic church architecture from the Middle Ages, the notion of God as "father" rather than judge, the use of vestments, the treatment of the eucharist with more dignity by placing it at the center of worship, and worship itself reflecting a sense of drama—all of which was anathema to Evangelicals.

Intellectual historian Perry Miller spoke of the Second Awakening outlook of Americans as "Romantic nationalism," and of its religious core as "romantic evangelicalism." The Second Awakening, occurring in the context of the Age of Romanticism and bearing the vivid imprint of Jacksonian Democracy, is often viewed as an interaction between the eighteenth-century *Age of Reason* and the nineteenth-century *Age of Romanticism.*

Revivals with evangelical preaching were considered uniquely American during the early 1800s. Frontiersmen craved emotionalism and were attracted to the fact that every person could achieve salvation through his or her own personal will by submitting to the lordship of Christ—which provoked a ready acceptance of revivals. They continued to flourish throughout the century and were the principal means of unprecedented membership growth in American Protestant denominations. Perry Miller said, "the dominant theme in America from 1800 to 1860 [was] the invincible persistence of the revival." It set the tone for the era. Miller noted further:

> In the west...the Presbyterian church fragmented... Stone led his followers into a "Christian" body which joined with Thomas and Alexander Campbell... But these denominational conflicts, though they make up the substance of denominational histories were not of great importance in the area of religious mentality. There, the simple fact of the revival was central. Whether it produced formal unity or created new churches was of less import than the omnipresence of the revival.[7]

Modern evangelicalism, an elastic term, emerged in the late 1730s and held persistently to a consistent core of beliefs: first, personal conversion as the central event in the spiritual life of Christians; second, no higher authority than the Bible; third, the importance of living lives of service, especially evangelism; and fourth, Christ's death provided atonement for all persons, not just a select few. David Bebbington, a widely respected authority on Evangelicalism, defined those four convictions or attitudes as *Conversionism, Activism, Biblicism,* and *Crucicentrism;* and also as Cross, Bible, Conversion and Activism. These convictions, he pointed out, "do not exist in the same proportions or exert the same effects in all times and places." The Evangelical movement was diverse, exhibiting a large variety of expressions—fundamentalist, charismatic, dispensational, radical, etc.—differing in theology, denomination, and geographic location. Evangelicalism brought religion to the people in language they could understand, making the gospel seem more accessible and more liberating while generating a more compelling spirituality. It achieved this by relying on intuition and inspiration rather than learning and doctrine–"fervent evangelicalism" without intellectual discipline. It scorned complex theology on the ground that it was not understandable to the common man. *Evangelism addressed the emotions rather than the mind.* Vigorous evangelism was a powerful sociocultural force in America during the Disciples/Christians immediate post-union years, providing a fertile context for Disciples growth in numbers, expansion in geography, education, journalism, and finally in organizational development, a circumstance portrayed in alliterative terms by one Disciples historian as "Disciples growth in preaching, publishing, pedagogy and plea." Although excluded from membership in the Evangelical Alliance because they taught baptism by immersion as an act of obedience essential to salvation, "Disciples style," it is argued, "was virtually identical with that of Evangelicals."[8]

The essential characteristic of revivals since 1825, claims William McLoughlin, has been their effort to adjust the theological, ethical, and institutional structure of Protestantism to changes in American culture. According to McLoughlin, revivals, or awakenings, occur at times of profound cultural and ideological transformations. Revivals bring revitalization. They restore cultural energy and self-confidence. They maintain balance between tradition and change. Perry Miller reminds us that revivals were only in part the conversion of sinners; the more important objective, he says, was always "the quickening of the people of God to a spirit and walk becoming the gospel." Periodic reformulations of the cultural and religious ethos are therefore essential to the dynamic growth of a people adapting to change. An awakening involves people caught in a fading worldview converting their mind-sets and institutions to more relevant ways of understanding the changes occurring around them (e.g., from the Age of the Enlightenment to the Age of Romanticism). A revival, or awakening, is both a funeral and a christening, bidding farewell to some of the old, welcoming to some of the new.[9]

By McLoughlin's reckoning there have been five religious Awakenings in American history, dated roughly, but not strictly, as follows: the Puritan Awakening, 1620–1660, setting in place a Calvinistic worldview; the First Great Awakening, 1730–1760; the Second Great Awakening, 1795–1835; the Third Great Awakening, 1875–1915; and the Fourth Great Awakening, 1960–1990. Each one was national in scope, and each lasted about a generation.[10]

The First Great Awakening (1730–1760) saw the Calvinistic worldview of the Puritans being severely challenged by the new Rationalist ideology of the European Enlightenment. Economically, this period also experienced the advancement of the Industrial Revolution from a feudal, patriarchal agrarian system to a new bourgeois capitalist system. From this socioeconomic-religious blend emerged "evangelical Calvinism," described as "sectarian, comparatively democratic in polity, puritanical in morality and devoutly evangelical in theology." It was characterized by itinerant revivalism of which George Whitefield, the defining figure of American Evangelicalism, was the prime exemplar.

The Second Great Awakening (1795–1835), arising from the social dislocation spawned by the American Revolution and fueled by the Age of Romanticism, is considered the most influential revival of Christianity in the history of the United States, the sociocultural centerpiece of the middle third of the nineteenth century, and the means by which a largely irreligious America was evangelized. It began in the camp meetings of Kentucky and Tennessee. Congregationalists, Anglicans, and Presbyterians spearheaded the First Great Awakening, but Methodists, Baptists, and Disciples dominated the Second. It is estimated that three-fifths of all evangelists came from these three groups, operating in the West and South among the middle and lower classes, presenting a sectarian, emotional, and conversionist plea. Protestant membership in America increased sixfold between 1800 and 1860.

During the Second Awakening, American society passed through a cultural and political reorientation known as "Jacksonian Democracy." It is often described as the age of the common man; the age of egalitarianism, personal ambition, and materialism; an age of idealistic reform movements, pragmatism, self-reliance, industriousness, and optimism; a time of profit-mindedness, individual ingenuity, utopian social experiments, and unashamed anti-intellectualism. During this era the country moved from a republic to a democracy. Human rights took priority over property rights; majority rule became idealized. True to the Age of Romanticism, there was a growing contempt for intellect, sparked by the new belief that wisdom was intuitive. Jacksonian scholar John Ward declared, "Jeffersonians rested their case on the power of man's mind; the Jacksonians rested theirs on the prompting of a man's heart." Revivalism, a mirror expression of Jacksonian Democracy's belief in self-reliant individualism and enlightened self-interest, was optimistic and captivated by success, always measuring its work quantitatively by membership growth to satisfy the pressing requirement of the churches for more converts.[11]

Charles Grandison Finney (1792–1875), the originator of modern evangelical Protestantism in America, was the embodiment of the Second Awakening, especially its interdenominational expression. "A mass uprising, a release of energy, a sweep of the people which made it an expansion of that energy we call Jacksonian America," was Perry Miller's succinct description of Charles Finney's movement during the Second Awakening. By 1836 Finney dominated Protestantism. He had become a national institution, the dean of evangelists, characterized by one contemporary as "a Napoleon among his marshals." Mark Noll described Finney as the "crucial figure in white American evangelicalism after Jonathan Edwards." Finney was neither theologically educated nor supportive of ministerial education. In his view, "young men involved in the intellectual race lose the firm tone of spirituality…their intellects improve and their hearts lie waste." Finney institutionalized both modern revivalism and professional mass evangelism. As a result, itinerant evangelist preachers became respected leaders in the life of American Protestantism. They became professionals, a special branch of the ministry often licensed as home missionaries. The ministerial office transformed from pastor to evangelist. Traditionally educated ministers were left in the wake of the evangelists' flair. Many able preachers were driven from their pulpits into other professions. Sidney E. Mead wrote of this phenomenon: "The conception of the minister practically lost its priestly dimension as traditionally conceived, and became that of a consecrated functionary called of God, who directed the activities of the visible church."[12]

Through the influence of Finney, Lyman Beecher, Timothy Dwight, and Nathaniel Taylor, Evangelical Protestantism became a national religion, a powerful subculture, and an American tradition within the society. The tone and tenor of Northeastern evangelists were interdenominational, leading to the establishment of many benevolent and reform movements. This profusion of "Voluntary Societies" (e.g., The American Bible Society, Temperance Societies, etc.), spawned by New England interdenominational revival synergy marked a new form of church organization that became typical of American ecclesiastical structures as well as a means of nurturing democratic participation in institutional life, particularly among women and minorities.

To New Englanders accustomed to more genteel revivals, the camp meetings were barbarous emotional outbreaks, the work of the devil trying to discredit true religion, a human work rather than a divine work. They saw revival excesses as manipulative appeals to the emotions of illiterate, half-educated persons on the frontier. They believed uneducated frontier preachers were neither capable of preaching true religion nor of restraining the passions of the rough, unruly folk who preferred frontier life to civilized society. Presbyterians soon divided over the nature of revivals. They were dismayed by what they viewed as an uncivilized West and the crude, unorthodox religious behavior of the Methodists, Baptists, and what they called the Western offshoots of Presbyterianism (Campbellites and Stoneites) But the general public was not hugely disturbed by arguments between revivalists and anti-revivalists.[13]

The South contributed the camp meeting, including Cane Ridge in Kentucky, to the Second Awakening. In the antebellum South, according to W.J. Cash, an unrefined innocence of belief was fashionable. The Southern masses were strongly evangelical and thought of themselves as the last great bulwark of Christianity.

> The core and bulk of [Southern intellect] consisted of the Protestant theology of the sixteenth century and the Dissenting moral code of the seventeenth...the Southerner required a faith as simple and emotional as himself, a faith to terrify them with Apocalyptic rhetoric, a faith of primitive frenzy...in other words the faith of the Methodists, the Baptists and the Presbyterians (Disciples)... Their revivals in the first half of the nineteenth century achieved their greatest success in the South... The triumph of evangelical sects involved the establishment of the Puritan ideal. From the first great revivals onward, the official moral philosophy of the South moved steadily toward the position of the Massachusetts Bay Colony.

Baptists, Methodists, and Disciples were subsumed into a larger culture of Southern evangelism. The antebellum period was the most religious age in the history of the South, imprinted by camp meetings, family altars, Bible readings, dramatic conversions, and rigid orthodoxy. Theirs was a deeply romantic religious movement, and it is said to be the reason the South produced pulpit orators, yet did not produce a theologian of new ideas–with the possible exception of Alexander Campbell. Peter Cartwright (1785–1872), the best known of the Methodist circuit riders and the classic itinerant revivalist among Southern camp meeting prophets, revitalized the South after 1800. With his pocket Bible, hymnbook, and Methodist Book of Discipline, it is claimed he outshouted and outwitted the Baptists and Campbellites throughout most of the South. While the West contributed *romantic nationalism* and the North contributed *voluntary societies* to the Second Awakening, the South brought the *camp meeting* into the mix. While New Englanders were interdenominational and reform-oriented, the Methodists and Baptists of the South and West appeared more interested in building denominations. Disciples, through their passion for Christian unity, were more interdenominational while making feeble attempts toward denominational structure and generally avoiding participation in reform movements.[14]

   The Third Great Awakening (1875–1915) contained numerous elements of social and religious reorientation, including the fear that science was becoming the enemy of God's law; that the new social sciences, particularly Freudian psychological theories, were undermining the basis of Christian faith; that higher criticism of the Bible was displacing literal inerrancy; and that Darwin's theory of evolution would destroy Christian faith. Out of this reorientation came liberal Protestantism, the Social Gospel, and the Federal Council of Churches on the one hand; and the development of fundamentalism on the other.

The era was marked by the 1870s revivals of fundamentalist Dwight L. Moody (1837–1899)–short, outspoken, bearded, and the most celebrated evangelist of his age. McLoughlin considered the late nineteenth-century revivals "the opening battle of the modernist-fundamentalist controversy." Moody's revivals are typically viewed as a response to the new sciences, to the Social Gospel, and to liberal Protestantism. He saw learning as an encumbrance to a person of the Spirit. He rejected Darwinism, higher criticism of the Bible, and modernism–holding fast to "Old Time Religion." Following Moody's death, Billy Sunday (1862–1935) became the champion of reactionary, nineteenth-century evangelical religious beliefs. He perfected the use of the revival, employing a professional group of meeting planners, musicians, advance agents, and finance committees, and developed a range of revival machinery (e.g., tabernacles, advertising campaigns) far more sophisticated than Finney or Moody could have envisioned. Fundamentalists rallied around the revivalism of Billy Sunday, making him a national prophet, while liberal Protestants, or modernists, took control of denominations and seminaries.[15]

The crisis of faith that arose during the 1890s was unlike anything Western culture had ever faced. Where fundamentalists bore witness to God through testimony, liberal Protestants bore witness through social action. Fundamentalists thought of religion as a direct relationship of the individual with God; the new liberals thought of religion as their relationship with God's children, "the Brotherhood of Man," each person spiritually and ethically united with his or her neighbor. Service to others, they believed, was the way in which a true Christian reached fulfillment. The new liberal Protestantism turned its attention from saving souls to elevating the moral condition of the whole human race through social services. But given their long history of protecting the unity of their Movement, restoring the ancient order, and pursuing evangelicalism during the Awakenings, Disciples were distracted–some would argue blinded–from prophetic witness, from actively addressing the social justice issues of the day such as the growing inequitable distribution of wealth, plight of industrial workers, child labor, or the advance of what Douglas Backmon identified as the "neo-slavery system" of debt peonage and Jim Crow laws.

The Second Awakening had portrayed humanity as free and unrestrained by the environment. But the Third Awakening, spurred by attempts to reconcile Darwinism and Christianity, spoke of God's power in the laws of nature. Critical analysis of the Bible, incorporating history, archaeology, anthropology, sociology, etc., drove many to join the fundamentalists, who held tightly to their belief in the literal inerrancy of the scripture. The late nineteenth- and early twentieth-century revivals increased church membership, gave impetus to the need for more sophisticated church organization, and stimulated the demand for a more highly educated clergy. But the revivals–overly emotional, theologically shallow–were also a divisive force, splintering congregations and splitting denominations. Their impact was greatest on small-town America and the rural poor, less so in urban centers.

It was within this powerful, subcultural context of evangelical revivalism, nourished by the Age of Romanticism, that the story of the Disciples evolved during most of the more than eighty years from 1832 to 1915. Disciples successfully blended the Christian message with the social realities of American culture and the social demands of the frontier. Despite their 1906 internal division and membership loss, Disciples prospered during the Second and Third Awakenings, and by 1915 could count a total membership of 1,142,000. "The Disciples," wrote Mark Noll, "evangelized America because they had translated the Christian message into an indigenous American idiom."[16]

Effects on Organizational Development

I cannot conceive of a kingdom without a constitution, an organization,
a joint and common interest, and a constant cooperation in reference to
its self-preservation and comfortable existence. If Christ have a kingdom
on this earth, it must be a community organized, united in common
interests, in harmonious concert, and conservative of its own integrity
and prosperity.

ALEXANDER CAMPBELL
The Millennial Harbinger, 1842[17]

The unfolding story of the Disciples' long quest for cooperation and organization began in an historic moment, August 1830. It occurred at Austintown on the Western Reserve in Ohio, the day the Mahoning Baptist Association, of which Alexander Campbell's Reform congregations were members, voted to dissolve. For Campbell's congregations it was a dramatic departure from being part of an association to stark independence. Nineteen years would pass between that day in August 1830 and October 1849, when the first Disciples general convention convened. The dissolution of the Mahoning Baptist Association's whole structure of unity and authority dismayed Campbell because he feared the Second Awakening would lure the congregations in all directions. Disorder and anarchy would follow.[18]

Evangelical reliance on inward experience of individuals contained the threat of what Richard Hofstadter called "anarchical subjectivism." Always, the tendency toward endless division and fragmentation resided in this kind of religion. The authority of evangelicals tended to be personal and charismatic rather than institutional, thereby requiring great organizing skill to keep the followers in a single faith community. Fortunately, the strength of Campbell's personality and teaching, along with annual fellowship meetings that did not conduct church business, held them together. He set to work almost immediately after the separation from the Baptists to bring some sort of order to the scattered and often frail Reform congregations. In the spring of 1831 he launched an effort toward organization with a series of seven articles in *The Millennial Harbinger* entitled "The co-operation of churches." In the first article, appealing to both scripture and reason, he discussed cooperation among congregations in New Testament times, concluding:

> It is the duty of churches to cooperate in everything beyond the individual achievements of a congregation… A church can do what an individual disciple cannot and so can a district of churches do what a single congregation cannot. The churches were districted in the age of the Apostles… Districts cooperated in contributing to the necessities of those who lived in another district…churches cooperated in choosing persons for the work of the Lord [who] were called the "messengers of the churches."

Citing 2 Corinthians 8, Campbell told of Paul instructing the "churches in Macedonia and Achaia" to collect contributions for the suffering poor in the "churches in Judea." The theme of cooperation, surprising to some of Campbell's followers, was carried through the entire series. Near the end of the series he stated:

> The kingdom of Jesus is one kingdom. The subjects of it meet in groups, called assemblies. These groups are placed in contiguous districts… It will be ever their duty to shine as lights in the world, to hold forth and sound abroad the word of the Lord.[19]

In 1831, the Reform congregations, formerly members of the Mahoning Association, met in New Lisbon, Ohio, on August 26 and approved a recommendation that "churches in each county should meet annually in one central place." Campbell's home county of Brooke, of course, implemented the suggestion and in 1834 joined with neighboring counties to hold a "General Meeting of Messengers" in Wellsburg, Virginia. Thirteen congregations participated in the historic meeting April 12, 1834. During its session, the gathering named five needs to be addressed:

- A systematic cooperation of the churches
- Better order in the congregations
- Congregational overseers to preside over them
- More general knowledge and teaching of the scriptures
- Proclaimers to proclaim the Word and teach the ordinances[20]

The question then arose, "How do we address these needs?" This question led to a debate on the problem of a perceived dichotomy between local autonomy and organic union, a debate on the wisdom of "cooperation," a debate preceding the Wellsburg meeting, and a debate remaining highly controversial and divisive throughout the remainder of the nineteenth century, the twentieth century, and into the twenty-first. It was argued the Reformation Movement had progressed so far without cooperative structures, and to create them at that moment might endanger the independence of the congregations as well as the principles of the Movement. Furthermore, the argument ran, such efforts of cooperation through the centuries had spawned detested ecclesial councils and creeds. The response to those arguments reasoned that abuse of an institution should never be justification against the use of it. Indeed, they argued, the Reformation Movement had progressed this far *because* of cooperation, consultations, and liberal contributions. It was asserted that if there had been more of it, the triumph of the Movement would have been much greater.[21]

According to the minutes, as written by Alexander Campbell, the cooperative argument carried the day:

> Establishing the principle of co-operation in such matters as cannot be effected by a single congregation, and by exhibiting that concern for the welfare of the brethren in small matters, furnishes a decisive argument for co-operation in the things pertaining to the greater wants and necessities of the brethren... The Acts of the Apostles throughout exhibit nothing more plainly in the history of primitive Christianity, than the spirit of cooperation... The Christian con-gregations, like so many families, have their internal and their external relations... Every family in one great community stands related to all the families in that community...and the whole of that community of families stands related to all other communities on earth... In the neighborhood of churches, they are all independent communities; but neighborhood association and co-operation are necessary to the prosperity of all.

The 1834 Wellsburg gathering approved ten resolutions, including the intent to cooperate on the collection of voluntary contributions and the selection of proper persons to be "proclaimers." In the eighth resolve the gathering referred to itself as "the congregations of disciples in this co-operation." Therein were the rudimentary beginnings of organization for cooperative work among Disciples.[22]

The 1832 joining of Disciples (Reformers) and Christians had increased the number of congregations and members, an increase that compounded the need for order and discipline. Coupled with the remarkable success of Walter Scott in the Western Reserve and the popularity of Second Awakening revivals, Campbell was moved to remark that the "influx of converts is greater than preparation for their growth and perfection." The expansion of Disciples stemming from the Second Awakening was largely responsible for turning the attention of Alexander Campbell and his Movement to the subject of cooperation, organization, and order. With the retirement of Barton Stone to Jacksonville, Illinois, in 1834, Campbell was the most influential figure in an unorganized Movement, embracing scores of churches with thousands of members in a half dozen states. Evangelists, periodicals, and schools, according to W. E. Garrison, "wove a fabric of mutual acquaintance and fraternity which they called a *Brotherhood*." Campbell managed to hold most of that Brotherhood together through correspondence, speaking tours, and *The Millennial Harbinger*. The impulse to evangelize was the primary cause of cooperation; and the principle of cooperation would lead ultimately to national organization.[23]

In 1835 Campbell first advanced the great concept of *covenant* as the most effective relationship between congregations and their overseers at both the local and national levels, a relationship he believed would safeguard both order and liberty. But 133 years would pass before the concept of covenant became a reality among Disciples as a creative approach to church governance. Three years later Campbell moved his emphasis from cooperation to thoughts of more specific organization in a series of four essays in *The Millennial Harbinger*, "The Senatorial Government of the Church." He used as his analogy the government of the United States. It was a call for a representative governance structure, someplace between chaotic anarchy and rigid dictatorship. In one article of that series, he wrote:

> There are extremes of congregationalism and monarchical despo-
> tism... Neither of these is the Christian institution. Mobocracy
> may become as tyrannical as unlimited monarchy. Both are to be
> eschewed for the same reasons.[24]

During the late 1830s district "cooperations" began to consolidate into statewide organizations, primarily for the purpose of evangelism. Cooperation meetings were common throughout the Movement. Coordination was essential within so scattered a group, prompting Campbell to become a highly vocal advocate of cooperation in county, district, state, and national organizations:

> We must plead for cooperation among all the citizens of Messiah's
> kingdom, in whatever pertains to its enlargement, prosperity, and
> ultimate triumphs. We want cooperation. Some of our brethren are
> afraid of its power; others complain of its inefficiency. Still we go
> for cooperation... We go for the cooperation of all the members...
> for their cooperation in heart and soul, in prayers, in contributions,
> in efforts, in toils.

This effort to reorient the membership to the need for organization stirred hostile reaction as well as strong support. Despite criticism, Campbell insightfully and courageously plunged ahead. In 1842 he published a list of five arguments for church organization:

- We can do comparatively nothing in distributing the Bible without co-operation.
- We can do comparatively little in the great missionary field of the world without co-operation.
- We can do little or nothing to improve the Christian ministry without co-operation.
- We can do little to check, restrain the flood of imposture and fraud committed upon the benevolence of the brethren by irresponsible and deceptive persons without co-operation.
- We can have no thorough co-operation without a more extensive and thorough church organization.

Typically, congregations in a state moved from "District Cooperations" to "State Conferences" to "State Christian Missionary Societies," adopting as their home mission objective "spreading the good news through evangelism." Pennsylvania established a state society in 1834, Indiana in 1839, and Kentucky in 1840. Campbell's most creative essay on church organization was written in 1843. It developed a hypothesis around an evangelist being sent to the Island of Guernsey and how the growth of membership and new congregations necessitated the development of a structure acting as one body for all the congregations on the island.[25]

David. S. Burnet (1808–1867), a colleague of Alexander Campbell, took the lead in organizing the American Christian Bible Society January 27, 1845, the first attempt to establish a Movement-wide organization. Shortly thereafter, he founded a Sunday school and Tract Society. The idea of a national convention of Disciples began to receive wide attention. Charles Louis Loos, a gifted Disciples leader and close collaborator of Alexander Campbell, wrote in the late 1840s, "It was urged on all sides, and by our wisest men, that it was of great importance that a closer acquaintance and fellowship of mind, heart and hand should now be established among us, because of the increasing number and the widespread extent of our people." Campbell, recognizing the need to disseminate Reformation ideals through evangelism, became the driving force behind the idea of a general convention. Some in the Movement were troubled by the absence of New Testament authority for creating such a convention, and they reminded Campbell of what he had written in the *Christian Baptist* opposing organizations beyond the congregation. Campbell responded that in things other than faith, piety, and morality the church was free, unshackled; and if it chose to do so, it could develop a convention or cooperation to advance the interests of a common salvation. This statement by Campbell is considered a landmark principle in the history of the Movement. By this principle, it was quite appropriate, in his view, for one generation to structure, and if needed, for another to restructure.[26]

The first general convention of Disciples was held in Cincinnati October 23–28, 1849, at the Christian Church on the corner of Fourth and Walnut Streets. Cincinnati was located at the center of the largest number of Disciples congregations at that time. Attending were 156 delegates from 100 churches and eleven states. The 1849 convention convened under the name General Convention of the Christian Churches of the United States of America, but adopted a constitution and resolved itself into the American Christian Missionary Society. Alexander Campbell was ill and unable to attend, a great disappointment to him after nearly two decades of work toward church cooperation and a delegate assembly. But he was elected president in absentia and served in the office for sixteen years while providing generous financial support for the Society's ministry. The convention had been planned as a delegate assembly, but due to confusion among those present about their status, everyone was declared a delegate and the convention abandoned Campbell's long envisioned idea of a representative, deliberative assembly in favor of a mass meeting. Disciples' conventions continued to be mass meetings until a representative assembly was instituted at the 1967 Assembly in St. Louis. "The Society" formed in 1849, wrote historian David Harrell, "was the herald of greater union and of ultimate division." With its creation, the "society" concept took root among Disciples, allowing acceptance of organization in practice, but repudiation of ecclesiastical structure in principle. This produced a long-term delay in creating a national representative body. The Society's mission was evangelism, the basic motivation for "cooperatives." But the Society, weak, ineffective, and claiming the loyalty of only a slender majority within the Movement at best, found itself immediately embroiled in controversy. Some called for another convention to discuss the legitimacy of conventions. Campbell responded, "In running out of Babylon [they had] run past Jerusalem." Despite the controversy, Campbell was pleased with the convention: "Our expectations from the Convention have more than been realized. We are much pleased with the result, and regard it as a very happy pledge of good things to come."[27]

Campbell wrote one final series of five articles on Church organization in 1853. He concluded that series with the words: "*Organization is indispensable. Organization is life and strength. Disorganization is death.*" Three years later Campbell would preside over the dissolution of the American Christian Bible Society and the American Christian Publication Society, both of which failed to command the support necessary to survive.

A decade later, Campbell was dead. In light of the remaining history of the nineteenth century, his advocacy for a national representative assembly seemed a losing battle. Two years after Campbell's death an attempt at unification occurred at Louisville when Moses Lard, William K. Pendleton, Ben Franklin, and William T. Moore proposed the "Louisville Plan," a representation strategy consisting of delegates from congregations to districts; from districts to states; and from states to a general national convention. The attempt failed. Again in 1909 a Committee on Reconstruction and Unification was appointed to develop a proposal for a delegate assembly to which all agencies would be organically related. It too failed. But a compromise grew out of it; and the non-delegate International Convention of Christian churches was established in 1917.[28]

Meanwhile, establishing volunteer societies became a national pattern with Disciples. Between 1860 and 1890, thirty-three missionary societies were founded. A few examples are cited briefly to illustrate the societal explosion ignited by evangelical growth during the Third Awakening of the last quarter of the nineteenth century. In 1874, Caroline Neville Pearre established the Christian Woman's Board of Missions for the purpose of improving the lives of women and children at home and abroad. The Foreign Christian Missionary Society was founded the following year. The Board of Church Extension was initially started in 1883 as a part of the ACMS; a Student Volunteer Movement was begun in 1886; the National Benevolent Association was chartered in 1887; Albertina Forrest established the Board of Education in 1894; and the Board of Ministerial Relief was established in 1895. These organizations did not appear as the result of denomination-wide planning or strategy. Rather, they appeared in ad hoc fashion, as the need demanded, and were often the brainchild of and financed by individuals. The cooperations, state societies, General Convention, and missionary and benevolent organizations would evolve into a cooperative work that profoundly effected the ethos of Disciples.[29]

Effects on Intellectual Development

The subject of an educated ministry is the greatest crisis in the last half of the nineteenth century.

ALEXANDER CAMPBELL
The Millennial Harbinger, 1853[30]

Scholars say of the Puritans that it was not the hand, the heart, or the pocket, but the mind they honored and that no other community of pioneers ever so honored study or respected the symbols of learning. But the Puritan ideal of the minister as an intellectual and educational leader steadily weakened in the face of evangelical ideals. As Evangelical Protestantism became the dominant cultural force in American civilization during the nineteenth century, respect for the mind declined among their ideals.

Intellectual historian Richard Hofstadter believed the American mind was shaped in the mold of nineteenth-century American Protestantism. One of the inheritances from the Awakenings, he argued, was the subordination of persons of ideas to persons of emotional power. Mark Noll concluded in *The Scandal of the Evangelical Mind,* "The scandal of the evangelical mind is that there is not much of an evangelical mind." Revivalists were emotionally intense, but intellectually thin. Rational religion and learned professional clergy suffered, while the forces of revivalism and enthusiasm became dominant. The question of learning having a place of priority in religion or being subordinate to emotion is a traditional and universal question within religion.

Mark Noll cited several effects of nineteenth-century evangelicalism: it created a lack of adequate Christian thinking about the world; produced no comprehensive Christian worldview; and produced no journal of public thought. Their colleges emphasized teaching at the expense of scholarly research and they rejected modernity and secular humanism. They supported a highly emotional, prosperity-driven, privatized, fundamentalist faith at the expense of good scholarship, deep theological inquiry, and responsible biblical exegesis. In her new analysis of nineteenth- and twentieth-century fundamentalism and education, Susan Jacoby concluded, "There is unquestionably a powerful correlation between religious fundamentalism and lack of education; between poor education and biblical literalism." They worshiped the Bible rather than using it as a means to an end and they loathed modern science, only wanting to love God with their hearts, not with their minds. The intellectual tension born of nineteenth-century evangelicalism and revivals became a contributing factor to division within the Disciples Reformation Movement. Jonathan Edwards and John Wesley defined evangelicalism as a conscious experience of the divine transformation of the will or human heart. Newell Williams wrote of the contrast with Alexander Campbell:

> Campbell's view that persons become religious not by the immediate work of the Holy Spirit, but by the Spirit working through the gospel demanded a higher view of the "means of grace" than that taught by Edwards and Wesley.

Nineteenth-century evangelicalism intensified the breeding of distinct factions within the Disciples Reformation Movement.[31]

America, the "promised land," attracted hosts of disinherited persons making it an ideal environment for religious revivalism. Forms of worship and religious doctrines of a church are to a great extent a function of social class. Upper classes usually desire more highly developed liturgical forms, a more rational religion. Lower classes are inspired by emotional religion. H. Richard Niebuhr provided insight into this issue: "An intellectually trained and liturgically minded clergy is rejected in favor of lay readers who serve the emotional needs of the untutored and economically disfranchised classes more adequately."

The religion of the unlettered and disinherited tends to stress inner religious experience over learned, formalized religion. It seeks inner convictions and feels little need for intellectual foundations, refined theological ideas, or aesthetic forms. While established churches, for example, thought of art, music, and architecture as leading the mind toward the Divine, evangelicals, relying upon inner experience, looked upon music, art, and architecture as barriers to the heart, as threats to the traditional religious authority of the Bible. These differences led to class conflicts, and to Disciples historian David Harrell's conclusion that "the institutional history of the church is largely a mirror of class conflict within the Movement."[32]

Sociologically, Disciples were predominantly semi-literate, Scots-Irish, frontier farmers; English, Welsh, German, a few French, a few African American, along with others intermingled within the membership. Some of the urban merchant class in Cincinnati, Pittsburgh, Lexington, and Louisville held membership with the Disciples as well, but the broad base of the Movement was a rural, Scots-Irish underclass. Describing the Disciples in 1839, Alexander Campbell observed, "We have a few educated intelligent men, as we have a few rich and powerful; but the majority are poor, ignorant and uneducated." Like the Baptists and Methodists, the Disciples used the methods of revival, emotional fervor, lay preaching, and ordaining their clergymen without requiring theological education. W. E. Garrison characterized the Disciples office of ministry during the early years as "loose and low."

In the first issue of *Christian Baptist*, however, Alexander Campbell expressed an early commitment to an educated clergy: "Authority does not rest in…the person saying he was moved by the holy spirit [*sic*]. To be called means 'go and learn the religion, learn the meaning and use of words, then I will send you to preach.'"

He established Buffalo Seminary in 1818, lodged it in his home, and handcrafted its curriculum to prepare students for ministry. Study included daily instruction in the scriptures, Hebrew language, mathematics, science, English grammar, and literature, with both morning and evening devotions bracketing their academic study. The faculty was composed of Alexander, Thomas, and Jane Campbell. He closed the school in 1823 because he thought the students were intellectually marginal and because so few entered ministry.

By the 1830s Campbell was recruiting as many preachers as possible to help establish new congregations and stay abreast of the demands and momentum of the Second Awakening. Horseback itinerants, visiting briefly at varying intervals, were sent in all directions, and he could not always be particularly selective about who was sent to preach the Word and organize the churches. Along with planting new congregations, he was faced with developing the already established and growing congregations. A tension developed: balancing the need for itinerant ministry sparked by the Awakening with the need for an ordained minister in a fixed location. Several, Tolbert Fanning among them, argued that there was no scriptural authority for a resident pastor or a "one man system." An additional tension surfaced: meeting the demands of autonomy for local congregations with the need for ecclesiastical order and accountability within the Movement. And there was the problem of congregations selecting their own poorly trained leaders over against what Campbell saw as the critical need for educated leaders.[33]

One parishioner wrote to Campbell:

> There is a set of men, now becoming pretty numerous going all round the country calling themselves Evangelists, some of them assuming to be planters of churches… They speak of the clergy as a set of blockheads… they abhor the priesthood. I believe our preachers and evangelists must be raised up by study. Those most eager are not generally the best qualified. Many who think well of your Reformation are…disgusted with this disorder.

Another writer grumbled:

> The name preacher is being used without explanation… When a Reformer tells his neighbor we are all preachers, the whole church are preachers–the people say it is a monstrous arrogance.

Campbell thoughtfully studied and developed Luther's concept of the "priesthood of all believers," but the concept was clearly not in universal favor and some thought the whole idea had created a leadership crisis. In the context of the democratic spirit of the Reformation Movement, hundreds of congregations and dozens of evangelists found themselves of many minds–and among them were those Campbell identified as "flaming literalists" and "infallible dogmatists," who claimed only those who accepted *their* version of the ancient order were of the elect. Thomas Campbell wrote a letter to Alexander: "the progress of the reformation has been much retarded for want of a competent knowledge on the part of the advocates, respecting the thing precisely intended." Alexander knew that his father had touched the root of the trouble, and as he watched this tendency of misrepresenting the principles of the Reformation Movement develop, sometimes in anger, but always in mounting distress, Campbell more than once expressed his frustration. In 1837 he warned:

> There is a growing taste for Opinionism in the ranks of Reformation. This must be quashed, or there will be an end to all moral and religious improvement. It has ever been the harbinger of schism, the forerunner of all discord, vain jangling and bad feeling. It has

ever been the plague of Christendom. *Unless the matter is better understood...we shall be broken to pieces.*

In 1839 he wrote:

Evangelists are ten times more expert in making converts than in putting things in order. Elders that rule well are rarer [*sic*] commodities in this day than Doctors of Divinity. I can find a hundred men that can preach down every ism in Christendom, for ten that can take care of a few sheep in the wilderness. Prophets now-a-days are more easily met than shepherds.

And again in 1842 he fumed:

To be called neither by God nor man to the work of a Christian minister, but by one's own impulse, is a humiliating reflection. The honor of being a Christian minister...is one that ought to be conferred not assumed... Many should blush who presume to speak by a divine call, for their ignorance of all laws of language, the force of words, the logical point in an argument, the meaning of the sacred style and their inaptitude to expound and apply the word of truth... The cause of Reformation is hurt by this class of unsent, unaccomplished, uneducated advocates who plead it. They are a most grievous pestilence and we have bled at every pore through the lacerations of many such.[34]

Campbell wrote at length about church leaders stating every well-organized Christian community ought to have its overseers, presidents, or bishops, and he further suggested the terms "bishop" and "elder" should be used as equivalent and convertible terms. Campbell suggested, too, that there ought to be deacons or public servants of the congregations. In *The Christian System,* he spoke of a threefold ministry: Deacons, Elders, and Evangelists. He saw this as the core of congregational organization. By 1853 he concluded, "The subject of an educated ministry is the greatest crisis in the last half of the nineteenth century." Two years later he wrote again, "on ministerial education I am only more and more convinced of the necessity and importance of it." But not all the membership agreed with him. A sizeable element within the Movement opposed the whole idea of an educated, learned clergy. Evil had fallen on the world, they proclaimed, since Adam and Eve sought knowledge, and, "we should seek salvation instead." They opposed building an order of ministry, feared the risk of concentrating power in the hands of one man, and complained about ministers whose "religion was more in their head than in their heart." One who wrote Campbell said, "You are reforming backwards!"[35]

Campbell's earlier anti-clerical writings had left a deep imprint on the Movement's thinking. But he believed the Movement was changing, and it needed different leadership for different times:

New-lights fifty years ago objected to a gifted man because he was educated and not immediately called at midnight from the plow, the anvil or the loom and divinely commissioned. The comparatively unlettered and uneducated community had influence and argued against education. The Age has advanced! The common people are not the common people of fifty years ago. Common people are more learned. Books and periodicals flourish. Education for evangelists is now indispensable, in keeping with the age... A professed Reformer needs the most enlarged mind, comprehensive Bible Learning. It is essential to his success.

He wrote often and specifically about the attributes of good leadership providing "watch-care" over a congregation. "The discipline of the church," he said, "is as essential to its moral health as its doctrine... To rule well is one of the most difficult attainments. It calls for meekness, candor, firmness, courage, patience... So peculiar is the assemblage of attributes requisite to ruling well, that they are more rarely to be met with than the gifts of eloquence and high analytic powers."[36]

Disagreement over the educational preparation of ministers would persist throughout the years following Campbell's death, with moderates demanding an educated, ordained, and competent clergy, and conservatives sounding the alarm about "priest-ridden sects" and ministers being trained at institutions staffed by "infidels and critics." The two sides failed to reach agreement due in part to the anti-intellectualism of the Second and Third Awakenings continuously inflaming the issue.

A ministry distinct from the laity developed only gradually within the Movement. After the Civil War and until the 1890s, those ministers who were educated generally acquired their learning from small Bible Colleges or small liberal arts colleges where they received three-year certificates for study in the Bible and the Liberal Arts. Levi Marshall, in 1875, was the first Disciples minister to apply to Yale. By 1887 there were three enrolled; and in 1901 there were eleven.

Founded in 1894, the Disciples Divinity House at the University of Chicago for a time became the intellectual center of Disciples under the leadership of the so-called "Chicago Liberals": Herbert Willett, W. E. Garrison, and Edward Scribner Ames, who were joined by Charles Clayton Morrison, editor of the *Christian Century*. The Campbell Institute, founded in 1896 by fourteen Yale seminarians who had transferred to the University of Chicago and who were influenced by the "Chicago Liberals," encouraged a scholarly spirit, contributions to Disciples literature, and a "quiet self-culture." It defined itself as a fellowship of thinkers, although conservatives regarded them as a clique of "shameless modernists," and added their opinion of the University of Chicago as "the greatest organized enemy of evangelical Christianity on earth today." Despite relentless criticism, the Campbell Institute by 1906 had generated a membership of 101 members;

and grew to 177 in 1911. For half a century it enjoyed substantial influence, particularly through its publication, *The Scroll,* criticized by J.W. McGarvey as "inspired by the three evil spirits of evolution, higher criticism and the new theology." The Awakenings left their legacy. In 1917, eleven years after the departure of the Churches of Christ, the Disciples claimed a total of 5,000 ministers. Only 45 percent were college graduates; 1600 had no college training and only half of those had more than a grade school education. Not until 1939 did the International Convention of Disciples of Christ adopt educational guidelines for ordination. As late as 1948 only 85 percent of Disciples ministers were ordained. And not until restructure in 1968 did Disciples begin to hammer out a theology and order of ministry.[37]

****

Protestant churches, newly energized by the Second Awakening, were engaged in intense denominational rivalry. The American frontier and American Protestantism witnessed the competitive creation of an educational infrastructure. The Jacksonian cultural ethos, the call for egalitarian patterns of thought, and the Second Awakening factored into the development of new educational institutions in the Disciples Reform Movement.

The contagion for college building was especially strong between 1830 and 1860, known as the "Golden Age" for founding small, rural denominational colleges, "hill-top colleges" typically with six to twelve professors and 100 to 300 students. In this competitive atmosphere Baptists declared that every state would have its own Baptist College, and soon Methodists voted to place a college in every annual conference.

All four founders of the Disciples Movement began their careers as educators. Each of them, Thomas and Alexander Campbell, Barton Stone, and Walter Scott would serve as president or principle of an academy or college, in addition to being highly respected teachers and authors. Disciples are known to have founded fourteen educational institutions prior to 1840, eleven of them established during the 1830s. Four were founded in Indiana and seven in Kentucky, with others in Ohio, Pennsylvania, and Virginia. Only one of the institutions, Bacon College, survived beyond the Civil War, but in 1858 it was rechartered as Kentucky University in Harrodsburg and merged with Transylvania University in Lexington. Most were academies, institutes, or seminaries, forerunners of the modern primary, middle, and senior high schools. Financed on a modest scale, they regularly solicited funds from congregations as well as individuals. They were privately organized, owned, and maintained by influential personalities within the Movement who were not accountable to any ecclesiastical authority–due to the absence of denominational structure. "Supreme independency," noted William T. Moore, "which controlled in the organization of churches, also controlled in the organization of colleges." Nevertheless, these institutions were regarded as part of the Movement.[38]

Alexander Campbell was a life member and served as a vice-president of Cincinnati's "Western Literary Institute and College of Professional Teachers." Among other members were two of Campbell's Disciples friends Robert Richardson and Philip Fall; William H. McGuffy, author of the *Electric Readers*; Rev. Lyman Beecher, president of Lane Theological Seminary in Ohio, and his son Henry Ward Beecher; Thomas Smith Grimke, a Carolina barrister whom Campbell often quoted; and the Rev. Bishop John B. Purcell whom Campbell contested in public debate. From his associations with the 222 members in the Institute and from his own extensive reading on education, Campbell developed an educational philosophy from the orthodox sources of his day that would shape the founding of educational institutions within the Movement for the remainder of the century. The components of Campbell's philosophy included: *Wholeness of Person, Moral Formation of Character, Biblical Studies, Non-Sectarianism, Perfectibility of Individuals,* and *Lifelong Learning.* The central premise of his six-part educational philosophy was the formation of moral character. The moral nature of persons, he argued, was superior to their intellectual and physical nature because it is in the moral nature of persons that the virtues of benevolence, justice, compassion, and generosity are developed and human excellence is achieved. "The formation of moral character, the culture of the heart," he wrote in 1840, "is the supreme end of education." Another feature of his philosophy was biblical studies. He was convinced that the study of the Bible was essential to a comprehensive literary education and the safeguarding of ethics. When Old Main at Bethany College was built in 1858, only one item was placed in the cornerstone–a Bible.

He viewed sectarianism as neither religion nor morality and saw it as one of the greatest defects of the educational system. In Perry Gresham's phrase, Campbell viewed sectarian education as a "contradiction in terms." And Campbell was a staunch supporter of lifelong learning. "Man is never out of his pupilage," he advised, and later added, "Every student that has attained graduation…is merely licensed to become his own teacher and pupil." Armed with this philosophy, which anticipated many of the educational reforms of Horace Mann and was twenty-five years ahead of other major college reformers, nineteenth-century Disciples became zealots in the creation of new institutions of learning. According to the study of Disciples Colleges by Floyd Reeves and John Russell in 1929, "There seems to have been one single controlling purpose in the minds of those who were responsible for the founding of Disciples colleges. That purpose was the provision of opportunities for training the leadership for the communion." Secondary motives also proved important, including local boosterism, sectionalism, and the market demand for teachers and for technically skilled workers.[39]

Between 1840 and 1866, individual constituents founded 115 educational institutions. Of that number, 83 would be considered high schools today, predecessors of the public high school and representing a transitional stage in American education. No charters, no catalogues, and few records remain to testify they existed, but their contribution to the literacy of the Movement is incalculable. These academies and institutes made their contributions over a short historical period, quickly became obsolete, and were soon crowded out of existence by the rapidly expanding public school system. The strongest among them made a gradual transition to two or four-year colleges. Thirty-two of the 115 institutions were colleges, rooted in the settled ways of rural communities where they attempted to insulate themselves from what they thought to be the evils of urban America. These colleges mirrored the educational model offered at Bethany College, founded on Campbell's philosophy. Disciples' colleges were among the earliest schools to pioneer the concept of coeducation and female education. Graduates were attracted to teaching and ministry, with law a close third. The mortality rate among these new schools was 80 percent, a rate that would last throughout the century, evidence that the number of colleges founded was too great for the Movement to support. William T. Moore observed: "It is remarkable that any of these colleges have lived. Many of them have certainly lived at a half-dying rate." Campbell was quick to realize there were more institutions than the movement could support:

> We should be glad to see a flourishing University in every state in the union, sustained by our Christian brotherhood. But, according to my political economy, we cannot now have a model one for an age to come, because we are lavishing our means on too many experiments, or un-matured projects… We must pay the price of wisdom in the school of folly, and leave our children to wish… that their fathers had been more wise.

Disciples' enthusiasm for establishing colleges often outstripped their resources to sustain and their ability to manage. W. E. Garrison graphically described the result:

> Soon the prairies were scattered with the bones of dead colleges whose very names have been forgotten. It is not surprising that the Disciples of that period little realized what it took to make a college, in money, scholarship and constituency.[40]

The Civil War stands as a watershed in the history of American higher education, separating the era of the small, sectarian college from the era of the large, land-grant, state-owned, secular universities. The post-Civil War industrial boom triggered the rise of the university responding to the demands for vocational and specialized education in a capital-driven, free-market economy. They were founded by politicians and industrialists rather than clergy, and administered by professional academics instead of ministers. But the Disciples Movement was not idle. Between 1867 and 1899 the Movement established seventy-nine colleges and seventy-four academies and institutes. The border states of Kentucky and Missouri accounted for twenty and eighteen colleges respectively, while the South established a total of twenty-five colleges, fifteen of those in Tennessee, the heartland of the future Churches of Christ. Eventually, the Movement founded 215 colleges and universities along with 207 academies and institutes, a total of 422 known institutions. Among those are Drake University, Texas Christian University, Butler University, and Bethany College.

The relationship between the church and the colleges and universities has continuously evolved–from free and independent institutions, to a period of ecclesiastical oversight, to loose affirmation through an association structure, to a highly vocal lobby constituted in a Board of Higher Education, to the present relationship of "Covenant." The multiplication of institutions and competition for finances and students prompted the 1894 establishment of a nine-member Board of Education in the American Christian Missionary Society. It received no funds for its work. Mrs. Albertina Forrest was appointed coordinating secretary. She prepared a groundbreaking report on the colleges entitled "The Status of Education among Disciples," containing a long list of deficiencies, pointing out, for example, that none of the colleges and universities had sufficient endowment; among all the faculty in all the colleges only one faculty member held a Ph.D.; and 42 percent of the faculty had no graduate training at all. Degree requirements were vastly different, prompting early twentieth-century demands from the church for uniform standards, academic accreditation, state convention approval for the funding of any new Disciples educational institution, and a national fund-raising effort for college endowments. Despite all the deficiencies, Disciples colleges and the Movement during the nineteenth century made four distinct and unique contributions to American higher education.

1. Disciples colleges were among the earliest schools to pioneer the concept of co-education and female education.
2. Considered by many its most original contribution was the establishment of Bible chairs, divinity houses, and schools of religion at state-owned colleges and universities, founding a greater number than any other religious body.
3. Disciples originated and advanced the concept of "campus ministry" on state-owned campuses. The first was the Campus Ministry at the University of Michigan in Ann Arbor, established by the Christian Woman's Board of Missions in 1894.
4. Study of the Bible was given a significant place in undergraduate curriculum. Several Disciples colleges today still hold to the requirement of 3 to 6 hours in biblical studies. Several designate it an elective.[41]

In 1910 an Association of Colleges of the Disciples of Christ was established to bring schools into closer relationship and serve as a consultation resource. Then in 1914, thirty-seven institutions agreed to affiliate with a new Board of Education of Disciples of Christ. The 1938 incorporation of a new Board of Higher Education, consolidating both the former Association and Board into a single entity, separated higher education from the Missionary Society. It had forty-two board members, later expanded to seventy-seven, including the heads of each institution. The work was *funded by assessments of member institutions,* not the church, and the Board functioned as a "lobby" pressing the church with its demands and concerns. The Board's existence lasted for forty years (1938–1978).

****

One other measure of the intellectual effects emitted by the Second and Third Awakenings is the nature of the literature produced by Disciples during the time of their evangelical growth and expansion. Disciples, unlike most denominations, have a comparatively complete listing of their nineteenth-century literature, with inventories compiled during the first half of the twentieth century. These inventories include Claude Spencer's *Periodicals of the Disciples of Christ* (1943) along with his *An Author Catalogue of Disciples of Christ* (1946); J.W. Monser's *Literature of the Disciples of Christ* (1906); W.E. Garrison's *Literature of the Disciples of Christ* (1923); and A.T. DeGroot and E.E. Dowling's *Literature of the Disciples of Christ* (1933). From these sources we learn Disciples published 1,160 periodicals and 12,500 books, pamphlets, and state newspapers by the time of the 1946 inventory. For the most part it was a literature written for the church, *not* for scholars; a literature advocating and defending theological positions; and a literature little read outside the Disciples Reformation Movement. Intellectual inbreeding was indeed a weakness of the Movement. The Awakenings helped shape and reinforce a set of convictions held by the more conservative wing of the Movement as well as hardening the moderate opposition, thereby contributing to inter-Movement tensions, clashes, and confrontations, setting moderate progressives against conservatives, both of whom aired their differences through periodical literature. The very nature and tone of the Awakenings subordinated learning and dulled the intellectual life of Disciples.[42]

Between 1830 and 1860 Disciples intellectual life centered in Bethany through the writing and speaking of Alexander and Thomas Campbell, Robert Richardson, W. K. Pendleton, and nearby Walter Scott. With the fading of this Bethany group, the center of intellectual activity moved to editorships. Because of their influence in shaping popular opinion, Disciples editors are often referred to as the Movement's nineteenth-century bishops. Leroy Garrett remarked they had "printers ink in their veins," while W. E. Garrison noted: "The editor's chair has come nearer to being a throne of power than any other position among Disciples; Disciples do not have bishops; they have editors."

Disciples relied upon a fraternity of editors and journals for guidance and direction. During the transitional middle period of Disciples history, they were the ones, wrote William Tucker, "who linked the founders to the present." Ronald Osborn reminds us, however, "While historians customarily note the influence of editors during the Disciples' first century, they have accorded insufficient recognition to the professors of Bible and the minister-presidents of the colleges." This latter group included such persons as W. K. Pendleton, C.L. Loos, J. W. McGarvey, Robert Milligan, Ely von Zollars, Clinton Lockhart, and Frank Marshall, to name only a few. They wrote the textbooks used in the colleges where some of the ministers were trained, and also wrote the Bible lessons published in the periodicals as well as serving as the headline speakers at most Disciples gatherings. Their influence has long been understated.[43]

Between 1830 and 1840 twenty-eight periodicals were published within the Movement, only ten of which survived more than ten years. Each had its own version of the ancient order. Of this group, three were distinguished: *The Christian Messenger, The Evangelist,* and *The Millennial Harbinger,* published by Barton Stone, Walter Scott, and Alexander Campbell respectively. For thirty years the *Harbinger* was unquestionably the most powerful force among Disciples. But by the end of the 1830s Campbell was aware that too many weekly and monthly periodicals was one of the chief causes of misrepresentation of his Reformation principles. He believed that "two or three [papers] well supported and judiciously conducted, would exert a better influence and do more good than the dozen now in being." In 1839 he published an article in the *Harbinger* entitled, "Too Many Periodicals"; again in the 1841 *Harbinger* he wrote of this problem: "They have done much injury to the cause of reformation. All claim equal freedom of speech and writing what they please;...not all are equally competent to instruct, equally free from error not equally worthy of public confidence."

With the coming of the Civil War and the discontinuance of the United States mail service to confederate states, the *Harbinger* lost its Southern subscribers, a radical reduction from which it never recovered. This was compounded by competition from other periodicals that began to appear. By 1870 the *Harbinger* ceased publication.

Two periodicals, regularly taking exception to Campbell's positions, commenced publication in the mid-1850s, *The Gospel Advocate* in 1855 and *The American Christian Review* in 1856. William Lipscomb and Tolbert Fanning launched *The Gospel Advocate* in Nashville, Tennessee, calling it a periodical "for southern people." Shortly, David Lipscomb, William's brother, became coeditor with Fanning. They resurrected *The Gospel Advocate* in 1866 after a hiatus due to the Civil War, giving as the major reason for republication, "we had not a single paper known to us that Southern people could read without having their feelings wounded." Consequently a sectional journalism was born. Benjamin Franklin, an exceptionally successful evangelist who was responsible for 8,000 baptisms, and who was a great, great, great nephew of the American statesman Benjamin Franklin, founded the *Review* in Cincinnati for "common people." It was harsh, exclusive, condemning, and dogmatically anti-society and anti-college. Both the *Advocate* and the *Review* advocated strict, legalistic Christian primitivism; they opposed the use of organs in worship; they opposed the establishment of missionary societies; and both questioned the wisdom of cooperative work.[44]

Many Disciples, in the words of James Lamar, demanded a "wiser, sweeter, better advocacy, an advocacy that should exhibit the apostolic *spirit* as well as the apostolic *letter.*" In April 1866, thanks to the leadership of future United States President James A. Garfield and the philanthropy of Thomas W. Phillips, *The Christian Standard* began publication. Phillips, a close associate of Alexander Campbell, served Bethany College as a trustee for more than forty years. Isaac Errett (1820–1888), who had fulfilled the role as coeditor of the *Harbinger* and as corresponding secretary of the ACMS, agreed to edit the *Standard.* His incisive mind, synonymous with the views of Alexander Campbell, brought a progressive spirit to the publication. The first issue of the *Standard* in 1866 carried the news of Campbell's death less than a month before. In 1870, a book publisher in Cincinnati offered to underwrite the periodical. Errett accepted the offer and relocated. From the 1870s to the early 1900s the *Standard* acquitted itself as the most powerful weekly among Disciples, commanding wide respect, although constantly under attack by David Lipscomb, J. W. McGarvey, and Ben Franklin. It was an advocate of Christian union with a mind and voice that understood Christian liberty; it favored open communion, supported the creation of an "Inter-denominational Congress" in 1885, and advocated, "Let the bond of union among the baptized be Christian character in place of orthodoxy… acknowledge the liberty of all." James DeForest Murch called Errett, "a leader of understanding, insight and broad vision," and David Harrell judged Isaac Errett's influence as "unequaled in the church in the 1880s." Historian Mark Toulouse names Isaac Errett "the premier leader of the second generation," and W. E. Garrison said of the *Standard*'s influence: "More than to any other journal and person, it was to the *Christian Standard* and Isaac Errett that the Disciples were indebted for being saved from becoming a fissiparous sect of jangling legalists."[45]

The Christian-Evangelist is the oldest continuously published journal among Disciples of Christ. In broad summary, it began as *The Christian* in 1874, then merged with *The Evangelist* and was renamed *The Christian-Evangelist* in 1882. It then merged with *World Call* in 1974 to become *The Disciple,* a publication that ceased publishing in the month of March 2002 and was immediately followed in April by the magazine we know today as *DisciplesWorld,* a publication launched by several Disciples, including James Suggs, Robert Friedly, and James Reed. James H. Garrison became coeditor of *The Christian-Evangelist* in 1869 and later editor, investing nearly six decades of his life in the publication prior to his death in 1931. It too was a forceful publication, taking the same positions as Errett in unstinting support of cooperation, Christian unity, and liberty. It supported higher criticism, refusing to stifle biblical scholarship. In fact, Herbert Willett (one of the so-called "Chicago liberals") was engaged to write the Sunday school lessons for *The Christian-Evangelist,* much to the dismay of conservatives. Garrison did not reject science; rather, he saw it as compatible with Christianity. On Darwinism, for example, he ultimately published his conclusion that "the great host of educated Christians look upon evolution as God's method of creation." *Christian Standard* and *The Christian-Evangelist* generated intellectual stimulation and formed a highly influential counterpoint to *The Gospel Advocate.* Errett and Garrison were enthusiastic loyalists to the Disciples Reformation Movement. After Errett's death, however, the *Standard* fell into conservative hands and became an organ for the Christian Churches/Churches of Christ. Shortly before his death in 1888, Errett wrote a letter to Garrison recounting their shared journey:

> We have stood shoulder to shoulder in all the conflicts through which the society has passed and the two most effective instrumentalities in educating our people and bringing them into active co-operation in spreading the Gospel...have been the Christian Evangelist and the Christian Standard...you and I have always worked on the same lines, in perfect harmony.[46]

Many other lesser periodicals, such as *Lard's Quarterly,* inspired and motivated by the controversies of the time, appeared briefly to sharpen the discussion on some of the issues in the protracted debates between moderates and conservatives, but then quietly disappeared. The Awakenings contributed grist for the essays and articles, induced several individuals to become editors, and helped crystallize the positions of debaters in both camps.

The notable contributions to Disciples literature, beyond the periodicals, during the nineteenth century were written primarily to defend theological views. Beyond Alexander Campbell, Robert Richardson is considered the most perceptive thinker and most lucid writer of the early period of Disciples history. From the near endless inventory, most scholars identify three publications as indispensable:

- Campbell, Alexander, *The Christian System* (1835)
- Milligan, Robert, *Exposition and Defense of the Scheme of Redemption* (1868)
- Richardson, Robert, *Memoirs of Alexander Campbell* (1868)

Study of the Disciples Reformation Movement finds its baseline in these writings coupled with the major periodicals cited above. They were among the very few Disciples books read outside the Movement until the end of the century, when the works of Peter Ainslie, Herbert Willett, and Charles C. Morrison were widely consulted beyond Disciples borders, helping to lift Disciples out of their long cultural isolation, and helping to penetrate the intellectual atrophy created by the experience of the Second and Third Awakenings.

The Road to Disunion

We cannot and will not regard them as brethren.

DANIEL SOMMER
The Address and Declaration
August 18, 1889

Ceaseless controversy born of fundamentalist-modernist issues tormented the Reform Movement from its beginning through the 1906 partition and even beyond. The 1906 rupture within the Disciples Movement has been interpreted by successive generations of observers and historians in a wide variety of ways: theologically, sociologically, economically, politically, intellectually, or as the result of human fallibility and powerful personalities. Historic understanding of events, particularly causation, is relative, not absolute, because interpretation is offered in light of the times in which it is written. When the *Mona Lisa,* for example, was first viewed in the sixteenth century it was seen as a great work of realism. In the age of nineteenth-century Romanticism, it was viewed as a work of mystery and symbolism. In the early twentieth century Sigmund Freud viewed it as a psychological creation. Interpretation of the causes of division among Disciples will continue, with new interpretations emerging in each new age.

The Civil War

Some scholars suggest the political, economic, and social forces unleashed by the Civil War were the true catalysts for division within the Disciples Reformation Movement. Clearly the Civil War fixed an enormous strain upon the Movement. And the heaviest strain of all was the dispute over slavery. Modern theologians suggest the Civil War generation was poorly prepared theologically to provide a critical examination of the racism that underlay the debate on slavery and the status of African Americans; was poorly prepared to confront the religious and moral implications of the war; and was equally poorly prepared for the intellectual (Darwinism) and social challenges (urbanization, non-Protestant immigrants, unequal distribution of wealth, and other convulsions of capitalism) that came after the war. Church historian Mark Noll called it a theological tragedy. An individualistic, literalistic biblical orientation was unable to speak to the issue of slavery—and has long stunted Disciples witness on issues of social justice. With no higher religious authority than personal interpretation coupled with the doctrine of biblical literalism, conservative Disciples were left with essentially two choices: condone slavery or reject biblicism. Moderate-progressive Disciples, including Campbell, who attempted to exercise religious statesmanship, worked to temper the debate, to find an elusive middle ground.

Citing sources from the era, David Harrell's research reveals that in 1851 Disciples owned 101,000 slaves, which on a per capita basis made them the leading slave-owning religious body in the United States. Both Stone and Campbell owned slaves, both opposed slavery, and both freed their slaves, although Campbell claimed not to be an abolitionist: "I have always been anti-slavery, but never an abolitionist." Most persons at the time feared religious havoc from so-called "Bible scorning abolitionists." From Campbell's perspective, slavery was a mutual bondage. "Masters, sometimes as well as slaves, hug the chains that enslave them," he wrote. During the 1840s he advocated a gradual emancipation using legal and moral means. He saw slavery as a matter of political opinion, on which Christians may differ and still be united. This moderate, nondecisive, middle-of-the-road position, while credited with holding the Movement together, was unsatisfactory to extremists on both sides. Some Northerners thought he should come out firmly for immediate emancipation and in their outrage organized an anti-slavery Christian Missionary Society in 1854, separate from the ACMS. Some Southerners, when Campbell advised them to rid themselves of slavery, canceled their subscriptions to *The Millennial Harbinger* and told Campbell to mind his own business. Although, as Lincoln noted in his second inaugural address, both sides "read the same Bible," their separate interpretations of the Bible ran to the extreme, leaving little common ground between the letter and spirit of the scriptures. Warfare was their final resort.[47]

Feelings ran at fever pitch. Families divided. The sons of both Alexander Campbell and Barton Stone fought in the Confederate army. Benjamin F. Fall, Confederate chaplain during the war and a staunch Southern Disciple, denied Yankees in the Movement were his brothers and claimed he wanted first chance to shoot them. Some Northern ministers wanted slaveholders to be treated as horse-thieves and advocated hanging all confederate leaders. The ACMS, meeting in Cincinnati in 1861, passed two resolutions supporting the Union, which deeply offended the Southern congregations in the Movement. And the peace agreement at Appomattox Court House had scarcely been signed when Tolbert Fanning recommended a "consultation meeting" of Southern Christians *only,* because we need to "work separately for a season." Exemplary of the raw feelings was the episode of the 1855 founding of Northwestern Christian University (later, Butler), a college in a free state established as a challenge to and as distinct from Bethany, a college in a slave state, even though their key recruiting and fund-raising turf overlapped. The Northwestern charter claimed it was established for "youth of all parts of the United States, especially the states of the Northwest." "Northwestern," it was stated in a letter from John Cox, secretary of the Northwestern Board to Alexander Campbell, "was in a free state, and that students attending it would not be brought into contact with habits and manners that exist in populations where slavery exists." Campbell was incensed, charging that Northwestern was grounded in "political freesoilism." The controversy lingered on into the Civil War, an episode reflective of larger sociopolitical forces at work within the Movement. As Campbell's reformation grew in number and geography, it encompassed the rivalry of sections and their attempts to deal with the great domestic questions of the day. Northerners held a more denominational, socially active concept of Christianity. Southern Disciples emerged from the war extreme sectarians with a pronounced sectional orientation.[48]

But did it divide the Movement? Within a year of the war several leading Disciples figures published their eyewitness opinions about its effects on the Movement. Robert Richardson saw the Movement as still "a united people." Moses Lard released an article in his quarterly in 1866 in which he declared that although the fierce ordeal of a horrendous war had caused tension within the Movement, it effected no division. "From what cause, then, can we as a people divide? I am free to confess I see none," he concluded. Lard noted further, "The Methodist body in this country divided into a northern half and a southern half. Such a division as this is with us absolutely impossible." David Lipscomb appealed to Northern Disciples in his *Gospel Advocate* to help their Southern friends "who cry for the bread of life," implying oneness as a Movement and an attendant obligation to respond. From the Missouri frontier came word from T. M. Allen "notwithstanding the defection, troubles and afflictions that prevail in our land, we are yet a united people." In 1868, W. K. Pendleton, writing in *The Millennial Harbinger,* replied to those who thought the Reformation Movement might be in danger of dividing: "No sign or fear of division among us; there was never a more indissoluble people." Despite the war, despite the tension and animosity, and despite the obvious existence of two factions, a tenuous unity seemed to prevail, at the very least a group consciousness, a sense of fellowship. Institutionally, it remained one church as it faced the post-war era. Ronald Osborn said the two sides persisted together because of Alexander Campbell. Benjamin Franklin insisted, however, there was a "schism in feeling." But in the years immediately following the war, with feelings bruised and bloodied, and with several small-scale local schisms surfacing from year to year, the leaders of both larger factions made an effort to stay unified, despite rifts or symptoms of fissure beneath the surface.[49]

During the first half of the twentieth century the interpretations by professional historians expressed pride in the belief that unlike other denominations the Disciples, having sizeable membership in both the North and the South, had been the only major Protestant body that did not divide. Earl West, Oliver Whitley, and Robert Fife, each representing a different branch of the original Disciples Reform Movement, all echoed the same theme. Garrison and DeGroot, devoting little space to the question of separation, claimed the Movement had come through the Civil War without division. But in the 1970s, historian David Harrell presented statistical evidence proving that nearly two-thirds of the 156,658 members of the Churches of Christ that separated in 1906 were in the eleven former Confederate states and most of the remaining members were in former border states. Harrell argued that Churches of Christ were, to a significant degree, the product of post-war sectional prejudices; and they emerged from the war committed more strongly than ever to extreme sectarianism, the same sociological forces that gave birth to *The Gospel Advocate,* a periodical commenced, according to Isaac Errett, "with an appeal to men of Southern blood and proposed cooperation among them only." The South, Harrell said, supported its own periodicals, its own institutions, and its own spokespersons. He considered this a tacit, or *de facto* separation. "In fact, if not in theory," he wrote, "the Disciples of Christ were divided by the Civil War." Subsequent general histories by Lester McAlister and William Tucker and by Henry Webb, influenced by Harrell's research, cited the Civil War in their writings as a powerful element contributing to the division of the Movement.[50]

Historian Leroy Garrett reviewed seven Ph.D. dissertations written between the years 1922 and 1972 addressing the question of division within the Disciples Movement. Among the causes commonly identified in those thesis, according to Garrett, were legalism of the radicals; a power struggle among editors following Campbell's death; conservatism within the Movement; legalism, literalism and anti-ism; sectionalism and noncooperation; restorationism; and the exclusivism of the Churches of Christ. The Civil War was not emphasized in these dissertations as the cause of the division.[51]

It may be fairly stated that the Civil War did not formally or institutionally divide the Movement into two separate churches. (It remained one church through the post-war era.) But the strain of war pounded the fellowship, wrecked the ACMS, intensified the Movement's ongoing controversies, caused the moderates to lose control of the Movement, and, although certainly not the sole or overriding cause of division, was clearly a potent and formidable factor contributing to the eventual separation in 1906. The struggle for the theological heart of the Movement existed *before, during,* and *after* the Civil War, creating under the surface a breach of cultural, sectional, and mental worlds within the Movement that at times surged, at times subsided, but always persisted and never disappeared.

Instrumental Music

The organ became a matter of dispute in nearly all frontier denominations soon after the instrument began to appear in 1860. Disciples, however, seemed to argue about the issue more vigorously than others. J. H. Garrison noted with amusement, "Disciples have a morbid fondness for controversy." Ben Franklin had even opposed the use of printed notes for singing; but it should be mentioned that many parishioners could read neither musical notes nor words. Moderates believed the organ enhanced worship, adding beauty and inspiration. Conservatives countered there was no authorization for the instrument in the New Testament. They referred to it as the "infamous box" or the "wheezing, grunting instrument" and warned they would not fellowship with "organ grinding churches." Some resorted to the theft of organs from churches; others attacked the instrument with hatchets and in new church construction doors were deliberately designed narrowly to prevent an organ from passing through. Moses Lard inveighed: "Let every preacher resolve never to enter a meeting-house of our brethren in which an organ stands... Let all who oppose the organ withdraw from the church if one is brought in."[52]

Moderates saw the organ as a sign of progress, a nonessential matter of opinion; conservatives viewed it symbolically as a betrayal of religious principle, the desertion of an essential matter of faith. Some interpreters have given the issue an economic underpinning. Citing the inequitable distribution of wealth, they state that congregations in the defeated South could not afford organs, that they resented the middle-class affectations of Northern congregations. The anti-organ posture became a convenient way to push for division. The "editor-bishops," of course, entered the fray, stirring emotions surrounding the issue by circulating their interpretations among their readers, a tactic viewed by some as an excuse to divide the Movement. Both *The Gospel Advocate* and *The American Christian Review* were anti-organ; Isaac Errett, through *The Christian Standard,* said it was too insignificant a question to divide a religious body—that it was *not* a question about the integrity of worship but simply a question of aiding the singing of the church, a question on which there may be many opinions without affecting the integrity of those who differ. Alexander Campbell died before the issue reached the time of its greatest consequence in the 1870s and 1880s, and there was not a national organization of sufficient strength to resolve the issue. However, the musical instrument controversy was more of a surface disturbance created by a deeper undercurrent of theological, cultural, and sectional rivalry.[53]

Missionary Societies

"*Silence* of the scriptures" became a key factor in support or nonsupport of Missionary Societies or any other organization beyond the local congregation. The founding of the American Christian Missionary Society in 1849 marked the weak beginnings of national organization, although it did not evolve into an "instrument of coherence" until the twentieth century. Equally important, the founding also exposed early signs of an internal difference in interpretation of Reform Movement principles. Legalistic conservatives, alarmed by the founding of the ACMS, said scripture was *silent* on the issue. They claimed the congregation was the only scriptural organization and creating societies beyond it threatened congregations' independence. Benjamin Franklin insisted, "The first demand…is a request that we show a 'thus saith the Lord' for…Societies." Tolbert Fanning scolded Campbell in 1854, stating that when he allowed the ACMS to elect him president he was shorn of his strength, just as Samson was when he allowed Delilah to cut his hair. Jacob Creath Jr. expressed the desire to have the following epitaph inscribed on his tombstone:

> Here lies Jacob Creath, who opposed all Societies to spread the Gospel except the individual churches of Jesus Christ, because he believed such Societies to be destructive of the liberty of the churches and of mankind.

And one correspondent wrote to the *American Christian Review,* "We want *more faith* and *less machinery, more work* and *less talk,* more faith and less planning."[54]

Moderates believed there were Christian responsibilities that reached beyond the local congregation and could only be met through cooperation. And where the scriptures were *silent,* they believed the church had the right to exercise its own enlightened judgment. They sought to be adaptable without compromising the historic principles of the Movement. William K. Pendleton stated the moderate position in his address to the 1866 meeting of the ACMS:

> Let it not be said, then, that the Disciples of Christ are to take the silence of Scripture on a given subject as a positive rule of prohibition against all freedom of action or obligation of duty. No rule could be more productive of mischief than this. That large freedom of thought and action, and that resistless spontaneity of benevolence, which makes a Christian a living power for good wherever he goes, would be cramped and stifled by so narrow a principle, till Christianity would become a timid and cringing thing of forms, and afraid to expand itself in free and God-like charities.

Christian Standard and *The Christian-Evangelist* were strong advocates of societies, while *The Gospel Advocate* and *American Christian Review* were strong opponents. Alfred DeGroot credited *The Christian-Evangelist* with saving the principle of church cooperation through societies for the Disciples of Christ. Whereas the organ issue was decided congregation by congregation, the society issue could not be decided in that fashion. Alexander Campbell's judgment and ACMS presidency were not strong enough to carry the day, and with his death, leaders like Ben Franklin reversed their positions and the anti-society forces of reaction were released. The organ and missionary societies were not defining themes, claimed Richard Hughes; they were symbols that became divisive issues only *after* the Movement produced two irreconcilable traditions.[55]

The Second Generation

Barton Stone died in 1844, Thomas Campbell in 1854, Walter Scott in 1861, and Alexander Campbell in 1866. A choice of direction inevitably confronts the second generation of all reforms. The Movement had to decide if it should cement the views of the founders and hold solidly to the traditions of the old order, or if it should venture intellectually, be open to change, and exercise flexibility by adapting its ministry to the newly emerging sociocultural environment of post–Civil War America: westward expansion, political reconstruction of the nation, influx of immigrants, urbanization, scientific discovery (Darwinism), and industrial transformation. Leaders of the second generation lacked the personal force of the founders. They lost the vision of the founders ("In essentials unity, in opinions liberty, in all things love"), transformed their opinions into essentials, hardened essentials into exclusivist positions, became ineffectual in building consensus, and were ultimately not able to consolidate the membership. From the original vision they lost the element of "love" that, in Campbell's words, "maintains unity of Spirit in the bonds of peace." Part of the Movement veered one direction; part of it veered another.[56]

Ronald Osborn noted one of the key factors holding the Movement together was the living leadership of Alexander Campbell. "When he was removed," wrote Osborn, "Disciples were left with neither a fixed position nor a dynamic principle of coherence… even though they grew for a while, at Campbell's death they immediately began to fall apart. No one succeeded him, for his leadership was charismatic, not official, and the leaders who came after had diverse spirits." And Leroy Garrett concluded, "Men cause divisions; not things."[57]

Theology

Most modern scholars account for the division of the Movement on theological grounds more than any other factor. They claim the Movement was ruptured ideologically, though not geographically, long before the Civil

War. The basic theological issue was a "loose" versus "strict" interpretation
of Reform principles, "Where the Scriptures speak, we speak; where the
Scriptures are silent, we are silent"; and, "In essentials unity; in nonessentials, liberty; in all things, charity." Disciples scholar Stephen England
believed the divisions that finally came are traceable to a "multiplying of
essentials" by conservatives, with almost everything in the New Testament
becoming essential, *even its silences.* Where the New Testament was silent, the
issue was considered forbidden. There was no room for liberty of opinion.
England concluded that controversies seethed beneath the surface for four
decades, before erupting into an open split.[58]

   Almost from the beginning, the Disciples Reform Movement contained
its moderate-progressive and conservative wings, due primarily to the
contradictory themes of unity and restoration. The moderate-progressive
wing (main body of the Movement) was strong in support of the *unity*
principle, more inclined to view restoration as a methodology, more
denominational and socially active in its concept of Christianity, more
inclusive, and more open to progress and change. The conservative wing
revered *restoration* as a principle, not a methodology; was more exclusive;
was extreme in its sectarianism; and was intent on preserving the ancient
order. David Harrell argued, "Strife between the two caused the fringes
to fatten into sizable, obstinate factions." Campbell's own progression of
thought created a theological ambiguity within the Movement that fueled
the conflict. Some characterized him as schizophrenic; others labeled him a
"rational super-naturalist." While most applauded his maturing thought and
his openness to learn, others believed he had lost his way and abandoned
the original principles of the Movement. They severely criticized him.
Historian Richard Hughes concluded:

> Campbell had raised up followers who, at many points, stood
> diametrically opposed to one another. Tragically, he found himself
> related to both but estranged from both, standing in the middle
> of their contentions but able to do little or nothing to reconcile
> their disputes. By the mid-1850s, the numbers in each of the two
> principle groups he had spawned were legion, though they had not
> yet congealed into separate and recognized denominations.[59]

Two episodes illustrate the building theological rupture. In 1837 a
lady in Lunenburg, Virginia, wrote to Campbell inquiring if there were
Christians in other faith groups and if the name Christian could be applied
to someone who had not been immersed. Many consider the exchange
of letters between the two the most significant piece of correspondence in
the history of the Movement. Campbell responded at great length but was
very specific about the question of immersion:

> I cannot…make any one duty the standard of Christian state or
> character, not even immersion… I do not substitute obedience to

one commandment for universal or even general obedience. And should I see a sectarian Baptist...more spiritually minded, more generally conformed to the requisitions of the Messiah, than one who precisely acquiesces with me in the theory or practice of immersion as I teach–doubtless the former rather than the latter would have my cordial...love as a Christian. So I judge and so I feel... There is no occasion, then, for making immersion, on a profession of the faith, absolutely essential to a Christian... He that infers that none are Christians but the immersed...greatly errs... I think in so reasoning I am sustained by all the Prophets and Apostles of both Testaments.

His response, published in *The Millennial Harbinger,* set off a controversy both far-reaching and intense. He received a flood of mail, in protest and in support. Supporters viewed it as a "Manifesto of Toleration." Critics, pained by its content, thought he had relinquished the most vital point of the Reformation Movement by claiming that immersion was not essential to being a Christian. Campbell responded with two articles on "Christians among the sects," and suggested that readers consult his writings in *Christian Baptist* in which he had asserted, "This plan...of confining all goodness and grace to our noble selves and the 'elect few' who are like us...; to associate with a few...as the pure church, as the elect, is evangelical pharisaism." According to Eva Jean Wrather, he always believed the chief greatness of the Reformation Movement lay in its inclusiveness–in unity and toleration–and therefore cited as his most urgent reason for having delivered "such an opinion at this time":

Some of our brethren were too much addicted to denouncing sects and representing them en masse as wholly alien from the possibility of salvation–as wholly antichristian and corrupt... I felt constrained to rebuke them over the shoulders of this inquisitive lady. These zealous brethren gave countenance to the popular clamor that we make baptism a savior, or passport to heaven.

Not long before receiving the letter from Lunenburg, he wrote, "There is not a society on earth more truly catholic and evangelical than the churches of the current reformation." He emphasized that he was building on "catholic and apostolic principles...for union in all things essential; forbearance in all matters of opinion; and Christian love in every thing, whether faith or opinion...*we have not a known article in our faith that is not broad as Christendom* [Campbell's italics]." Then he asked his brother-in-law to write a series of ten essays supporting his position. The issue raged on for three years, becoming more and more intense until Campbell simply stopped publishing letters and responses. The episode exposed an ideological rupture within the Movement, with the more inclusive Disciples recognizing other Christians as equal, while the more exclusive conservative minority insisted they had restored the *only* true church and the requirement of *immersion was essential.*[60]

The second episode occurred twenty years later, March 1857, when Robert Richardson, long-time personal friend of Alexander Campbell, professor at Bethany College, and associate editor of *The Millennial Harbinger,* began a series of articles entitled "Faith *versus* Philosophy." Believing that philosophy should not be substituted for Christian faith, he argued that no intellectual system should be allowed to take the place of an inner quality of life, that spiritual life cannot be reduced to a process of reasoning. In a private letter that same year, Richardson, sounding like an advocate of the counter-Enlightenment, had expressed his disagreement with Alexander Campbell on this same issue:

> The philosophy of Locke with which Bro. Campbell's mind was deeply imbued in youth has insidiously mingled itself with almost all the great points in the reformation and has been all the while like an iceberg in the way–chilling the heart and benumbing the hands and impeding all progress in the right direction.

Richardson, seeking to liberate the Movement from literalism and fearing strict legalism and rationalist extremism would lead to the Disciples future destruction, used as an example Tolbert Fanning, editor of *The Gospel Advocate* in Nashville, who he described as "destitute of poetry and barren of imagination." He criticized Fanning and those who used the Bible as a scientific handbook because, in his view, they failed to understand that the "Divine word addresses itself to our higher spiritual nature." Richardson further charged that using the Bible like a legalistic instruction manual does not honor the Bible; it honors a philosophical perspective (Lockean) *imposed upon* the Bible. Tolbert Fanning, a confirmed Lockean who was convinced the Movement's paramount purpose was replicating the primitive church, was enraged and believed Campbell (who had written much the same thing as Richardson in *Christian System*) had departed from the principles of the Movement in favor of denominationalism. Fanning launched a hostile counterattack on Richardson, denouncing him, and by implication Campbell, as having "abandoned the simplicity of truth for…idle fancies." Richardson, however, charged that Fanning was the one who had abandoned the principles of the Campbell Movement for sectarianism:

> It is when a system of philosophy is made the basis of religious thought; when the Scriptures must be interpreted so as to agree with it, and when the dogmas thus deduced are imposed upon men as the orthodox Christian faith, that it becomes…sectarianism.

He further claimed that Fanning and his conservative adherents made "the Bible either a rubric which prescribes forms and ordinances or a species of mere logical machinery," thereby distorting and perverting Campbell's intent beyond all recognition. The exchange between the two inflamed the sectarian publications in the Movement and inundated Campbell with correspondence. Fanning was so unnerved by the attack he traveled to Bethany to speak with Campbell who, in his attempt to reconcile the two and calm the Movement, closed the columns of *The Millennial Harbinger* to further discussion of the matter, and reprimanded Richardson, who, after nearly three decades in Campbell's employ, resigned from the *Harbinger* and from Bethany College. But Campbell soon changed his mind; issued a full and public apology to Richardson in the May 1858 *Harbinger,* and subsequently confided to a friend that Elder Fanning was "intent on a war with us." The Richardson/Fanning debate centered on the difference between a literalistic and practical religion. Fanning, the most commanding figure among Southern Disciples, reflected their mind-set, and spoke to and for that constituency when he insisted that the legalistic search for the ancient order was the heart of the Movement. The controversy sparked similar debates throughout the Brotherhood on such issues as open communion, the meaning of baptism, the title "Reverend," the "one man system," and the education of ministers. Richard Hughes concluded the Richardson/Fanning debate was "nothing less than a prelude to outright division."[61]

The Movement was repeatedly shaken by questions of theology and doctrine: "Is the church primarily an *inclusive* or an *exclusive* community?" "Is the church imprisoned by scriptural *silence,* or can it be receptive to the Holy Spirit and exercise its enlightened judgment?" "Can the church respond to changing circumstances without sacrificing its principles of Reform?" Controversy continually swirled around these questions from the 1830s to the official partition in 1906 and beyond, questions that predated and followed the Civil War. Although sectional, social, cultural, and political issues coupled with a weaker second-generation leadership contributed heavily to the rupture within the Movement, the principle ground for their divisive debates was consistently theological, the Movement's problem of first magnitude that was continuously hardened and sharpened by sectional, cultural, and political divergence.

Conclusion

Divergent paths were evident as early as the 1830s. By 1880 two distinct groups within the Movement had taken shape. All the incidents and issues described above gave definition to the schism. *The American Christian Review* declared in 1883, "The dissolution of our people seems inevitable." During the 1880s, Daniel Sommer succeeded Benjamin Franklin as editor of *American Christian Review.* It was Sommer who began to refer to the conservative wing as "The Church of Christ." In the late eighties he decided to throw down the gauntlet by organizing a public confrontation. At least 6,000 conservatives traveled to Sand Creek, Illinois, August 18, 1889, where

Sommer shared his "Address and Declaration" with the gathering on the evils of Disciples: choirs, societies, preacher-pastors, and "other objectionable and unauthorized things." He closed the address with the statement, "We cannot and will not regard them as brethren!" For the first time, matters of opinion were made a test of fellowship. While some considered the "Address and Declaration" an affront to the spirit of Thomas Campbell, Sommer plunged ahead, confident that a new church was being born:

> The Sand Creek Declaration is being adopted, and those who will not do right are purged out as old leaven. In course of a few years the Church of Christ will be entirely separated...there will be no more fellowship with [Disciples]....Hallelujah.[62]

By 1897, David Lipscomb, long a holdout against division, had become an exclusivist. In August he criticized Disciples for including in their Year Book "hundreds of churches and thousands of preachers and communicants that do not belong to [the Disciples Movement] at all or have any more interest in it or sympathy for it than any other denomination." Disciples' scholar Arthur Murrell concluded that the division of Disciples should be dated, August 1897. The Church of Christ had two fathers, Daniel Sommer in the North and David Lipscomb in the South. Lipscomb gave leadership to the larger membership within the conservative constituency and Sommer's effort could not have succeeded without Lipscomb's eventual support. One year later, 1898, J. H. Garrison closed the columns of *The Christian-Evangelist* to debate with *The Gospel Advocate.* There was no official organization within the Movement with the power to announce a separation. But in 1906 Lipscomb received a letter from S. N. D. North, director of the U.S. Census Bureau, asking if the Churches of Christ should be listed separately. And Lipscomb responded:

> There is a distinct people taking the Word of God as their only rule of faith, calling their churches "churches of Christ"...distinct and separate in name, work and rule of faith from all other bodies or people.[63]

Coexistence was at an end. The partition, developing for several decades, was official.

Founding Fathers

Thomas Campbell
1763–1854

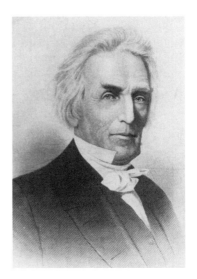

Alexander Campbell
1788–1866

Barton Warren Stone
1772–1844

Walter Scott
1796–1861

James O'Kelly and Elias Smith

Monument placed to honor James O'Kelly (1735–1826) and his Christian Churches at the site of his Old Lebanon Church in Surry County, Virginia.

James O'Kelly founded a community of faith named the Christian Church in 1794. With the help of Rice Haggard he developed six principles to guide the new church, five of which appear on the back side of the monument pictured above. The sixth principle stated: "The union of all Christians to the end that the world may believe."

Elias Smith (1769–1846), early founder of Christian Churches, a common fellowship of cooperation with the O'Kelly churches. He is considered the father of religious journalism in America.

Barton Stone and Cane Ridge

Cane Ridge Sacramental Occasion, August 6–12, 1801, often called the great Cane Ridge Revival.

Old Presbyterian Cane Ridge meeting house near Paris, Kentucky; Barton Stone was ordained here October 4, 1798, and served as pastor until 1804. It is the site of the Cane Ridge Sacramental Occasion.

Portrait of Barton Stone as a young minister at Cane Ridge.

The Last Will and Testament of the Springfield Presbytery, June, 1804. Pictured above is an 1808 reprint.

Thomas Campbell's Ahorey Church and Home at Rich Hill, Ireland

The Ahorey Church near Rich Hill, Ireland, where Thomas Campbell served as minister, 1798–1807.

The Ahorey Church in 2007.

The commemorative plaque placed in the church tower constructed in the twentieth century to honor the service of Thomas Campbell.

The home of Thomas Campbell and his family in Rich Hill when Alexander was a small boy. The home also served as a school where Thomas, and later Alexander, both taught.

Interior of the church at Ahorey.

University of Glasgow

Attended by Thomas (1783–1786) and Alexander (1808–1809) Campbell

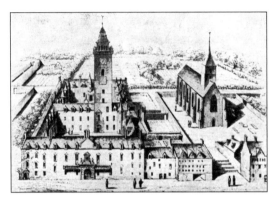

Early rendering of the University of Glasgow, similar to its appearance when Thomas and Alexander studied there.

Many times Alexander Campbell climbed the famed lion and unicorn staircase on the outer quadrangle of Glasgow University.

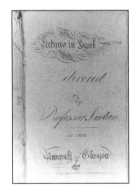

Alexander Campbell's personal notebook containing his notes from the lectures in logic heard in the class of George Jardine.

The ticket used by Alexander Campbell for admission to George Jardine's class on logic.

University of Glasgow Faculty
Thomas and Alexander studied with some of the same faculty.

John Young (1774–1820), Professor of Greek.

Andrew Ure (1778–1857), Professor of Natural History.

George Jardine (1774–1827), Professor of Logic and Moral Philosophy; he was Alexander Campbell's favorite professor.

Greville Ewing (1767–1841), one of Glasgow's most distinguished ministers and close friend of Alexander Campbell during Campbell's attendance at the university.

Thomas Reid (1710–1796), author of "Principles of Common Sense," 1764; Thomas Campbell was a student in his classes.

Hibernia Shipwreck

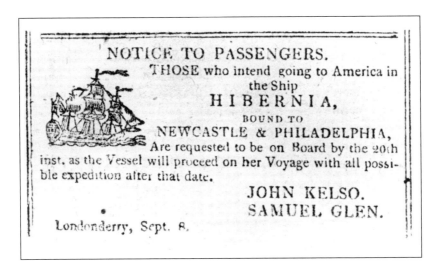

Notice of the Hibernia's departure in the *Belfast News Letter,* Sept. 9, 1808.

Notice of the Hibernia shipwreck in the *Belfast News Letter*, Oct. 21, 1808.

The *Declaration and Address*

On August 17, 1809, the Christian Association of Washington was formed. During the two weeks immediately following, Thomas Campbell drafted the *Declaration and Address.* A photo of an original copy appears here. It is preserved in the Campbell Archives at Bethany College.

The printing press on which the *Declaration and Address* was printed (above) is presently exhibited in a newspaper office in Washington, Pennsylvania.

Brush Run Church

Brush Run Church was formed May 4, 1811. The first service, June 16, 1811, was held in the building sketched above, constructed on the Gilcrist farm near the junction of Brush Run and Buffaloe creeks. Alexander Campbell was ordained in this building January 1, 1812, with Thomas Campbell officiating. Worship services were held here until 1828.

Selina Bakewell near the time of her marriage to Alexander Campbell.

Brush Run church as reconstructed from the original lumber in the early twentieth century near the Campbell home in Bethany.

Alexander Campbell at age 30. Earliest known portrait of Campbell.

The *Christian Baptist*

The sixteen-foot shed in which the *Christian Baptist* was printed. It was built in 1823 on the banks of Buffaloe Creek a short distance from the Campbell home.

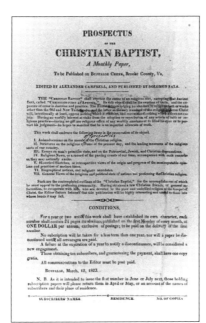

Prospectus for the *Christian Baptist*.

The Millennial Harbinger

The print shop constructed in the early 1830s by Alexander
Campbell to house his new magazine, *The Millennial Harbinger.*

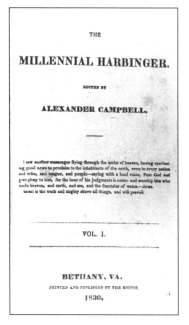

The first page of *The Millennial
Harbinger* as it appeared in 1830,
Vol. I.

Early Writings of Alexander Campbell

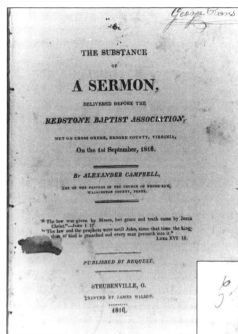

Alexander Campbell's famous Sermon on the Law, 1816.

Alexander Campbell's translation of the New Testament, 1826.

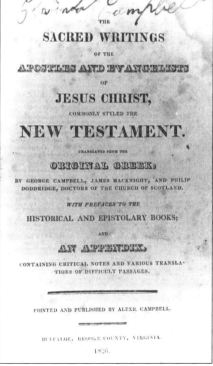

Alexander Campbell in 1829

Artist's sketch of Alexander Campbell's debate with Robert Owen on April 13, 1829, in Cincinnati.

Alexander Campbell was elected a delegate to the Virginia Constitutional Convention, October 5, 1829 to February 1, 1830. He is seated seventh from the right on the back row. James Madison is standing. Seated immediately in back of him is John Marshall. James Monroe is in the speaker's chair on the left of the picture.

Home of Alexander Campbell

Photo of the Campbell home in the early 1860s. The family, including Alexander Campbell, is standing on the front lawn.

Photo of the Campbell home following its total refurbishment in 1990.

The Campbell Study.

Selina and Alexander Campbell in their later years.

Alexander Campbell in his study, 1858.

19th Century Leadership

Robert
Richardson
(1806–1876)

John Rogers
(1800–1867)

"Raccoon" John
Smith (1784–1868)

John T. Johnson
(1788–1856)

Phillip S. Fall
(1798–1890)

Charles L. Loos
(1823–1912)

Robert Milligan
(1814–1875)

Lewis L.
Pinkerton
(1812–1875)

President James A. Garfield
(1831–1881)

John W.
McGarvey
(1829–1911)

Robert Moffatt
(1836–1908)

William K.
Pendleton
(1817–1899)

Ely Von Zollars
(1849–1916)

Selected Disciples Editors
19th & 20th Centuries

Issac Errett
Christian Evangelist

James H.
Garrison
Christian Standard

Marcia Melissa
Goodwin
*The Christian
Monitor*

Benjamin
Franklin
*American Christian
Review*

David Lipscomb
Gospel Advocate

Tolbert Fanning
Gospel Advocate

Moses Lard
Lard's Quarterly

George Walker
Buckner
World Call

Charles Clayton
Morrison
Christian Century

James Merrill
The Disciple

Robert Friedly
The Disciple

Verity Jones
DisciplesWorld

Disciples Women: 19th Century

Emily Tubman (1794–1885), generous Disciples philanthropist who supported many causes including colleges and Negro evangelism.

Selina Bakewell Campbell (1802–1897), solicitor of funds for missions and Disciples women's work, author, wife of Alexander Campbell.

Caroline Neville Pearre (1831–1910), founder of the Christian Woman's Board of Missions, 1874.

Anna Atwater (1859–1941), President of CWBM 1908–1920, and the first Vice President of the United Christian Missionary Society in 1920.

Martha "Mattie" Yonkin (d. 1908), a founder of the National Benevolent Association in 1887.

Ladonia "Doni" Hansbrough, a founder of NBA, which she served for more than fifty years as corresponding secretary.

Disciples Women: 20th Century

Jesse Trout (1895–1990), Co-founder of the World CWF and its first Executive Secretary 1955–1961.

Mae Yoho Ward (1900–1983), missionary, mission executive, advocate of social justice, beloved colleague.

Fran Craddock, Vice President of ICWF 1974–1978, Executive Secretary at Department of Church Women, 1975–1987.

Jean Woolfolk, first woman Moderator 1973–1975, first woman General Unit President (Church Finance Council).

Joy Greer, Moderator 1981–1983

Marilyn Moffatt, Moderator 1991–1993

Recent Quadrennial gathering of Disciples Women

Charise Gillette, Moderator 2003–2005

Missions Building, built by CWBM

Foreign Christian Missionary Society

Archibald McLean (1849–1920),
President of the Foreign Christian
Missionary Society.

Dr. Albert L. Shelton

Dr. Albert Shelton treating a Tibetan boy.

Batang hospital in Tibet established by Albert Shelton.

Foreign Christian Missionary Society

Bolenge station in the Congo.

Dr. Royal J. Dye
(1874–1966)

Bolenge Day School
and church building.

Bolenge medical clinic established by Royal J. Dye.

Disciples Centennial 1909

Centennial gathering of an estimated 50,000 Disciples in Pittsburgh at Forbes Field in 1909.

Disciples' Polar Star

Three Disciples veteran advocates of Christian Unity in the twentieth century who became international symbols of the Age of Ecumenism.

Peter Ainslie III
(1867–1935)

Paul A. Crow Jr.
(b.1931)

Michael Kinnamon
(b. 1949)

African American Disciples: 19th Century

Jacob Kenoly
(1876–1911),
Missionary to Liberia

Sarah Lue Bostick
(1868–1948), founder
and president of the
Negro Christian
Woman's Board of
Missions.

Preston Taylor
(1849–1931), minister,
writer, businessman,
founder, and president
of the National Christian
Missionary Convention.

Founding of the National Christian Missionary
Convention, Nashville Tennessee, 1917.

Samuel Buckner
(1820–1904) organized
the "Mother Church," the
first First Christian Church
among African Americans in
Bourbon Co., Ky., 1861.

Southern Christian Institute, founded in 1875. It
nurtured several generations of African American
leadership for the Disciples.

African American Disciples: 20th Century

Carnella Barnes,
first African
American
President of
ICWF, 1974-78.

Syble Thomas,
President of the
World Christian
Woman's Fellowship,
1988-1992.

Brenda Etheridge,
President
of ICWF,
2002–2006.

Jackie Bunch,
President ICWF
1994–1998.

Walter Bingham, first
African American
Moderator of the
General Assembly,
1971–1973.

John Compton, first
African American
Regional Minister
(Indiana), First African
American General Unit
President (DHM).

King David Cole,
Moderator General
Assembly, 1989–1991.

Emmett Dickson,
beloved leader of African
American Disciples.

William K. Fox, first African
American Deputy General
Minister & President.

Cynthia Hale, Pastor
of 5,000-member Ray
of Hope Congregation,
past President of
National Convocation,
Vice Moderator of
General Assembly.

Disciples Hispanic Expression of Church

Four preeminent leaders of the Latino expression of the Disciples:
David Vargas, Lucas Torres, Domingo Rodriguez Figueroa, Luis Fererrer.

Daisy Machada,
professor, Dean,
scholar in Latino
Disciples history.

Obra Hispana.

Asian American Disciples

David Kagiwada (1929–1985), a founder of the Fellowship of Asian American Disciples, 1978 (now NAPAD); first moderator of FAAD.

John Soongook Choi (1933–2002), founder and first Moderator of Korean Disciples Convocation; a founder of FAAD (now NAPAD), 1978.

Geunhee Yu, Executive Pastor for North American Asian Ministries since 1992.

Lian Jian, Director of Chinese Disciples Ministries.

April Lewton, Moderator of North American and Pacific Asian Disciples (NAPAD), 2004.

Tim Lee, Moderator of Korean Disciples, Moderator of NAPAD, scholar in Asian Disciples history.

Kim Tran, Director of Vietnamese Disciples Ministry.

Itoko Maeda, first Japanese missionary assigned by UCMS.

NAPAD convocation 1996; GMP Richard Hamm presiding at the table.

Restructure

Drafting the "Provisional Design." W. A. Welsh chairing the session, with Kenneth L. Teegarden, Administrative Secretary, and committee member Virgil Sly. Rough draft of structure on the chalkboard behind chairman Welsh.

Williard Wickiser
(1900–1974)
Father of Restructure.

A. Dale Fiers
(1906–2003),
Soul of Restructure.

Kenneth L. Teegarden
(1921–2002),
Architect of Restructure.

Kansas City
General Assembly,
1968, voting
approval of the
"Provisional
Design."

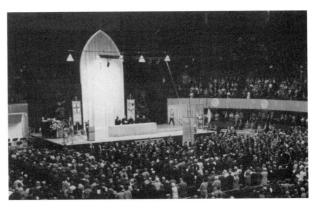

Restructure

Dale Fiers, First General Minister and President, 1968–1973, (center) and his staff: Gertrude Dimke, Kenneth Teegarden, James Suggs, Robert Friedly, and Howard Dentler.

Granville Walker (1908–1991), Chair, Commission on Restructure.

Kenneth Teegarden, second General Minister and President, 1973–1985, (center) and his two deputies, Howard Dentler and William Howland.

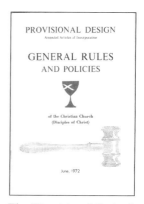

The "Provisional Design"

Early 20th-Century Leaders of Disciples Thought

Herbert Willett
(1864–1944),
author, dean,
professor.

Edward
Scribner Ames
(1870–1958),
author, dean,
professor.

Winfred E.
Garrison
(1874–1969),
dean of Disciples
historians.

Cynthia Pearl Maus
(1880–1970), author
of
*Christ and the
Fine Arts.*

Stephen J.
England,
(1895–1987)
author, dean,
professor.

Ralph Wilburn
(1909–1986),
author, dean,
professor.

William B.
Blakemore
(1912–1975),
author, dean,
professor.

Ronald Osborn
(1917–1998),
author, dean,
professor.

Leaders of the International Convention

Graham Frank (1873–1954),
General Secretary 1913–1946.

Gaines M. Cook (1897–1983),
Executive Secretary 1947–1964.

Post-Restructure Years

John O. Humbert,
GMP 1985–1991.

John Humbert receiving on behalf of the Disciples a gift of $8 million from the estate of Ethel Fiers Brown, sister of Dale Fiers. At the time it was the largest bequest ever received by a Protestant church body.

Richard Hamm,
GMP 1993–2003.

Richard Hamm's first General Assembly, Pittsburgh, 1995.

154

Post-Restructure Years

The closing of the Missions Building, January 1995.

The new Disciples Center in Indianapolis, 1995.

The Portland General Assembly, 2005, and the election of Sharon Watkins as GMP.

Sharon Watkins, General Minister and President, 2005–present.

CHAPTER V

Cooperation through Mission, Christian Unity, and Cultural Expressions

Cooperation through Mission

It is the glory...of the first convention ever assembled of our brethren, that then and there they unanimously resolved in the name of the Lord to...organize and put in operation a society for spreading salvation and civilization over all lands, as far as the Lord will give them the means and the opportunity... Of all the other projects of the age, this is the chief. All other benevolent associations are subordinate to this.

ALEXANDER CAMPBELL
ACMS presidential address

Archibald McLean (1849–1920), descended from Scottish highlanders in the rugged Herbides and born on Prince Edward Island in the same year the Disciples birthed the American Christian Missionary Society, is the man most remembered for developing the Reform Movement's cooperative missionary enterprise. W. E. Garrison called McLean one of the greatest missionary statesmen of all time. McLean, who rejected strict restoration with its refusal to cooperate with other Protestants in mission work, became a moderate convinced that cooperative missions fostered fellowship. Prophetically, he viewed the mission field not only as a place for humanitarian work and carrying out the great commission, but as a place for productive connections with other Christians, a place for the powerful promotion of Christian unity. In McLean's view, missions and unity were inseparable. From around the world he heard the missionaries call for "union," call for the removal of sectarian competition, call for "cooperation" among the churches on the mission field. He served as one of twelve American representatives to the 1920 International Foreign Missionary Conference in Geneva, Switzerland. Placing the principle of unity in the context of foreign missions is seen as one of his greatest contributions to the Disciples Movement. He proved that a Society, even one regularly criticized by ardent restorationists, could be efficient and successful. Because of his success, agencies gained wider acceptance and affirmation within the Movement.[1]

The American Christian Missionary Society began its history with a biblical underpinning from Alexander Campbell, who from the first issue of *Christian Baptist* insisted the church was a "missionary institution." He wrote again in 1854: "We shall, therefore, regard it as a fixed fact, that the Church of Jesus Christ is in her nature, spirit and position, necessarily and essentially a missionary institution." It began too, with the often quoted poetic words of Walter Scott, "Leave your footprints in the snow of the frozen North... Trace your pathways into the flowery pampas... Tread over the golden sands... Go to those who water their steeds in the Rhine; to those who drink from the Seine, or who bathe in the Nile, the Niger, the sacred Ganges [and] the Indus." The support of words, however, did not generate matching support from either a theology of mission or dollars necessary to keep missionaries in the field. Mary R. Williams, described by Alexander Campbell as a "Christian lady of large mind and still larger heart," was the first missionary appointed by the ACMS, sent in 1850 to Palestine. Her support came through individual contributions solicited by Selina Campbell from Disciples women. Dr. James T. Barclay (1807–1874) was assigned to Jerusalem in 1851; Alexander Cross (1811–1854) to Liberia in 1854; and Julius O. Beardslee (1814–1879) to Jamaica in 1858. With the exception of the untimely death of Alexander Cross, the other assignments failed due to lack of financial support from local congregations and the ACMS. By 1870 the Disciples did not have a single missionary in the field.[2]

To address the financial problem, Disciples leadership advanced a new approach. The Louisville Plan of 1868 was an attempt to structure the church with delegate representation from the congregations to thirty-six districts; districts in turn would send delegates to eleven state societies and the states would elect delegates to a General National convention. Special agents were assigned to raise missionary offerings from the congregations. These dollars were to be sent to the district; the district would keep one-half for local evangelists and send one-half to the state society; the state society would keep one-half and forward the remaining one-half to the ACMS or the General Christian Missionary Society. Theoretically, one-fourth of the offerings would go to each of the four entities: congregation, district, state, and general. But the money rarely got out of the district and almost nothing reached the ACMS. This circumstance was compounded by the fact that many simply ignored the plan because of their objection to the idea of organizations beyond the congregation. By 1874, the silver anniversary of the ACMS, missionary offerings had reached a new low, producing a crisis. "In all the wide foreign field," wrote McLean, "we do not have a single herald of the cross. Jerusalem and Jamaica [are] deserted; Liberia [is] forgotten."[3]

In response to the crisis, Caroline Neville Pearre (1831–1910) led a group of seventy-five women from nine states in establishing the Christian Woman's Board of Missions. The constitution (formatted largely on the model of the Congregational Woman's Missionary Society) was adopted October 22, 1874, at the General Convention in Cincinnati. The Board took an offering of $430 at its first meeting; had receipts of $5,050 in 1880; and by 1900 offerings and individual gifts totaled $106,722. Their first CWBM missionary, William H. Williams (1842–1928) was assigned to Jamaica, arriving in 1876. CWBM soon sent missionaries to France (Annie Crease, 1880) and four young women to India (1882); and in 1883 began publishing their own magazine, *Missionary Tidings*. Lorraine Lollis wrote in *The Shape of Adam's Rib*:

> Our women were more original than they realized at the time. They became the first woman's board to do both home and foreign work, to employ both men and women, to manage their own business, to choose their fields of service, to own property, and to raise and administer their own funds.

Leadership in the Reformation Movement itself was overwhelmingly male and white. Women, youth, and post–Civil War African Americans were essentially excluded from participation in the Disciples body politic and therefore sought expression in parallel structures. This is a significant factor in the creation of the Christian Woman's Board of Missions. The Movement was known throughout the membership as "The Brotherhood," an irony accenting the locus of mission with the "sisters." This dynamic persisted through the twentieth century among women in the Christian Women's Fellowships, who often thought of themselves as a "church" apart. Within the latter day Disciples Home Missions structures, women's work is still sometimes perceived more as a cultural expression component than other program units.[4]

The CWBM pioneered the Bible chair movement in 1894 at the University of Michigan, consulted with other religious bodies, became one of the first Disciples organizations to use the term "ecumenical," established an orphanage in Puerto Rico in 1900, and founded the College of Missions in Indianapolis in 1909–offering graduate programs in missionary education including medicine, colonial government, and international law. By 1919 enrollment in the College of Missions reached forty-seven, and by 1921 it increased to fifty-five. In 1927 the teaching operation was transferred to Kennedy School of Missions at Hartford Seminary Foundation. The CWBM continued to send missionaries, including three appointments in 1905: Jacob Kenoly (1876–1911) to Liberia, Dr. Samuel Guy Inman (1877–1965) to Mexico, and Willis J. Burner (1870–1957) to Argentina. The Board cooperated as well with the ACMS in the establishment of home missions, including the Hazel Green Academy in 1886, the Chinese Christian Institute in 1891, and the Mexican Christian Institute in San Antonio in 1913. Helen E. Moses (1853–1908) became president of the CWBM in 1900, holding the position until her death. The International Christian Women's Fellowship (ICWF), a descendant of the CWBM, was organized in 1953. This network of Christian Women Fellowships then produced the Quadrennial Assemblies beginning in 1957, becoming the place in the general church where there is continuation of the CWBM tradition and theological contributions of stewardship, service, worship, prayer, and mission education.

The Foreign Christian Missionary Society, conceived at the same General Convention as the CWBM, organized one year later at the 1875 General Convention in Louisville, an action of the whole convention, not simply a men's movement. At the moment of its creation, according to Archibald McLean: "There was a sense of the Divine presence, a conviction that what was being done was in harmony with the purpose of God in the ages." Isaac Errett (1820–1888) was elected president. The FCMS immediately began to deploy missionaries to Christian lands rather than to so-called non-Christian lands, mostly because no one wanted to serve in non-Christian lands. Among those sent were Henry S. Earl (1832–1919) to England in 1875, Dr. A. O. Holck (1844–1907) to Denmark in 1876, Jules Delaunay to France in 1878, and George N. Shishmanian (1837–1922) to Turkey in 1879. During these early years the secretary of the FCMS operated out of a Cincinnati storeroom belonging to Standard Publishing Company. Staff used boxes as chairs and their knees for desks. The FCMS sent two missionaries to India in 1882, assigned two to Japan in 1883, one to China in 1886, and one to the Philippines in 1897. Following the death of Isaac Errett in 1888, Charles Louis Loos (1823–1912) became president of the FCMS, serving until 1900 when Archibald McLean, who had been secretary of the Society since 1882, accepted the presidency and served until the 1919 consolidation into the United Society. The *Missionary Intelligencer,* with its large circulation, served as the monthly of the FCMS.

Two of the Disciples most famous missionaries were appointed by the FCMS near the turn of the century. Dr. Royal J. Dye (1874–1966) received assignment to the Bolenge station, Belgian Congo, in 1899, where he established a medical clinic and found himself in a persistent rivalry with the Bantu witch doctor, Bosekola. With her book, *Bolenge,* published in 1909, Eva Dye made the little missionary outpost of Bolenge the most widely known mission station in the minds of lay Disciples. It was located in a commanding position in the great Congo basin, squarely on the equator, near the mouth of the Bosira River as it feeds into the Congo. The land surrounding it was a flat marsh for hundreds of miles, causing the language of the native Bantu tribes to lose the words for hills and mountains. In 1903 Dr. Albert L. Shelton (1875–1922) went to Tibet. Shelton helped develop the Batang medical clinic. He was described by Peter Morgan as the twentieth century's David Livingston, by Douglas Wissing as one who possessed an "adventurers heart and a missionary's soul," and by another as a "prototype for a more pious version of Indiana Jones." He spent twenty years as a medical missionary in the Tibetan borderlands, becoming known as a revered doctor, respected diplomat, fearless adventurer (constantly exploring and collecting art treasurers), and one of the West's first interpreters of Tibetan culture. Driven by the goal of establishing a medical mission in Lhasa, the seat of the Dalai Lama, Shelton ultimately received an invitation to Lhasa. While finalizing his entry to Lhasa in 1922, Shelton was murdered near the notorious 9,500-foot-high Khuyuk La pass by a band of brigands from the Seven Tribes of the Sangen. His wife Flora preserved the story of his ministry in *Shelton of Tibet*, published the following year. By 1900 the FCMS was supporting 111 missionaries in nine countries. There were 6,000 converts in 79 churches in 113 stations. Medical missionaries were treating an average of 40,000 patients annually in four fields.[5]

Meanwhile, the ACMS, often called the Disciples "mother of cooperating organizations," reconstituted itself as an agency for homeland missions. Robert Moffett (1836–1908) helped establish the Church Extension Fund as part of the ACMS in 1883. Within five years 1,628 congregations without buildings had been identified and in order to address the demand, the Fund became the Board of Church Extension in 1889. It located in Kansas City, near the region where many of the new congregations were waiting to be constructed. Initially loans were generally $250 at an interest rate of 6 percent, but in 1892 the loan level was raised to $1,000. The Board began offering architectural services in 1897. But the most famous event associated with the Board's early history was the 1893 horseback ride by Guthrie pastor E. F. Boggess (1869–1931) during the Cherokee Strip land run in Oklahoma, staking out land claims for churches in the county seats and railroad towns across the newly opened territory. By 1900 the Board had financed the construction of 600 congregations in twenty-eight states at a total cost of $305,000. The assets of the Board, approximately $5,000 at its 1883 founding, had grown beyond $172 million by the year 2007.[6]

In 1887, Matilda "Mattie" Younkin (d. 1908), Landonia Hansbrough, Sophia Kerns, and Elizabeth Hodgen (first president)–along with several other women–helped charter the Benevolent Association of the Christian Church, better known to twentieth-century Disciples as the National Benevolent

Association. The General Convention, however, did not recognize it until 1899. According to the memoirs of the corresponding secretary, Landonia Hansbrough: "It was in the spring of 1886 that we first began talking of this great venture of faith–the venture of helping the helpless."

Beginning in 1894 its work was publicized through their periodical, *Orphan's Cry*. The Easter offering was designated to support its work. In 1889 the first NBA site appeared in St. Louis. Soon there were facilities in Denver, Jacksonville, Cleveland, Dallas, and Atlanta–formed, like the early colleges, by generous Disciples individuals rather than through a church-wide plan. NBA experienced enormous growth through the succeeding decades. By 2003, NBA was serving persons in more than ninety facilities.[7]

A Ministerial Relief Fund took form in the early 1890s. The General Convention meeting in Dallas, 1895, built on that small beginning by creating the Board of Ministerial Relief in Indianapolis, with Howard Cole as President. The new board, legally incorporated in 1897, received the Christmas offering designated to support its work. By 1901 the Board assisted fifty-eight retired ministers with receipts of approximately $9,700. In 1928 the Board renamed its ministry The Pension Fund of the Disciples of Christ; and again in 1972 its name was revised to The Pension Fund of the Christian Church (Disciples of Christ). By 2007 the Pension Fund claimed assets in excess of $2.6 billion, with 5,674 persons receiving pension benefits and an additional 7,265 participating members who were preparing for retirement.[8]

The Christian Board of Publication was chartered in April 1911. R. A. Long had purchased the Christian Publishing Company from J. H. Garrison in December 1909, bringing *The Christian-Evangelist* into the "brotherhood publishing house." For the first time Disciples had a publishing house and a national journal that belonged to Disciples rather than to a private publisher. Long was named president of the self-perpetuating board and J. H. Garrison remained as editor of *The Christian-Evangelist*. CBP, as it was called, began producing curriculum materials for the congregations in 1920 and was the major source of book publishing for Disciples throughout the twentieth century. The book-publishing arm of the house would become known as Bethany Press and ultimately as Chalice Press, yet most would continue to call it CBP.

Thus the tradition of organizations carrying out ministry beyond the local congregations is a long one. As early as 1875 a resolution approved by the General Convention urged:

> We most cordially invite these organizations (FCMS & CWBM) to a close alliance with the ACMS in every practical way; and still we look forward hopefully to the time when such a cooperation of our churches shall be secured as may enable us to resolve these organizations into one.

With the passage of time the total of "special day" offerings grew to fifteen. Some said that no agency felt respectable unless it had a "special day" in the calendar set aside for a financial appeal to support its cause. The growing demand to reduce the number of special day offerings paired with the rising call for simplifying the network of boards and societies resulted in the appointment of a Calendar Committee during the Buffalo convention in 1906. This committee followed a succession of appointed committees on coordination, one having proposed unification as early as 1893, but it was regarded as premature. The new committee proposed that all boards and societies unite in one organization with one board, but its report was postponed for several years. In the interim, a planning process for the 1909 centennial celebration in Pittsburgh coupled with the success of the 1913 Men and Millions movement convinced many rank and file members, along with Movement leadership, that Disciples were capable of successful cooperation. A Committee on Unification was appointed at the 1917 International Convention in Kansas City, and two years later, at the Cincinnati Convention, it submitted its recommendation for a cooperative venture named the United Christian Missionary Society. The success achieved from congregational cooperation through these boards and societies changed the "the self-identity of the 'brotherhood' to a group of congregations engaged in joint ministry." These centers of ministry, state and general, increasingly worked in collaborative fashion, which prepared the way for the 1920 merger of the ACMS, the CWBM, and the FCMS into a single structure–the United Christian Missionary Society. Reporting on the important structural creation of the UCMS, the 1928 *Survey of Service* noted:

> Awkwardly and with many embarrassments, as is inevitable in a democracy, and especially a religious democracy that breaks into a panic at the mere mention of ecclesiasticism, the brotherhood began to take the business of the brotherhood into its own hands.[9]

The new structure brought together the ACMS, the CWBM, the FCMS, the Board of Church Extension, the National Benevolent Association and the Board of Ministerial Relief into a single organization under the guardianship of a twenty-two-member board of trustees. Because the CWBM held more assets than any other board and because it feared merger would remove women from leadership, the composition of the new board was negotiated to be 50 percent female and 50 percent male. Frederick Burnham, president of the ACMS, was named president, Archibald McLean and Anna R. Atwater (1859–1941), presidents of the FCMS and CWBM respectively, were named vice presidents. The UCMS legally incorporated June 20, 1920, and located in St. Louis, Missouri.

The early years of the UCMS were rife with internal controversy. The boards of Church Extension, Ministerial Relief, and National Benevolent

Association described themselves as "captive" organizations. Although the merger was well intended, these boards refused to transfer their assets to the UCMS and continued, as they had before the merger, to agitate for separation. Control of staff, budget building, distribution of gift income, geographic location of their operations, leadership clashes, and misunderstandings, all of these issues contributed to constant bickering within the UCMS. By the early 1930s it was decided separate boards might administer their functions more efficiently. All three organizations independently incorporated and established control of their own financial assets, their own staff, and their own boards (Pension Fund 1928, NBA 1933, and BCE 1934). This internal structural differentiation within the UCMS would become a major characteristic of twentieth-century organizational development in American Protestant denominations. The increasing number of specialized agencies governed by secular considerations coupled with the growth in managerial personnel reflected this trend. Most said it enhanced efficiency; others claimed it disenfranchised local congregations by creating a social distance between congregations and the agencies, breeding conflict over the question of authority. Disciples would eventually address this bedeviling issue through restructure.[10]

As noted in the opening quote by Alexander Campbell, "Christianizing" and "civilizing" were initially placed on equal footing, a traditional missionary concept. The arrogance of the concept, the tendency to judge primitive societies in terms of modern values, and the dismissing of remote civilizations as inferior contributed to the negative reaction toward these missionaries when they arrived in another culture and tried to foist upon it a Judaeo-Christian outlook that recognized no values besides its own. Gradually, however, Disciples put aside their notion of cultural superiority and began to rethink their ministry as one of social justice, world order, and cultural partnership.

Stephen J. Corey (1873–1962), president of the UCMS, attended the 1928 International Missionary Council in Jerusalem. After the conference he recorded these prophetic words in his personal diary: "Indigenous, self-governing, self-operating, self-supportive–the burning topic in Jerusalem; shift from paternalism to partnership." Corey's unpolished private notation contained the future course of world mission, a direction that would not come to full fruition until after his time as president. Soon the watchwords were service (*diakonia*) and fellowship (*koinonia*), the building of human community through a relational approach rather than an evangelical approach. Through the efforts of Virgil A. Sly (1901–1978) and Harry B. McCormick (1884–1974), "The Strategy for World Missions" was produced in 1950 and published five years later. While still not a full theological basis for mission, it guided mission work toward a Christian witness of the mission of God, rather than maintaining a simplistic exportation of Disciples missions.[11]

Despite controversies within and without, the UCMS performed a successful ministry for fifty years: providing a period of organizational experiment, providing experience with designing and modifying structural patterns, and providing both time and means to develop a cooperative mind-set, all highly significant in preparing the way for an impending restructure of the church. Between the age of "editor-bishops" and restructure, the UCMS leadership functioned as the voice of promotion and influence for Disciples. Its various missionary publications were consolidated into *World Call.* In 1947 88,000 native Disciples members were in missionary outposts served by 2,500 native workers.

The removal of NBA, BCE, and the Pension Fund necessitated an internal reorganization of the UCMS. By 1951 the Society was structured around four divisions. Virgil A. Sly, assisted by E.K. Higdon (1887–1961), Mae Yoho Ward (1900–1983), and Donald West (1912–1974), chaired the Division of Foreign Missions. It provided support for 221 missionaries, 382 Bible schools, 341 mission schools, fifteen hospitals, twenty-three dispensaries, and ninety-six missionary candidates in training. The Division of Home Missions, chaired by Willard M. Wickizer (1899–1974) with fourteen assistants including Clark Buckner, James Sugioka (1907–1978), James Crain (1886–1971), and John Frye (1895–1983), gave oversight to 135 workers in home missions, eighty home mission pastors, eleven migrant staff workers, and six home missions institutions including the Yakama (current spelling) Indian Christian Mission, All Peoples Christian Center in Los Angeles, the Mexican Institute, and the Southern Christian Institute. The Division of Christian Education, under the leadership of George Oliver Taylor (1902–1982), assisted by Parker Rossman (1919–) and Marion Ross (1896–1966), supported fifty religious education field staff and forty-two missionary education field staff. It supported 337 summer conferences, forty-two student centers, four Bible chairs, and 161 World Fellowship Youth meetings. Finally, there was the Division of General Administration under the presidency of A. Dale Fiers (1906–2003) assisted by Spencer P. Austin (1909–1984), Jessie M. Trout (1895–1990), Louise Moseley, and Francis Payne. It was responsible for resources, interpretation, men's work, treasury functions, and general administration of the entire UCMS. And by the late 1950s, under the leadership of A. Dale Fiers and Virgil Sly, the Society had further refined "The Strategy for World Mission," guided in part by Dale Fiers' declaration: "Mission churches and the institutions associated with them must be helped to move as rapidly as possible from mission direction and support–to self-direction and support." The missionary enterprise was moving inexorably from paternalism to partnership and beyond.[12]

In 1928 the whole UCMS operation moved physically from St. Louis to Indianapolis, occupying the vacated College of Missions Building. Indianapolis would remain the chief center of Disciples organized life from that time through the present. Of special importance to the generation of

Disciples in the first half of the twentieth century, the UCMS demonstrated that "cooperation" could work through an efficient structural organization for missions at home and abroad.

The Great Depression brought financial constraint but also significant new initiatives. By December 1932, the deficit of the UCMS had reached $1,126,952, forcing a reduction in field staff, the withdrawal of missionaries from various stations, and substantial reductions in salaries. The UCMS staff in Indianapolis went two months per year without pay. In 1942 the Society, through careful stewardship of limited resources, paid the last of its depression indebtedness. Every agency, state organization, and higher education institution had suffered during this period. One of the saddest moments came with the closure of Cotner College in Lincoln, Nebraska.

But new initiatives abounded. In 1930, R. A. Long, a Kansas City lumberman, through his generous contributions, helped found the National City Christian Church Corporation in Washington, D.C., for the purpose of constructing a national church on Thomas Circle. The Board of Higher Education functioned as a department within the UCMS from 1934 to 1938. The formation of the College Association of Disciples of Christ prompted the Board to separate from the UCMS in 1938. Dr. Harlie Smith (1900–1970) accepted appointment as secretary of the new Board. The Disciples Peace Fellowship, established at the San Antonio International Convention in 1935, has continued to function as the conscience for Disciples on world peace. The Home and State Missions Planning Council of the Disciples of Christ organized in 1938 to coordinate the common interests of the States and the Division of Home Missions. Williard Wickizer provided leadership for the Council, which met annually as an interagency organization. The Council published *The Church Functioning Effectively* (1946) by Orman L. Shelton and *Christian Worship: A Service Book* (1953) by G. Edwin Osborn, the combination of which contributed to a standardization of local organization and worship in hundreds of congregations. And in 1939 the Richmond International Convention appointed a committee to study the preservation of Disciples historic materials. At the St. Louis Convention in 1941, the constitution of the Disciples of Christ Historical Society received approval, with J. Edward Moseley (1910–1973) as president, and Claude E. Spencer (1898–1979) as curator, with the collection to be housed at Culver Stockton College. In 1957 the Thomas W. Phillips family of Newcastle, Pennsylvania, donated the necessary funds to build the T.W. Phillips Memorial in Nashville, Tennessee, as a permanent home for the Historical Society, and the staff moved into their new quarters the following year.[13]

One of the most significant achievements during the Depression era was the creation of Unified Promotion on July 1, 1935. Spencer Austin said the reason for its formation "was a response to pressures from congregations and local Church leadership that desired more statesmanlike, more Christian, more equitable and more effective way of financing the God-given mission of the Church–locally, regionally, nationally and globally."

In development since 1931, its approval by formal vote came at the Des Moines International Convention in 1934. This was the first time joint promotion had been achieved in the long history of Disciples. The new entity, under the leadership of Clarence O. Hawley (1890–1963), stimulated cooperation in budget making among the various agencies, with allocations made by a Commission on Brotherhood Finance. Through educational promotion aimed at building understanding of the total Christian enterprise, Unified Promotion effectively increased giving to cooperative boards and agencies. In a denomination not noted for generous stewardship to its organizations beyond the local congregation, the record of Unified Promotion proved to be the most steady among the many methods of fund raising attempted before or since.[14]

Canada

Structural cooperation also developed between Disciples in Canada and Disciples in the United States. The very name of the church, in its entirety, includes both the United States and Canada–*The Christian Church (Disciples of Christ) in the United States and Canada.* In his two earliest histories of the Movement, *Religion Follows the Frontier* and *An American Religious Movement,* W. E. Garrison did not include Canadian Disciples in either the indexes or the narratives. But in 1948 Garrison and Alfred DeGroot noted the strength of Canadian Disciples had exceeded 9,000 members in seventy-nine congregations and proceeded to include Canadians with comparatively extensive coverage in their *The Disciples of Christ: A History.* Lester McAllister and William Tucker in their 1975 *Journey in Faith* equaled the coverage of Garrison and DeGroot. At this writing, sixty years after Garrison and DeGroot's history, the Disciples' strength in Canada has plummeted to slightly over 1,000 participating members in twenty-three congregations.

Year	Congregations	Total Members	Participating Members
1965	81	8,909	6,286
1968	5,254	3,338	[restructure]
1970	44	4,888	2,887
1980	38	4,686	2,613
1990	36	4,092	2,506
2000	27	2,912	1,765
2007	23	1,776	1,069

Data from Year Books of the Christian Church (Disciples of Christ) 1965–2007.

Rooted in Haldanian, Scotch Baptist immigration, the oldest Disciples congregation in Canada was founded at River John, Nova Scotia, in 1815 in the home of James Murray. Several congregations were founded during the 1830s: Halifax, 1832; St. John's in New Brunswick in 1834 by George Garretty (1811–1890); and numerous founding's in Ontario, including Toronto in 1838. Due to the spatially enormous, sparsely settled expanse of Canada, development of the Disciples Movement there was slow. It began in the rural, thinly populated Maritime Provinces: Nova Scotia, New Brunswick, and Prince Edward Island. Very little development occurred in Roman Catholic French Quebec, while the most successful expansion was in Ontario–with many years of slow development in the prairie provinces of Manitoba, Saskatchewan, and Alberta, as well as in the mountainous province of British Columbia.[15]

> A meeting of delegates and brethren took place at Equesing… There are about 16 congregations in various parts of the (Ontario) province which were represented by delegates.

This announcement, earliest evidence of Canadian cooperation, appeared in the August 1843 issue of *The Millennial Harbinger*. Cooperation between Canadian Disciples and the ACMS began in 1853. Alexander Campbell, at age sixty-six, visited Ontario in 1855, staying at the home of Disciples cooperative leader James Black (1797–1886), and giving Canadian Disciples development a boost. In 1886, the "Cooperation of Disciples of Christ in Ontario" was established, heir of the earlier cooperative initiative in 1843. Its purpose was evangelism and founding new churches. The Ontario Christian Woman's Board of Missions was founded in 1887 with similar purpose. These cooperative ventures naturally spawned an anti-society movement led by James Beatty of Toronto. But the Maritime Provinces created a Christian Missionary Society in 1855, and the western provinces later developed multiple societies between 1905 and 1910.[16]

Across the years, Canadian Disciples created eighteen periodicals, beginning with the *Christian Gleaner* (generally a reprint of *Christian Baptist*) in 1833. Its best-known publication was *Canadian Disciple,* founded in 1923. Several educational institutions were also established, most of them by Independents and Churches of Christ. At the annual meeting of the Ontario conference in 1921, George Stewart (1875–1958) called for national church unity, an All Canada Movement. During the year that followed, an All Canada Team visited congregations in each of the provinces. At the annual Ontario conference in 1922, the All Canada movement was approved. The six-point program included: closer cooperation, appointment of an All Canada secretary, placing the headquarters at Toronto, development of Sunday school literature, development of a children's program, and stewardship education.[17]

From the mid-twentieth century, Disciples of Christ in Canada have been in steady decline. Despite the decline, Canadian Disciples contributed several significant twentieth-century leaders to the Movement, in particular

Archibald McLean (1849–1920) and Jessie Trout (1895–1990). Cooperative efforts exist between the Churches of Christ and the Christian Churches–Churches of Christ, and in recent decades they have founded several new congregations. The Disciples of Christ recently selected a new regional minister, Cathy Hubbard, to lead their cause.

Cooperation through Christian Unity

If this movement is of God, He will not forget us; if it is not of Him, we desire it to be forgotten; but, believing that it is of the Lord, we are students of the problem of Christian union above all other issues in the Church.

PETER AINSLIE III
The Message of the Disciples for the Union of the Church, *1913*[18]

Disciples began with the insight that Christians should be united. Christian unity was referenced in the 1804 *Last Will and Testament,* which declared the presbytery "sink into union with the body of Christ at large." The defining feature of the *Declaration and Address* of 1809 proclaimed, "The Church of Christ upon earth is essentially, intentionally and constitutionally one." Disciples, from their earliest days, held an unshakable passion for the ideal of Christian unity, described by Barton Stone as our "Polar Star." In our own time, Kenneth L. Teegarden (1921–2002) said of this ideal:

> The ideal of Christian unity is to Disciples of Christ what basketball is to Indiana, hospitality is to the South and nonviolence is to Quakers. It is our middle name. It is the distinctive cause that has been the [Disciples] reason for existing.[19]

Although they thought they were launching a reform movement to unite Christians, the founders underestimated the power and popular appeal of denominationalism. The roots of denominationalism can be traced to the sixteenth-century Protestant Reformation. Attempts to renew the Catholic Church from within by Martin Luther, John Calvin, and John Knox led to the fragmentation of *church* into *churches*. When these churches immigrated to America, "denomination" became the organizational pattern emerging from the religious freedom guaranteed by the Constitution's separation of church and state. Martin Marty describes the denomination as an "invention of Anglo-American Christianity, designed to make possible free and equal church life in the era of voluntary religious association; and that it now appears to many to be obsolete." "Since 1910," continued Marty, "denomination has stood as a symbol for that which retards the expression of Christian Unity." Denominationalism, according to Sidney Mead, shaped American Christianity. He identified several influences that configured American denominationalism: the absence of history, the voluntary principle, evangelical mission, revivalism, heart religion, and intense competition. Winfred E. Garrison described denominationalism as "the guarantor of religious freedom." But H. Richard Niebuhr viewed denominationalism as stifling the dynamic unity of the church. The traditions, he said, became self-serving denominations rather than structures of the universal church. Denominationalism, wrote Niebuhr, "represents the accommodation of Christianity to the caste-system of human society… The division of the churches closely follows the division of men into the castes of national, racial and economic groups."

Charles Clayton Morrison also denounced the denominational system because he believed it (a) wasted Protestant resources, (b) provincialized Protestant mentality, (c) denied breadth of outlook to the local church, (d) stunted the missionary expansion of Christianity, and (e) denied the freedom that is in Christ. Other critics have written that denominational separations look to the past for justifications of division, rather than to the future hope that all may be one. The visible unity sought by Disciples founders was far more arduous, complex, and exasperating than they envisioned. Throughout the whole of Disciples history, entrenched denominationalism has been the ecclesial environment in which ecumenical witness has attempted to recover the meaning of Christian community.[20]

General consensus holds that between the 1832 union of Christians and Disciples (Reformers) and the opening of the twentieth century few advances of significance toward unity occurred. Of course, there was a series of overtures to the Baptists (1841, 1866, 1895, and into the twentieth century in 1903–10, 1929, and 1946–52), but the two bodies were never able to achieve visible unity. Disciples also participated in several other notable nineteenth-century efforts that crossed denominational lines. In 1872, the International Sunday School Association began issuing Uniform Lessons used by several denominations. Disciples were involved in this effort through the person of Benjamin B. Tyler (1840–1922), who became president of the ISSA in 1902. Disciples also participated in cooperative agencies in which the common life of American Protestantism found expression: the Foreign Missionary Conference of North America, the Home Missions Council, the Young People's Society of Christian Endeavor, and the International Council of Religious Education supported through the leadership of Robert M. Hopkins (1878–1955) and Roy G. Ross (1898–1978). Although the number of nineteenth-century interdenominational ventures was limited, Disciples explored them all.

The twentieth century, by contrast, is often called the "Age of Ecumenism." The word *ecumenism,* wrote Paul Crow Jr., comes from a family of classical Greek words: *oikos,* meaning a "house," "family," "people," or "nation"; *oikoumene,* "the whole inhabited world"; *oikoumenikos,* "open to or participating in the whole world"; and *koinonia,* "one fellowship."

Ecumenism represents the universality of the people of God; it is not a monolithic uniformity; it is a spiritual reality of shared love and a common trust in Christ. Progressive Disciples have long been strong ecumenists. Their appreciation of ecumenism is empowered by the belief that no single Christian community possesses the whole Christian truth; each adds theological insight to a full understanding of faith.

When the Federal Council of Churches of Christ in America organized in 1908, Disciples were charter members. James H. Garrison (1842–1931), in fact, suggested the organization's name. It provided a means for American churches to retain their separate identities, but work together in "conciliar" fashion. Disciples were active in it from the beginning. The World Missionary Conference in Edinburgh, 1910, in which Disciples participated, is recognized as the first concrete manifestation of the modern ecumenical movement. That same summer, British and American Disciples sponsored an Anglo-American Conference on Christian Union in London. Among the Disciples attending were Archibald McLean, Charles Clayton Morrison, and J.H. Garrison. The ecumenical movement found further expression in a series of gatherings between 1925–1938: two Universal Christian Life and Work Conferences at Stockholm (1925) and Oxford (1937), two Faith and Order conferences at Lausanne (1927) and Edinburgh (1937), and a conference on World Christianity at Jerusalem (1928). These conferences provided the genealogy for the World Council of Churches constituted at Utrecht, Netherlands, in 1938. Disciples were vigorous participants in all of these. Back in 1908 Charles Clayton Morrison purchased a struggling magazine that published interdenominational interests. *The Christian Century,* under Morrison's editorship, became thoroughly ecumenical, highly successful, and earned international acclaim. The theme for the Disciples 1909 Centennial, "The Union of All Believers...," stood as a befitting introduction to open the ecumenical century.[21]

Peter Ainslie III (1867–1934), a Disciples minister, was a towering presence among early twentieth-century ecumenists. It was said he possessed "a soldier's courage and the shepherd's gentleness." The son and grandson of Disciples ministers, his father, Peter Ainslie II, a Bethany College graduate and friend of Alexander Campbell, served as an evangelist for the Movement. Ainslie III, born in the tidewater region of Virginia, reached the mid-point of a forty-year ministry at Baltimore's Christian Temple Christian Church in 1910. He served as president of the General Convention of Disciples of Christ at their October 1910 Topeka gathering where he delivered a presidential address entitled "Our Fellowship and the Task," urging Disciples to reclaim their ecumenical purpose. The Convention took two important actions: the first called for a World Conference on Christian Unity, and the second established a permanent general Disciples ecumenical agency named the "Council on Christian Union" to be placed on equal footing with the missionary societies. Promoting Christian unity at home and throughout the world would be its purpose. With a generous contribution from R. A. Long, Ainslie launched a publication in 1913, named *The Christian Union Quarterly.* It became a leading ecumenical journal of its day. In 1916 he changed the organization's name to the Association for the Promotion of Christian Unity, a name that subsequently evolved into the Council on Christian Unity in 1954. Under all its names the Council played an enabling role in linking Disciples to all conciliar agencies of cooperation. Ainslie became the central figure in the Faith and Order movement, served as a delegate to the 1925 Stockholm Conference, a participant in the 1927 Lausanne Conference, and helped sponsor the American conference on Organic Union in 1920. Herbert Willett said of Peter Ainslie III, he was "a singular compound of gentleness and inflexibility," and in pursuit of the principles of Christian unity he was both "fearless and aggressive." Ainslie advocated an open pulpit, open communion, and open membership; and he regularly charged that churches were "captive to the powers of denominational idolatry." Consequently, he seemed always at the center of controversy. Among his prolific writings is *Message of Disciples for Union of the Church,* a compilation of his 1913 Yale lectures on ecumenism that remains one of the Disciples valuable sources on Christian unity.[22]

During the nineteenth century Disciples mostly took the position of proclaiming a sectarian heritage arrived at in isolation rather than dialoging in reciprocity with other bodies of faith to share in mutual strengthening. But in the twentieth century Disciples became more open, more receptive, and found expression in inclusive movements by contributing leadership and finance to support conciliar ecumenism. Their focus shifted from a divided Christendom to the needs of the world. Edgar DeWitt Jones (1876–1956) served as president (1936–1938) of the Federal Council of Churches; and Jesse Bader headed the FCC Department of Evangelism. Bader was the pivotal leader in founding the World Convention of Churches of Christ in 1930 to facilitate fellowship and dialogue among the three branches of the Campbell-Stone Movement, and in initiating the observance of World Wide Communion Sunday in 1940. Disciple Mossie Wyker (1902–1988) served as President of the Federal Council of Churches Department of United Church Women. The first World Council of Churches Assembly, held in Amsterdam, August 22–September 5, 1948, counted 140 churches from forty countries attending. Disciples were charter members and their delegation to the historic Amsterdam Assembly included George Walker Buckner (1893–1981), Gaines Cook (1897–1993), Harry McCormick, Hampton Adams (1897–1965), Alfred T. DeGroot (1903–1992) and Magruder E. Sadler (1896–1966). At the 1948 assembly, Peter Ainslie III received high commendation by being named one of the "Twelve Apostles of the Modern Ecumenical Movement." In short order the National Council of Churches organized in 1950 as a successor to the Federal Council of Churches. Again, Disciples were charter members. Disciples layman J. Irwin

Miller (1909–2004) served as president (1960–1963) of the NCC; and three Disciples–Roy Ross, Joan Brown Campbell and Michael Kinnamon–have been appointed General Secretary of the organization.

Some claim that Disciples ecumenical involvement has been "primarily restricted to leadership and those conversations rarely reach congregations, where involvement has been marginal." It should be noted, however, that a sizeable body of Disciples leadership has been engaged for decades in state and local councils of churches, arranging exchanges of ministers and inter-congregational visitations as well as joint mission initiatives. Disciples have always been active participants in United Ministries in Higher Education, ecumenical campus ministry, the World Student Christian Fellowship, student Christian Movements, united churches on the mission fields, and the ecumenical publication of Christian education resources–all important ecumenical seedbeds so often overlooked.

Howard E. Short (1909–2007) and William Barnett Blakemore (1911–1975) represented Disciples at the famed Vatican II (1962–1965) where the landmark *Decree on Ecumenism* called for a deeper "spiritual ecumenism." The *Decree* proclaimed in part:

> There can be no ecumenism worthy of the name without a change of heart. For it is from newness of attitudes, from self-denial and unstinted love, that yearnings for unity take their rise and grow toward maturity… This change of heart should be regarded as the soul of the whole ecumenical movement.[23]

Many view Vatican II as the single most significant event within Christendom during the 500 years since the Protestant Reformation.

In 1960 four churches collaborated in founding the Consultation on Church Union. Edwin Gaustad referred to the Consultation as "the most ambitious effort to shape the destiny of institutional religion in America" during the 1960s. The Disciples joined by official vote in 1962. Forty years later, January 20, 2002, COCU's expanded membership of nine churches voted to end consultation and begin living into unity, renaming itself Churches Uniting in Christ, sharing life in faith, sacraments, mission, and combating racism. Paul A. Crow Jr. (b. 1931), named the first full-time General Secretary of the Consultation in 1968, continued in that post six years. Another Disciple, Michael Kinnamon, served as General Secretary of Churches Uniting in Christ from 1999 to 2002.

Paul Crow accepted the presidency of the Disciples Council on Christian Unity in 1974, succeeding George Beazley Jr., a position he would hold for the next quarter century. Few people in the world, during the last four decades of the twentieth century, saw more of the modern ecumenical movement. Author of numerous articles (particularly in the Council's journal *Midstream*), books, and countless lectures, he became a major prophetic voice in the universal church: traveling to every part of the globe, becoming a world presence in the Christian unity movement. At home, determined that Disciples would not become a narrow, provincial expression of the body of Christ, he insistently reminded Disciples of their ecumenical heritage. Among Crow's numerous accomplishments are the launching of an international dialogue with the Roman Catholic Church in 1977, starting an international visitors exchange with the Russian Orthodox Church in 1987, and an international dialogue with the Evangelical Lutheran church in Finland in 1996. He led in the reactivation of a dialogue with the United Church of Christ in 1977 that ultimately developed a Declaration of Ecumenical Partnership in 1985 leading to a Declaration of Full Communion in 1989, and to the founding of a joint Global Missions Board in 1996. Peter Ainslie III and Paul Crow Jr., controversial in their times, often voices in the wilderness, are recognized as the two preeminent Disciples advocates of Christian unity in the twentieth century. Others, such as George G. Beazley Jr. (1914–1973) and Michael Kinnamon made significant contributions to the ecumenical movement. Ainslie and Crow established themselves as international symbols of the Age of Ecumenism.[24]

At the dawn of the twenty-first century, Robert Welsh (b. 1946), who succeeded Paul Crow as president of the Disciples Council on Christian Unity in 1999, gave leadership to the launching of a dialogue with the Evangelical Lutheran Church in America (1999), and a dialogue with the Reformed and Moravian Churches (2002). He has led the Disciples into a full partnership with the Alliance of Baptists, the United Church of Christ, and the Christian Church (Disciples of Christ), formed in 2001 to "deepen ecumenical friendship." Disciples were among the first to join the Christian Churches Together in the USA, which began in September 2001 and now claims a membership of thirty-four communions representing 100 million members. The first Executive Administrator of CCT was a former General Minister and President of the Disciples, Dr. Richard Hamm (b. 1947). Its mission is "to enable churches and Christian organizations to grow closer together in Christ in order to strengthen Christian witness in the world." By the turn of the century both NCC and WCC faced serious financial constraint resulting in severe program cutbacks. In 2007 internationally respected Disciple Michael Kinnamon, author of a dozen books on ecumenism, including *The Vision of the Ecumenical Movement: And How It Has Been Impoverished by Its Friends* (2003) and *The Ecumenical Movement: An Anthology of Texts and Voices* (1997), was elected General Secretary of the National Council of Churches. His election sparked new hope for the future of NCC.

At a World Convention executive committee meeting in 2000, Richard Hamm declared "the three streams of the Stone-Campbell Movement have lied about each other for years and have otherwise conducted ourselves in ways that are anything but demonstrative of a commitment to Christian unity and we need to stop it." A flurry of conversation ensued, ultimately leading to a formal Stone-Campbell dialogue that Robert Welsh has helped shape and maintain. The Global Christian Forum (begun in 2000) is another new body in which Disciples formally participate along with nearly sixty other families of faith. Its purpose is "to create an open space wherein representatives from a broad range of Christian churches can gather to foster mutual respect and explore common challenges." Welsh, a member of the leadership team of the Global Christian Forum, helped plan their November 2007 gathering in Nairobi, Kenya, attended by 240 Christian leaders from seventy-two nations representing 95 percent of the world's Christian population, the most diverse range of churches and confessions ever assembled to explore the gift of Christian unity.

Ecumenism in the twenty-first century carries many definitions. Among the descriptive terms in common use are: cooperative unity, spiritual unity, organic unity, practical unity, visible unity, communion of communions, ecumenical partnership, full communion, and conciliar ecumenism. Some scholars suggest a new ecumenism is emerging that is able to define its terms with greater precision and creativity, thereby giving rise to new ecumenical principles. Michael Kinnamon raised the question, "Do we speak of unified diversity or diverse unity?" It is clearly the latter, he advised, "we learn from the legitimate diversity of our given oneness." William Tabbernee proposed ecumenical redefinition should focus on "differences" to discover it's meaning: the difference between unity and uniformity; the difference between disagreement and disunity; the difference between comparative ecclesiology and ecumenical theology; the difference between ecumenism and interfaith dialogue; and the difference between koinonia and cooperation. Understanding those differences, suggested Tabbernee, lifts up principles of a new ecumenism; embracing diversity, accepting controversy, using ecumenical theology as the hermeneutical norm, avoiding an isolation of Christian ecumenism, and sharing a common life should be the intentional goals of all ecumenical engagement. Applying these five principles, it is hoped, will help steer the twenty-first–century church toward its hallowed goal of visible unity.[25]

Cooperation through Multicultural Expressions

Rivers need not and do not always divide; they can and do often connect. They present challenges to us to build bridges. Beyond them often lie great and wonderful promised lands.

ROSA PAGE WELCH (1901–1994)[26]

Developing Disciples multicultural solidarity with a growing racial/ethnic diversity of cultural expressions in the United States and Canada (at this writing totaling approximately 80,000 members, or an estimated 11 to 12 percent of Disciples total membership) has been a historic challenge. Each expression is organized into a separate structure while maintaining full participation within the Disciples' core design. Guided by the principle of "the church of Christ upon earth is essentially, intentionally and constitutionally one," racial/ethnic cultural structures are viewed as "multiple expressions in one body," a participatory interdependence in which each contributes spiritual gifts and religious experience to the whole of "pro-reconciliation/anti-racism church," with the intention of avoiding becoming spiritual ends in themselves. Their individual stories are best read in conjunction with each other as a means of comparing their developmental trajectories, as a means of insuring an uninterrupted continuity for each individual story, and as a means of adding strength and range to the combined heritage of Disciples ethnic expressions.

All are engaged at different stages in the journey toward wholeness. The search for wholeness with ethnic expressions has generally been conducted by offices within the Disciples Home Missions (formerly Division of Homeland Ministries), heir to the spirit and programs of the old ACMS, and an heir to the *cooperative tradition* in Disciples heritage–a powerful tradition that spawned the "society" concept; that urged the earliest forms of structure; that unceasingly advocated inclusiveness rather than independence; that produced the twentieth-century restructure; and that gave birth, nurture, and shape to the development of ethnic expressions. The search for wholeness has commonly followed a line of progression from paternalism to partnership to self-determination to integration: from establishment of congregations and social service centers with the assistance of Disciples resources and leadership, to regional and general networking, to the creation of staff positions and board participation within the organized structure, to general organized racial/ethnic/cultural expressions in partnership with Disciples, which include ethnic caucusing, ethnic self-resourcing, and finally ethnic self-determination within the Christian Church (Disciples of Christ). This sequence of mutual exploration has been supported with meager resources, both in finance and in numbers of personnel, several of whom entered the home mission field relying upon their own financial capital and ingenuity. We are all Disciples regardless of racial/ethnic/cultural heritage, which, at times, is expressed differently in music, worship, preaching style, languages, and support structures.

Native Americans

In 1830 government preparations were underway for the infamous removal of the Cherokee from their ancestral lands in Georgia to a newly created Indian Territory on the Western frontier. The very first issue of *The Millennial Harbinger* carried an article written with a touch of sarcasm by Alexander Campbell expressing strong opposition to "Indian Removal."

The "rights of man," one would think are any thing and every thing which any body and every body pleases to make them, if we yield to the opinions of those who maintain that any state in the Union has a right to seize the property and exile or banish the owner, because he is red or yellow, or some other unfashionable color…; have treaties any sanction, any validity, any faith? Have the parties to any covenant or compact any right? Or is it the right of the strong always to plunder the property of the weak? Has one man…the right to seize the farm of his neighbor and give him a tract on the moon or in No Man's Island? All this, and even more than this is assumed by Georgia in reference to the Cherokee Indians.[27]

But then Campbell's pen fell strangely silent. Although the *Harbinger* continued publication for the remaining thirty-six years of Campbell's life, he did not write another article on the subject of Native Americans. Although Campbell considered Jonathan Edwards his favorite theologian, he obviously did not internalize Edward's great passion for the Native American. Likely, his Southern friends cautioned him to leave the subject of removal alone or risk a schism within the Movement—an early instance of Disciples' concern for unity overpowering their concern for social justice.

Through the years, beginning in 1832, he printed correspondence received from a minister devoted to the Native Cherokee, James Jenkins Trott (1800–1868), a former ordained Methodist preacher who became a Disciple, husband of a Cherokee woman, and self-appointed missionary. Agitation surrounding the removal question caused the Georgia legislature to pass a law forcing all citizens to take an oath of support for Georgia laws. Trott refused to take the oath and was arrested along with ten others on March 12, 1831. He and the other two missionaries in the group were released because they were thought to be federal agents Christianizing and educating the Indians. But the Georgia governor insisted they take the oath. Still they ignored the governor's plea and were arrested again on July 7; two were sentenced to four years in prison and Trott reported to the *Harbinger* his banishment from the territory: "I have been arrested, chained, imprisoned, condemned, reprieved and banished from the territory of the State, because I refused to take what I believe to be an unconstitutional and impious oath."

From 1831 to the deportation in 1837 known as the "Trail of Tears," he continued to minister to the Cherokee in Georgia. During this time he suffered imprisonment again for opposing the 1835 removal treaty of New Echota. One of his daughters died during the forced migration to Indian Territory. After a twenty-year absence from the Cherokee, the ACMS, in 1853, officially appointed Trott as a missionary to the tribe, subject to his finding his own sources of financial support. He arrived in Indian Territory November 1857, investing $1,500 of his own money to start a Christian

Mission. He envisioned a mission, not only to the Cherokee, but also for all Native Americans of the West. Trott's correspondence to the *Harbinger* in 1860 advocated his dream of establishing such a mission in Indian Territory ("inhabited by Creek, Chickasaw, Choctaw and Cherokee tribes numbering about 100,000... The Baptists, Presbyterians, Methodists and Moravians have many churches and hundreds of members... We have about 75 Disciples in the Cherokee nation."). Trott solicited Campbell's support. Campbell responded succinctly at the conclusion of Trott's printed letter, assigning the matter to individual opinion.

> We heartily commend these earnest words of our devoted and much loved Bro. Trott to the generous Christian philanthropy of our Brethren. The support and success of this mission hangs upon their liberality.

The Civil War forced the ACMS to retrench and there is no record that any financial assistance was ever given to Trott. He died in 1868. The ACMS had reached low ebb and the CWBM had not yet appeared. In 1874 J. Ellis and Murrel Askew (one-fourth Choctaw) began missionary work among the Chicasaw. They planted fifty-four congregations, none of which are known to have survived. In 1884 the ACMS funded a mission to the Creek Indians in Indian Territory, assigning Isaac Mode, from the Creek capital at Okmulgee, as missionary. That same year R. W. Officer, sponsored by a Disciples congregation in Paris, Texas, began work with the Choctaws. He planted an industrial school and an orphanage, representing the first attempt to found an industrial mission as distinguished from an evangelistic mission or a congregation. Like other missionaries, starving for support, he appealed to the *Christian Standard* and *The Gospel Advocate* to help raise funds. The following year found the ACMS providing financial support to Prairie City, a church organized among the Cherokee. The Society attempted work in Indian Territory among the Choctaws and the Cherokees again in 1890 led by missionary W. B. Stinson. And in 1871 E. M. Gibson was sent by the ACMS to Washington Territory to work among the native Makoh.[28]

From 1843 to 1846, immigrants, enduring the hardships of the Oregon Trail, poured into the far Northwest. The immigration included scores of Disciples. In fact, one observer noted, "The Campbellites and the fern are taking the Willamette Valley!" The 1847 massacre of Dr. Marcus Whitman and his wife Narcissa at their Waiilatpu mission among the Cayuse likely inhibited any intended Disciples initiatives toward the many Native American tribes in the region. Sixty-five years later, in 1912, W. F. Turner, pastor of the Disciples congregation in Yakima, Washington, developed an immediate and sympathetic interest in the Yakama Indians, recording in his writings: "The tribe was living in the restraint of a reservation and in a strange isolation from the mass of citizenry—a tribe apart."

He invited Frederick W. Burnham (1871–1960), president of the ACMS, to visit the Yakama reservation. A number of conferences followed, resulting in an agreement among the ACMS, the West Washington Christian Missionary Society, the congregation at Yakima and a council of Native Americans. The ACMS purchased eighty acres of land for $8,800; the Yakima congregation raised $3,500 and the Indian Council pledged $2,000 to establish a mission named "American Tepee Christian Mission," a name later changed to the "Yakama Indian Christian Mission." It was to be patterned after the Episcopalian Wind River Mission in Wyoming, a mission that had been visited by both Burnham and Turner. A board of four local Disciples and three Native Americans governed the Yakama operation. The cornerstone of the mission building was placed on June 26, 1920, with Mrs. Lester Pearne, sister of the old Yakama chief, White Swan, turning the first spade of earth. The new building was dedicated in the fall of 1921. Thirty-nine children enrolled. The mission continues to operate in 2007, and is known as the Yakama Mission School for Native American children. It is the lone surviving work of Disciples among Native Americans.[29]

Disciples' several sporadic efforts left few abiding results. The primary reason was lack of structure. Most missionaries went into Indian Territory of their own accord without an organization to back them, and no assured support. Recruiting a minister for a newly planted congregation that wanted to become permanent was a huge challenge, because Disciples polity grew out of congregational authority. The problem of finding a minister was viewed as a responsibility for the congregation. Consequently, only one permanent congregation (Atoka, Oklahoma) survived the early missionary period. Another, founded on the Osage reservation in 1907–First Christian Church in Hominy, Oklahoma–continues to exist with ninety members at this writing. It should also be noted that, as of 2008, there is a forty-six-member Native American congregation in formation at Benton, Illinois.

Disciples' ministry to Native Americans is accurately described as weak. Ironically, the lack of a strong missionary effort may have ended up being something of a positive. Protestant and Catholic mission work among Native Americans in many instances is believed to have bred destructive effects: a degeneration of Native cultures, societies, and institutions–in some cases warfare and even extinction.

Hispanic Americans

Many writers, especially Herbert Bolton, have recorded the heroic story of the Roman Catholic Jesuits, often referred to as Black Robes, in the American Southwest. David Weber called them "Conquistadores of the Spirit." The deeds and influence of Jesuit missions formed traditions of substantial weight and must be viewed as more than an irrelevant prelude to the arrival of Disciples. In the fall of 1572 Pedro Sanchez and fifteen

Jesuit companions reached Mexico City and began an unbroken work of nearly two centuries. Over those two centuries it is estimated that 3,000 Jesuit missionaries came to New Spain, for an average term of twenty to twenty-five years.[30]

They were the primary agents in transforming a large native population from nomadic to sedentary life, with attendant cultural changes. Each mission, an integral part of the Spanish strategy for conquest and pacification, was an agricultural unit of the Spanish frontier containing its own carpenter shop, blacksmith shop, spinning and weaving rooms, corrals for the stock, fields, and irrigation ditches. The Black Robes, individually, fulfilled multiple roles as theologians, teachers, college founders, explorers, cartographers, ethnologists, linguists, and historians. They were responsible, too, for religious instruction of the people in the form of a daily round of drill in the Catechism, prayers, and sacred music. Black Robes were required to learn the native languages of the region where they were sent to serve.

Soon the Jesuits began extending their reach 1,000 miles northward, across Durango and Chihuahua into what would become New Mexico and California. The Black Robes did not only explore the borderland beyond the Rio Grande, they occupied it "river by river, valley by valley, canyon by canyon, tribe by tribe," wrote Herbert Bolton, "moving into the wilderness ahead of the prospector, miner, soldier, cattleman and trader."[31]

Historians referred to the area north of the Rio Grande, the outer limits of Nueva España, as "borderlands." Bolton made the insightful observation that this region was more than a physical or geographical environment; it was a "social environment," created by Spain through the use of Jesuit missionaries to establish *misiones,* the soldier to establish *presidios,* and *colonos* to establish civilian settlements. Many of the folk in today's western Mexico and in the borderlands of the United States are direct descendents of ancestors who experienced the age of the Black Robes.[32]

For two centuries, the Jesuits essentially operated a tightly controlled, miniature theocracy. Their objective was to Europeanize their converts, much as Alexander Campbell wrote in the nineteenth century when he called for both "Christianizing and Civilizing." The church of the Jesuits, and later the Franciscans, was a complex cultural institution. It brought education, vocational stability, fellowship, and direction to a social order where few other institutions were available. By the 1830s, the lineaments and distinctive social features that had been there for generations set the old Jesuit-Franciscan culture apart from the younger Anglo American culture beginning to enter the land and confront its traditions. The land was heavily populated by Tejanos (a poor class of mixed races with a Roman Catholic religious base—*la sangre española, india y negra*) and located between the southern boundary of the Louisiana Purchase and the Rio Grande, a land in which Indian, Spanish, Mexican, and American traditions crossed. Mexico, which received its independence from Spain in 1821, considered this a borderland, a buffer zone. When the Mexican constitution was written in 1824, it stated clearly, "The religion of the Mexican nation is and will remain Roman Catholic." As Euro Americans began the process of attempting to separate this borderland from Mexico, they discovered the language, social divisions, legal system, and religious tradition had changed little from the time of the Jesuit expulsion. By 1827 some 12,000 Euro Americans had illegally crossed into the region that, in less than a decade, would become known as Texas.[33]

The first Disciples interaction with Hispanics and Tejanos appears to have been through a sixteen-year-old boy, Jose Maria Jesus Carvajal (1810–1874), who heard Alexander Campbell speak in Kentucky. Jose traveled to Bethany, where he lived with the Campbell family for four years, returning to his San Antonio home in 1830. For a time he preached and distributed Spanish language Bibles, but soon directed his energies toward political freedom and revolution in the northern states of Mexico. His religious efforts left no documented lasting impact. From February 24 through March 3, 1836, the most famous event of the Texas rebellion against Mexico occurred at an old Franciscan mission in San Antonio known as the Alamo. Approximately 200 American settlers and Tejanos were killed by the Mexican army led by General Antonio Lopez de Santa Anna. Shortly thereafter, Santa Anna's army was defeated at San Jacinto, setting the stage for Texas independence. Historian David Weber tells of the Alamo's symbolic significance:

> The lore surrounding the battle of the Alamo provides the clearest examples of how the Texas rebellion…has been romanticized… In American pop culture, the Texas fight for independence has come to represent a triumph of Protestantism over Catholicism, of democracy over despotism, of a superior white race over a degenerate people of mixed blood, of the future over the past, of good over evil.

In reality, a Mexican province had been lost to Euro American settlers.[34]

The Treaty of Guadalupe-Hidalgo in 1848 gave nearly half of Mexican territory to the United States (roughly the states of Texas, New Mexico, Arizona, Colorado, Utah, Nevada and California). The Mexicans who lived in that territory instantly became Mexican-Americans. Four decades would pass before the Disciples Reform Movement, relying upon Spanish-speaking American missionaries and bilingual Tejanos to translate, stepped gingerly into the borderlands. Disciples mission work moved slowly due to the presence of Roman Catholicism as a state religion integrated into a long-established social order, coupled with the Disciples' heritage of less-than-even-modest financial resources for mission work and Alexander Campbell's anti-Catholic bias. The *Missionary Tidings* of the CWBM reported in 1888 that a Disciples Mexican Mission had been established in

San Antonio with "feeble support." Disciples missionaries in the borderland were few in number and did not possess the intellectual boldness, discipline, or vigor of the Black Robes. Yet attempting something as unpretentious as founding a single congregation or social service center provoked criticism by later scholars for being either too "paternal" or not being paternal enough in supporting Hispanic mission work; and for having a Eurocentric complex that marginalized Latino culture. While these criticisms obviously contain truth, critics have not placed Disciples mission work in the full historical sociocultural context of the region or within the larger nineteenth-century conventional missionary practices of Protestantism; nor do they place Disciples work with Hispanics within the experimental frame of Disciples polity or within its total missionary enterprise, particularly its financial constraints.

In 1899, Pastor Ignacio Quintero organized the Mexican Christian Church in San Antonio. And in 1913, on the suggestion and persuasion of Disciples medical doctor Samuel Guy Inman (1877–1965)–born on a farm near the Trinity river in Texas–and with the support of the CWBM, a social service center, the Mexican Christian Institute (known since 1953 as the Inman Christian Center), was established to provide a medical clinic, a day nursery, a kindergarten, and a range of educational courses for the Spanish-speaking community. It was started in a densely populated ghetto district described as containing "muddy streets, no playgrounds, no health facilities. This area was isolated from the rest of the total community; housing conditions were unbearable. All the Mexican people spoke Spanish."

It ultimately gained recognition as the "second most important settlement house in Texas." Today the center manages six apartment complexes for the elderly and the physically and the mentally challenged. By 1919 a Mexican State Convention took form, consisting of eight Hispanic congregations: one in Lockhart, one in Robstown, two in San Antonio, two in Sabinas, and two in Mexico.[35]

In 1899, the FCMS and CWBM sent missionaries to Puerto Rico, founding a Disciples orphanage there in 1900. Puerto Rico had become a territory of the United States in 1898 as result of the Spanish-American war. Early in the twentieth century Disciples had recruited leaders educated in Mexican schools to lead newly established congregations, but by mid-century Disciples were relying heavily on ministers educated at the Evangelical Seminary of Puerto Rico and ordained in Puerto Rico to give leadership to the founding of congregations in the Southwestern and the Northeastern United States, as well as providing leadership to create programs, services, and general structures for Hispanic Disciples congregations. Beginning in 1969, the oversight of Hispanic Ministries within the Division of Homeland Ministries took a significant turn when Byron Spice, the executive with responsibility for Hispanic ministries and advocate of the "acculturation" missionary model of ministry for Hispanics, invited the first Hispanic,

Domingo Rodriguez (1918–2006) to be director of the Office of Programs and Services for Hispanic and Bilingual Congregations of the Division of Homeland Ministries. Rodriguez was the former pastor of three Christian churches in Puerto Rico, and La Hermosa Christian Church in New York; former executive secretary of the Churches of the Disciples of Christ in Puerto Rico; past vice president of the World Convention of the Churches of Christ; past president of the Evangelical Council of Churches in Puerto Rico; and past president of the board of Trustees and Board of Publication of *Puerto Rico Evangélico.* When Rodriguez arrived at DHM, there were eighteen Disciples Hispanic congregations in the continental United States and Canada. Lucas Torres succeeded Rodriguez in the DHM position in 1973; and David Vargas followed Torres in 1978. All three of these leaders–Rodriguez, Torres, and Vargas–were born, raised, educated, and ordained in Puerto Rico. Luis Ferrer, also born in Puerto Rico, but raised, educated, and ordained in the United States, succeeded Vargas in 1983. This succession of leaders clearly demonstrated Disciples dependence upon Puerto Rican leadership. More importantly, Hispanic congregations were inspired by their own leadership to launch an era of expansion.[36]

Byron Spice, National Director of Home Mission Ministries in the UCMS and former missionary to Mexico and Paraguay, authored an important study in 1964 entitled *Discípulos Americanos.* He candidly expressed his philosophy of missions along with his frustrations regarding Hispanic ministries. Spice made several references to the strength of the centuries-old Spanish Roman Catholic heritage, its hold on the minds of Hispanics, and the difficulty of breaking through the tradition to increase Disciples membership.

> With their Roman Catholic background, and as a result of the anti-protestant campaigns of the clergy in many areas, some Spanish-speaking people would quite literally rather die than go to a clinic housed in the same building with a protestant church.

> They come to our [church], but when they are old enough to be confirmed, they go to the Catholic church.[37]

He hoped Hispanics would "grow into the culture," although he added, "Acculturation is difficult to measure and varies in degree from city to city." He acknowledged that many Spanish-speaking people feel they are in a cultural "no man's land," caught between cultures. Spice recommended that paternalism not be used as the method of implementing acculturation because it was flawed for both the supervisors and the congregations.

> Prejudice and paternalism are qualities that make supervision ineffective. They are apt to blind one…
>   Paternal benevolence, once sought, is cast aside. Authority is rejected. Independence and freedom are of prime importance.

Rules and restrictions are avoided; yet financial assistance is needed and sought.

It is no longer believed that individuals must relinquish their cultural or ethnic identities in order to be acculturated into the mainstream. Rather, it is now understood that an individual can be competent in more than one cultural setting. Ricardo Ainslie, an authority on Latino acculturation, reasons new bicultural and multicultural models recognize that immigrants should engage the majority culture; but they do not need to give up their cultural identity. The complex lives of immigrants, he argues, *require* engagement with more than one culture.

Latinos are often called "hemispheric citizens" living in a transnational framework, a sociopolitical force both in the United States and in their home countries. The term "Latino" is a relatively new term, designating a cultural category of Caribbean and Latin American descent, but without any racial significance. It includes white, black, and every combination thereof. It is a term used in the United States, but not outside. Latinos are said to be "a work in progress"–"made in the U.S.A." A general demographic configuration of the 35 million Hispanics in the United States today reveals approximately: 58 percent Mexican, 10 percent Puerto Rican, 5 percent Central American, 4 percent South American, 4 percent Cuban, 2 percent Dominican, and 17 percent all other.[38]

The Hispanic Caucus grew out of a national Hispanic planning event in the summer of 1975. This body created the National Hispanic and Bilingual Fellowship of the Christian Church (Disciples of Christ) and planned its first national assembly in 1981. The process of organizing additional area conventions followed: the Midwest convention in 1978, the Southeast convention in 1990, and the Pacific Southwest convention also in 1990. Conventions in the Northeast and Southwest existed previously.

Dissatisfaction grew among Hispanic leaders regarding their place within the Disciples structure. Hispanics lobbied for an office that would report directly to the Disciples General Board, rather than through a Division of the Church. Consequently, in 1991 (finalized in the summer of 1992), the Central Pastoral Office for Hispanic Ministries was established and the person occupying the office given the title of "National Pastor" (the word *national* being chosen because it referred to the fact that Hispanics considered themselves a nation within the United States). From this point Hispanics could select their own leaders who would be primarily accountable to them. David Vargas served as National Pastor until 1993. Lucas Torres continued the work until his retirement in 1999, succeeded by Pablo Jiménez, elected in 1999, and Huberto Pimentel, elected in 2006.

Obra Hispana (Hispanic Ministries), serving nearly 200 congregations (as reported by the Hispanic ministries office, 166 congregations as reported by the Disciples *Year Book and Directory*) and numbering slightly more than 12,000 persons in 2007, is structured around six conventions (regions) that meet biennially in a National Assembly. The Central Pastoral Office for Hispanic Ministries serves Hispanic congregations "in a collaborative partnership with Disciples general units, regional offices and Hispanic conventions." The National Pastor manages the office, whose responsibilities include raising funds from Hispanic congregations, from the Disciples Mission Fund, and other church sources; pastoral care for Hispanic ministers, lay leaders, and congregations; developing programs for Hispanic congregations; and being an advocate for Hispanic congregations. A twenty-member board of directors, four-fifths of whom are elected by the conventions, gives oversight to *Obra Hispana.*[39]

By comparison to the Jesuit network of missions three centuries before, the Disciples have developed a relatively small Hispanic mission effort. It is, however, a new effort, barely a century in the making. It has evolved from paternalism to partnership and is preparing to move beyond. With a heterogeneous Latino population in the United States–called by Daisy Machado a rainbow people because of their rich mixture of culture, bloodline, and national origin– having grown from 14 million in 1980 to 35 million in 2000, the number of congregations and the ministry will continue to expand.

Asian Americans

In 1898 Archibald McLean issued "A Plea for Missions in America," in the form of a chapter in his book *A Circuit of the Globe.* "The Gospel," he said, "must be carried into every city and hamlet of this broad land." He continued: "Wherever men go to mine gold or silver or copper, or to raise corn or wheat or fruit, or to engage in any form of work, there the ministers of the Gospel must go and preach the unsearchable riches of Christ."[40]

The writing struck a nerve with Disciples, especially in relationship to their ministry within ethnic cultural expressions. Stray congregations and social service centers began to sprout in several areas of the country during the late 1890s and early 1900s for the purpose of supporting evangelical and pastoral work among racial/ethnic/cultural minorities throughout the nation.

Disciples' ministry to Asians first began in 1891 when the CWBM opened a mission for Chinese immigrants in Portland, Oregon. Jeu Hawk, a Chinese minister, agreed to lead the work beginning in 1892. The Chinese Christian Institute was established in San Francisco in 1907 and grew to a level of several hundred members, but the Chinese Exclusion Acts forced it to close in 1924. It would be sixty-seven years [1990] before a local congregation in Alhambra, California, would rekindle this ministry.

During the 1920s, some 6,000 Filipinos migrated to Los Angeles from the Ilocano region of the Islands, where Disciples missionaries had been working since the late nineteenth century. Dr. and Mrs. Royal Dye started a Sunday school class for Filipinos at First Christian Church in Los Angeles in 1928, and in November the California state board endorsed Silvestre

Morales, a native Filipino, to establish a Filipino fellowship. It served fifty members. Soon a Filipino Christian Center organized and by 1933, with the assistance of the UCMS, a Filipino Christian Church also formed, with Morales as pastor.[41]

In 1901 a night school for Japanese young men established its presence at Broadway Christian Church in Los Angeles. The school offered lessons in English and Bible instruction. Under the sponsorship of the CWBM, the Japanese Christian Church with ten members formed in Los Angeles in April 1908 with Teizo Kawai, a native evangelist from Japan, as pastor. That fall a Japanese Christian Home for boys appeared, followed in 1914 by the establishment of the Japanese Christian Institute–both in Los Angeles. Japanese students at the University of California in Berkeley established a Japanese Christian Church there in 1914. By 1942 there were nine flourishing Japanese congregations in existence. All were forced to close, however, due to anti-Asian sentiment spawned by World War II, resulting in the internment of Japanese Americans. Asian communities and Asian ministries suffered greatly, and in some cases were destroyed. Among those held in internment camps was Gertrude Fujii, who later became a professor of English at UCLA and secretary of the Board of Directors of the Disciples Division of Higher Education during the 1980s. Following World War II, several California Japanese Disciples, under the leadership of Kojiro Unoura who succeeded Teizo Kawai, joined with the UCMS in forming the West Adams Christian Church in Los Angeles. It supported two congregations–one for Issei (first-generation Japanese immigrants born before 1924), the other for Nisei (children of the first-generation immigrants and the first generation of Japanese to be born in the United States.) For the next three decades, Disciples Asian ministry remained essentially dormant until a wave of new immigrants from Asia came as result of the Immigration Acts of 1965 that allowed up to 30,000 people to immigrate to America from each Asian nation. Contemporary Asian Americans were victims of racial discrimination, yet simultaneously agents of change as they proceeded to shape their own destinies.[42]

In 1956, Itoko Maeda (1918–2008) was the first missionary of Japanese descent to be assigned by the United Christian Missionary Society. Luz Bacerra, hired by the Department of Church Women in 1977, was the first person of Asian ancestry to work in the General Offices of the church. Harold R. Johnson (b. 1921), Program Executive for the Division of Homeland Ministries arranged the first consultation on Asian ministries. Johnson identified with the Asian world during his 1972 visit to numerous Asian countries. He wanted to return, but was persuaded by Joseph Smith that Asians in America were being neglected and someone needed to address the issue at home. Holding a special passion for redemptive work with Japanese Americans, Johnson took the lead. The first consultation convened in Indianapolis in July 1978 with the purpose of raising Disciples consciousness regarding Asian ministries, affirming Asian identity, and addressing the needs of Asian Disciples ministry. The meeting gave birth to the Fellowship of Asian American Disciples (FAAD), a new organization that changed its name at the second consultation in April 1979 to American Asian Disciples (AAD) and appointed David Kagiwada (1929–1985) and Janet Casey-Allen to edit its newsletter.

AAD gained full recognition as a Disciples partner institution at the 1984 meeting of the General Board of the Christian Church (Disciples of Christ). The AAD decided to meet in biennial convocations. At their third convocation in 1989 AAD identified its guiding principles as establishing new congregations, developing ministerial leadership, and fostering representation on the Disciples many boards.

At an October 1989 consultation on Asian ministries the AAD executive council decided on a strategy of targeting a specific Asian-language group. They selected Koreans because of the rapid rise in Korean immigration. Koreans had arrived in large numbers in the early 1970s, establishing the first Korean congregation at the Los Angeles Wilshire Christian Church in 1976. The 1991 General Assembly in Tulsa, Oklahoma, voted to establish a position for American Asian Ministries. On February 1, 1992, Geunhee Yu, a Vanderbilt Ph.D., accepted appointment to the position. In 1992 there were only eight Asian congregations, but by 2006 both the number and pluralism of Asian congregations had increased to either ninety-five congregations (as reported by American Asian Ministries Office) or fifty-eight congregations (as reported in the Disciples' *Year Book and Directory*), plus a rich and growing variety of thirteen different ethnic and linguistic groups: Chinese, Japanese, Filipino, Korean, Vietnamese, Indonesian, Mongolian, Indian, Burmese, Laotian, Taiwanese, Cambodian, and Samoan totaling approximately 3500 members.[43]

Min Zhou, Chair of the Department of Asian American Studies at the University of California, claims in her 2007 study, *Contemporary Asian America,* that few Americans of Asian ancestry would identify themselves as Asian, and fewer still as Asian American. She states that, *privately,* they link their identities to specific countries of origin. And joining a religious congregation offers a place that helps reinforce identity. Zhou's studies reveal that early Asian immigrants were mostly low-skilled laborers, but today's immigrants, particularly since 1965, have far more diverse backgrounds. "Differences in national origin, timing of immigration, affluence and settlement patterns," she writes, "profoundly effect the formation of a pan-ethnic identity." Recent arrivals, for example, are less likely than those born, raised, and acculturated in the United States to identify as Asian American. An increasing number of persons of Asian origin in the United States, however, lean toward multiple identities–a private one and a public one. *Publically,* Asian Americans, numbering 11.7 million in the 2000 census, were emerging in American society as a cohesive, self-identified racial group.

To be more inclusive by welcoming Asian Canadians and Pacific Islanders, the ninth convocation of AAD in 1996 renamed itself the North American Pacific Asian Disciples (NAPAD). Korean Disciples made up 75 percent of NAPAD congregations. In 1995 Koreans founded their own fellowship, Disciples of Christ Korean Ministries Fellowship (renamed Korean Disciples Convocation in 2000), naming Soongook Choi (1933–2002) as its moderator. NAPAD formulated a ten-year action plan including a five-point covenant at its 2000 visioning conference. In 2001 a proposal to relocate the office of NAPAD ministry in the Office of General Minister and President of the Christian Church (Disciples of Christ) did not succeed, therefore remaining in Disciples Home Missions. NAPAD began a process of restructure seeking "a new identity with self-determination."

African Americans

The largest non-European cultural expression within the Disciples is African American, with congregations numbering either 431 (as reported by the National Convocation Office) or 407 congregations (as reported by the Disciples *Year Book and Directory*) and containing approximately 65,000 members (several North Carolina congregations do not report to the *Year Book*) in 2007. It should be noted that four huge African American congregations represent approximately 45 percent of the total African American membership. In addition, there are 110 French-speaking Haitian congregations—located primarily in Florida, New York, and Canada—listed separate from Hispanics and African Americans. Haitian is the fastest growing minority group among Disciples.

Only a dim outline of the unrecorded history of African Americans, gleaned from the memory of venerable ex-slaves such as G. A. Goins, from cornerstones of aging church buildings, and from oral traditions, is available to help us understand the period prior to the Civil War. Mere glimpses can be recovered. We are aware, for example, that African Americans were part of the Movement from the beginning. Several (mostly slaves who accompanied their owners) participated in the famed gathering at Cane Ridge in 1801. We know too, that African Americans were members of both founding congregations: Cane Ridge and Brush Run. According to ex-slave Robert Jordan, "I saw Mr. Campbell many times with his own hands, baptize colored men and women." By 1852 the Cane Ridge congregation in Kentucky had a membership of 124, seventy-one of whom were African American. We also know that the Second Great Awakening exerted a powerful influence upon African Americans, generating black spirituals and gospel music, bringing "hope, self-respect, justice and moral order" to slaves along with occasional opportunity for institutional leadership in churches. As a rule, in the pre-Civil War period, slaves attended church with their masters, but they were relegated to the balcony or rear pews or stood outside the doors and windows. They were baptized into a subordinate membership, not elected to elderships (although a few became deacons) and they were served communion after the whites. Masters, freedmen, and slaves, however, worshiped together at the same church building, listening to the same sermon. Despite an estimated 7,000 African American Disciples (5,500 in mixed congregations and 1,500 in black congregations) by 1861, there were very few all-black or "colored" congregations. Negroes were normally members of white congregations.

An ordained ex-slave, educated at Transylvania University, Lexington, Kentucky, who adopted the name of a Disciples founder, Alexander Campbell, established the first "colored" congregation in 1834 at Midway, Kentucky, to which, it is reported, he soon added 300 members. Within three years of the founding, he accumulated sufficient resources enabling him to purchase the freedom of his wife, Rosa. In 1838 the first Disciples African American church was established on free soil, organized at Pick-erelltown, Ohio, with Henry Newson serving as pastor. It became famous as an Underground Railroad station.[44]

The views of the founders on the question of slavery, so often misinterpreted or misunderstood or simply unknown, deserve mention. All Disciples founders–Thomas Campbell, Alexander Campbell, Barton Stone, and Walter Scott–are recorded as having occasionally offered modest religious education to African American slaves during the antebellum years, beginning with Thomas Campbell as early as 1819. Two of the founders owned slaves. Barton Stone inherited slaves when he married his second wife. Stone wanted to free them but could not do so in Kentucky because they would be placed back into slavery immediately. So he moved to Jacksonville, Illinois, where he could give them their freedom in a free state. Stone was a radical abolitionist who advised nonparticipation in the process of American government because of the existence of slavery.

Alexander Campbell inherited slaves when the Brown farm was deeded to him. He purchased two additional young brothers who had no family, James and Charley Pool, with the promise to free them at age twenty-eight. Campbell freed all his slaves, stating, "I have set free from slavery every human being that came in any way under my influence or was my property." He presented a resolution at the Virginia Constitutional Convention in 1829 to abolish slavery, but it failed by a vote of 73 to 58. In the late 1840s he attempted to abolish slavery in Kentucky when the state was rewriting its constitution. Again he failed. Part of his Kentucky effort included–at his own expense–publishing a pamphlet, *Tract to the People of Kentucky,* opposing slavery and circulating it throughout the state at the time of its constitutional debates. His *political* position on slavery was expressed freely and without reserve:

> I most sincerely and conscientiously, for many years,…have
> been so much opposed to American slavery because of its abuses

and liabilities to abuse–because of its demoralizing influence upon society through these abuses–because of its impoverishing operations upon the states and communities…that I am a candid and fearless advocate in my political relations, of a state constitutional termination of it by a gradual approach.

In a series of thirteen articles on the subject, eight entitled "Our Position to American Slavery," published in 1845 after long study and one year after the Methodist Church divided over the issue, his position, "not as a politician or economist but as a *Christian*," was made public:

- Slavery is not condemned in the Bible; therefore slavery *is a matter of opinion, not of faith*; slaveholders should not be excluded from the church. Slavery is not a test of Christian fellowship. The Bible sanctions the relation of master and slave.
- Slavery is economically and morally dangerous; Christians may properly oppose it. Slavery is not in harmony with the spirit of the age nor the moral advancement of society.
- Christian unity is more important than political agreement.

Many Disciples of the period, like Campbell, were anti-slavery moderates–opposed to what was considered the radical wing of the abolitionists, who were also outspoken critics of organized religion and advocates of women's rights–favoring *gradual* emancipation through legal and moral means. Campbell was repelled by the frenetic publications and disputatious conduct of uncompromising abolitionists, believing them as great an evil as slavery itself. His lodestar statement, "I have always been anti-slavery, but never an abolitionist," echoed the language used by Abraham Lincoln in 1837 to author a protest to a bill before the Illinois Legislature regarding the issue of slavery: "The institution of slavery is founded on both injustice and bad policy… The promulgation of abolition doctrines tends rather to increase than to abate [slavery's] evils." But the moderate anti-slavery position became increasingly unsatisfactory, and Campbell's attempt to be a moderate on the subject as well as a judicious church leader caused him to be criticized by the immoderate extremists as both "anti-slavery" and "pro-slavery." Fearing the issue could divide the young Movement, as it had the Methodists, Presbyterians, and Baptists, Campbell–like many of his contemporary religious colleagues, including Lyman Beecher, who asked Presbyterians to prohibit discussion of slavery because it would break the "silken ties" between Northern and Southern Presbyterians–hoped a mediating position would hold the Disciples together as one people. He fell back on the formula of Meldinius, "In essentials unity, in non-essentials (opinions) freedom, in all things charity." An unyielding commitment to Disciples unity was more important to him than his unequivocal opposition and personal aversion to slavery. In his words, *My grand object*

is to preserve unity of spirit among Christians of the South and of the North. He
stated further:

> Every man who loves American union, as well as every man who
> desires a constitutional end of American slavery, is bound to prevent
> as far as possible, any breach of communion between Christians at
> the South and at the North.

Less than twenty years later, President Abraham Lincoln would echo
Campbell's words:

> *My paramount object in this struggle is to save the Union,* and is not either
> to save or to destroy slavery. If I could save the Union without
> freeing any slave I would do it, and if I could save it by freeing all
> the slaves I would do it…. What I do about slavery I do to save
> the Union… I intend no modification of my oft-xpressed personal
> wish that all men everywhere could be free.

Both Campbell and Lincoln felt tension between their personal wishes and
what they considered "a higher obligation." In the context of his passionate
concern for Christian unity and his desire to be biblical in all things, using
the Meldinian formula seemed logical to Campbell. Christians could differ,
he believed, but remain united.[45]

The 1863 emancipation came to mean religious separation as well
as civil separation. "Negroes" were encouraged to organize into separate
bodies. R. H. Peoples reminds us, however, "the separation of the two
into distinct churches was a gradual process." Partly due to exclusion from
participation in Disciples structures, African American Disciples evolved
into a "parallel universe." This was manifested in the development of
Assembly churches in North Carolina with their bishops and alternative
structures. The walls of separateness did not begin to break down until
Disciples restructure in the 1960s, with conscious attempts to include African
American and other Disciples from excluded groups in staff positions and
on general unit and regional boards.

Between 1866 and 1876, black evangelists Samuel Buckner (1820–1904)
and Alexander Campbell, both from Midway, established thirty African
American congregations in Kentucky. Evangelists in North Carolina
baptized 3,000 new members. Seven congregations were established in
Georgia, where Mrs. Emily Tubman gave financial support to employ a
black evangelist. Nine were started in Tennessee; and twenty in Mississippi
were created primarily through the efforts of the Mississippi Negro evangelist Elder Eleven Woods (also known as Levin Wood) from Jeff Davis
Bend, Louisiana. The Baptist church in Grand Gulf, Mississippi, a cotton
landing and loading town where Woods had founded the first black Disciples
congregation in the state, had civil authorities arrest Woods for heresy.
The judge required Woods to preach a sermon for him; satisfied, the judge

released him. By 1876 African American congregations had been established in fifteen states. The principal sources of financial support were donations, including money, land, buildings, and legal advice from benevolent individuals such as Ovid Butler in Indianapolis, Indiana; offerings from local congregations; and finally meager support from Disciples state and general missionary societies. However, setting a special offering for African American home mission work did not occur until 1891.[46]

The first post-war national convention of "colored" Disciples was held in 1867 when Rufus Conrad founded the American Christian Evangelizing and Education Association in Nashville, Tennessee. That same year Charles Loos and Robert Milligan formed the Freedman's Missionary Society; but due to lack of support it ceased to exist in 1870. Preston Taylor (1849–1931) and H. Malcom Ayers organized a more permanent national convention for black Disciples in 1878. From the end of Reconstruction in 1876 to around the turn of the century, the height of the "Jim Crow" era and also the era known culturally as the Age of Black Renaissance–the age of W.E.B. DuBois, Frederick Douglass, and Booker T. Washington–African American Disciples suffered through a painful time as they addressed three priorities: evangelism, organization of conventions, and education. Robert Jordan wrote of their needs:

> After the Negro was housed in his own churches, problems of maintenance, evangelism and education confronted him. Most of the leaders could not read. They had been trained to remember that which was told them. To preach and sing was all they knew. To develop worship programs, finance undertakings and develop leadership to continue the work, left them bewildered.

To address these issues, black leadership constituted numerous area and state conventions. They met regularly in national gatherings for fellowship and cooperative planning. At least three periodicals were launched to help inform the membership: *Assembly Standard, Christian Soldier,* and *The Gospel Plea.* Several educational institutions were established, although only three survived into the twentieth century. One of these was the storied Southern Christian Institute founded in 1881 near Edwards, Mississippi. The Institute, under the aegis of the ACMS, took great pride in having graduated Jacob Kenoly (1876–1911), son of former Alabama slaves, second of thirteen children, who became a famous missionary to Liberia. SCI merged with Tougaloo College in 1954, located in Jackson, Mississippi.[47]

Among the outstanding African American Disciples leaders was a husband and wife team, Mancil (1864–1928) and Sarah Bostick (1868–1948), pioneers in home missions and founders of numerous congregations in Arkansas and neighboring states. But the most inspiring leader of African American Disciples during this period was Preston Taylor, born into slavery in Shreveport, Louisiana, November 7, 1849. At age fifteen he enlisted as a drummer with the Union Army and participated in the siege of Richmond and Petersburg, Virginia. He witnessed the surrender of Lee to Grant at Appomattox in 1865. After the war he attended school, became a porter on the Louisville and Chattanooga railroad, and at age twenty became an elder in a black Disciples congregation in Kentucky founded by Samuel Buckner. Taylor decided to enter the ministry and for fifteen years served as minister to the High Street Christian Church in Mt. Sterling, Kentucky. When the Big Sandy railroad was being built from Mt. Sterling to Richmond, officials refused to hire Negro labor. Taylor bought two sections of the work and provided employment opportunities for African Americans. In 1883 he was named National Evangelist by the General Christian Missionary convention, but given little support. He also began editing a column entitled "Our Colored Brethren" for the *Christian Standard.* Having previously worked four years for an undertaker to supplement his income, he decided in 1888 to establish his own mortuary and by 1899 purchased thirty-seven acres that would become Greenwood Cemetery near Nashville, Tennessee. He became widely known for his generous philanthropy. Booker T. Washington wrote of Taylor: "Through his own warm and tender feeling for suffering humanity, individual help, solicitations from friends, he was enabled to feed, warm, and clothe almost a thousand suffering poor people and shield them from the cold."

On August 5, 1917, forty-one persons from fourteen states, responding to a call sent out by Preston Taylor, gathered in Nashville. It was the first meeting of the National Christian Missionary Convention, and Preston Taylor accepted election as President. It adopted the purpose of "self-expression, cooperation, and to develop an informed laity and learned clergy to lead in a Christian world." Attending the gathering were Robert Hopkins of the ACMS; Anna Atwater of the CWBM; Stephen Corey of the FCMS; and Joel Baer Lehman, former president of Southern Christian Institute, named in 1912 Superintendent of Missions and Schools for Negro work in the CWBM. The National Christian Missionary Convention became an auxiliary to the Disciples International Convention. At the 1920 NCMC gathering, Taylor's address, reflecting his tenacious spirit, included the famous remark, "Push and pull until the fullest realization of our work is realized." He died in 1931, leaving his estate to the National Christian Missionary Convention.[48]

In 1900 there were 307 African American Disciples congregations scattered across twenty-one states, with more than 33,000 members. By 1914 the membership had grown to 48,000. J. B. Lehman had a significant impact upon African American Disciples. In 1913 he launched a campaign to raise a "jubilee gift for mission." Favoring a paternalistic approach to his work, Lehman selected black pastors and evangelists, determined their length of service, deployed them to eighteen states, expected them to raise funds from the congregations, and provided to each one a modest stipend of $16.66 to $50 per month. During Lehman's tenure Jarvis Christian Institute was established in Hawkins, Texas, in 1913, under the auspices of the CWBM. The school, later becoming a College, provided education for blacks. Lehman, the primary negotiator for purchasing the properties and guiding the establishment of Jarvis, also determined the budget, employed the personnel, and involved himself in the day-to-day operations of the school. [49]

When the total number of black congregations reached 500 in 1944, an expanded partnership was created between the NCMC and the UCMS. Following restructure in 1969 the African American membership abandoned their annual assemblies in favor of a biennial National Convocation of the Christian Church (Disciples of Christ), placing the Administrative Secretary of the Convocation in the office of General Minister and President. The old NCMC was dissolved and black administrators, including the beloved Emmett Dickson and Lorenzo Evans, transferred into the new DHM structure serving the whole church. This enabled African American congregations to receive program services through a united structure. By 1973 the first African American, Walter Bingham (1921–2006), became moderator of the Christian Church (Disciples of Christ). John Compton (1925–2003) became the first black regional minister elected in 1979; and in 1982 he became the first black general unit president leading the Division of Homeland Ministries. The grand old servant of African American Disciples during the modern era was Dr. William K. Fox (1917–2005), Administrative Secretary of the National Convocation and Deputy General Minister and President—succeeded in later years by William Hannah, John Foulkes, and Timothy James.[50]

During the last half of the twentieth century a new generation of seminary-educated African American leaders brought many changes to the life of this cultural expression. By 2005, an African American female, Lois Artis, became one the candidates considered for the office of General Minister and President.

World War II was an important benchmark in what Leon Litwack calls the "African American odyssey." It is considered the opening event in the civil rights revolution that followed. Langston Hughes gave poignant statement to this fact in the opening line of his poem *Jim Crow's Last Stand*: "Pearl Harbor put Jim Crow on the run." The civil rights revolution stands out as a signature event in the late twentieth century. Litwack wrote of it:

> In the 1860s, and a century later in the 1960s, two major struggles, two major civil conflicts were fought over the meaning of freedom in America: over the enslavement of black people and over the legally sanctioned repression of their descendants, over the bonds of slavery and the bonds of segregation and economic strangulation.

Litwack noted, however, that despite court decisions, legislation, and confrontations, racism persisted and the nation remained "separate and unequal." But the civil rights revolution provided the environmental context for a newly evolving relationship between African Americans and the Christian Church (Disciples of Christ) during those decades.[51]

In May 1989, an African American Network of seventy black Disciples met in Indianapolis as "an open/voluntary connection…committed to sharing information regarding issues affecting African American Disciples of Christ." They concluded African American Disciples could enrich the wholeness within the body of Christ by affirming African American heritage, values, and identity and by sharing resources. Among the largest Disciples congregations, with memberships each over 2,000 in 2008, are four African American congregations: *Ray of Hope* in Atlanta, *Light of the World* in Indianapolis, *Mississippi Boulevard* in Memphis, and *New Direction Christian Church,* also in Memphis.[52]

The journey toward wholeness continued. Rosa Page Welch wrote eloquently, "Rivers need not divide. They often connect." An African American Disciples educator and vice-moderator of the Disciples, Dr. Ann E. Dickerson (1936–1975), just a few weeks before her untimely death, elaborated upon this thought with profound insight.

> If the Christian Church (Disciples of Christ) in the United States and Canada is to experience a wholeness, it must accept the legitimacy of black thought, black opinion, and black worship styles. The spiritual and evangelical nature of the black church, as expressed among Disciples, provides renewal of an evangelical spirit within the church that goes even beyond the gift of blacks to the church.[53]

CHAPTER VI

Division and Restructure

The Road to Disunion: 1968

We sound a call to all Disciples:

*That we sink into oblivion the particularisms that divide us as a people
and rally ourselves to a supreme and common effort for the realization of
Christian unity, beginning each one with himself...*

*That we evaluate our differences by treating them for what they really
are, opinions which are subjects for free and open discussion, and which
all are free to accept or reject, answering only to Christ...*

*That we rise to a new sense of our mission and our mission to the world,
noting their essential interdependence; for only if the Churches hear our
Lord's prayer for unity may we expect the world to believe.*

COMMISSION ON RESTUDY,
International Convention, 1948

Although overwhelmingly approved by the San Francisco International
Convention in 1948, the report of the Commission on Restudy, a serious
attempt at internal unity, eloquent in presentation and fourteen years in
the making, was met with a deaf ear. In fact the movement's journalists
essentially ignored it. The 'Commission on Restudy of the Disciples of
Christ,' appointed in 1934 by the International Convention to reconcile a
growing breach within the "Brotherhood," contained some of the movement's most influential figures. A representative few are named here to
demonstrate the quality of leaders that authored the report:

Ames, Edward Scribner
Buckner, George Walker Jr.
Burnham, F. W.
Corey, Abram E.
Elliott, Virgil L.
England, Stephen J.
Errett, Edwin R.
Fortune, A. W.
Frank, Graham
Garrison, Winfred E.
Harmon, Henry G.
Jones, Edgar DeWitt
Kershner, Frederick D.

Lemmon, Clarence E.
Long, Robert A.
Miller, Raphael H.
Morrison, Charles Clayton
Murch, James DeForest
Sadler, Magruder E.
Shelton, Orman L.
Sias, G. Gerald
Smith, T. K.
Sweeny, Zachary T.
Walker, Dean E.
Wells, L. N. D.
Welshimer, P. H.

The year 1948 marked a juncture slightly beyond the mid-point in what Stephen J. Corey labeled *Fifty Years of Attack and Controversy*, fifty years of gradual disintegration of a relationship between the Christian Church (Disciples of Christ) and the Christian Churches–Churches of Christ (also known as Independent Christian Churches, Undenominational Fellowship of Christian Churches–Churches of Christ, and Direct Support Christian Churches–Churches of Christ, but most commonly as "Independents" in order to distinguish them from "Cooperatives"). Historians have suggested several dates for the official separation, ranging from the first North American Christian Convention in 1927 to the restructure of the Christian Church (Disciples of Christ) in 1968. Some, including A. T. DeGroot, say the separation came with the publication of a directory of ministers in 1955 by the "Undenominational Fellowship of Christian Churches–Churches of Christ." Others suggest it did not become official until publication of the *Year Book* of the Disciples of Christ in 1971, the first not to include Christian Churches–Churches of Christ in the listing–by request of individual congregations. Still others, like James DeForest Murch, cite as the major turning point the election of Clarence E. Lemmon, an avowed advocate of open membership, as president of the International Convention in 1942 over the objection of a vocal minority. Murch further cited the Study Commission's failed effort to bring reconciliation through its 1948 report as another turning point. Officially, no complete break of fellowship occurred in 1927, nor on any of the other dates until the conclusion of restructure in 1968, probably the most reasonable date to fix the official division, despite the fact the Disciples' *Year Book* declined to acknowledge it for three years while exerting efforts toward reconciliation.[1]

Stated in different ways by different scholars, historians say that three traditional points of disagreement produced the second division within the Movement: (a) the theological development of Modernism; (b) the twentieth-century emergence of ecumenism; and (c) open membership.

These points of disagreement, however, appear rooted in an underlying contest for power and authority within the Movement; an increasing level of educational attainment by a sizeable portion of the Movement's moderate/progressive ministers (two very different paths to ministerial education existed–Disciples via seminary and Christian Churches–Churches of Christ via Bible College); and a societal shift from a small town to a cosmopolitan mind-set.

Theological Development of Modernism

Transforming developments in American intellectual life, particularly the demanding historical and literary analysis of scriptures, were deeply troubling to legalistic restorationists. Progressives, on the other hand, found their imaginations fired by openness to new truths. Conservatives viewed the modern methodology of "Higher Criticism" (the use of scientific historical method to determine authorship, date, and circumstances for writing; literary style; together with the use of findings through archaeology; etc.) as intolerable. Alexander Campbell advocated reading the Bible and analyzing it like any other book. But to twentieth-century scholastics the Bible was the product of divine revelation, not subject to this sort of human analysis. Edwin V. Hayden maintained in his *Fifty Years of Digression and Disturbance* the divisive issue was simply the "acceptance or rejection of the Bible as the Word of God."

M. Eugene Boring, in his 1997 *Disciples and the Bible: A History of Disciples Biblical Interpretation in North America,* provided insightful perspective on the conflict over "modernism" by comparing two prominent figures in the movement: John William McGarvey (1829–1911) and Herbert Lockwood Willett (1864–1944). Boring thoughtfully concluded: "In these two men, their institutions, writings and careers Disciples may see an embodiment and reflection of themselves…at the turn of the century."

J. W. McGarvey, symbol of the old tradition of biblical scholasticism, was born in Kentucky, raised in Illinois and enrolled at Bethany College at age eighteen. He studied with the first-generation faculty of the college, including both Thomas and Alexander Campbell. After graduation he pastored in Missouri until 1862 when he responded to a call from the Main Street Christian Church in Lexington, Kentucky. The College of the Bible soon moved to Lexington and in 1865 President Robert Milligan appointed McGarvey its first professor of Sacred History. He remained a commanding figure in the college until his death. During those years he created a model of ministerial education, yielding two generations of Disciples ministers.[2]

Herbert Willett–symbol of the newly emerging methodology for interpreting the scriptures, born and raised in Ionia, Michigan–fell under the formidable influence of his family's pastor, Isaac Errett. At age nineteen Willett entered Bethany College, graduating with both an A.B. and a M.A. in 1887. The second-generation faculty taught him the Bible was inerrant and he should reject biblical criticism. President Woolery, however, advised Willett to continue his education at an eastern university. He subsequently enrolled at Yale in 1891, and found it a transforming experience. He moved on to the University of Chicago where he earned a Ph.D. in 1896–the first Disciple to earn the Ph.D. degree. He pursued post-doctoral work in Germany. From 1894 to 1921 he served as Dean of the Disciples Divinity House at the University of Chicago where he taught the first course ever offered in Disciples History.[3]

Both men were scholars, theologians, educators, and published authors. Their differences, however, were pronounced. McGarvey, fixed and rigid, represented the conservative, rural, traditional mind-set of America. Peter Ainslie III, a student of the legalistic McGarvey, said of him, "had he become a lawyer he would have been one of the greatest lawyers of his time." He lived all his life in the country, most of it in the small town of Lexington where the population did not reach 10,000 until 1900. Willett, committed to growth and change, spent his maturing years in Chicago (pop. 1,700,000 in 1900), New Haven, and Berlin, thereby forming a more cosmopolitan, progressive perspective. He read German and knew personally some of the "higher critics." McGarvey believed truth to be absolute. One authoritative answer existed for every question. Exclusive in perspective, he saw church history as a story of decline from the days of the New Testament church, and believed higher criticism (which he labeled "rationalistic destructive higher criticism of the Germans") to be an enemy from which he had to protect his students and the church; and he criticized the scientific theory of evolution as evil. Boring quotes McGarvey as having written in his "Biblical Criticism" column for the *Christian Standard,* "The Scriptures are not to be tested by the science of chemistry, or that of astronomy, or that of geology, or that of mathematics, but by the science of logic… Reason must determine for us whether the Bible is from God."

Herbert Willett, driven by the concept of growth toward a higher truth, believed in relativism, exhibited an inclusive perspective, saw church history as a story of progress revealing new insights, and saw higher criticism as a tool to enlighten lay understanding of the scriptures. He welcomed evolution as a door to new truths. In Willett's classes at Chicago students were taught on a graduate level of instruction, encouraged to explore a variety of sources in a large library, prodded to listen to many points of view from a variety of faculty, and make up their own minds. Students were required to study the biblical languages of Greek and Hebrew. McGarvey's College of the Bible, by contrast, was a center of pedagogical indoctrination with instruction on an undergraduate and junior college level. Students who studied under McGarvey were required to use his four volumes *Class Notes on Sacred History* as their textbook. Colby Hall, a former student who became professor and dean of Brite College of the Bible, recalled, "Never did he suggest we use the college library." Bible colleges did not offer graduate work, the ministerial track being combined with college undergraduate studies. Students at Lexington were rarely referred to books beyond the Bible or those written by McGarvey. The library did not need to be large or up to date. It was reported in 1905 that fifty-six books were added to the library and only 240 books circulated during the whole year. Students used an English translation of the scripture rather than engage in intense use of biblical languages. Boring summarized this educational model:

> The College of the Bible of that era was not a research center but a propaganda institution. McGarvey…saw his function as teacher to serve as a guardian for the ministry and the church. He would read the critical studies digest and respond to them, and deliver the results to his students and the church at large, whom he did not encourage to read and think for themselves. McGarvey stood between the critics and the people, to guard them, because he did not respect or trust them. "Father McGarvey" might better express this paternalistic kind of populism better than "Brother McGarvey."

By way of comparison, Boring offered Willett's descriptive judgment of higher criticism:

> The Higher Criticism has forever disposed of the fetish of a level Bible; it has destroyed doctrine of verbal inspiration; it has set in proper light the partial and primitive ethics of the Hebrew people; it has relieved the church of the responsibility of defending ancient social abuses which received popular and even prophetic sanction in Old Testament Times; it has made faith easier and more confident;…it has enabled us to understand the varying testimonies to the life of Jesus and the divergent tendencies of the apostolic age; and most of all it has explained the seeming contradictions and conflicts of biblical statement which were in former periods the target of…successful attack.[4]

The question troubling Disciples was: *Should they continue to follow the path of McGarvey or should they adopt the new methodology and worldview of Willett?* The approaches were irreconcilable, and the choice between the two polarized the Movement. A growing number of Disciples ministers elected to study beyond their undergraduate degrees and several chose Yale, Harvard, Princeton, Union, and the University of Chicago. By 1920, 105 Disciples had seminary degrees from Yale and forty-eight from Chicago, numbers that continued to grow and provide a key source of leadership for progressive Disciples. Among them were Edward Scribner Ames, Minor Lee Bates, Stephen J. Corey, A. W. Fortune, W. E. Garrison, Burris Jenkins, Frederick Kershner, Clinton Lockhart, Raphael Miller, Herbert Moninger, H. O. Pritchard, L.N.D. Wells, and Herbert Willett. A few formed the Campbell Institute at the University of Chicago and issued a periodical called *The Scroll.* The *Christian Standard,* now the confirmed voice for the McGarvey methodology, resented the apparent superior learning at Chicago and sensed a threat to the old model of biblical scholasticism. It relentlessly attacked the Campbell Institute and its magazine. Members of the Institute were repeatedly called "High Brows," "Radical Liberals," "Unbelievers," "Heretics." and "Infidels." With scorn and derision, McGarvey regularly attacked Willett's weekly Sunday school commentary, written for *The Christian-Evangelist*; and the *Standard* launched a concerted effort to prevent Willett from being a speaker at the 1909 centennial celebration of Disciples. Willett remained on the program and spoke to an overflow audience. When the *Standard* discovered one of its employees, Herb Moninger, favored higher criticism, he was dismissed.[5]

The death of McGarvey in 1911, coupled with the departure of nearly all College of the Bible faculty members by retirement or death within three years, resulted in the hiring of a new faculty. The new faculty–A. W. Fortune (1873–1950), William Clayton Bower (1878–1982), George Hemry (1874–1924), and Elmer E. Snoddy (1863–1936)–were sympathetic to new methods of biblical research and new methods of teaching, including library research, extensive reading, and graduate level education. Many of the students at the College of the Bible had only a high school education or modest preparatory training. They found adjusting to the new methods difficult. A few students began reporting comments of the professors to the Academic Dean, Hall Calhoun, who had been groomed for the presidency by McGarvey and thought he should have been named to the post when McGarvey died. The information from the students was then forwarded to the *Christian Standard*. Appalled at the thought of progressives teaching at their beloved College of the Bible, characterized by George Beazley Jr. as the "stronghold of scholasticism," proponents of Disciple scholasticism (insistence on traditional doctrine), in April 1917, used the *Standard* to call for a "heresy" investigation on the claim new faculty were "modernists." The so-called "heresy trial" became a sensation among Disciples. Three issues were at stake: (a) academic freedom, (b) the right to teach higher criticism, and (c) trustworthiness of the trustees. In May the professors were exonerated of all charges, but the *Christian Standard* continued its vigorous attacks on the faculty of the College of the Bible through 1919, when it shifted its focus to the United Christian Missionary Society.[6]

The outcome was threefold: (a) a deepening estrangement between two factions within the Movement; (b) a shift in thinking for many in the Movement about how to approach the Bible, about theology, and about how ministers ought to be educated; and (c) establishment of the new theology as the predominant intellectual force among Disciples for the next forty years. Following the heresy trial at the College of the Bible, conservatives established two new institutions in 1923: McGarvey Bible

College in Louisville and the Cincinnati Bible College in Cincinnati. This was a harbinger of coming separation. Within a year they merged into the Cincinnati Bible Seminary. Meanwhile, the Disciples Divinity House at the University of Chicago became the intellectual center for Disciples and would remain so for several years. The new methodologies of ministerial preparation took root in most Disciples houses of learning, a model committed to intellectual openness. Ronald Osborn observed of the new methodology leaders: "Through their teaching and writing, and that of their students, they brought home to Disciples, too long isolated from the currents of contemporary thinking, the full impact of liberalism."[7]

Emergence of Ecumenism

Ecumenical stirrings gave religious identity to the twentieth century, but were viewed with alarm by the conservative element within the Disciples Movement and by their unrivaled periodical, the *Christian Standard*. In some respects the issue appeared to resurrect old tensions between *restoration* and *unity* within the Stone-Campbell Movement. The conservative element subordinated Christian unity to restoration of the primitive church, believing legalistic and exclusive conformity to the beliefs of the one true church was the primary goal of the Movement. The progressives, including the moderate/liberal mainstream of the Movement, with a more inclusive spirit and a commitment to the essential oneness of the church, held the ideal of Christian unity as the primary focus of the Movement. They were open to creative cooperation with other religious bodies. They further believed restoration had never achieved unity. It had only led to *division* over the interpretation of what restoration of the New Testament Church means. After long years of study both W. E. Garrison and A. T. DeGroot concluded the restoration principle was "divisive and not unitive." And David Harrell argued the dual plea of restoration and unity proved to be impractical. After the Civil War, Disciples chose either one or the other. As a methodology for unity, the restoration principle proved ineffective.[8]

Edwin V. Hayden cited "Federation in interdenominational activities" as one of the most provocative causes of the second division within the Movement. The Federal Council of Churches of Christ formed in 1905, with the Disciples participating as a charter member. Moderates believed the witness for unity could be strengthened by contact with other Christians. J. A. Lord, editor of the *Christian Standard* and considered by many the father of the second division in the Movement, remained convinced Disciples should not become a part of such organizations, stating "federation was a tacit approval of and concession to denominationalism" and Disciples support of the new organization compromised their nondenominational position. For progressive Disciples, federation and cooperation were synonyms, a way to avoid becoming exclusivist. Conservatives argued federation diluted the one true and pure church. From the conservative vantage point, it compromised the restoration plea and especially their position on baptism by immersion. A. T. DeGroot argued pointedly, "recognizing the denominations led to the creation of Church of Christ Number Two." He also argued:

> The Independent position...is to stand apart from the existing Christian world and to show by its life and deeds so superior a type of character that all others will join them in unconditional surrender.[9]

Opposition to interdenominational cooperation focused on the proposed United Christian Missionary Society, which restorationists saw as a means to advance the ecumenical vision of the moderate progressives. As the 1919 International Convention approached, the *Christian Standard* opened a campaign against the proposed United Christian Missionary Society. In a series of six articles entitled "Shall there be a United Missionary Society?" it claimed the new organization was an "ecclesiasticism," adding, "The conflict between the Restoration advocates and Restoration wreckers will be hot, and it will continue for...years. The propagandists [Campbell Institute and *Christian Century*] are struggling for supremacy."

By 1925 the *Standard* established an adjunct publication to specifically focus on accusations that the "Brotherhood" was "fostering denomination-alism," "cultivating ecclesiasticism," and "substituting a sectarian combine for New Testament unity." The earlier "meeting of protest" called to precede the 1919 convention included discussion of such topics as "Relation of our Co-operative agencies to the Inter-Church World Movement" and the "Attitude of Restoration Movement Toward present day Union Movements." It also discussed conservative dissatisfaction with ecumenical comity arrangements in the mission field of Mexico, which they saw resulting from "denominationalism" and the "willingness to see our own church work supplanted by others." A reallocation of districts and exchange of mission stations in Mexico had occurred in 1919 to reduce overlapping and competition with the Methodists. The *Standard* aggressively recruited persons to attend the pre-convention congress. This was the first of the Restoration protest congresses preceding each convention until 1922 when they became "competitive" conventions, and later in 1950 "permanent and separate" conventions. J. H. Garrison criticized the protestors for calling a separate congress, urging them instead to go directly to the floor of the convention. They did both. The convention debate in 1919 was long and bitter. Due to conservative fears that "modernism" was infecting the church, the debate was laced with charges that the progressive Disciples were delivering the Movement into the hands of "German rationalism." While the convention overwhelmingly approved the UCMS, those who opposed the measure did not accept defeat. Unable to impose their view in an open and democratic forum, they proceeded to attack the UCMS as a "monolith beyond control." The Society was referred to as the "UCMS Octopus," an "infidel organization," an "infidel oligarchy," "a towering super-organization unknown to the New Testament," "a deadly poison virus," "betrayers," and "You See a Mess." The *Standard's* "everlasting nagging, snarling and faultfinding" toward the UCMS would continue for fifty years. Despite the attacks, Disciples' literature and their expanding participation in all newly emerging conciliar organizations reflected a deepening commitment to cooperation and ecumenism.[10]

Open Membership

The issue of open membership was an echo from nearly a century before when controversy erupted over the 1837 Lunenburg letter. The question had then been asked, "Can the unimmersed be called Christians?" And Campbell responded yes, the "pious unimmersed" could be called Christian. Even with this response most nineteenth-century Disciples did not practice open membership, although Brush Run and a few other congregations accepted the unimmersed throughout the nineteenth century. Cooperation with other religious groups continued apace. In time, the more progressive members of the Movement began to reason that if the "pious unimmersed" could be *called* Christians they ought to be accepted into membership. Yet if they accepted the nonimmersed, they were approving a form of baptism other than that practiced in the New Testament. On the other hand, if they refused to accept unimmersed, they were deepening the divisions within the body of Christ. Conservatives believed there was no choice. Everyone, in their view, had to be immersed to be part of the one true church.

Baptism by immersion was the normative mode of baptism in both progressive and conservative Disciples congregations. Conservatives, however, loudly opposed the practice of allowing unimmersed persons to become "associate members" of a congregation. They called it a manifestation of "modernism." The conservative *Christian Standard* abhorred the practice, while the progressive *Christian Century* praised it. Influenced by an ecumenical mix in the mission fields, most Disciples missionaries became progressive in their thought, and challenged the conservative way of thinking by welcoming the practice of open membership. In 1917, reports from certain mission fields indicated selected missionaries were practicing open membership. In light of the growing cooperation of denominations on the mission fields, the practice seemed reasonable to missionaries. L. N. D. Wells observed:

> A person comes from another place to a place where there is only a Disciples church. You let him pass the emblems, teach a class, and fully fellowship with him, but you say, "I will not put your name on the church roll." I can't find anything between Genesis and Revelation that says anything about a church membership

roll except, "The Lord added to the church daily them that were being saved." Little attention is paid to a church roll on the mission field. God's people fellowship each other whenever they come together.[11]

For nearly two decades there had been union churches in cities like Tokyo, Manila, Nanking, and Shanghai, affording the opportunity for people with different religious beliefs to meet together for common worship.

But the matter sparked a vicious feud. It is said this issue generated more controversy among Disciples than any other issue in the twentieth century. The increasing numbers of congregations that actually practiced open membership did so without publicizing the fact for fear of controversy. Along with its angry editorials, the *Christian Standard* promoted a series of regional restoration congresses and "indignation" meetings to discuss the issue. John T. Brown, a UCMS employee who sympathized with the *Standard,* announced in 1921 that he would tour the mission fields to investigate for himself the work of the missionaries. Upon his return, he presented a report of approval to the UCMS; but then presented a lengthy report of disapproval to the *Standard.* The unfavorable report appeared in the October 1922 issue—irrespective of the fact the UCMS had approved a policy statement in 1922 reminding missionaries to receive into their membership "only those who are immersed," and vowing not to "appoint or continue in service" those who practiced open membership.[12]

At the 1925 International Convention in Oklahoma City, a resolution came to the floor, stating:

> Any person…now in the employment of the United Christian Missionary Society…who has committed himself or herself to belief in, or practice of, the reception of unimmersed persons into the membership…the relationship of that person to the UCMS will be severed as an employee.

Following two days of discussion the motion passed, over the strenuous objections of moderates and progressives who viewed it as intellectual policing, an infringement on freedom of thought. Trying to address the dismay and confusion in the mission field, where Brown's trip had been viewed as a "ridiculous travesty of Christian ethics" and where missionaries now feared heresy trials, the UCMS attempted to steer a middle course by declaring the resolution was "not intended to invade the right of private judgment, but only to apply to such an open agitation as would prove divisive." In the judgment of historians, the Society "lost on both counts. At home [its] actions failed to mollify the conservatives. On the Mission field [its] pragmatic response to issues at home caused Disciples to stand on the sidelines while in 1928 united churches were launched successfully in both China and the Philippines."[13]

By 1926, enraged by the UCMS interpretation of the resolution, the *Standard* and its adjunct publication, the *Touchstone,* aroused their readers to attend the Memphis convention "to save the 'brotherhood.'" The restoration congress met in the downtown Pantages Theater, appointed a Committee on Future Action and ultimately received funding from the *Standard* to assist with the next convention. It was the moment of birth for the North American Christian Convention. Within a decade the NACC would declare in the *Standard* that the NACC "cares nothing about unity with any one else."[14]

In 1934, with emotions inflamed on both sides, the convention formed a "Commission on Restudy of the Disciples of Christ" with the appointment of excellent leaders from both sides of the controversy. The Commission labored for fourteen years, finally bringing its report to the 1948 International Convention. But by this time, the sense of mutual respect for a common "Brotherhood" had soured; the warring parties had become indifferent. Neither side seemed interested in preserving unity. And the basic points of the report satisfied neither side. The report affirmed the restoration plea, claimed agencies were compromising congregational autonomy, identified immersion as the baptismal norm despite the contrary practice of a "considerable number of churches," denounced the acceptance of denominationalism and reaffirmed the concept of "Movement," and affirmed unity only through restoration. The strongest part of the report is found in its eloquent conclusion calling for internal unity. The failure of the report to rally strong support is now viewed as a decision to divide. 1948 seems to many the year when separate fellowships crystallized. The process of restructure, twenty years later, brought official partition when, variously estimated, 650,000 members in 3,500 congregations (only 3 percent of which contributed to Disciples outreach) withdrew from the "Brotherhood." The prolonged controversy resulted in a schism expressing itself in separate conventions, separate missionary support, separate groups of schools, separate periodicals, and a separate doctrinal plea.[15]

Restructure

Renewal is not just change. It is bringing the results of change into line with the continuity of our mission as the church. This is why we refer to restructure and renewal as a process. It is an endless interweaving of continuity and change, conserving the meaningful aspects of a rich and enduring tradition, but realizing it must be a tradition facilitating its own continuous renewal.

KENNETH L. TEEGARDEN
Administrative Secretary, Commission on Brotherhood Restructure
Acceptance address, 1965[16]

Kenneth Teegarden said the compelling factor in his decision to accept appointment as Administrative Secretary resided in his belief that there was a widespread general acceptance of the need for reorganization and reform. He proceeded to define the nature of the restructure process as noted above in the introductory quotation, a statement still viewed as the most incisive definition anyone has given before or since. Teegarden soberly declared not to be naïve about the outright attacks that would be made on restructure and its process.[17]

At the time of his selection as Administrative Secretary of the Commission on Brotherhood Restructure, Teegarden served as Executive Secretary of the Arkansas Christian Missionary Society. In the capacity of State Secretary he had successfully managed restructure of the region of Arkansas, leading to his selection as an original appointee to the 126-member Commission on Brotherhood Restructure in 1962.[18]

The first Administrative Secretary was George Earle Owen (1908–1993), a part-time appointment on short-term loan from the UCMS, due to an absence of funds to underwrite the position. One year later, in 1962, A. Dale Fiers (1906–2003), president of the UCMS, followed Owen as Administrative Secretary. Kenneth Teegarden succeeded Fiers.[19]

Background and Context

Inspired by the success of cooperative initiatives in the 1930s, 1940s, and 1950s, and prompted by the fact that several state societies had begun to reorganize themselves into unified entities with delegate assemblies, the Council of Agencies appointed several ad hoc committees in the early 1950s to study interagency relationships and unification. In 1958, Willard Wickizer (1899–1974), chair of the UCMS Division of Home Missions and often credited with being the "Father of Restructure," delivered to the Council of Agencies an address entitled, *Ideas for Brotherhood Restructure.* This insightful set of remarks compelled the Council to action. A brief excerpt reflects the flavor:

> [Only] in very recent days, has anyone dared to suggest that what the Disciples of Christ needs to do is to look at its total organizational structure and attempt a major restructuring that would result in more effective cooperation. Now it would seem that we have reached a degree of maturity as a religious body when such a restructuring might be faced with some hope of success.[20]

> We must come to appreciate the fact that freedom carries with it responsibility and that free persons in Christ must cooperate effectively with other free persons in Christ to accomplish those things we cannot do alone. In restructuring the brotherhood we must preserve the principle of voluntarism on the one hand, but must magnify the principle of responsibility on the other. That we have had too much of the former in the past and not enough of the latter goes without argument, but we must not be guilty of destroying the one to achieve the other. Responsible

discipleship within the framework of freedom should always be our organizational goal.

Too frequently in the past we have wanted to prove our freedom by refusing to cooperate when all the time we could have proven it just as well and far more constructively by cooperating together for the advancement of God's kingdom. Of this I am sure, it is high time our brotherhood take a look at its organized life in its totality and restructure it according to a basic plan. For too long we have been willing to add patch on patch, never moving according to a carefully worked out master plan. I believe the mood of our people would support such an undertaking at this time.[21]

With a century-long genealogy of failed attempts, what prompted the leadership during the 1950s and 1960s to believe they could succeed in a restructure effort where so many before them had met defeat? The Disciples of Christ Historical Society conducted interviews with forty-seven leaders of restructure twenty-five years after completing their work. They identified reasons for attempting restructure, and five general responses emerged.

First, it was noted by some the World Council of Churches urged all member denominations to study their structures in light of post-World War II social changes. Each denomination was to consider two questions: "Does your structure facilitate the fulfillment of the mission of the church?" "Is the structure of your church responsive to the culture and to the world of the 1950s and the 1960s?" Several member denominations began evaluating their structures and making modifications. Sydney Ahlstrom, in his *Religious History of the American People,* noted "progressive organizational reform" in some of the denominations during that era, and called it a sign of promise. By this reckoning, the Disciples' initiative in restructure did not occur in isolation, but was part of a general religious undertaking.[22]

Second, from 1920 to 1950 the increased number of Disciples agencies, both state and national, resulted in a complex, multilayered system with less than adequate coordination and accountability. Many congregations thought they were being imposed upon by state and agency financial appeals while others thought the congregations behaved as if the meaning of church began and ended with them. Sharp pleas from congregations and from the Council of Agencies demanded that an alternative be found to the freewheeling way of carrying out the mission: some practical and efficient means of cooperation. The agencies and states needed an integral unity, a responsible mode of making decisions, some sense of accountability to replace the "mine is mine and yours is an afterthought" mentality. Seven states had already begun the process of unification and had developed delegate assemblies. By 1962 the number of states with delegate assemblies doubled, which helped spur the national societies and boards to do likewise. Recent decades birthed a growing hope for an efficient, connecting relationship among congregations, states, and agencies, a hope for some form of representative delegate assembly that could engender at least modest accountability. Frustration with the lack of coordination—and the resulting desire for a major overhaul into a more efficient ecclesial architecture—was cited most often and by most people as the single most important reason for attempting restructure in the 1960s.[23]

Third, Disciples had no theology of church beyond the local congregation. But in the 1930s, 1940s, and 1950s they were, in practice, maturing into church, into something more than a loosely knit collection of congregations with agencies simply materializing as a need arose. Through the early years of Disciples history, an inadequate understanding of church produced an inadequate structure. A growing sophistication among seminary-educated Disciples clergy in the twentieth century brought a new understanding of the nature of church—what it ought to be, what it could be. Despite the growing conviction church was something more than the sum total of local congregations, Disciples did not have a way to speak as church. Yet a hunger for church persisted, a hope the Christian Church could become a reality, a hope for recognition that church existed in regions and in general agencies just as surely as in local congregations. The concept of church, well down the list of reasons at the outset of restructure, gained force as the process unfolded, and became its most compelling feature.[24]

Fourth, the growing strength of the ecumenical movement caused some to seek restructure as a prerequisite to full participation in the ecumenical movement, its councils, and its collaborative ventures. Fueled by a virtual explosion of ecumenical activity, including the establishment of the World Council of Churches in 1948, the National Council of Churches in 1950, the Consultation on Church Union in 1960, and Vatican II beginning in 1962, the momentum of ecumenism stimulated the quest for restructure in the minds of a fair number of Disciples.[25]

Fifth, the United Christian Missionary Society was a powerful Disciples agency, often resented, particularly by Independents, because it was so much larger, had so much more budget, so much more programmatic material, and exercised so much more authority and leadership than other agencies or states. Thought by some as being too big, restructure was sought by at least a few to trim back, if not break up, the UCMS.[26]

There were other reasons as well. In July 1962 Dale Fiers addressed the first meeting of the Commission on Brotherhood Restructure with remarks entitled "An Apologetic for Restructure." He began with the declaration, "[restructure] involves a fundamental reordering of Brotherhood life with principles that arise out of a fuller understanding of Church." He proceeded to identify, from his front line experience, four reasons he believed led Disciples to restructure: (a) reaching a climactic point in the long cooperative history of growing together; (b) discovering a dynamic "sense of church," the basic concept emerging in the Brotherhood's midst; (c) moving the

Movement toward unification in the state societies; and (d) insisting that appropriate unification must be achieved at the general level or the whole process would be incomplete. Then he concluded, "Church is more than a local congregation—and appropriate expression of its life must be developed at all levels structurally, functionally and promotionally. Failure to achieve this objective for Disciples of Christ is to miss the challenge of restructure in our time." It required a leader of spiritual force who had the deep respect of the people to be able to stand against one of the most cherished traditions of the Movement and say, "the local congregation is not the fullest expression of church."[27]

Each of these forces held its place in the list of motives for seeking restructure in the 1960s. Together, they made the possibility of success appear more probable than ever before, even in the face of hostile anti-institutionalism in the nation at large. Most persons who supported the restructure effort were motivated by multiple reasons, some by all of them. In the beginning, the primary impetus for restructure came from the practical need for coordination. Less powerful was the theology of church, yet in time it became the premier objective and the most telling force advancing restructure.

The Process

Process, for Disciples, is equal in importance to the end result. During the period 1962–1968, the Commission on Brotherhood Restructure, one of the great creative assemblages of modern Disciples history, met annually. Its Central Committee, composed of eighteen members, and later twenty, and still later twenty-seven, met three to four times annually, and the five-member Executive Committee met, on average, three times per year. In addition, the Commission structured itself in task forces to carry out its work:

1. Preparation of Documents dealing with Restructure [W. B. Blakemore, Chair]
2. Theological Evaluation of Recommendations [Ronald E. Osborn, Chair]
3. Program Structures of the Brotherhood [James A. Moak, Chair]
4. Promotional Structures in the Brotherhood [Spencer P. Austin, Chair]
5. Structure of the Local Church [Jo M. Riley, Chair]
6. Ecumenical Relationship of the Brotherhood [Virgil A. Sly, Chair]
7. Restructure Participation Meetings [Harrell A. Rea, Chair]
8. Nature, Design and Authority[W. A. Welsh, Chair]
9. Ministry [Paul S. Stauffer, Chair]

A dedicated and determined group of Disciples leaders undertook a bold venture in ecclesial ideals. In education, ecumenical perspective, involvement in Brotherhood life beyond the congregation, and urban location of their congregations, the members of the Commission and its Central Committee reflected the characteristics of cooperatives. Church historian Anthony Dunnavant in his seminal work, *Restructure,* provided a useful profile of the Commission: 34 lay persons, 91 ministers; 17 women, 108 men; 30 from congregations of 500 members or fewer and 95 from those that were larger. Dunnavant also analyzed the eighteen-member Central Committee, concluding it was representative of the Commission at large:

- Thirteen of the eighteen were ministers.
- Nine of the thirteen ministers received their theological education at non-Disciples institutions (Chicago, Yale, Union).
- Four of the thirteen were local pastors, two were state secretaries, four were national agency staff, three were educators.
- Four of five lay members were members of national agency boards.
- Twelve of the eighteen were active in the National Council of Churches, four in the World Council of Churches and fifteen in the Council on Christian Unity.
- Thirteen of the eighteen members were from cities with populations of more than 250,000; no one from a city less than 25,000.

Chair of the Commission was Granville Walker (1908–1991), a Ph.D. graduate of Yale, former Chair of the Bible department at Texas Christian University, author of *Preaching in the Thought of Alexander Campbell,* and pastor of the 3,500 member University Christian Church in Fort Worth, Texas. The appointed composition of the Commission and the Central Committee, a gathering of talent unlikely to be surpassed, became a subject of criticism for some; but to constitute the Commission otherwise, with a profile adverse to recent cooperative trends, would likely have resulted in adding still another failure to the historic list of unsuccessful attempts to achieve Alexander Campbell's vision of effective organization for Disciples.[28]

At the start of its work in 1962, the Commission requested a budget of $52,000 for its' ministry, but was granted only $20,000, thereby creating an annual scramble for funds that always left it undersubscribed. Until Kenneth Teegarden came to the post of Administrative Secretary, it was uncompensated. But with his arrival a budget of $64,000 was finally approved and funded to support the Commission's work. Slightly more than $18,000 of that amount paid for travel expenses for the Commission and its committees. Another $18,000 was budgeted for interpretation. A third budget component of $18,000 underwrote the salaries of Dr. Teegarden and his secretary, along with insurance, pension, taxes, and housing. The final $10,000 covered postage, equipment, office supplies, telephone, printing, rent, and cost sharing in Missions building. At the end of his first year total budget expenditures of $57,375 were reported, with a surplus of $6,625.[29]

In his opening remarks to the June 1965 Commission meeting, Teegarden advised, "we must enjoin the task of interpretation in a more definitive way." Working in collaboration with James Suggs, the professional director of interpretation for the Commission (an extension of his paid role as director of the Office of Interpretation for the International Convention), Teegarden used the next several months to prepare and circulate a thirty-two-page study booklet, *The Direction in Brotherhood Restructure.* Copies of this piece were mailed to every congregation as well as distributed at thirteen regional assemblies. Three restructure leaflets were authored and printed, of which 275,000 copies of each were distributed church wide. The filmstrip, "Brotherhood Restructure: A Process of Growing Up," was produced, with a copy placed in every state and area office, while brochures describing the filmstrip were sent to every congregation, with copies of the strip made available for use upon request through the office of the Commission. A special edition of *The Christian* was arranged based on the study booklet, with reprints available in quantity for congregational distribution. Further, a schedule of articles appeared in *World Call* during 1966. Robert Friedly became a member of the interpretation staff in 1966 to cover the regular responsibilities in Jim Suggs' portfolio, thereby allowing him to concentrate on restructure interpretation. This immense interpretation effort transpired through the desire to assure full and accurate information circulated to all publications, congregations, state societies, and agencies.

An International Convention was not held in 1965. In lieu of a Convention several regional assemblies, or mini-conventions, were organized, each of three days' duration: four in the East, four in the South, and four in the West. Collectively, these mini-conventions attracted a total of 15,000 people. Each geographic cluster had a team assignment. Dale Fiers was the team leader for assemblies in the East; Howard Dentler (b. 1922) for assemblies in the West; and Kenneth Teegarden for assemblies in the South. In each of the mini-conventions the thirty-two-page booklet, *The Direction of Brotherhood Restructure,* received an in-depth review, generating informative interaction between the teams and those who attended. The booklet identified seven principles guiding the work of the commission.

1. The Brotherhood seeks structures rooted in Christ's Ministry
2. The Brotherhood seeks structures that are comprehensive in Ministry and Mission
3. The Brotherhood seeks structures by which Congregations may fulfill their Ministries
4. The Brotherhood seeks structures that are responsibly Inter-Related
5. The Brotherhood seeks structures that manifest both Unity and Diversity
6. The Brotherhood seeks to be Ecumenical
7. The Brotherhood seeks to be faithful in Stewardship[30]

It is estimated that from 1965 through 1968 Kenneth Teegarden conducted restructure sessions before approximately 340 Disciples associations, boards, institutes, councils, states, areas, regions, and organizations; 150 local congregations; and three International Conventions (Dallas, St. Louis, and Kansas City)–reaching a total of at least 40,000 persons. The massive effort of 1965 succeeded in placing the purpose and work of restructure on the radar screen for large segments of the membership.[31]

By June 1965 the Commission had been in existence three years, and the Board of Directors of the International Convention voted in February to "request the Commission on Brotherhood Restructure to exert every effort to complete their basic work by the St. Louis Convention, October, 1967." One of the prominent themes of discussion in the June meeting centered on the question of an intermediate manifestation of church–region, zone, diocese, state, area, district, or no intermediate body at all. Late in the plenary session national, regional, and congregational "manifestations" were proposed and approved. The word *manifestation* was used to help the membership avoid thinking in terms of "levels" of church life, and particularly to relieve congregations from thinking of themselves as the bottom level, subservient to the other two. Rather, everyone was on an equal playing field, one church without top or bottom.[32]

Kenneth Teegarden, as Administrative Secretary, prepared the first draft of a "pre-constitutional document." A second draft, accompanied by an invitation for written comments, circulated in February to all Central Committee members. As scheduled, the "pre-constitution" or "provisional design" document (as yet unnamed) was presented to the Central Committee in March 1966. The committee granted approval to present the document to the full Commission in July, to the Dallas International Convention in October 1966, and to the St. Louis International Convention in 1967. A second motion instructed the Executive Committee to prepare a report on the steps needed for the provisional establishment and implementation of the Christian Church constituting assembly.[33]

On Tuesday, July 5, 1966, in Cincinnati, Ohio, "A Provisional Design for the Christian Church (Disciples of Christ)" was presented to the 112 members attending the Commission on Brotherhood Restructure. Following a period of questions, clarification, and general comment, the Commission divided into six small groups and spent an entire day editing the document paragraph by paragraph, noting their suggested revisions–which a re-writing committee, led by Teegarden, incorporated into the document that evening. On Thursday, July 7, in plenary, the "Provisional Design" was reviewed once again, with approval coming paragraph by paragraph. W.B. Blakemore (1911–1975), along with six others–Ronald Osborn (1917–1998), Kenneth Teegarden, Granville Walker, Dale Fiers, W.A. Welsh (1917–1996), and Albert Pennybacker–labored for weeks contributing language for the preamble. The preamble, in reality the *Covenant* in preamble language, appears today in congregational bulletins, in the *Chalice Hymnal,* and Disciples literature across the church. The concluding motion came from Dale Fiers, "That the final article be approved as amended…[and] that the "Design" be submitted to the Dallas assembly." A seven-word sentence appeared in the minutes recording one of the most important benchmarks in Disciples history — *"The entire document, as revised, was approved."*[34]

Two more years of labor remained. The next major test was later that same year, at the Dallas International Convention, 1966. At the business sessions in Dallas a panel of commissioners seated on the platform before the convention were peppered with questions about the "Provisional Design." At the end of the final session came a vote of approval to receive the document and transmit it to congregations, agencies, regions, and institutions for study and response, with the goal of provisionally constituting the international manifestation of the church under the "Design" at the 1967 St. Louis International Convention. The Dallas vote of more than two-thirds in support of this action constituted an affirmation for the Commission, and more importantly for the church. Significantly, the Dallas assembly approved representative assemblies (Teegarden always corrected anyone who used the term delegate instead of *representative*) for the future, with each congregation represented by at least two voting representatives and an incremental increase if the membership exceeded 750. A later modification set representation at two per congregation plus one for each additional 500 participating members over the first 500 or portion thereof.[35]

The Commission established a consultative process between the Central Committee and the state and area secretaries to help define the work of regions and regional ministers. A Task Committee on Regions, chaired by W. A. Welsh was confirmed; and at the November meeting the Commission voted to invite all State Secretaries not on the Commission to participate. During the remaining months of its existence much of the Commission's effort focused on the issue of regions. It fell to Kenneth Teegarden during these months to negotiate a merger between the National Christian Missionary Convention and the International Convention. The negotiation was successful. Emerging from this was the National Convocation. Significantly, the Administrator for the National Convocation came into the office of the General Minister and President and several Convocation staff positions for ministerial support and education relocated to the Division of Homeland Ministries—along with an endowment to support them. Raymond Brown remembered real differences of opinion, but Kenneth Teegarden "stayed in there and worked until he found a solution agreeable to everybody."[36]

When the Commission met January 11, 1967, Teegarden reported 225,000 copies of the "Provisional Design" were in circulation, with orders still being received at a steady pace, pushing the publication of the "Provisional Design" into its third printing. Of the 9,000 responses in hand on that date, only a small percentage was negative. He further reported delivering a presentation on *The Role of State Ministers and State Organizations in Interpreting and Implementing Restructure* to the Conference of State and Area Secretaries and Board Chairmen. Following his address the Conference passed a recommendation to the Commission asking the schedule for restructure to be relaxed, stating not enough preparation time remained for any action to be taken at the 1967 St. Louis Convention. The Commission, after considering the recommendation, thought otherwise. It moved ahead with the St. Louis Convention as planned. One of the significant achievements was assuring that the process continually moved forward.[37]

As the drive toward approval of the "Provisional Design" gained momentum, and with the St. Louis Convention a short time ahead, opposition groups intensified their campaigns of criticism. Anthony Dunnavant described four groups, identifying the tension among them as growing out of their interpretation of the purposes of the Movement: *unity, restoration, liberty,* and *mission.* Each group appeared to emphasize one of the four ideological options as the guiding light for restructure. The *unity* group, according to Dunnavant, actually carried out restructure. The *mission* group, Disciples for Mission and Renewal, led by Missouri pastor Charles Bayer (b. 1927), based their opposition on the belief the Disciples were addressing the wrong issue. "I really didn't think our problem was ecclesiology. I thought our problem was the loss of our sense of mission," Bayer said, "I referred to our problem as a heart problem, not as an orthopedic problem. Simply getting the bones right wasn't going to help." In the 1965 plenary of the Commission, Bayer further commented, "I hope restructure will bring renewal at every level. We have been called primarily to minister to the world as a servant people, and not to be democratic." This group did not really oppose restructure. They wanted it to go further. Teegarden described the Bayer group in a neighborly tone, as a "counter-balancing influence that kept the process from focusing entirely on 'how will it function best organizationally.'"[38]

The *restoration* group, called The Committee for the Preservation of the Brotherhood, was headquartered in Canton, Ohio. They operated anonymously with a return address of Box 1471. Teegarden referred to them as "our friends at Box 1471." This group, led by James DeForest Murch (1892–1973), represented the "Independent" point of view, critical of Disciples cooperative organizations for half a century. They wrote and distributed letters to all the congregations. They also sent their newsletter, *Restructure Report,* along with printed pamphlets such as "The Truth about Restructure." These publications brimmed with false claims, contending, among other things, that restructure would cause congregations to lose their property and lose their right to choose a minister, and that the proposed General Board and Administrative Committee in the new structure were nothing more than ecclesiastical courts. The statements were willfully misleading, confusing to some congregations, causing a few to withdraw; however, they had almost no effect on cooperative congregations. It was estimated that of the 8,000 Disciples congregations, approximately 4,000 were cooperative, 1,000 were unknown, and 3,000 were of an independent cast never supporting the current Disciples structure financially or any other way. In a long letter of response to Lesley L. Walker on this subject, Granville Walker noted sharply, "[This group] might be rallied to almost anything of a negative character. Many of these churches are already identified with the independent movement and could care less either about what is proposed in Restructure or how we are currently organized."[39]

The *liberty* group identified themselves as the Atlanta Declaration Committee, led by Robert Burns (1904–1991) and Robert Shaw. Burns, long-term pastor of Peachtree Christian Church in Atlanta, Georgia, was a member of the Commission on Brotherhood Restructure as well as a member of its Central Committee from 1963 onward. Their deep concern was congregational autonomy and the protection of congregational rights. On May 4, 1967, as support became increasingly evident for the "Provisional Design," the Atlanta Declaration Committee circulated a document throughout the Brotherhood entitled "Atlanta Declaration of Convictions and Concerns." It contained inflammatory accusations, describing restructure as an authoritarian, connectional system that would endanger congregational liberty; warning it controlled from the top down; claiming the right of congregational voting representatives would be taken away; stating congregations would have no voice in the selection of the General Minister and President; and alleging regions could prevent congregations from calling a minister of choice or from withdrawing. The statements were patently false and were countered repeatedly by the Commission, but to little effect. Kenneth Teegarden said of the Atlanta group, "It was the one primarily responsible for keeping on the [table] all the time the local autonomy issue."[40]

In early summer 1967 the Atlanta group demanded a meeting with members of the Commission. The date of August 3 was mutually agreed and seven commissioners: Granville Walker, Myron Cole, Ronald Osborn, Dale Fiers, Harrell Rea, Forrest Richeson, and Kenneth Teegarden traveled to Atlanta. Most of the meeting was an interrogation, with the Atlanta group raising their standard questions and the Commissioners responding. The Commissioners held firm in their refusal to use the word "autonomy" in the "Provisional Design." They were convinced no part of the body of Christ can be autonomous; free, yes, but not autonomous. There were responsibilities to the larger Christian community. At one point a question surfaced about Winfred E. Garrison's widely referenced "Fork in the Road" address delivered at the Pension Fund breakfast during the 1964 Detroit International Convention. The commissioners were asked if Disciples were taking the wrong fork. Kenneth Teegarden responded: "I will not accept the concept that we have come to a 'fork in the road.' The choice of participation under the 'Provisional Design' lies with the individual and with the congregation."[41]

The Commission worked its way through these four ideological alternatives toward restructure and determined which of the four to choose. The Panel of Scholars, writing prior to the work of the Commission, rejected *restoration* when it declared, "The notion that the New Testament is a constitution for the church is repudiated by biblical scholars generally," and that restoration "was no longer tenable in the light of current understanding of the New Testament." The *liberty* group influenced the restructure process through their advocacy of congregational freedom. The *mission* group helped counter-balance, preventing an exclusive focus on organization. The *unity* group waged the offensive for restructure.[42]

The St. Louis International Convention gave triumphant approval to the "Provisional Design" in October 1967. It was the first representative assembly–a long-thwarted Disciples aspiration to strengthen the congregational voice in governance–that had at last become a reality. Howard Dentler, a devoted and competent member of Dale Fiers' professional staff, reported 5,093 registered voting representatives from 1,967 congregations. In addition, there were 4,482 non-voting members who brought the total of local congregations present to 2,133–only 166 of whom, by their own choosing, did not have a registered representative. Of the 5,093 voting representatives, 1,750 were ministers. The business sessions, rated excellent by 91 percent of the participants, had an average attendance ranging from 4,000 to 4,700. The Convention majority vote by congregational representatives in favor exceeded well beyond the two-thirds requirement, with fewer than seventy-five votes in opposition. Following this "congregational approval" came the two-thirds majority approval from states, areas, and agencies, achieved prior to the September 1968 Assembly in Kansas City. By April 1968, eleven general agencies had approved the "Design," more than the two-thirds requirement; and five states had approved, Georgia being the first by a representative vote of 155 to 10.[43]

The "Provisional Design"

Anthony Dunnavant suggested in his closing three-chapter analysis of restructure that it supplanted the society concept of polity and recovered the concept of *covenant*. It abandoned restorationism and created an ecumenically oriented church. It offered a new unity of self-understanding tied together by covenant as parts of one church. Restructure, in his view, was a culmination of both a structural and ideological evolution, characterized by a basic continuity of structure, but with a dramatic change in organizational and ecclesiological language.[44]

In essence, only the ecclesiological language changed, expressing a new self-understanding as a "church in covenant." The number and structure of agencies, state societies, international convention, and institutions remained visibly and for the most part structurally the same, with the same leadership, staff, and geography and separate governing boards. *The only agency required to give up its programmatic existence was the UCMS*—an act of self-giving to the wholeness of church. But dramatic change occurred in what could *not* be seen, *covenant* and *church*. Disciples had found a new, vital, and creative means of linking everything in their structural life—including the promise that links one age to its successor.

The General Assembly became the final organizational authority for the church. According to Ronald Osborn, that authority was "a persuasive authority of truth and goodness among a people in covenant to do the will of God." The General Assembly achieved status as a broad, proportional representative and deliberative body composed of congregational, regional, and institutional representatives. The General Board, the most important *structural* outcome, contained an elected membership: one-third to one-half of whom were to be ministers, and at least one-half lay; one-half from regions, one-half from the Assembly at large. It was subordinate to the General Assembly to which it submitted recommendations. The "Provisional Design" also provided for an Administrative Committee—the program planning, implementation, grievance, and promotional body. It was composed of half lay, half ministers, with three-fourths of its membership drawn from the General Board and containing the officers of the church: Moderator and two Vice Moderators (voluntary), plus the General Minister and President, Secretary, and Treasurer (salaried).[45]

The "Provisional Design" also set forth the rights of congregations in clear and certain terms. Congregational responsibilities were less clear and certain.

> Among the rights recognized and safeguarded to congregations are the right: to manage their affairs under the Lordship of Jesus Christ; to adopt or retain their names and charters or constitutions and by-laws; to determine in faithfulness to the gospel their practice with respect to the basis of membership; to own, control and incumber their property;…to establish their budgets and financial policies; to call their ministers; and to participate through voting representatives in forming the corporate judgment of the Christian Church…all financial support of the general and regional programs of the [church] by congregations and individuals is voluntary.[46]

Administrative Units were established by the General Assembly to meet responsibilities of the church in its witness, mission, and service to the world. Each unit was charged with facilitating policy decisions of the Christian Church. They were to be called "divisions," and the members of their boards were to be elected or ratified by the General Assembly. Each developed its own by-laws, elected its own administrative officers, and administered its own financial affairs. But they were to be something more than "agencies" owing allegiance only to self-perpetuating boards composed of focused-interest individuals.[47]

The least developed portion of the "Provisional Design" dealt with regions. Regions were to establish, receive, and nurture congregations and to extend the ministry of Christ in witness, mission, and service. The "Provisional Design" added that the church, to establish regional structures, might use geographic, sociological, cultural, and political boundaries. The following amendment was recently added to the section dealing with modification of regional boundaries:

> The process of reshaping regional boundaries (even if only one congregation is affected) includes the participation and approval of the parties [congregations & regions] involved, the Administrative Committee, the General Board and the General Assembly.

By providing veto power to regions or congregations, the amendment overtly reinforced the old concept of autonomy, a resurgent attitude in recent Disciples history during repeated negotiations regarding the allocation of funds for mission. Irrespective of the authority and recommendations of the General Assembly, approval of regional reconfiguration currently resides with the regional expression of church.[48]

After six years, the Commission on Brotherhood Restructure presented "A Provisional Design for the Christian Church (Disciples of Christ)" to the convention in Kansas City, Saturday afternoon, September 28, 1968. It was 3:35 p.m. when the Moderator, Ronald Osborn, called for a vote on Resolution #55, the most significant organizational action of Disciples in 136 years. It seemed like the entire auditorium stood to vote "yes." The assembly, at the invitation of Dr. Osborn, broke into the doxology. In the history of Disciples, this was one of its most storied moments, a stunning improbability, one of the rare triumphs of structural politics.

Dale Fiers offered a benedictory conclusion to the long and arduous process. He told those assembled the church could not deal with structure and mission in isolation from each other. He expressed his conviction that the Brotherhood had been led by the Spirit to develop a more theologically and pragmatically sound structure. Then he ended the long quest with the words, "I pray that we will bring to the mission new resources of commitment and spiritual power which arise out of an obedient response to the divine call to be the church."[49]

Reflections

During subsequent decades, members of the Commission were frequently asked about restructure, about how effective or ineffective they thought restructure had become, and about several important issues that arose during the course of developing the "Provisional Design." T.J. Liggett

(b. 1919) wrote to Dale Fiers in 1999, posing a series of questions about restructure. Fiers answered with candor.

Question 1: What was achieved?

The dream of becoming church and transcending the society concept was gloriously achieved… Another unique achievement was the basis of membership in the church. The region does not consist of member congregations, nor the general manifestation of member regions. Each person is a member of all three.

Question 2: Where did we fall short?

We fell short on integrating the regional manifestation of the church, but I don't know that we could have done differently at the time. The three manifestations evolved as I expected but not with the *esprit de corps* I had hoped.

Question 3: What price did we pay?

We lost a lot of momentum in the areas of program planning and promotion. I think a tremendous price was paid in the breakup of the United Society. I am sure it was the right thing to do but my heart aches every time I think of it. It was absolutely essential to the full realization of the dream. Virgil Sly and T. J. Liggett are to be credited with the most magnificent demonstration of the surrender of position and power and prestige I have ever witnessed. We lost 2,700 congregations. Sadly, this was part of the price.

Question 4: What have we learned?

We were on target in building into the design provision for continuing reform and renewal. We learned it is a recurring need to interpret the "dream" to each new generation lest we forget its primary objective to be a worthy manifestation of church within the Church Universal.[50]

Kenneth Teegarden was interviewed in the spring of 1990, a little more than two decades after the fabled Kansas City Assembly. The first question directed to him focused on the concept of "church" as the foundation of restructure. Teegarden accurately responded, "There was a maturing of thought with most of us throughout the beginning of the process… We were about halfway through the process when we began to see an ecclesiological concept emerge that said, we are not churches–we are Church." The documents of restructure reveal that Dale Fiers first introduced the concept at the second Central Committee meeting in January 1962. In that session he spoke extemporaneously when the question, "Why Restructure?" was raised. So impressed was the committee with Fiers' succinct analysis that they asked him to develop a full address on the subject, resulting in "An

Apologetic for Restructure," delivered to the full Commission six months later. Dale's 1962 statements came more than two full years prior to the famous set of three lectures presented by veteran scholar Ronald Osborn (1917–1998) in Louisville, July 1, 1964. In his first lecture, "The Calling of the Church," Osborn turned to the servant poems and songs of Second Isaiah, *Behold my servant…in whom my soul delights…bring forth justice to the nations.* In the second lecture, "The Nature of the Church," he declared, "The church properly understood is both institution and event, both organization and community, both form and spirit, it is both catholic and body. Its divine character inheres in both sides of each affirmation." Life must have structure, he proclaimed: "Spirit requires a body to give it a place to function." The third lecture, "Building the Church," contained his oft-quoted characterization of church corporate life: "It is something far more than a convention, far more than a policy of cooperation, far more than an association of churches. It is the *church,* as surely as any congregation is the church. It is not yet the whole church–but it is the *church.*"[51]

The lectures were powerful, producing an epiphany, the most dynamic moment in the work of the Commission. It was a seismic shift in Disciples ecclesiological self-understanding. The lectures crystallized the Commission's thinking around the concept of church and from that moment this became the driving force behind their work. So powerful were these lectures they were quickly published in booklet form, *Toward the Christian Church,* and distributed throughout Disciples congregations and regions. Because of the wide circulation, many Disciples were under the impression the concept of church had been Osborn's. The concept, of course, can be found in Campbell's writings; but it was Dale Fiers who reintroduced it to Disciples during the restructure discussions. Ronald Osborn performed the invaluable service of embedding this guiding principle in the heart of the Commission and expanding their grasp of its meaning through the force of his pen and rhetoric. Kenneth Teegarden was quite accurate in saying the thought of the Commission on the concept of church matured with the process.

Teegarden also commented on the question of "congregational auton-omy." Aware the question of autonomy had derailed all previous attempts to develop cooperative structure, he responded, "From the beginning there were fears that restructure was going to interfere with the autonomy of congregations… We did not try to attack autonomy; we conscientiously and consciously did not use the word in the *Design,* but recognized the church in all its manifestations. The concept of local determination was so inherent to the Disciples' understanding of Church that we were not about to displace that concept, but make it a more mature concept." Reference was made to the Atlanta Declaration Group, and Teegarden assessed the impact of their role: "It kept the process from being one of full enthusiasm to move forward to the fullest kind of covenantal concept. Instead of being able to begin with what is the most fruitful possibility, we had to say what is the most fruitful possibility that is favorable to [all elements]." The Commission wanted to make the point that the work and witness of the local congregation did not *end* with the congregation; it was a unit of the body; but not the whole body. But in the final draft, due to the Atlanta influence, congregational *rights* were detailed in the "Provisional Design"; *responsibilities* less so. Restructure was so intent on reassuring congregations of their autonomy that it fell short on knitting them together as a manifestation of church. This deeply aggrieved Teegarden, Fiers, and others, yet it seemed the only way the "Provisional Design" could be approved. When so many congregations were planning to leave after restructure, Teegarden tried to prevent it. It was not the minor loss of funds that troubled him; it was the loss of half the membership he believed needless.[52]

"Covenant," Teegarden emphatically and repeatedly proclaimed, "is the most significant accomplishment of restructure." For Disciples, the authority of the church is understood through covenant; God initiates covenant and members affirm this through the preamble to *The Design*—"We rejoice in the covenant of love which binds us to God and one another." It is a call for trust, compassion, and forgiveness. It was the heart of Restructure, the heart of biblical faith: *God and God's people bound together in a solemn promise.* It was clearly a biblical concept and therefore not at all unexpected for Disciples to express their restructure in covenantal relationships. One of the important intentions of restructure was to replace "autonomy" with "covenant." Teegarden defined the meaning of covenant this way:

> [Covenant is] the very beginning of the nature of the church of which we are a part. We are a community bound by covenant... our relationships are not hierarchical, they are not constitutional; they are covenantal! In our theological understanding of the word, we do not think of it as contractual...'I will be your God and you will be My people'...we will be congregations together forming a region, we will be regions and congregations living together in covenant to form the Christian Church in a general manifestation. As a whole church we are bound in covenant to the whole church of Jesus Christ. *We were not just establishing a structure; we were establishing a covenantal community.*

God brings the covenant-community into being, and together with God and with one another, Christians assume a sacred bond. In his distinguished work, *The Faith We Affirm,* explaining the preamble (the actual statement of covenant) to *The Design,* Ronald Osborn, one of the preamble's architects, declared "through covenant God binds us to one another, to the whole body of Christians and to all humanity." He added:

> Suspicious of organizational structure that might attempt to impose its will on the congregation...for more than 100 years Disciples tried

to carry on their common life as if there were no church beyond the local congregations. They organized societies, associations, boards and conventions…secular corporations organized under civil law. They were not ecclesiastical bodies, not the church. Through all those years some of the greatest apostles and saints of the movement had no ministerial titles. They preached, they sacrificed…they wore out their lives for the churches–but were called corresponding secretaries, executive secretaries, [etc.]… This kind of pious subterfuge could not be sustained forever.

Following restructure, bound to God and to all God's people in sacred covenant, we cannot think of Christian community as limited to a congregation or a particular denomination. Through covenant, Disciples speak today of their life together as *Church,* and view their leadership as ministerial and ecclesiastical–serving the church at large. Many leaders from the restructure generation believed the church did not do enough to communicate to the post-restructure generation the meaning of covenant or firmly root the fact Disciples had become a covenantal church.[53]

Finally, in regard to regions–from the beginning an intractable dilemma–Teegarden responded, "The regional manifestation was spelled out as complete as was possible. It was left as an unfinished task." The Commission spent more time and energy on this topic than most others but was never able to pull it all together to everyone's satisfaction. Teegarden commented on the difficulty of finding common ground for regions: "You cannot have the same kind of regional expression in the Southwest as in the region of Utah." As to the plan for fewer and larger regions, Teegarden wrote in 1975:

The whole idea of fewer regions is based upon two primary principles: one, that all entities seeking to fulfill regional responsibilities should be viable operations from numerical and financial standpoints; and secondly, that larger geography will require new understanding of administrative functions from a central location, with pastoral care and oversight dispersed. At the very heart of the concept of fewer regions is the proposition that administrative functions should be coordinated at fewer locations, [reducing] duplication of effort, and that pastoral care and concern should be operative at the nearest and most personal level possible. Unfortunately, the terminology of *larger regions* rather than *fewer regions* has been used and the implications have not been adequately discussed.

The deeper concern was structural development among regions being determined more by economic circumstances than church planning within the context of covenant. When a large number of congregations announced plans to leave the Brotherhood if restructure was approved, several thought state secretaries should be doing more to educate and change the opinions of those congregations. Teegarden met with the state secretaries and pleaded with them to help congregations understand that the pamphlets coming from Atlanta and Canton were misleading. His failure to move the secretaries to action profoundly affected him. In the Commission he continued to work hard analyzing numbers, developing regional diagrams without reference to state lines, trying to adjust boundaries in his quest to discover the most effective regional configuration. New geography and new language were not readily acceptable to the state leadership of that generation, who tended more toward preserving rights and territory than toward developing a new vision of region.[54]

Both Kenneth Teegarden and Dale Fiers wanted desperately to redefine and strengthen the role of regions. Neither had envisioned regions clinging so tightly to their autonomy, boundaries, and size of staff. Neither regions nor general units chose to take the lead in a teaching role to assist with the understanding of covenant, the understanding of church, and the general implementation of restructure. Consequently, the various manifestations were all initially unsure of the new structure, creating tentativeness in their early attempts to become church. On the question of the initial implementation of restructure, regional leadership did not help local pastors catch the vision of sending informed members to General Assembly. General Assembly materials were sent sixty days in advance with the thought that congregations and their voting representatives could research, study, and debate the issues, thereby creating a better prepared constituency that could be brought together in assembly to debate from informed points of view. Voting representatives were not to arrive "instructed," but "informed." It was seen as a regional responsibility for both general and regional assemblies.[55]

With restructure, Disciples had accomplished something unprecedented, and did so in the face of great historical odds. Kenneth Teegarden warned in 1965 the new structure would look "barbarous" to some; to others it would seem "less spiritual and lacking the values of the old way." In the years immediately following restructure it became fashionable and conventional to be critical: restructure did not go far enough, or it was entirely too connectional; restructure developed too quickly and more time was needed, or the restructure process moved too slowly. If membership declined, it was the fault of restructure; if offerings sagged, it was the fault of restructure; if a planning glitch occurred, it was the fault of restructure. People became particularly adept at tracing the roots of any controversy to a restructure fault. Moving from autonomy to covenant was found to be complicated. The hardness of tradition seemed at times invincible.

But Teegarden also assured, "our people will not let such impressions distort their judgment. They will reject the notion that the Brotherhood has fallen victim to some nefarious plot." Through the peoples' judgment, expressed in representational forum, the "Provisional Design" within a decade became *The Design* of the Christian Church (Disciples of Christ); and by its own approved procedures it was successfully amended in 1969, 1971, 1973, 1975, 1977, 1979, 1983, 1984, 1994 and 2005! The expansive consequences of *church* and *covenant* slowly took root; and it was ultimately determined unnecessary to have a constitution in addition to *The Design.* The covenantal structure among Disciples, at this writing, has reached its fortieth birthday! This remarkable thing happened because, in Kenneth Teegarden's words, *"Growth and maturity in responsible structures enrich freedom."*

The restructure generation produced a document that ranks with the *Declaration and Address* and the *Last Will and Testament of the Springfield Presbytery* as a seminal Disciples text. But it was not conceived to be eternal. Kenneth made that plain when he described restructure as *"an endless interweaving of continuity and change–a tradition facilitating its own continuous renewal."* The "Committee on Structure and Function" was inserted into *The Design,* later to become the "Task Force on Renewal and Structural Reform," because of absolute certainty about the continuous need for reform and renewal. *The Design* was neither immutable nor immaculate, but it is regarded as the most significant achievement in the modern history of Disciples–Willard Wickizer its *father,* A. Dale Fiers its *spirit,* and Kenneth L. Teegarden its *architect.*

CHAPTER VII

A Community in Covenant

Gaines M. Cook:
Prelude to a Community in Covenant

There is a growing maturity in our churchmanship which is thoroughly consistent with our congregational polity, wherein our congregations may find corporate expression in programs of outreach for which they are willing to assume responsibility, on the same basis that that they provide for the program of the local parish.

GAINES M. COOK
Our Brotherhood *International Convention Address, Miami, 1963*

Gaines M. Cook (1897–1983) was born and raised on a farm near the prairie town of LeRoy, Illinois, midway between Bloomington and Champaign/Urbana. The citizens of LeRoy numbered approximately 1,200 in 1897, the same year the first telephone arrived in that small rural community linked together by dirt streets. Young Gaines grew up in the local Disciples congregation, earned a B.A. from Eureka College in 1921, and his B.D. from Yale in 1925 in preparation for ministry. He was pastor of several congregations in Illinois, including Bloomington, and one in New York, Fisher's Island Union Chapel; he also served as a member of the Board of Trustees of the College of the Bible in Lexington (now Lexington Theological Seminary) and as Chairman of the Home and State Missions Planning Council. After becoming State Secretary of the Ohio Christian Missionary Society, where colleagues described him as "an able and efficient executive," he became president of the National Association of State Secretaries. He also served as a member of the General Board of the National Council of Churches, where he held numerous positions; and was the only Disciple to serve among Disciples delegates to each of the first three assemblies of the World Council of Churches. In 1946 he left his position as State Secretary, where he served fifteen years, to become the first full-time Executive Secretary of the International Convention following the retirement of part-time General Secretary Graham Frank. He took with him his secretary of ten years, Gertrude Dimke (1910–2003), who would give thirty years in service to three general church chief executives: Gaines Cook, Dale Fiers, and Kenneth Teegarden.[1]

Gaines Cook came to his position as Executive Secretary of the International Convention immediately following World War II and the 1946 approval of the Disciples' "A Crusade for a Christian World." The Crusade set a goal of establishing 200 new congregations in three years and raising $14 million for mission. The Crusade, separately incorporated and chaired by L. N. D. Wells (1876–1963), was the largest program ever attempted by the Disciples up to that time. It reached most of its goals and raised $8,000,000 with another $2,000,000 in "accepted goals." By 1946 Disciples recognized the acute need to coordinate the ministries of their several agencies and state missionary societies. The official purpose of the International Convention as stated in its constitutional preamble, "facilitating closer cooperation among the various agencies," coupled with its slogan, "Building a Brotherhood through Voluntary Cooperation," foretold the need. The office of executive secretary, traditionally responsible for overseeing the planning for the annual conventions, printing the *Year Book,* and representing Disciples in ecumenical gatherings, took on new expectations. With Cook's appointment the office became a full-time position housed in Indianapolis with an intensified degree of seriousness attached to its slogan and constitutional purpose.[2]

The Great Depression and World War II generated a welcoming social environment for interagency cooperation. A call was issued in 1948 for a commission to review the organizational structures and programs, leading to the formation of the Council of Agencies in 1949, along with the National Church Program Coordinating Council in 1953. "Organizing" was suddenly in vogue, manifesting itself within many groups throughout the church, including hundreds of congregations that began reorganizing themselves around Orman Shelton's book on functional departments, *The Church Functioning Effectively.*

The newly organized Christian Men's Fellowship (CMF) held its first national meeting at Cane Ridge in 1949; and the Christian Women's Fellowship (CWF) became a department in the UCMS in 1950, evolved into the organization of the International Christian Women's Fellowship in 1953, and held the first Quadrennial meeting at Purdue University in 1957. From 1954 to 1956 Wilbur Cramblet chaired a Committee on Brotherhood Organization and Interagency Relationships. In 1956 the Movement changed its name from the International Convention of Disciples of Christ to the International Convention of Christian Churches (Disciples of Christ). During the same year the Panel of Scholars was constituted to give theological self-understanding to the Movement at mid-century. In the final years of the 1950s, the "Decade of Decision," a Brotherhood-wide long-range plan for the 1960s was planned and approved. The flow of these events culminated in the famous July 1958 meeting of the Council of Agencies in Canton, Missouri, where Willard Wickizer delivered his pivotal address resulting in the appointment of a Study Committee on Brotherhood Structure. The following year, the International Convention at Denver approved a recommendation to appoint a Commission on Brotherhood Restructure. By 1963, Gaines Cook could state in his final address to the International Convention:

> The word "structure" seems unfamiliar to Disciples of Christ. "Cooperation" and "organization" are familiar words because they represent voluntary expressions of our corporate life... These voluntary expressions have been recognized as having churchly significance... Agencies–state, national and world–each recognizes that it cannot be a self-contained organization appealing to local congregations for support, just because it happens to be doing the kind of work in which it is interested. Rather, it would recognize itself as a specialized expression of the total church [performing] a service which no local congregation acting alone could possibly implement.[3]

This eighteen-year prelude, encompassing the tenure of Gaines Cook as Executive Secretary of the International Convention, was a time crowded with an aggressive, impassioned, spirited sequence of cooperative events in an important organizational evolution leading finally to the appointment of "The Commission on Brotherhood Restructure."

A. Dale Fiers:
Assembling the Community in Covenant

*Let all be done decently and in order... A clear mandate rests upon
us to develop relationships and structures which are compatible with
the nature of the church... The extent to which we are able to re-order
our organizational structure in harmony with developing insights into
the nature of the church ...will be one of the major factors of advance
and progress. Our search for structure can never be satisfied short of
the manifestation of the full unity in the church for which our Lord
prayed... We can never be content to stumble and crawl into church
union out of weakness [or] to live isolated from the church's great
struggle for wholeness. We must never let ourselves think we can carry
the responsibility for Christ's mission to the world on our own shoulders.*

A. DALE FIERS
Installation Address, 1964[4]

Dale Fiers (1906–2003) was born in the rural county seat town of
Kankakee, Illinois. At age seven he and his family moved to West Palm
Beach, Florida. His father, owner of a construction business, gave oversight
to the construction of a new Christian Church in West Palm Beach where
young Dale's mother, an ordained minister, served as associate pastor. An
outstanding high school athlete, he was named to both Florida all-state
football and baseball teams. Choosing ministry as his life's work, he enrolled
at Bethany College in 1925. After his first pastorate at Shadyside, Ohio,
he continued his preparation for ministry by enrolling in seminary at Yale
University in 1931 where he studied with several renowned professors,
including H. Richard Niebuhr. After graduating in 1935, he became
minister of congregations in Hamilton and Newark, Ohio, before being
called as senior minister in 1945 to the 1,800-member Euclid Avenue
Christian Church in Cleveland. During those years he served as a board
member of the Board of Higher Education, Council on Christian Unity,
and the UCMS, as well as a trustee of both Butler University and Bethany
College. He was elected to the General Board and executive committee of
the National Council of Churches, and as a delegate to the New Delhi and
Uppsala assemblies of the World Council of Churches.[5]

In September 1951 Fiers became the fifth president of the United
Christian Missionary Society, a position he held for thirteen years. The
policy governing foreign missions was "Paternalism to Partnership to
Autonomy." Within a year, following his world tour of Disciples missions
and his publication of *This Is Missions,* he wrote for *World Call:* "Missions
must be helped to move as rapidly as possible from mission direction and
support to self-direction and support." During his final two years in the
UCMS presidency, he served simultaneously as Administrative Secretary

of the Commission on Brotherhood Restructure and Executive Secretary of the International Convention, succeeding Gaines Cook. Holding these three offices placed him in the persuasive position of diplomatically prodding the commission processes to *develop* the "Provisional Design," judiciously guiding the convention processes to *approve* the "Provisional Design," and wisely shaping the smooth transition from the UCMS in order to *implement* the "Provisional Design." Many Disciples, then and now, agree that his balanced and thoughtful statesmanship in these positions was absolutely essential to the success of restructure. He exhibited exceptional skill at influencing the spirit of the process. With the approval of the "Provisional Design" at the 1968 Kansas City Convention/General Assembly, Dale Fiers was named the first General Minister and President of the Christian Church (Disciples of Christ). Faced with helping the church live into its new ecclesiology, he managed the challenge with acumen and wisdom.[6]

Dale Fiers' decision to resign as president of the UCMS, the largest and strongest unit in the church, to become Executive Secretary of the International Convention, as T. J. Liggett (Fiers successor at UCMS) remembered, was "a very important decision personally and substantively. It sent a powerful message to everyone. Dale's leadership provided an incarnation for restructure."

Kenneth Teegarden attached the same importance to the event, adding: "Dr. Fiers was universally recognized as a spiritual leader who imbued the process with spiritual depth. His enormous personal integrity, strong commitment to Disciples traditions, administrative experience and pastoral concern made him the single most important person to the success of restructure." And Joseph Smith commented:

> I believe restructure really began when Dale Fiers decided to give up the presidency of the UCMS... Dale Fiers was Mr. Disciple as president of the United Society and executive Secretary of the International Convention and I think that is one reason restructure carried...we had a good sense of carry-over through Dale, a sense of unity and doing something together under the leadership of this man.

Dale Fiers' decision to resign as president of UCMS, a creative act of statesmanship, should be viewed as an ultimate act of commitment to restructure, a bridge of continuity to the new structure, and an act of spiritual discipline. Dale recalled, "it was a watershed decision for me. My passion was the search for an expression of 'church,' not a group of societies. Yet I loved the United Society, and every time I revisit the moment, I have to justify it all over again." The venerable regional minister of Ohio, Herald B. Monroe, wrote of Dale:

> In a period of uncertainty and change I cannot think of anyone superior to Dale Fiers to whose leadership I would more willingly

pledge my support and entrust my church… This is not a time
for the timid nor cautious to lead… Dale quietly manifests such
unmitigated courage that he inspires the rest of us to do what
we know our Lord wants us to do. All are aware that when he
sees clearly his Christian duty, he will say in a quiet, determined
voice, 'We simply must do this!,' regardless of how painful the
consequences may be. I am grateful for a leader from whom no
timid note is likely to be heard as we move into new times.[7]

Awaiting Dale Fiers was the task of launching the newly restructured
church in covenant, at that point only a theory. The first order of business
was dismantling the UCMS. Dividing the UCMS into the Division of
Overseas Ministries, the Division of Homeland Ministries, and a Christian
Church Services unit (communications, *Year Book,* building maintenance,
technical assistance)–along with the transfer of capital, personnel, and other
responsibilities to the general church and to the new regions–constituted a
monumental and controversial act. T. J. Liggett became the last president
of the UCMS and presided over the asset division, finally completing it
in 1971.

The new General Assembly had to be planned. Bringing the General
Board and Administrative Committee into existence had to be quickly
accomplished. Building a sense of church within the cabinet (composed of
general administrative unit presidents) presented a significant challenge.
Both Kenneth Teegarden and Gertrude Dimke recalled the early cabinet
meetings, convened without guidance from *The Design*, as "trying."
According to Teegarden, "They said essentially we want to cooperate, but
we have our own task to perform–Dale was very patient with them." This
same feeling was equally pronounced when he attempted to bring cohesion
to the body of regional ministers, again without any real guidance from
The Design. It was also Fiers' responsibility to define and pioneer the role
of General Minister and President. Again, Teegarden recalled:

Dale shaped the title; his style of ministry was reflected in it; he
was both pastoral and administrative in his nature; and he applied
this title to his staff as a whole. There was no sense of personal
promotion; you could never question his honesty; there was never
a question about who he was. He was a strong and obvious leader,
but not a domineering or dominating administrator. He was thought
of primarily as a minister with caring concern for others and a deep
commitment to "church."[8]

Left over from the work of the Commission on Brotherhood Restructure
was the subject of ministry. It had been hoped that the Commission would set
standards for Disciples ministers. *The Design* contained a section on ministry
that recognized an "Order of Ministry," but left the establishment of policies
and criteria for the order to the General Assembly. Fiers, during his first

year as General Minister and President, appointed a Task Force on Ministry. It labored two years on the issue, bringing its report entitled "Policies and Criteria for the Order of Ministry" to the 1971 General Assembly in Louisville. Among the recommended criteria were the requirement of theological education along with "growth in personal character, Christian insight, spiritual formation and disciplined commitment to ministry." A new and important policy in the document placed authorization of ordination in the hands of the region, to be carried out in concert with the congregation. The right of the congregation to call a minister was not denied; but the congregation did not have the right to ordain persons into the ministry of the whole church without regional authorization. The policy recognized one order of ministry for transmitting Christian tradition from generation to generation through the time into which Disciples ministers were to be ordained. The 1971 General Assembly in Louisville approved the "Policies and Criteria for the Order of Ministry;" and amended it in 1977 to include policies and criteria for "candidacy," focusing on their spiritual, moral, intellectual, and emotional capacities. Revisions were made to the document in 1981 relative to the criteria for maintaining ministerial standing. In 1985 the policies were amended again to affirm the right of all manifestations of the church to call ministers and the freedom of ministers to accept or reject the call, and also provided for the mutual recognition of ministers of the Disciples and the United Church of Christ. A major revision of the document is underway in 2008 attempting to align with the proposal of the Churches Uniting in Christ and the World Council's *Baptism, Eucharist and Ministry*. Conservative-oriented Disciples are critical of this progressive advance from nineteenth-century origins to a formal order of ministry. Historian Anthony Dunnavant complained that "ecumenical imitation" "disfranchised" and "desacralized" Disciples elders and the diaconate while "clericalizing" Disciples ministers. In reality, Disciples elders and deacons perform a unique function at the Lord's table that in most other churches is reserved for ordained ministers. Dunnavant concluded:

> From the middle twentieth century forward Disciples ecumenical involvement...increasingly favored communions with highly clerical traditions of ministry... Cut off from their roots, Disciples have recently tended to order their ministry, to too great a degree, by imitation–by the superficial appropriation of symbols and practices adopted from admired ecumenical conversation partners.
>
> Reform and ecumenically oriented Disciples, however, applauded the creation and development of an order of ministry that gives universal acknowledgement to Disciples' ministers, that expresses a continuity with the church at large and that recognizes ministers serve entire bodies, not just a congregation or organization which employs them.[9]

One of Fiers' prized early initiatives as General Minister and President was mounting a capital campaign for mission within the newly covenanted church. The needs assembled from all units and regions of the church totaled $200 million. Before the campaign could be launched, it had to be approved. But internal conflicts among general administrative units, regions, and higher education institutions caused the church to withdraw from the effort. "This failure," said Dale Fiers, "was one of my bitter disappointments. My sad conclusion was that we were not yet enough of a church to make a church-wide effort."[10]

Dale Fiers, a civil rights activist who marched with Martin Luther King Jr., is credited with conceiving the idea of "Reconciliation," originally an urban emergency program. The response of the new church was heartening and prophetic. The Reconciliation fund, established in 1968, evolved into Reconciliation Ministry with a Pro-Reconciliation/Anti-Racism initiative in the early 2000s.

Fiers, a man of generous spirit and prayerful self-discipline, assembled the "community in covenant" and put the new structure in working order. His most important contribution as General Minister and President was teaching Disciples that structure should be viewed far more as an expression of an ideal than as a practical concern for economy. He helped Disciples learn that structure is an expression of church, a means to unity, a way to participate in the totality of church, a channel to ecumenical oneness. This contribution will remain his compelling legacy. At age sixty-seven, after serving one full term as General Minister and President, he announced his intention to retire in 1973.[11]

Restructure towers over the landscape of modern Disciples history like a mountain range, and A. Dale Fiers looms over the era as its central figure. He is fittingly regarded as the most important Disciples leader of the twentieth century.

Kenneth L. Teegarden:
Realization of a Community in Covenant

The Provisional Design has worked well. It is a flexible document befitting a pilgrim people. It has protected our freedoms while underscoring our responsibilities. It has bound us together, not by law, but by covenant.

KENNETH L. TEEGARDEN
State of the Church Address, 1977[12]

Kenneth Teegarden (1921–2002), a fourth-generation Oklahoman and a sixth-generation Disciple, often characterized his boyhood years in Cushing, Oklahoma, with the words, "Church was all I knew." He possessed extraordinary talent as a high school debater, twice named by the University of Oklahoma as one of the top ten high school debaters in the state. Following high school graduation in 1938, at age sixteen, he began his undergraduate work at Oklahoma A & M with the intent to become a lawyer. He completed ninety hours of course work, concentrating in American History and government, state and municipal government, political parties and European history. By the end of his second year he decided to change his career to ministry: "I was interested in a more personal way of working with people, and at a deeper level of existence, than their legal defense." He transferred to Phillips University where he completed both his B.A. and M.A. degrees. He later earned a B.D. degree from Brite College of the Bible in Fort Worth, Texas. Kenneth held several pastorates in Oklahoma, Texas, and Arkansas, including First Christian Church in Vernon, Texas, and First Christian Church of Fort Smith, Arkansas. In addition, he participated extensively in numerous agencies of the "Brotherhood" beyond the congregation: Recommendations Committee of the International Convention, Board of Directors of NBA, Seminary Council of Phillips University, chair of the Arkansas Council of Churches, Board of Directors of the Board of Higher Education, to name only a few. He served as regional minister of Arkansas; was elected and earned high national recognition and respect as administrative secretary of the Commission on Brotherhood Restructure; and subsequently became the regional minister of Texas.[13]

When Dale Fiers announced his retirement, the search began for his successor. The list of nominated candidates contained eighty-seven names, and Kenneth Teegarden received more nominations than anyone in the pool. Following a protracted two-year process, Teegarden was elected to the position at the October 1973 General Assembly in Cincinnati. The way in which the press covered his election was a matter of amusement. *The New York Times* ran an unfortunate headline, "Disciples of Christ Choose New Leader." *Playboy* picked up on it, and noted in their next issue, "We were afraid it would come to this one day."

Teegarden–learned, incisive thinker, humanely generous, orderly, engaging–often referred to his title, *General Minister and President of the Christian Church (Disciples of Christ) in the United States and Canada,* as the longest title in Protestantism. But during the restructure process, the title, according to Teegarden, "was selected very intentionally. It was to be ministerial and administrative. The first part of the title, 'general minister,' defined the responsibility for spiritual oversight and nurture of the whole church; and 'president'–not in the sense of having very much authority– identified the duty of administration." Disciples were absolutely petrified at the thought of investing authority in ecclesiastical offices. Robert Cueni observed recently, "Disciples are not structured for ease of leadership."[14]

When Teegarden assumed the office of General Minister and President in 1973, he found himself presiding over a Protestant denomination in a newly arrived post-denominational, post-Protestant age. This overriding social reality would compound every issue he faced. His twelve years as General Minister and President were marked with several challenges to the new "covenantal" polity: a threat to covenant from units and regions during implementation of the "Provisional Design"; a threat to covenant from the question of ordaining gays and lesbians; a threat to covenant from the question of "policing" or "disavowing" congregations in light of the Jonestown massacre; and a perceived threat to covenant because the church took action on social justice issues.

Implementation of the "Provisional Design"

Teegarden immediately faced the task of completing the implementation of the "Provisional Design." It would be a constant theme during his twelve years in office, particularly in his first term. Reading about it today may leave the impression that it was the only subject receiving attention. But Disciples were heavily engaged in multiple ministries while living into their new structure, and to maximize their ministry they needed to get their house in order as quickly as possible by completing the transition to a covenantal community. Six years had passed since approval of the "Provisional Design" in Kansas City, yet many parts of the church were still stepping gingerly into the new covenantal structure, trying to find their way.

In the fall of 1973, a five-year survey of the progress of restructure was conducted among general administrative units and regions. This report, submitted to the Committee on Structure and Function, awaited Teegarden's arrival for action and response. The Committee, believing itself empowered through the "Provisional Design," exercised substantial initiative and functioned like a mini-commission on restructure. Chaired by Jean Woolfolk, it contained a powerful membership of nineteen persons. Many of them served on the Restructure Commission, and some had been key leaders in shaping the "Provisional Design," which stated, "The General Assembly, upon recommendation of the General Board, shall establish or recognize by constitution or contract administrative units."[15]

Nearly all provisional general units in the 1973 survey reported revisions in their by-laws complying with the new "Provisional Design." The Board of Church Extension, however, said its relationship would be contractual, and consequently made no by-laws change. The 1972 "Provisional Design" stated specifically that general administrative units "shall be called divisions," and the Committee on Structure and Function urged consideration of a divisional concept upon general units. Two new divisions were incorporated in 1972–the Division of Overseas Ministries and the Division of Homeland Ministries. Their charters and by-laws were subsequently approved by the Committee, by the General Board, and then by the Cincinnati General Assembly in 1973. The National Benevolent Association, in 1973, approved the name Division of Social and Health Services, but kept NBA as its programmatic title. Also in 1973 the Board of Higher Education launched a self-study that over the next five years led to the creation of the Division of Higher Education in 1977, converting itself from an association of dues-paying institutions to a division of, by, and for the church, funded by the church rather than the institutions.[16]

Some of the ministries of the general manifestation, such as finance and ecumenism, involved all of the programmatic units and identified themselves as "councils." Unified Promotion, under the leadership of Spencer Austin, reconstituted itself as the Church Finance Council in 1973. And the ecumenical arm of the church already carried the name, Council on Christian Unity. The Disciples of Christ Historical Society chose to keep society status because the society concept had acceptance by all three branches of the Stone-Campbell Movement in the nineteenth century. Since DCHS still served all three, a concept change might somehow alienate one or both sister branches, all of whom shared a common heritage. The Christian Church Foundation came into existence in 1969, designing its charter and by-laws in concert with the "Provisional Design." One other new general unit, Christian Church Services, emerged during the dismantling of the United Christian Missionary Society, placing all overhead management and functions in a single location. The eclectic group of General Units greeting Teegarden in 1973 included three boards, three divisions, two councils, a society, a foundation, a general services unit, and the Pension Fund. Five years later one board (Board of Higher Education) had converted to a division; and the ministry of the services unit was deployed to other units.[17]

The Committee on Structure and Function struggled to determine the most effective means to realign units. They considered it axiomatic that structure flows from the functional requirements of mission. They were equally convinced that structure informs and shifts the character of mission. Assured the church was free to preserve, delete, reorder, and form new structures appropriate at any point in its history—the committee believed itself empowered to effect such change through the General Board and General Assembly. Structures, it asserted, were to be used like tools so long as they are useful; then adapt them or dispose of them as demands and opportunities require.

As hard as the Committee on Structure and Function labored, general unit structural changes turned out to be modest during the time Teegarden served as General Minister and President. All claimed to be motivated by a greater understanding of the wholeness of church, a spirit cultivated by regular meetings of the Cabinet, the Council of Ministers, the Administrative Committee, and the General Board—all of which brought units, regions, and congregational representatives into regular interaction with each other. Most general units claimed the new identity resulting from restructure resulted in stronger ecumenical relationships with their counterparts in other religious bodies. One of the important contributions Kenneth Teegarden brought to general units, and thereby to the church, was his unceasing nurture of collegiality and mutual general unit support of a single mission. Interrelatedness and common sharing became a natural part of general unit life during his years. The cabinet bonded, growing in confidence, collegiality, and churchliness. But few were willing to entertain suggestions of structural change. By 1976 the Committee on Structure and Function ceased its efforts to realign general units. The February minutes of 1976 stated, "the Administrative Committee and the General Board are the appropriate place for continual prodding of the general manifestation for more effective structures for mission."[18]

The committee divided into several subcommittees to address regional realignment. In the 1973 Progress Report fifteen provisional regions adopted new constitutions and by-laws in compliance with the "Provisional Design." Many formally changed their names from "association" or "missionary society" to "The Christian Church (Disciples of Christ) in [State name]." Several developed regional structures variously called districts, clusters, areas, or consultations. Most of the regions had formal ecumenical relationships with councils of churches and many enjoyed working relationships with judicatories of other communions. Ten regions gave very favorable evaluations for the over-all effects of restructure, emphasizing particularly the growing sense of church. On the other hand, several regions thought it was too early to determine the effects of restructure. Others believed the new demands on regions were too costly in both time and money; some expressed fear about what they called a growing centralization of power in the church; but the largest and most pervasive complaint by many regions was their dislike of the model "fewer but comparable" regions suggested by the Committee on Structure and Function.[19]

The Committee operated on the understanding, as stated in the "Provisional Design," that all general units and state organizations were *provisional.* And the "Provisional Design" stated clearly in the case of regions: "The General Board shall initiate procedures for reorganization of existing state and area organizations as regions of the Christian Church."[20] The Committee on Structure and Function set to work on the task, just as it did on general units. Chair Jean Woolfolk sent a letter in October 1972 to all regional ministers with a list of eleven suggested guidelines for initiating regional realignment. The second guideline articulated the intent: "With responsibility to the General Board, the Committee on Structure and Function may properly take initiative in suggesting consultation between two or more present provisional regions." The ninth guideline declared,

"Regions should be established so that their strategy, resources, program and administration may be more effective and efficient in the accomplishment of mission."[21]

The committee soon proposed the concept of "fewer and more comparable regions." John Wolfersberger produced for the committee a thoughtful paper on the concept, in which he proposed as a model for discussion, nineteen regions with a minimum of fifty-five areas, each area containing approximately sixty-eight congregations. He noted that in the 1970 census there were 243 metropolitan centers with 50,000 or more persons. Furthermore, 68 percent of the nation's population lived in those centers. Wolfersberger also noted that most Disciples lived, at that time, in the eastern half of the United States and below the 43rd parallel–the northern boundary of Iowa. Within that geography were twenty-seven states and twenty-five Disciples regions, containing 3,297 of the 3,782 participating congregations, and 761,606 of the 881,467 participating members. In addition, $14 million of the $16 million given to outreach came from that geography. The density of Disciples in the eastern United States, he surmised, offered a manageable geographic configuration.

The western part of the United States provided a different picture with only three territories of relative density–Colorado, California, and the Northwest. Wolfersberger's study considered the placement of the Interstate highway system, areas of major newspaper circulation and trade centers. He pointed out, at that time, Disciples had twelve regions with one hundred or more congregations, nine regions with sixty to one hundred congregations, and fifteen regions with fewer than fifty congregations. One region had as few as three congregations. He concluded his study with the assurance "fewer but more comparable regions" did not mean *small* regions would be absorbed by *large* regions, but *new* regions could be formed along new demographic and cultural lines, rather than state lines. Areas, he suggested, should be identified first. The boundaries of the region around them would be determined later. Regions, therefore, would be developed from the center outward, rather than the reverse.[22]

In October 1973, Kenneth Teegarden reviewed the progress report on General Units and regions, and proceeded to prepare a six-page paper reviewing the concept of "fewer and more comparable" regions to help engage regions in study and reflection. His review spoke of a model describing the central office of the region as a "regional resource center," and the areas as "pastoral and nurturing entities." The area, containing as many as seventy-five congregations, was *not* to be a fourth manifestation of church in the sense the term was used in the "Provisional Design," but a legitimate churchly structure finding its integrity within the organizational life of a region and in its proximity to the congregations within its boundaries. He suggested eleven functions for a region, eight functions for an area, and fourteen advantages of "fewer and more comparable" regions. Among the fourteen advantages were (a) being more nearly equal in size and strength would enable a more efficient fulfillment of mission and purpose, (b) the church could more easily decentralize some functions of general units, (c) a greater ethnic and gender diversity would become possible for regional staff, (d) excessive parochialism would be discouraged, (e) close pastoral care would be available through areas, (f) increased specialized skills and services would become available through a regional resource center, (g) a greater flexibility for renewal would be created by allowing easier boundary adjustments of areas within regions in response to growing urbanization, (h) duplication of several administrative and programmatic functions could be reduced, and (i) the cost of publishing both regional and area papers might be minimized by publishing one regional paper with a section provided for area material.[23]

There were positive reactions from several quarters of the church, but discussion of the concept of "fewer and more comparable" with regions over the next several years turned negative. Regional and area leaders advocated a preference for "diversity in size, shape, and structure as the better way to serve congregations and church mission, rather than 'fewer and comparable.'" Like the Commission on Restructure, the Committee on Structure and Function invested enormous time and energy in research and consultation with regional leadership on the subject of regional realignment. But across the twelve years of Kenneth Teegarden's tenure, only two regional realignments occurred. New Mexico and Texas merged into the Southwest Region; and Utah and the Central Rocky Mountain Regions agreed to share the same regional minister. When Teegarden retired in 1985, Utah was still listed in the *Year Book and Directory* as a separate region. In the final analysis, the Committee on Structure and Function during Teegarden's years as General Minister and President experienced only limited success in its repeated attempts to realign both the general and regional manifestations of the church.[24]

The colleges and universities also raised questions about how they were to be related to the restructured church. In 1973 a coalition of Disciples colleges in Missouri appealed their financial allocation and called for legal arbitration. Plans were laid for the creation of a court with James Noe, Moderator of the Church, to serve as judge. On the recommendation of Kenneth Teegarden, the General Board, in May 1975, appointed a Higher Education Evaluation Task Force. It recommended a twenty-four-point covenantal relationship between the institutions and the church: twelve responsibilities placed upon the church and twelve responsibilities placed upon the institutions, embodying the principal of mutual interpretation, mutual supportive services, a mutual community of faith and reason, and a mutual acceptance of the Campbell philosophy of wholeness of person. The task force also recommended a four-part funding formula for annual distribution of funds to each college and university that accepted the covenantal relationship: (a) $30,000 as a base or historic figure, (b) $10 for every full-time student, (c) $100 for every student who was a member of the Christian Church (Disciples of Christ), and (d) $500 for each graduating student who enrolled in an accredited seminary. The task force report was approved at the 1976 meeting of the General Board. Implementation occurred in 1977 when the board of trustees of each of the thirteen institutions approved and each president signed the covenant and accepted the formula. At this writing the covenant and formula have been in operation thirty years (1978–2008).[25]

Proposals to amend the "Provisional Design" appeared at nearly every General Assembly during Teegarden's tenure. Five resolutions to amend were considered at the General Assembly in 1973. Four resolutions to amend came in 1975, only one of which was approved. And in 1977 the Kansas City assembly voted to drop the word "Provisional" and simply call the document *The Design.* It was further determined at the 1977 assembly that a constitution was unnecessary. Amendments regarding the setting of priorities and General Board representation were presented in 1979. No amendments were proposed in 1981. In 1983 the General Assembly amended *The Design* to allow four ecumenical representatives to be elected to the General Board. And a request came in 1975, referred to the Committee on Structure and Function, to reduce the size of the General Board. The committee rejected the request to downsize the Board–but the request later received approval by the general assembly in 2005, along with a significant revision of *The Design.* All in all, the enduring yet malleable *Design*, crafted by the commission on restructure in 1968, has stood the test of time.

During the 1970s and early 1980s, Kenneth Teegarden coached Disciples in their successful quest to learn *The Design*'s meaning and how to use it constructively for effective self-governance, notwithstanding a few cases of clever manipulation by some manifestations. In his state of the church address to the 1977 Kansas City General Assembly where the word "Provisional" was dropped, Teegarden proclaimed to the 11,000 Disciples in the great hall:

> When [the Christian Church (Disciples of Christ)] is gathered as we are now, it is not just a collection of individuals who come to a convention, not even a collection of local churches, but a church–a distinctive, recognizable, working part of the church universal. And we have life, and hope, and responsibility for each other to prove it… A Provisional Design has worked well. It is a flexible document befitting a pilgrim people. It has protected our freedoms while underscoring our responsibilities. It has bound us together, not by law, but by covenant.[26]

Ordination of Gays and Lesbians

With the rise of the gay-liberation movement in the 1960s, homosexuals asserted their right to bring their sexual orientation into the open and demanded this disclosure not be treated with discrimination. It forced churches to confront the problem of human rights as it affected gays, both in and out of ministry. Many church groups in 1977–1978, including Episcopalians, Presbyterians, and Disciples, conducted studies of the subject in light of changing moral values and the findings of modern scientific and biblical research on sexuality. Episcopalians released their twenty-two-page report in August 1977; and the Presbyterians' report, accompanied by a 150-page background paper and a twenty-page minority report, was released in January 1978. Both caused major debates and controversy within their respective assemblies and denominations.[27]

The Disciples controversy erupted at the Kansas City General Assembly, October 21–26, 1977. There were four resolutions before the Assembly dealing with the issue of homosexuality. One asked the assembly to oppose homosexuality as a lifestyle for Christians. It was rejected by a majority vote (2,304 to 1,538: 60 percent). The second resolution, while neither approving nor condemning homosexuality, urged the passage of legislation at all levels of government to end the denial of civil rights for reason of sexual orientation. The resolution received approval by a two-thirds majority vote (2,541 to 1,312). The third resolution, an eleven-page study document, came from the Task Force on Family Life and Human Sexuality under the aegis the Division of Homeland Ministries. Submitted for use by the whole church for research and reflection on the issue, the resolution generated considerable ferocity and rancor. The document did not endorse homosexuality, although some thought it an apologetic for a homosexual lifestyle. It set off a firestorm in the Assembly, including abuse of parliamentary procedures, emotional tirades, and threats of withdrawal from the denomination. At length, however, the study document was approved.[28]

The fourth resolution (No. 7744) asked the General Assembly "to deny ordination status to any candidate who declares he or she practices or prefers homosexuality as a lifestyle; such candidates be screened out; counseling resources be offered to such candidates; and the church remain open to the candidates change in lifestyle." The heat of five and one-half hours of earlier debate drained the energy from the representatives. They voted to refer the resolution to the Task Force on Ministry for further "investigation and study" and to prepare a report for the 1979 General Assembly in St. Louis.

The final gavel had barely sounded when bundles of unfriendly mail began to arrive in Teegarden's office. Many of the letters threatened withdrawal from the denomination; others threatened to cut off their financial support; still others said they were going to designate or restrict their giving. A number of letters requested the elimination of controversial issues from the General Assembly agenda. Some indicated they were not going to attend any more Assemblies.[29]

Teegarden did not believe discussion of social issues caused membership to decrease. He stated forthrightly in his State of the Church address in Kansas City:

> Occasionally we hear the claim that the involvement of the church in social issues is causing people to drop away. It is my personal belief that that is a myth we have concocted to cover our failures in evangelism… Lay people have fewer misgivings than clergy about social involvement. What really is stunting our growth is the failure of the church to be challenging enough.

Despite all the criticism, Teegarden never wavered from his belief that by helping the church deliberate issues of the day candidly in open assembly, he helped Disciples live out the gospel in their communities, and helped them understand religion as a source of personal and public morality. Freedom, he declared, could only be safe when diverse views can be debated openly. Controversy should not force abandonment of a system. Above all, he thought, religious discussion of the public issues should not be left exclusively to the Christian Right.[30]

For two years, Resolution 7744 became the consuming subject of the Task Force on Ministry. Over Kenneth's signature a survey instrument circulated to the chairs of all regional commissions on ministry. The survey results revealed none of the regions had knowingly ordained a candidate who claimed to be an avowed homosexual and they did not confront candidates about their lifestyle. The question of sexual orientation had not arisen. All said they had not and did not intend to ordain a homosexual person. And with strong unanimity the regions stated they did not want the General Assembly establishing content definitions for personal fitness, emotional stability, and maturity or standards of morality. None had studied the issue of homosexuality and few had in place a process for counseling and guidance.[31]

As 1978 progressed, several regions (Kentucky, South Idaho, Tennessee, Florida) began to consider resolutions prohibiting the ordination of homosexual candidates. In March, the Division of Homeland Ministries produced a study packet to supplement the study document approved at Kansas City for congregational use. That summer, a judge ruled Lexington Theological Seminary must award a degree to a homosexual student who had completed all the academic requirements. The judge stated the catalog phrases describing requirements were inadequate.[32]

In this environment, the Task Force on Ministry completed its report for the 1979 General Assembly in St. Louis. The report was widely reviewed, including all regions, prior to final submission to the General Board and

General Assembly. The task force noted, in sharp contrast with traditional consensus, some in the church now affirmed that homosexual practices could be an appropriate way of life for consenting adult Christians. For Disciples, the report stated, the broader topic of homosexuality and ordination was intertwined with the procedure whereby Disciples nurtured and authorized their ministry. Within Disciples ecclesiology, the nurture, certification, and ordination of candidates for ministry were the responsibility of the regions in collaboration with their congregations. The task force, therefore, developed a twofold conclusion: "(a) Recent studies have not convinced us nor the Church at large that ordaining persons who engage in homosexual practices is in accord with God's will for the Church, and (b) The Christian Church (Disciples of Christ) intends to continue the current pattern of assigning responsibility to the regions with respect to the nurture, certification and ordination of ministers. There is a reluctance among Disciples to have the General Assembly establish doctrinal or moral standards for ministers." The report implied, for that moment, the church would probably not ordain homosexuals, but it did not say the church should not or could not ordain homosexuals. While neither the task force nor the church was convinced ordination was in accordance with God's will, it was not within the spirit of *The Design* to forbid regions from exercising their best judgment in each individual case. The report recognized and affirmed the established procedures for examining candidates for ministry. The General Assembly approved the Task Force on Ministry report and the issue began to subside in light of other events, such as Jonestown, that temporarily overshadowed it.[33]

The Jonestown Tragedy

The preoccupation of the church with the issue of ordaining homosexuals was suddenly eclipsed on November 19, 1978, when news erupted about an unspeakable tragedy in Guyana, South America. A murder-suicide occurred, taking the lives of 913 people, including the life of a California congressman, Leo Ryan. Shockingly, the pastor, James W. Jones, had been ordained in Indiana as a Disciples minister, and the more than 900 dead were members of a congregation, People's Temple, affiliated with the Christian Church (Disciples of Christ) in the Northern California Region.

Disciples had no background in disciplining or defrocking ministers. Restructure, seemingly, had not provided the means to deal with such a situation. A minister or congregation could leave easily, but it was nearly impossible to "throw" somebody out. The regional commission on ministry in Northern California had decided in 1977 to confront Jones with charges and review his standing, but he refused to return from Guyana. They let the matter rest. Then the news broke. Within forty-eight hours of the tragedy Kenneth Teegarden issued a statement of concern for the families of the victims and for survivors. He also acknowledged the relationship of both the congregation and its pastor to the Disciples of Christ. Furthermore, he took what he felt to be an appropriate step of getting the question of denominational follow-up out of the hands of staff and into the hands of those who initiate and make policy. Questions were being raised about what Disciples were planning to do about People's Temple. Teegarden announced that he "would make an inquiry with the legislative bodies of the church as to whether there ought to be a procedure for disavowing congregations, a procedure we have never had."[34]

On March 12, 1979, Teegarden presented a four-page address to the forty-four-member Administrative Committee in which he elaborated upon six points.

a. Let us act with the good of humanity in mind, not the reputation of the church.
b. Having a policy to disavow congregations could not have foretold or averted Jonestown.
c. We ask the individual prospective member only if she or he believes in Jesus Christ. We offer relationship to congregations on the same basis and accept on faith the reply of each.
d. Disciples are bound by an understanding of the church as one. In tolerating differences of opinion we leave ourselves no measuring rod by which errancy can be determined.
e. Social witness should not be lost by the church because opponents tie it to the aberrations of Jones.
f. If we have shortcomings in relating to congregations it is at the point of shepherding, not policing.

The Administrative Committee reaffirmed Disciples congregational freedom, and vowed not to take steps "passing judgment on a congregation's ministry." The committee further recommended improvement in "shepherding" congregations by encouraging regions to establish an annual visit to every congregation and to request ministers to report annually on the ministry in which they are involved.[35]

Christian Unity and the United Church of Christ

Potential union between the United Church of Christ and the Christian Church (Disciples of Christ) was a proactive issue during all of Teegarden's twelve years. Conversation between the two churches and their antecedents dated to 1912. Their mutual history extended back to James O'Kelly and Elias Smith in the early nineteenth century. In 1957, a union occurred between the Evangelical and Reformed Church (which itself was a result of the union of the Evangelical Synod of North America and Reformed Church in the United States in 1934) and the Congregational Christian Churches (which had previously formed through the uniting of the Congregational Church and the Christian Church in 1931) to form the United Church of

Christ. Disciples held their 1912 conversations with the Congregational Church and later participated as a consultant when the UCC developed a constitution in the late 1950s. In 1961, the UCC General Synod voted to begin union conversations with Disciples "at the earliest mutually convenient time." Official conversations began immediately and continued until 1966, when bilateral discussions were delayed in favor of energetic participation in the Consultation on Church Union that envisioned a wider union based upon an emerging theological consensus. In 1971, the General Assembly of the Christian Church (Disciples of Christ), meeting in Louisville, received a resolution calling for an "acceleration of conversations with the United Church of Christ, looking toward early union." Concluding that the work of COCU was a longer-range process than originally thought, Kenneth Teegarden and Robert Moss, presidents of their respective church bodies, together proposed in 1975 a resumption of union talks.

The General Synod and General Assembly in 1977 approved a joint resolution authorizing a two-year period of exploration at all levels of church life regarding union. At the end of two years, the two churches authorized a six-year (1979–1985) study of baptism, the Lord's supper, mission, and ministry and appointed a joint steering committee with Kenneth Teegarden and Avery Post (successor to Robert Moss as President of the United Church of Christ) as cochairs. "Progress," reported Dr. Teegarden in 1980, "is both good and slow." It is slow, he continued, because "everybody realizes that church union is not going to occur because of some legislative acts at denominational headquarters from the top down."

Covenant Study Packets were prepared by the joint steering committee and 11,000 were sold during 1981 and 1982 alone. In partnership, regional and conference ministers invited 700 congregations to participate in a special study process. Over 625 accepted. Disciples and UCC congregations were paired to share in the study together. A joint meeting of the Disciples Council of Ministers and the United Church of Christ executives occurred in February 1983, involving the leadership in the covenantal process. In fitting closure to Teegarden's last General Assembly as General Minister and President, the 1985 Des Moines General Assembly approved the establishment of an "ecumenical partnership" between Disciples and the UCC, thereby making a firm commitment to become one church, leaving any actual union to be worked out gradually and naturally through a "shared life." The General Synod approved the same resolution.[36]

Teegarden's correspondence contained a sprinkling of letters opposed to the talks, usually stating they did not want Disciples to "join" the United Church of Christ. He answered them courteously, but firmly. "I am glad you feel free to express any dissent you may have. This characterizes the kind of church we are–one that has unity with diversity… What is being explored is whether or not our two churches, which have so much in common from the beginning, should seek to discover whether God wills for us to be one church. It certainly would not be a matter of either *joining* the other. If it ever comes about, it will be because of our faithfulness to the Bible which records Jesus prayer that all his followers should be one."

By way of epilogue, in 1989 both the Synod and the Assembly passed a resolution declaring that "a relationship of 'full communion' now exists between our churches." Both church bodies began to hold occasional joint gatherings of the General Assembly and General Synod, the first in 1993 in St. Louis and the second in Kansas City in 2001. And in 1995 the General Synod and the General Assembly both affirmed a common Global Ministries Board of the Christian Church (Disciples of Christ) and the United Church of Christ.[37]

Social Justice

Kenneth Teegarden believed the church needed to stand with the poor and the outcasts and to be an advocate of human rights, an instrument to alleviate world hunger and a maker of peace. Early in his tenure as General Minister and President he wrote, "For the church not to be actively involved in seeking to secure basic human rights for people everywhere is really a denial of the fundamental precepts of Christianity." Then he added, "Separation of Christianity and humanism is unscriptural. It diverts us from the ministry of servant-hood."[38]

In all five General Assemblies held during his years as General Minister and President resolutions regarding human rights and peace with justice appeared on the docket. At the 1979 gathering two lengthy reports were received from the Division of Overseas Ministries and approved: one on world hunger, the other on human rights. There were also resolutions to end the arms race, to support the Equal Rights Amendment, and to urge the church to be a witness for world peace. In 1981 the Assembly approved the designation of a "Peace Sunday"; a resolution supporting the establishment of a "Peace Academy"; and a resolution advocating a nuclear arms freeze. The 1983 General Assembly debated and approved resolutions opposing apartheid in South Africa by use of divestiture with corporations doing business in South Africa; opposing the Mid-East arms race; supporting human rights in Iran; assuring asylum in the United States as required by law; and expressing appreciation to the Roman Catholic Bishops for their statement on world peace.[39]

An achievement especially prized by Kenneth Teegarden was the 1985 publication of *Seeking God's Peace in a Nuclear Age*. In the preface, he explained his rationale for originating the project: "The church has a responsibility to provide its members guidance for their ethical thinking. I appointed a Panel on Christian Ethics in a Nuclear Age...to reflect upon those issues and to share with the membership the results of that reflection." The panel, appointed in 1983 and chaired by T. J. Liggett, worked two years on the subject, publishing their result in May 1985, to coincide with the International Year of Peace. Teegarden thought, "*Seeking God's Peace in a Nuclear Age* may be the most significant thing to come out of the Disciples' 'peace with justice' priority." The little eighty-five-page volume was circulated widely to boards, committees, units, and regions of the Christian Church (Disciples of Christ). Ronald Osborn called this work the "high water mark" of Kenneth Teegarden's years as General Minister and President. And T. J. Liggett, who chaired the panel, wrote to Dr. Teegarden, "the coming generation of Disciples will recognize your emphasis on a Christian witness for Peace as the most enduring contribution of your leadership."[40]

The period of Teegarden's ministry saw more than thirty resolutions come before the General Assembly regarding civil liberties, human rights, hunger, and peace with justice. Sixteen of those were resolutions regarding peace with justice, twice as many as would appear during the next twenty years. He did not personally sponsor them, but a sizeable portion came from general units with whom he regularly communicated. Disciples, aware of his position on such matters, knew they could count on his support. He had written openly to the membership:

> It seems to me that it is the responsibility of leaders of the congregation to give people an opportunity to deepen their faith by confronting the knotty moral and theological questions. That is as much a ministry to them as calling on them when they are sick. There is no question that social action and social issues have caused some problems in congregations in the past decade. But the agonies and ecstasies of arriving at decisions of faith should be what the gospel is all about.

Two-thirds of the sixty resolutions on international relations considered by the General Assembly between 1971 and 2003 came before the Assembly during his tenure. His determination that the church should witness on the subject is clearly manifested in the high volume of resolutions addressing peace, justice, and social issues during his time as General Minister and President. It is also manifested in the ministry he performed with Disciples' cultural expressions. He helped bring into existence the Hispanic Caucus in 1975, and also the Hispanic Bilingual Fellowship in 1981 that led the way to the establishment of the Hispanic Central Pastoral Office in 1992. In 1978 he helped establish the Fellowship of Asian American Disciples, then the American Asian Disciples in 1979, and the partner relationship with AAD in 1984 that ultimately evolved into the establishment of American Asian Ministries in 1992. It was during Teegarden's tenure that the church elected its first African American Moderator, Walter Bingham, and its first African American Regional Minister in 1979, John Compton, who was also the first African American to head a general unit, DHM, in 1982. These initiatives did not happen by accident; they required the full commitment and support of the General Minister and President.[41]

Policy on World Missions

Kenneth Teegarden's years as General Minister and President were marked with a major policy transformation in the Division of Overseas Ministry. Robert Thomas, the president of DOM, thought the proper description of the modern missionary era should be the "servant stage" of the Disciples century-long heritage in the mission field. Disciples originated the concept of self-administration under Dale Fiers leadership of the UCMS. Robert Thomas now sought to construct a theological and philosophical framework for this new "servant stage." Thomas, an insightful and enlightened leader, understood the wholeness of church. The policy he sought and of which he was the predominant author could easily have been developed by staff and approved by the DOM board with no further involvement from the General Board or General Assembly. But after a four-year period of crafting the new policy statement, Thomas demanded it be sent forward to the General Board and finally to the General Assembly at Anaheim in 1981. The policy received overwhelming approval—and consequently *formal ownership by the whole church.* Following an extensive historical overview the document articulated twelve theological principles for overseas ministry. Among those principles were: missionary commitment is grounded in God's love for all humankind and Christ's liberating resurrection; the church exists for the sake of the world, not itself; Discipleship makes Christians aware they belong inescapably together; the gospel includes the obligation to denounce all that hinders wholeness; the church is called to identify with the oppressed, the poor, the prisoners, and the sick; social action and evangelism are one; the church is called to stand against that which destroys people; and the church is called to support people who suffer on behalf of justice and freedom.[42]

Teegarden called these principles "thoroughly Biblical, evangelical, radical and recognizing the Christian as servant, not master, the mission as losing one's self, not gaining." The approval of the policy represented a major achievement for Disciples world mission, and also for the polity of restructure that proclaimed the "wholeness of church."

Closure for the Restructure Generation

When Dr. Teegarden took office in 1973, veterans of restructure composed the General Cabinet: W. A. Welsh, Robert Thomas, Kenneth Kuntz, William Gibble, William Martin Smith, Rolland Sheafor, William Miller, James Suggs, Spencer Austin, James Reed, Roland Huff, and George Beazley. In 1973 George Beazley unexpectedly died on a trip to Moscow and was succeeded by Paul Crow. Spencer Austin retired in the mid-seventies. Jean Woolfolk followed Austin.

The veterans were beginning to retire. By the time he left office, only James Reed of the original cabinet leaders mentioned above remained, along with Deputy General Minister Howard Dentler. A whole new generation sat at the table. The same pattern was true of regional ministers. By 1985 a majority of the restructure generation had retired, and Teegarden found himself surrounded with a substantially new group of leaders. In his final State of the Church address at Des Moines in 1985, he made note of this circumstance: "Of the 128 people who made up the Commission on Restructure…one of five of them is now deceased. More than half the rest are retired. In the regions, 91 percent of the regional ministers who were serving at the time of the adoption of our new covenantal relationship are gone from their posts. Ten of the eleven presidents of the church's general administrative units have also changed." A look back across his twelve years disclosed *The Design* had been implemented and amended. The concept of a representative General Assembly was accepted and functioning. The colleges and universities were in covenant. The church was learning to confront moral and ethical issues in the society around it. The issue of ordaining gays and lesbians had been addressed. The Covenantal Partnership with the United Church of Christ appeared ready to move toward "full communion." And the first wave of post-restructure leaders of regions and general units were assimilated into their positions. Kenneth Teegarden's final words to the 1985 Assembly set the course for the future: "We come to Des Moines with the responsibility to end one era and initiate another. For the last 25 years we have been 'becoming church.' It is time to close one era and enter a new one. Now we put aside *becoming* and begin to *be*."[43]

CHAPTER VIII

Into the Twenty-First Century

Sociocultural Challenge

We have a problem, Disciples. This is no time for denial. Neither is it a time for panic. This is a time for honesty and frank recognition, for our best thinking, our best work, our deepest prayer, our fullest commitment, and our realization that we are utterly dependent upon God.

RICHARD L. HAMM
From Mainline to Frontline, *1996*[1]

Disciples reached the high-water mark of their twentieth-century membership in the year 1957–1,951,820 (including both Disciples and Independents). At this writing, fifty-one years later in 2008, the total membership figure stands at 691,160, an approximate 64 percent decline. (Participating membership declined from 1,639,495 to 448,316 during those same years, a decline of 73 percent.) The largest loss–351,000 total members and 641,474 participating members–occurred between the years 1958 and 1968. This was during the restructure process marked by a major withdrawal of Independents. Since 1970–71, the date the *Year Book and Directory,* at the request of Independent congregations, stopped including Independents, the trajectory of total membership loss has averaged about 19,500 per year as reflected by decade in the chart below; during the same time frame participating membership declined at a rate of about 12,500 per year. In 2008 Disciples had approximately 600 congregations with 125 or more in worship. The process of Independent congregation withdrawal continued until 1993, and Resolution 9516 approved in 1995 established a process for deleting nonreporting congregations.

Decade	Total Membership loss	Participating Membership loss
1958-1968	-351,172	-641,474
[Restructure: Withdrawal of Independents]		
1970-1980	-211,620	-138,473
1980-1990	-161,384	-83,757
1990-2000	-222,326	-154,963

Based upon a review of data from Disciples Year Books, 1950 to 2007

Based on the research of Roger Stump, certain "demographic" factors contributed to the decline and are cited by Newell Williams in *A Case Study of Mainstream Protestantism*. Between 1971 and 1980, Disciples congregations, reflecting the denomination's small-town orientation, were less likely to grow in counties where population growth was less than the national median, in counties where Independent Christian Churches were present and in counties where the combined membership of Presbyterians and Methodists declined. Nearly half of all Disciples in 1971 (point of division with Independents) lived in counties having all three of these conditions; three-fourths lived in counties with at least two of these conditions. The largest numerical increase among Disciples up to the time of restructure occurred in ten counties, each containing a major city. Urbanization played a key role in Disciples growth during the first half of the twentieth century, a growth driven by large and prosperous urban congregations. But these same urban counties suffered the largest Disciples membership decline during the last third of the century.

The percent of mission support of general units and regions contributed by congregations grew from the early 1950s until 1990, with a stable percentage during the late eighties. In 1957 total giving from 8,080 congregations was $73 million, of which $8.6 million–or *12 percent*–was given to Disciples mission beyond the congregation. In 2008 the total giving from 3,754 congregations was $432 million, of which $25.2 million–or *5.8 percent*–was contributed to Disciples regions, units, colleges, and seminaries and the Office of General Minister and President. Congregational outreach giving actually increased in aggregate, but more was given horizontally rather than vertically, with more money actually given, in some years, to non-Disciples causes and special mission projects such as Habitat for Humanity than to the Disciples Mission Fund. The trajectory by decade cited on the next page reveals the percentage allocated through congregational stewardship to the Disciples Mission Fund (formerly Basic Mission Finance and Unified Promotion).

The claim of bureaucratic and denominational hierarchy expansion is a myth. In reality the size and influence of the general expression of Disciples diminished as financial constraints deepened.

Year Book	Total Cong. Giving	Disciples mission	Percentage
1957	$73,000,000	$8,600,000	11.7%
1960	84,900,000	10,600,000	12.4%
1970	108,700,000	15,300,000	14%
1980	200,400,000	27,400,000	13.6%
1990	306,300,000	30,000,000	9.7%
2000	389,000,000	31,000,000	7.9%
2008	431,700,000	25,250,000	5.8%

Based upon a review of data from Disciples Year Books, 1950 to 2008

Beginning in the 1960s, the national environment became less supportive of mainline Protestantism (increasingly called "oldline" Protestantism or the Protestant Establishment), less dependent on it as a political force, and less needful of it as a cultural support system. In 1967, Protestantism commanded the preference of 67 percent of the population; by 1991 preference had fallen to 56 percent; in 2003 the preference was 46 percent. Membership within the seven mainline denominations between 1965 and 1992 decreased 20.3 percent. One analyst characterized the time as a "rapid evaporation of denominational loyalty"; another called it a time of "religious disestablishment and the mainline Protestant loss of a position of privilege in the wider culture"; a third said, "Religion lost its power as an integrative force in America"; and Sydney Ahlstrom concluded the " sharp crescendo of social strife seemed to demonstrate that time honored structures of American church life were *irrelevant* to the country's actual condition." "The seeming social irrelevance of the church," he added, "brought profound and widespread disillusionment to the ministers in nearly all denominations." Most analysts concluded American religion had entered a "post-Protestant" era, an age also labeled anti-institutional, anti-establishment, and anti-intellectual. The basic issue, wrote Leonard Sweet, was "the decline of Protestantism as a popular religion." An old religious order, some said, was passing. Others claimed the society had entered a post-Christian era. All of these forces effected Disciples membership, compounded by a deliberate campaign on the part of Independents using "fear" of impending restructure to influence congregations to withdraw before restructure was implemented.[2]

Protestantism had long been part of the "tripartite" religious base of the United States—Protestants, Catholics, and Jews. But in the last third of the twentieth century, Protestantism became conflicted and challenged by a new and virulent strain of the Christian Right, characterized by Susan Jacoby in her recent study *The Age of American Unreason* as "a resurgence of militant, anti-secular, anti-intellectual Fundamentalism." Jacoby argues the growth of fundamentalism came at the expense of mainstream Protestantism, accelerating across four decades into the 1990s and giving birth to the Christian Right. Simultaneously, Protestantism faced, for the first time, a growing religious pluralism within the nation. By the 1980s Protestants were dividing more along political lines than denominational lines. Membership in evangelical churches exploded, claiming a quarter of the nation according to the research of Robert Wuthnow, Wade Roof, and Bruce Schulman. During the 1950s beliefs and values of mainline churches were "virtually indistinguishable from the culture." Even the motion picture industry produced movies like *The Ten Commandments*, *Quo Vadis*, *The Robe*, and *Ben Hur.*

For maturing Baby Boomers in the 1960s and 1970s, denominational religion became a low personal priority. A new secular world emerged, characterized not so much by an absence of religion but rather by a "continuing multiplication of new options"–some religious, some spiritual, and some anti-religious. A robust religious pluralism offered options ranging from Sufi dancing to Gregorian chants, including Muslim, Buddhist, Hindu, Sikh, Sun Myung Moon's Unification Church (Moonies), David Koresh and the Branch Davidians, Hare Krishna, Elizabeth Clare Prophet's Church Universal and Triumphant in Montana, Zen, Jim Jones' Peoples Temple, Yoga, Reiki, Sri Chinmoy–an endless and ever increasing list. Wade Roof found the number of Transcendental Meditation adherents in the United States to have become equal to the number of Presbyterians. With 1,200 mosques and Islamic centers attracting in excess of six million Muslims in 2001, Muslims outnumbered (taken separately) Jews, Presbyterians, Episcopalians, Disciples, and other traditional religious groups. Due to immigration and conversion, two of the most rapidly growing religions in the nation are Hinduism and Buddhism. In her 2008 study *Liberty of Conscience,* philosopher Martha Nussbaum states it is inaccurate to characterize America today as either a Christian or a Protestant nation; it is pluralistic.

Martin Marty wrote of the modern age as one of "a bewildering religious pluralism," while the *Encyclopedia of American Religion* reported that, at the time, 1,200 different religious groups active in the United States. During the late twentieth century American religion struggled in a pluralistic world in which new forms of belief and unbelief continuously appeared and contended with each other. Leonard Sweet said of the period, "Protestants found themselves inhabiting a religious landscape of unbelief and over belief." The result of religious pluralism for Christianity, claimed Charles Taylor, was a "retreat from the public square." Several analysts began to use terms like "Christian Nominalism" or "Minimal Religion" to define Christianity in this era.

If the "New Age" generation became part of a church other than "evangelical," they were more likely to join nondenominational groups, trans-denominational groups, parachurches, cults, or no church at all.

Americans with no formal religious ties doubled between 1990 and 2001, from 14.3 million to 29.4 million. Baby Boomers' "local" understanding of church–linked with their unfamiliarity approaching a virtual absence of knowledge regarding denominational programs, policies, and traditional religious language–called into question the allegation of "social justice advocacy" as a cause of denominational decline.

Most religious historians cite secularism as the *major* cause of Disciples membership decline along with the decline of other mainline Protestant bodies in the late twentieth century–*not* competition from the Religious Right, *not* the social justice component of the Disciples agenda, *not* internal liberal/conservative theological confrontations, *not* exclusively demographic shifts, and *not* restructure. While these factors contributed, secularism drew people away from the Disciples and other mainline denominations, weakening the Protestant establishment as a personal religious priority.[3]

Charles Taylor, in his 2007 Templeton Prize–winning work, *A Secular Age,* described the late twentieth-century religious environment as a time of "disaffection and distance from religion." Religious belief enjoyed an unchallengeable status in earlier decades, a status presently subordinated to the powerful new phenomenon–secularization. Into the 1950s, religious belief was so interwoven with social life that one was not conceivable without the other. Joining a church, said Taylor, was more about social identity than about God. Consequently, an inflationary membership growth following World War II began to dissipate in the late 1950s. Meanwhile, mainline denominations began to grow older, members were dying, and strategies to replace their numbers were inadequate, particularly the near absence of new church establishment. Decline in numbers, influence, and status was not a surprising result.[4]

Meanwhile, many Baby Boomers desired to be "spiritual, but not religious." "New Age Spiritualists" viewed spirituality as a quest, an intense search for an adequate spiritual life, placing high value on individual intuition and instinct while rejecting institutional religion. Although feeling a need for spirituality, they were illiterate concerning the sources that support spirituality: the language of faith, spiritual disciplines, theological teachings of the church, multigenerational communities of support, spiritual systems, and biblical knowledge. Wary of denominations, they desired to explore the Christian faith without preconditions–a circumstance referred to by Taylor as the "beginning of a new age of religious searching." Wade Roof defined Boomers as a "generation of seekers," empowering *self,* rather than *community,* to direct spiritual life. Their beliefs and wide range of new modes of religious practice were outside religious orthodoxy– reflecting the shift from institutional religion to spirituality.

A sizeable body of literature appeared on this spiritual revolution, as well as on the new phenomenon labeled "emerging church": Wade Roof, *Spiritual Marketplace*; Paul Heelas et al., *The Spiritual Revolution*; Robert

Wuthnow, *After Heaven*; Gibbs and Bolger, *Emerging Churches*; D. A. Carson, *Becoming Conversant with the Emerging Church*; Don Kimball, *The Emerging Church*; and a host of others. New Age and postmodern persons did not think of the church as a place, a bureaucratic structure, a meeting, a time, or Sunday-focused. They thought of it as a way of life. Their beliefs were eclectic and diverse; they were well-educated, young in age (18–34), and their buzzwords included *postmodern, emerging, seekers, mission, spiritual,* and *deconstruction.* Traditional rites of passage such as baptism and marriage (or, if they married, they often chose a venue other than church) were bypassed. Taylor concluded that denominations in twenty-first–century America would continue to have great difficulty maintaining their membership because they were not holding the young.[5]

The combined loss of membership and mission dollars within the Disciples created an ethos of stress. When the structure came under severe financial constraint, the competition and wrangling among and between general ministries and regions intensified. Carping about absence of leadership in all areas of church life became a denominational sport; complaining about perceived weaknesses of the General Minister and President, from Dale Fiers to Sharon Watkins, became commonplace–criticized by one historian as "the failure of professional leadership"; and, as expected, many cited "structure" as the heart of the problem, claiming that although Disciples governance is supposedly a binding agreement identified as "covenant," Disciples behavior is more like a "confederation," an alliance in which parties keep their independence, do not pledge mutual accountability, and if they do not feel obliged to abide by a General Assembly resolution they ignore it. Yet to invest more power and authority in Disciples ecclesial structures would have been viewed as a betrayal of members most deeply held principles, and not to do so made many governance issues virtually impossible to solve. For example, the stress incurred through membership and financial loss produced a series of unsuccessful attempts to formulate a new means of distributing limited mission dollars. But, throughout the 1990s and into the twenty-first century, regions and general ministries were unable to engage their creative energies to achieve mutual support and accountability, the very soul of covenant.[6]

John O. Humbert:
Transition to a New Order

*We are moving toward establishing a priority for the church as we
look toward the 1990s. I have listened to the people in the pews and
pulpits in twenty regions. The members of the general board engaged in
envisioning what the future ought to be for Disciples. We have carefully
studied the Division of Homeland Ministries research on the views of
our people. The Council of Ministers and the Administrative Committee
have had strong input into the substance of the proposed priority... For
a period of six years the Christian Church (Disciples of Christ) will
focus on—developing vital congregations as dynamic faith communities
in prophetic, redemptive and reconciling ministries to the whole world.*

JOHN O. HUMBERT
"Proposed New Church Priority," 1987[7]

John O. Humbert—open, ingratiating, intuitive—was elected to succeed
Kenneth Teegarden in the position of General Minister and President at
the Des Moines General Assembly in 1985. Humbert, a sixth-generation
Disciple, claimed a lineage of Disciples distinction. Within two weeks of
Thomas Campbell's emigration from Ireland to Washington, Pennsylvania,
in 1807, two families followed from his Ahorey congregation: those of
Thomas Hodgens and James Foster, whose wife, Martha, was the daughter
of Thomas Campbell. Both Thomas Hodgens and James Foster were great-
great-great-grandfathers of John O. Humbert. Both were charter members of
the Brush Run congregation and the Christian Association of Washington.
Foster participated as a deacon in Alexander Campbell's ordination at Brush
Run and was himself ordained an elder by Alexander Campbell.[8]

An ordained Disciples minister can be found in every Humbert generation from James Foster to John Humbert, including his grandfather and
grandmother Humbert (Godlove Orth and Mary Eleanor "Ella"). Ella was
invited to speak at the 1909 International Convention at Pittsburgh, but
was pregnant with their son Royal and sent her address, "The Investment
of Life," to be read in her absence. John Humbert's father, Morton
Dale Humbert, and Morton Dale's three siblings—Harold, Royal, and
Madge—were all ordained Disciples ministers. The family line from James
Foster through John Humbert and his niece produced a total of fifteen
ministers.

John Orth Humbert, born October 1927, spent his first year in Richmond, Missouri, where his father M. Dale pastored the Christian Church.
The following year began the Humbert family migration to the rural Ohio
towns of Ravenna and Bellefontaine, where young John was raised. At age

eight he spent a summer with his grandparents in the state of Washington and began third grade that September at the Yakama Indian Christian Mission. At Bellefontaine High School John Humbert exhibited the skills of a natural athlete, lettering in football, basketball, baseball, and track. During those four years he also attended Disciples summer youth conferences at Wilmington, where counselors and faculty included Myron Cole, Gaines Cook, Dale Fiers, Herald Monroe, and John Updegraff. At the summer conference of 1945 young John Humbert made the decision to invest his life in ministry, rather than coaching.[9]

To prepare for ministry, he enrolled at Butler University on an athletic scholarship and was a member of the varsity basketball team. Meanwhile, his father moved to a new ministry in Niles, Ohio. In the fall of 1947 John transferred to Youngstown State, serving nearby student pastorates in Hanoverton and Augusta. Following his 1949 graduation, John entered the College of the Bible at Lexington, Kentucky, to pursue graduate theological education. Professors Dwight Stephenson and Howard Short especially influenced Humbert's intellectual development. On Christmas Eve 1950 he fell ill with tuberculosis, underwent surgery, and spent the next four months in a tuberculosis sanitarium where medical diagnosis speculated he would die. But he survived, resumed his education in 1952, graduated with honors from the College of the Bible in 1954, and accepted a position as organizing pastor of a new church start in Dayton, Ohio (1954–1962). There he built the membership to 300 and constructed two buildings. While pastoring in Dayton, he accepted appointment by Gaines Cook to serve as program director of the International Convention, a position he held until 1966. John became senior pastor at North Chevy Chase in 1962; at Euclid Avenue in Cleveland in 1970; and accepted the position of Deputy General Minister and President under Kenneth L. Teegarden in 1977. His responsibilities included serving as representative to general unit board meetings, staff liaison to the Task Force on Renewal and Structural Reform, and ex-officio representative to the Executive Committee of the Conference of Regional Ministers and Moderators, as well as providing staff oversight for coordinating the Task Force on Funding Criteria for Seminaries and developing program and worship for the General Assemblies. He viewed his term and role as General Minister and President as a "bridge to the future," a bridge between restructure and post-restructure.[10]

Christology

A developing tension between Disciples with evangelical leanings and Disciples engaged in social justice activities existed at the time of John Humbert's election. Many were critical of the advocacy for social justice, holding to a belief the church lost members because of it. Evangelism, they claimed, was being neglected. Humbert spoke directly to the issue in his installation address, identifying the center of the tension as christology. He admonished Disciples not to settle for a fragmented confession. "Christ," said Humbert, "is both Lord *and* Savior; *Lord* of the whole creation including social and political systems, social justice and liberation; and *Savior* of a person's inner will and heart." This call to the full biblical richness of Jesus Christ would become the touchstone of Humbert's ministry. T. J. Liggett, moderator of the church during Humbert's first two years, affirmed this view in the introduction he wrote for Humbert's 1987 book, *A House of Living Stones.*

> In classical prototypes, the ministry can be conceived in both priestly and prophetic forms...the former concerned about the vertical relationship with God and the latter about the horizontal relationship with fellow human beings–Humbert rightly affirms the place of both...spirituality and ethics are not to be separated... There is no place in the religion of Jesus for privatized religion that is self-serving and aloof from the vicissitudes of the world.

At the 1985 Assembly in Des Moines a resolution urged acceptance of belief in biblical infallibility. The General Board submitted a substitute resolution affirming the centrality and inspiration of the Bible. Richard Bowman, pastor of the congregation submitting the original resolution and deeply offended by the substitution, within two years formed a group known as Disciple Renewal. The group submitted a resolution [8728] at the next General Assembly declaring Jesus Christ as the only path to salvation. The Commission on Theology received the resolution by referral, formulated a response, and reported to the 1989 General Assembly "eligibility for salvation is God's decision and human judgment in the matter is inappropriate to the gospel–human judgment cannot place parameters on the grace of God." Disciple Renewal people were again indignant. This time the question, referred to Reference and Counsel, was modified to include the words "no statement of faith speaks for everybody in the church. The report is one resource...for study and response." When final approval of the report came, Dr. Humbert asked for personal privilege to lead the Assembly in reading the Preamble to *The Design.* Later in the same Assembly, the Special Rules of Procedure for General Assembly were amended to read "A Sense-of-the-Assembly resolution is out of order and shall not be considered...when it contains doctrinal statements as a *test of fellowship.*" By 1990 Disciple Renewal had employed a full-time executive, Kevin D. Ray, and soon was publishing its own journal, *Disciple Renewal,* with its stated purpose of "changing the theology of our denomination." It later developed its own pastoral placement process, established its own national and regional assemblies, its own seminary ties, and links to its own missionaries.[11]

Tension between Congregations and Leadership

A perceived distance between congregations and leadership of the church, an issue common to all mainline Protestantism at the time, presented a second challenge to Dr. Humbert. Newell Williams, who later researched the matter, discovered fundamental differences between the worldviews of laity and clergy. On the question of inerrancy of scripture only 14 percent of clergy believed in biblical inerrancy compared to 48 percent of the laity; on the question of abortion 73 percent of the clergy believed in pro-choice while only 14 percent of the laity held that view; 79 percent of the clergy supported gay rights, but only 34 percent of the laity did so; and 83 percent of the clergy supported federal welfare for the poor compared to 10 percent of the laity. Clearly, a gap existed between laity and clergy on issues of theology and social justice. More important, the gap between laity and clergy accented the long-standing difficulty of general and regional leadership to effectively communicate the agenda of the church to the congregations and members in clear, biblical, theological terms. Leonard Sweet wrote of the circumstance, "there was a foot on the hose in the flow of information from clergy to laity, from seminary to sanctuary, from denominational staff to congregations." Congregations, believing church bureaucracies were out of touch, increasingly distrusted them.[12]

Sensitive to this tension Humbert, in his installation address, committed to a series of listening conferences across the church. He subsequently conducted listening conferences in twenty regions; led futuring sessions with the General Board; participated in dialogue sessions with the Council of Ministers; and presided over a four-day retreat with the General Cabinet. This process led him to propose a priority for Disciples: "To develop vital congregations as dynamic faith communities in prophetic, redemptive and reconciling ministries to the whole church." It was resoundingly approved by the 1987 General Assembly.[13]

Humbert, eager for all parts of the church to work together, organized a church-wide planning conference, offering access, participation, and shared decision-making on implementing the priority. Designed as a working conference of small groups, it intentionally brought together representatives from all three manifestations of the church in mutual collaboration on how to develop vital congregations. There were 675 participants in the conference, held at Lexington, Kentucky, June 1988. In addition, thirty-seven locations across the church linked into Lexington through DisciplesNet, the first significant use of computer technology by Disciples for church-wide planning. The conference based its work on the biblical images of vital congregations Humbert had identified from his study of the New Testament and which he shared with the conference: *confessing* congregations, *teaching* congregations, *caring* congregations, *worshiping* congregations, *sharing* congregations, *evangelistic* congregations, *reconciling* congregations, *ecumenical* congregations, *mission* congregations, and *peacemaking* congregations.[14]

Full Communion with the United Church of Christ

Ecumenical accomplishments of this period included General Assembly approval of the COCU Consensus of the Quest of the Church of Christ Uniting in 1989 and the opening of an ecumenical dialogue with the Russian Orthodox Church. Of particular significance was the 1989 approval of full communion with the United Church of Christ. In 1985 both the General Synod of the United Church of Christ and the General Assembly of the Christian Church (Disciples of Christ) approved a "declaration of partnership," stating, "we wish to express our unity in Christ by doing nothing alone which can be done together." Despite the opposition of Disciple Renewal, who characterized the United Church of Christ as "the most apostate denomination in the United States" (because it ordained gays and lesbians), a twenty-two-member partnership committee was appointed, with both church presidents, John Humbert and Avery Post, as members. In 1989 both the Synod and Assembly approved a proposed resolution proclaiming, "the relationship of full communion now exists between our churches." The foundation of the relationship drew on theological understandings reached in the COCU consensus and the *Baptism, Eucharist and Ministry* publication of the World Council of Churches. It contained five points of acceptance and cooperation.

1. Both churches confess that Jesus is the Christ, son of living God.
2. Members of both churches are members of the one universal church of Jesus Christ, and are members of the one body.
3. Members share in celebrating the Lord's Supper.
4. Ordained ministers of each partner church are ministers of the word and sacrament.
5. Both churches search for mutual ways of manifesting the common mission of witness and service.

The achievement of full communion with the United Church of Christ is viewed as a major milestone in Disciples ecumenical history. John Humbert thoughtfully cautioned, "This is not a substitute for full unity, but it is a practical way toward that unity."[15]

Indianapolis Office Facilities

The General Assembly in 1985 called for leaders to find and develop new facilities for offices in Indianapolis. Humbert appointed a "New Facilities Committee," naming Richard Knowlton as chair. An architect was retained and a site selected in the historic district on Indiana Avenue near the downtown canal. The architect designed a building specifically for this site and Lilly Endowment granted $4.2 million dollars to commence the project. The Indianapolis African American community leaders, with whom the church had consulted and received approval, subsequently decided the site needed to be preserved for black community development. The church purchased a new site two blocks further down Indiana Avenue. A new building design was completed and a model displayed at the 1987 General Assembly in Louisville. Bill Barnes, development officer at Christian Theological Seminary, agreed to become the chief fund-raiser for the new building. At the 1989 Indianapolis General Assembly, a parade of members walked to the new site for a dedication of the grounds. Near the close of Humbert's final year a capital campaign was launched to help underwrite the construction. When he left office in 1991 the project was still in place to move ahead although, with the exception of Lilly Endowment, neither the business community of Indianapolis nor the membership of the church seemed inclined to provide financial support for the project.[16]

Social Justice

At the outset of his term, Humbert made clear his unequivocal commitment to "the primary biblical mandate for reconciliation of the whole human family." He pledged to bring a woman to the General Minister's staff, and promptly named Rev. Claudia Grant as Deputy General Minister and President. Several resolutions were submitted and approved in support of social justice positions during the three General Assemblies of Humbert's six-year tenure. Among those were: a call for Preservation of the Family Farm System; opposition to Racism; reaffirmation of Disciples commitment to Civil Rights; and one that stirred the deep strength of feeling in Humbert—the Pledge of Resistance to prevent the Invasion of Central America. Counterrevolutionaries supported by the United States military were accused of being involved in the murders of forty-nine health workers, eighty-nine teachers, and 3500 children. Humbert, a member of the Advisory Board of the Christic Institute in Washington, D.C., had been regularly informed of U.S. arms shipments being sent to the Contras. He repeatedly wrote and visited members of Congress in an effort to persuade them to halt the practice. On Ash Wednesday, March 1987, working through the National Council of Churches, he led a service of worship on the steps of the Capitol. The small group of four (including Avery Post, president of the United Church of Christ, and Arie Brouwer, General Secretary of the National Council of Churches) moved into the Rotunda to continue the service, an act of nonviolent civil disobedience. They were arrested, held in jail for eight hours, then released. John Humbert presided at the subsequent press conference broadcast on CBS News explaining their actions. House Speaker James Wright, present for the news conference, spoke in support of their action. Later in the spring, Congress voted to end funding of the Contras and the June 1987 issue of *The Disciple* carried Humbert's explanation of the situation in Nicaragua, one of the most impassioned articles he ever authored. Based on chapters 44 and 45 of Isaiah he wrote, in part:

I believe the policy of the present U.S. Government toward Nicaragua and El Salvador stands squarely in contradiction to the tide of the God who acts in history to set people free. [The Ash Wednesday service] was the worship of the sovereign God who acted in the Babylonian captivities of history. It was a service of confession for our responsibility as a nation for taking so many lives...an intercessory prayer for our suffering brothers and sisters in Nicaragua... I believe that the God of the prophets, the God who is in Christ reconciling the world, is at work to set people free. For the sake of the very lives of our brothers and sisters in Central America let our government join the tide of the God who acts in history to set people free or, for God's sake, at least get out of the way!

In November 1987, Humbert led a delegation of eight Disciples leaders on a visit to Managua, Matagalpa, and Jinotega in Nicaragua. He declared to the people in Nicaragua: "We want to say as church we stand with you and support your commitment to the Lordship of Jesus Christ. As Christians we understand what the sources of peace will be." In Jinotega, the mayor had been kidnapped the week before their visit and bombings were still an occasional occurrence. Marcelino Davila, the old man who founded the Christian Mission Church among the poor in Jinotega, wrote a poem because it so moved him the church would make such a visit. And the people there proudly displayed news clippings telling of Humbert's arrest.[17]

At home, Humbert found certain Disciples disapproved of his action. Some canceled a few of his scheduled speaking engagements. Eighty percent of his correspondence on the subject, however, strongly supported his Nicaraguan stand and the Disciples Peace Fellowship honored him at the 1987 General Assembly for his actions. An amusing incident occurred when one delegate came to the microphone during a 1987 Assembly business session to voice opposition to Humbert's Nicaraguan actions and stated, "If Alexander Campbell were alive today, he would turn over in his grave."

The Election

By existing rules, John Humbert at age sixty-four could not stand for election to a second six-year term. He would be the last General Minister and President to view *The Design* through the eyes of one who helped create it. As staff liaison to the Task Force on Renewal and Structural Reform for eight years and as General Minister and President for six years, he heavily invested himself in preserving and strengthening a document he held in high regard. Although some thought the retirement rule restrictive, Humbert did not seek to have it modified.

Following several months of research and interviews the search committee nominated Michael Kinnamon to be the fourth General Minister and

President. The nomination, approved by the General Board and submitted to the 1991 General Assembly in Tulsa, Oklahoma, for official action, required 66 2/3 percent approval of voting representatives. Kinnamon, an ordained minister, held a B.A. from Brown University along with M.A. and Ph.D. from the University of Chicago. He served as executive secretary of the World Council of Churches Commission on Faith and Order (1980–83); assistant professor of theology at Christian Theological Seminary (1983–1988); dean of the faculty and professor of theology and ecumenical studies at Lexington Theology Seminary since 1988; and authored numerous books and articles on ecumenism. For progressive and moderate Disciples his nomination was exhilarating; but for Disciple Renewal and other conservatives his inclusive stand on the ordination of gays and lesbians was unacceptable.

It was widely rumored that on the day of the election, several busloads of delegates arrived from nearby regions to vote on the General Minister and President, left the following day, and did not participate in any other part of the Assembly. The rumor was untrue. The credentials committee reported that only three new persons registered on the day of the election. To date this was the only GMP election to use a secret ballot; all others have been by acclamation. A count of the votes revealed Dr. Kinnamon received slightly in excess of 66% of the vote, but was short of the required 66 2/3 percent (5,623 votes were cast: 3,679 for; 1,944 against [there were also 28 abstentions]–65 votes short of election . Following the announcement of Kinnamon's defeat, moderator King David Cole led the Assembly in prayer.[18]

Later in the Assembly, the Administrative Committee submitted the name of a Decatur, Illinois, pastor, C. William Nichols to serve an interim period of two years, thereby allowing the church to conduct another search process. Kinnamon's defeat spawned a deep sense of disappointment, because a substantial majority of representatives had voted for Kinnamon to be General Minister and President. Many, however, voted against Kinnamon without prejudice against him personally, but because they felt he was not the right person for the position at that time. In various ways 1991 is a line of demarcation in the modern history of Disciples. Momentum on the initiatives of the Humbert years stalled: the capital campaign fell short of its goals, the headquarters building was not constructed, the congregational priority faded, and the psychological impact of the defeat produced an air of cynicism about the ability of the Disciples ecclesial structures and processes to function, even though the election processes had functioned precisely as they were designed. The year also marked the beginning of a precipitous downturn in the percentage of congregational support for Basic Mission Finance to underwrite the ministries of the regional and general expressions of church. William Nichols spoke all across the denomination during his two-year interim, repairing emotional damage where he could, holding the manifestations together, and helping the membership fix their vision on the future. The search process moved forward, nominating Tennessee regional minister Richard L. Hamm to be the next General Minister and President. Hamm received an overwhelming mandate at the 1993 General Assembly in St. Louis.

The Humbert Years

Year Book	Membership	Congregations	Mission support	Percent of total giving
1985	1,137,340	4,301	$28,900,000	11%
[participating] 758,242				
1991	1,039,692	4,105	$30,500,000	9.8%
[participating] 681,246				

Richard L. Hamm: Beyond Restructure

If we commit ourselves to at least one thousand new congregations between 2000 and 2020 we will actually see an accelerated rate of revitalization in our existing congregations due to the renewed sense of mission such an effort will engender... One thousand new Disciples congregations begun between 2000 and 2020, each seeking to realize true community, a deep Christian spirituality, and a passion for justice, would be a significant step forward in faithfulness and growth.

RICHARD L. HAMM
2020 Vision, *2001*[19]

Richard Hamm entered his senior year at a Florida high school in 1965, the year Kenneth Teegarden became Administrative Secretary of the Commission on Brotherhood Restructure. Hamm became the first of the post-restructure generation of leaders. He was born in 1947 in Crawfordsville, Indiana, where most of his relatives lived on nearby farms on which he spent much of his time when not attending church activities at First Christian Church in Crawfordsville. At age nine, young Hamm and his family moved to St. Petersburg, Florida. They joined Mirror Lake Christian Church, the place of Hamm's baptism. Soon thereafter the family became charter members of Palm Lake Christian Church. His experience as president of the Tampa District CYF, president of the Florida State CYF, and attendance at CYF summer conferences, along with the influence of his pastor, Kenneth Dean, led Hamm to decide upon ministry as his future. Following high school, where he lettered in football, basketball, and track, he began his collegiate career at St. Petersburg Junior College. Hamm transferred to Butler University in Indianapolis for his sophomore through senior years, then enrolled at Christian Theological Seminary where he remained enrolled through the completion of his Doctor of Ministry degree, one of the last students allowed to complete a D. Min. without interruption following completion of his M.Div. CTS professor Clark Williamson significantly shaped his thought. Following graduation he became associate pastor of Central Christian Church in Kansas City, Kansas, then founding pastor of the Kansas City, Missouri, North Oak Christian Church (1975–1982), building it to 225 members. He served with distinction as senior minister of First Christian Church in Fort Wayne, Indiana (1982–1990), then accepted a call to be regional minister of Tennessee. Richard Hamm's election as the fifth General Minister and President of the Christian Church (Disciples of Christ) occurred in 1993.[20]

Process of Discernment

Hamm–imaginative, intelligent, filled with reforming zeal–introduced several initiatives in the life of the church, including the establishment of a General Commission on Ministry, biennial-planning sessions of the General Board, and active General Minister and President participation in the leadership selection processes for general units and regions to increase gender and ethnic diversity. One of his most influential innovations, however, was implementing the "Process of Discernment." Having observed in General Assemblies and General Board meetings the "debate and vote" approach resulting in numerous confrontations and internal division, Richard Hamm introduced an alternative concept in 1993–the "Process of Discernment." It provided a means, not necessarily to prepare the church for a vote, but to move the church toward reflection and conversation around issues for which there is little consensus. Among the purposes of discernment were (a) to provide a procedure for dialogue to occur in a context of spiritual disciplines, (b) to establish a process in which all perspectives participate and are heard, (c) to offer a modus operandi to be modeled in all expressions of the church, and (d) to produce useful resources to inform the whole church with the goal of achieving consensus. Pilot processes were begun during the 1990s on "Participation of Gay and Lesbian Persons in the Life of the Church," "Racism," and "The Authority of Scripture." Out of the discernment process on Racism, for example, grew the pro-reconciliation/anti-racism initiative, authorized and implemented by the General Board in congregations, regions, and general units. Some who want Disciples to be more proactive on social justice issues have viewed the process as a means to avoid taking a stand, a process that has weakened the prophetic voice of the church. Since the mid-1990s the number of social justice resolutions has decreased and most national staff positions responsible for social justice have been eliminated. Richard Hamm, however, believed few pay attention to mainline church resolutions because they do not represent a unified opinion. And, if the resolutions do not impact the culture, then why have them? The process is still in use, still being tested and refined. Disciples became pioneers in modeling this methodology. Variations of the approach are being used, at this writing, in most mainline denominations in the United States due to Hamm's advocacy of the method in every ecumenical setting in which he was a participant. Discernment, asserts Hamm, helps the church understand two things: not every issue is best addressed by "debate and vote," and thoughtful discussion of difficult questions can bring enlightenment to the whole church.[21]

2020 Vision

When Richard Hamm assumed office, he studied and compared the rate of new congregational starts with the number of congregations lost over a twenty-year period, 1979-1999.

Gains	Losses
237 new	534 closed
18 reentered	295 withdrawn
5 mergers	29 mergers
62 removed (resolution 9516)	
260 total	920 total

Noting the huge gap between gains and losses and realizing that Disciples had averaged only about twelve new church starts per year for twenty years, while losing on average forty-five congregations per year, Richard Hamm urged the church into a new venture of founding fifty congregations per year for the next twenty years, 2000 to 2020, a goal of 1,000 new congregations. In addition, he prodded the church toward clarity of mission. This goal, based on Micah 6:8 and New Testament witness, became the cornerstone of his *"2020 Vision": To be a faithful, growing church that manifests true community, a deep Christian spirituality, and a passion for justice.* General Assemblies tended to be freestanding events, each planned by a different program committee. Taking responsibility for the direction of the Assemblies, Hamm sought to connect each one to the next, building on the 2020 Vision. Hamm's vision, advocated throughout the church in his addresses (300 addresses in 120 regional visits) and in his book *2020 Vision,* proved to be a significant contribution to the life of Disciples. In the first two years 116 new congregations were started, most of them racially and ethnically mixed. By 2007 it was reported that 504 new congregations had been established, well ahead of the 2020 schedule. It is believed that about one-half of these congregations are new and about one-half adopted, congregations already in existence who decided to become Disciples and are counted as new.[22]

The 2020 Vision included three other priorities: becoming an anti-racist, pro-reconciliation church; leadership development; and an emphasis on Christian unity. In 1995, the General Assembly meeting in Pittsburgh voted by a huge margin to commit itself to continuing the "process of covenanting" as presented by the 1988 COCU document. Upset by the vote, due to their objections to COCU, Disciple Renewal issued a "Pittsburgh Proclamation," establishing an independent organization of conservative members of the Christian Church (Disciples of Christ). Disciple Renewal renamed itself "Disciples Heritage Fellowship" with Doug Harvey as executive director. The DHF claimed a membership of sixty-five congregations (about 2 percent of all Disciples congregations); published its own magazine; and distributed DVDs along with polemical literature attempting to recruit additional congregations.

The Harvest of Financial Constraint and Membership Loss

The ensuing few years have been described by some as "an oft told narrative of our demise," and by others as a painful but necessary transition leading into a period of renewal. Whichever view is correct, these years are part of the story and must be told to prepare for the future. Richard Hamm was decisively reelected to a second six-year term as general minister and president at the Cincinnati Assembly in 1999. The combination of membership loss and reduced financial support of mission, of which he became keenly aware in his first term, coalesced in a series of events during his second term approaching a level of crisis. A warning signal appeared in 1993–1994 when the church-wide capital campaign failed to reach its goal and the project of constructing a new headquarters building had to be abandoned. The land was returned to the city. Hamm, troubled with uncertainty about the future organizational shape of the church, managed the situation by finding a property to lease at a reasonable rate in downtown Indianapolis and proceeding with the sale of the old Missions Building that had served the Indianapolis units for nearly a century. He successfully convinced all general units in Indianapolis to join in occupancy of the leased building and arranged for an emotional service of closure for Missions Building. "The price we paid for moving out of missions building," said Hamm, "was heritage." But hundreds of thousands of dollars were saved due to maintenance and utility costs to heat and cool the old building. The failure of the capital campaign, however, was a clear signal of growing financial constraint.

It soon became apparent that not enough reconciliation offering was being generated to support the Reconciliation Ministry. Hamm attempted to operate it through the Office of General Minister and President, resulting in a huge deficit, addressed in 2004–2005 by restructuring the reconciliation program, reallocating general ministries mission fund dollars to restart the program, and paying the deficit through private fund-raising.

On April 1, 1998, Phillips University filed for Chapter 11 bankruptcy and closed its doors four months later. It was a stunning development for Disciples because the university had produced huge numbers of leaders through the decades from its founding in 1906. A widely held perception that the leadership of the school blamed the church proved damaging. But the church faced a financial struggle of its own and had been repeatedly assured things were well at the university. Neither the university's donor base nor the dwindling coffers of the church could save the school from closure. Once again, people across the Christian Church (Disciples of Christ) were bewildered. But the seminary survived the closing of the university and ultimately moved from Enid to Tulsa, Oklahoma.

Early in 2002 Christian Board of Publication announced it would discontinue publishing *The Disciple,* the journal of the Christian Church (Disciples of Christ). CBP, working ecumenically to no longer publish denominationally specific church school materials, was suffering serious financial constraint. It was another shock to the church psyche because *The Disciple* served as an important means of communication and it suddenly vanished without advance notice and with little consultation. James Suggs, a former president of CBP privately established a new magazine, naming it *DisciplesWorld,* by raising private funds and creating a twelve-member board to sustain its publication.

On February 16, 2004, the National Benevolent Association filed for Chapter 11 bankruptcy. NBA, founded in 1887, managed ninety-five facilities in twenty-two states housing 9,500 residents. Many in the church viewed NBA as the crown jewel in the Disciples constellation of ministries. About 75 percent of the clientele were senior adults, a major source of income for the operation. But NBA experienced four successive years of losses. Creditors were owed roughly $230 million, an amassed debt consisting primarily of tax-exempt bonds issued to finance expansion of mission in the upscale senior care business. The resulting cash drain from senior care assets coupled with the stock market decline, increased insurance premiums, and precipitous erosion in investment returns put NBA in technical default on the bonds. It was another distressing piece of news, described as "the most egregious event in our denomination's history." Disciples' self-confidence was further undermined. Many reasons were advanced for the declaration of bankruptcy. Some said a flawed business plan of long-standing was at fault; others claimed incompetent management and lack of openness and honesty; still others said it was due to a downturn in the stock market; and one widely repeated observation asserted that when a general unit becomes dependent upon the market it ceases to be a general unit (it becomes accountable to the market, not the church). Eleven NBA facilities were sold to Fortress Investment Group LLC; NBA discontinued management of the seventy-eight HUD facilities in December of 2004; five small facilities were retained. A reorganization plan was issued on April 15, 2005, and to its credit the newly restructured NBA paid all of its indebtedness with interest, fees, and expenses. Disciples were incredulous over such an unexpected development, particularly the senior adults housed in the facilities who had entrusted their savings, estates, and futures to NBA for long-term care. Many believed NBA had broken covenant with the church. The episode stood as another severe blow to Disciples, contributing to a deepening disillusionment and loss of optimism.[23]

Financial constraints on general ministries and regions worsened. Hamm concluded the issue was systemic, in part a flaw of restructure for not assigning clear fiduciary accountabilities to general units and regions serving the church as a whole. He invested an immense amount of time and energy (*three* proposed reorganizations of the Mission Funding system) in an attempt to repair mission funding–arranging, for example, a negotiating session involving the general units and regions. Bargaining in good faith, general units agreed to transfer 10 percent of their share of the Disciples Mission Fund to regions. This concession did not seem to satisfy the regions, eight of which decided to follow alternative routes of funding, thereby creating multple funding systems.[24]

Leaders of several mainline denominations experienced similar frustrations. The prime year for restructure was 1972 (four years after the Disciples) when the United Methodists, Presbyterians, and American Baptists all restructured. Some postmodern voices viewed the spate of restructures as a "trivialization" of church; others believed churches were being overseen by an "ecclesiocracy without ecclesiology." Many of the New Age saw a growing preoccupation with institutional concerns and procedural matters in the life of all Protestant churches and feared their identity no longer resided in theology, but polity. Hamm viewed *The Design* through the eyes of the post-restructure generation of Protestant leaders trying to lead churches that were in decline. Typical of the postmodern generation, Hamm became frustrated with structure, often recording those frustrations in his publications… "structures begin to demand service rather than remaining servants"; "bureaucratic governance with built-in structures is designed to avoid change"; "bureaucratic organizations are created to preserve important things but eventually tend to prevent needed change"; "excellent leaders are often used by a system to prevent change"; "obsolete organizational forms mean you end up doing huge amounts of maintenance work that is neither satisfying nor productive"; "church is an organism, not a machine"; and, "*The Design* was inherited from the World War II generation along with the assumption the church is properly organized and needs little tweaking." Hamm believed restructure ecclesiastically correct in its introduction of a more mature concept of "church" and its development of the idea of a "community in covenant." However, he also believed the new structure did not provide for the kind of accountability that might have made the new organization an effective expression of the envisioned body.

It appeared to him that old and stubborn autonomies were institutionalized in a way that made them more difficult than ever to address.

Convinced that structure needed modification, Hamm suggested several initiatives to reduce expenditures and to build accountability, among them downsizing the General Board's membership of 244 persons. The initiative was defeated at the 1997 Denver General Assembly. Reconceptualizing general ministries and regions was also suggested, but resisted. One success came in 2002: the consolidation of three regions (Arkansas, Louisiana, Mississippi) into the Great River Region. At their peaks in the 1950s and 1960s before the Independent split, Arkansas membership reached 17,196 in 119 congregations, Louisiana 6,843 in thirty-four congregations, and Mississippi 9,499 in ninety congregations. However, by 2002 the numbers had eroded: Arkansas had 8,904 members in sixty-one congregations, Louisiana 3,948 in twenty-three congregations, and Mississippi 4,439 in twenty-nine congregations. The three merged into a single region of approximately 17,000 members in 113 congregations. Expressions of appreciation came from across the church for this consolidation, despite the fact that economic constraint appeared to be the force driving the decision rather than mission planning or achieving greater accountability.

Hamm—emotionally, physically, and spiritually exhausted from ten years as general minister and president—decided to resign in 2003, two years before the end of his second six-year term, hoping it would cause the church to focus on the larger forces at work in its life, rather than spending its time "scapegoating." The resignation of a General Minister and President, however, seemed to add to the anxiety within the membership. At the 2003 General Assembly in Charlotte, North Carolina, W. Chris Hobgood, retired former regional minister in Arkansas and the Capital Area, was elected to fill a two-year interim while the church conducted a search for a new General Minister and President. It fell to Hobgood to deal with the NBA bankruptcy, its fallout, and reorganization. In 2005, following a protracted search, Sharon Watkins received nomination and subsequent approval by the General Board as the first Disciples female candidate for the position of General Minister and President.

Year Book	Membership	Congregations	Mission support	Percent of total giving
1993	1,015,568	4,301	$33,200,000	10%
[participating] 657,974				
2003	788,965	3,716	$29,900,000	7%
[participating] 505,717				

Sharon E. Watkins:
Championing the Quest for Reformation

"There are two wolves inside each of us," said the old Cherokee to his grandson. "One wolf is evil, vengeful, angry and full of self-pity. The other wolf is good. It represents love, hope, truth and compassion." "Which wolf wins, Grandfather?" asked the grandson. The old Cherokee replied, "The one you feed."
…How hard it is for us Disciples to feed the good wolf of hope. How hard it is for us to choose life… That is the part of the story we must learn to tell.

SHARON WATKINS
State of the Church Address, 2007[25]

When the 1968 Kansas City Assembly approved the "Provisional Design" of the restructured church, Sharon Watkins was beginning her freshman year in high school. She was born in 1954 in Wabash, Indiana. Her father, Keith, was a student minister in the nearby village of Somerset while completing his seminary degree at Butler School of Religion in Indianapolis. In 1956 the family moved to Sanger, California, a community near Fresno, so her father could pursue his seminary education at the Pacific School of Religion. During her childhood years, the family joined actively in the life of Richmond Avenue Christian Church in Richmond, California. When her father was appointed to a professorial position at Christian Theological Seminary, the family moved to Indianapolis, Indiana. They lived in the racially integrated Butler-Tarkington community near the seminary, where the neighborhood association resisted early signs of a white exodus. The Watkins family, along with most seminary and many university families, stayed in the neighborhood. Sharon attended a predominantly black high school, a formative and spiritually significant experience. Following graduation, she began college studies at Macalester College, St. Paul, Minnesota, during which she spent a semester in Avignon, France. She completed her B.A. degree in French and Economics at Butler University in 1975; and, neither desiring to teach nor enter a financial career, she chose to spend two years in Kinshasa, Zaire, under the auspices of the Disciples Division of Overseas Ministries and missionaries Bob and Jane Williams. Her job was to "create an adult literacy program for the United Protestant Church of 50 denominations and 200 languages." Still uncertain of what to do with her future, during 1979–1980 she served as a staff assistant in the Africa Department of the Division of Overseas Ministries in the Indianapolis Missions Building where everything came into focus when Dr. Robert Thomas, president of DOM, suggested she prepare herself for ministry. Watkins enrolled at Yale Divinity School, receiving her Master of Divinity degree in 1984. For four years she pastored Boone Grove Christian Church in Indiana until her husband was selected for a professorial post at Phillips Graduate Seminary. There were few places in Oklahoma at the time for a female to enter ministry. She accepted appointment as director of church relations at Phillips University, and later as director of student services at the seminary and as associate vice president for university relations at Phillips University. During those years she completed her Doctor of Ministry degree at Phillips Seminary. In 1997 she accepted a call as senior pastor of the Disciples Christian Church in Bartlesville, Oklahoma. While at Bartlesville she served as moderator of the Oklahoma Region, as a member of the General Board of the denomination, and as a member of the Stone-Campbell dialogue. In 2005 Sharon Watkins became General Minister and President of the Christian Church (Disciples of Christ), elected at the General Assembly in Portland, Oregon.[26]

Early Initiatives

Described as a pragmatic visionary–quick, receptive, flexible, candid– Sharon Watkins came to the office of General Minister and President with high expectations on the part of the membership. News from the church had been depressing for a long time. Disciples were anxious for change. In July 2006 the General Board directed Watkins "to lead the church in a prayerful examination of our mission and structure." Watkins accepted the directive, saying at the time, "The people are crying out, 'less structure, more mission.'" She appointed a seventeen-member "21st Century Vision Team," chaired by Cynthia Hale, to address the matter of mission and identity in the twenty-first century. The team produced a proposed statement of identity for the church to consider: "We are disciples of Christ, a movement for wholeness in a fragmented world. As part of the one body of Christ, we welcome all to the Lord's table as God has welcomed us." This statement of identity is to be undergirded by twelve principles of identity that at this writing remain under development.

Approved revisions to *The Design* were implemented in 2006, including the reduction of the Administrative Committee by one-half, and trimming the General Board in size to sixty-six voting members. Change began to occur within the ministries themselves, the first being a deployment of the Church Finance Council responsibilities to other general ministries. The Council on Christian Unity opened a new structural exploration of its own; and the National Benevolent Association presented itself in a new form, Disciples Benevolent Service, of substantially reduced size. "Mission," rather than mere structural change, it was claimed, drove these reorganizations. Undoubtedly, economics played a role. Sharon Watkins expressed the view that there "is a true readiness to reorganize, not linear and sequential, but happening as it will." In her judgment "the more we tinker with the system, the more we tinker with the things that don't matter," later adding, "spending time on funding issues within a tangled mind-set of distrust and despair is a dreadful misuse of energy and the church must turn to something new and better." Watkins responded to the second half of the General Board 2006 directive (examination of mission *and* structure) by recommending to the April 2008 meeting of the General Board a document entitled "Principles of a Plan of Mission Alignment," calling for a Task Force to develop recommendations on structure that will allow the mission of the church to "take wings and fly." The General Board named seven principles to guide the work of the Council: mission-driven and priority-focused, Design-guided and whole-church oriented, future-leaning, modeling unity and celebrating diversity, good stewardship, empowering networks, and encouraging partnerships. Further, the General Board instructed the Council to work toward three specific outcomes: (1) define the appropriate role of the General Board, (2) enhance partnerships, funding, and mutuality in a context of growing racial/ethnic diversity, and (3) streamline the general ministry infrastructure. Subsequently, Watkins appointed a twelve-member "Mission Alignment Coordinating Council" to be chaired by the Moderator, Newell Williams. The Council, beginning its work in June 2008, provided three general ministries realignment models on the church Web site, requesting comments, questions, suggestions, and ideas from the entire membership. The Council planned to bring its recommendations to the General Board and General Assembly in 2009.[27]

The new Administrative Committee convened in January 2007, and the downsized General Board met for the first time in April. The General Board was lean, more youthful, and more engaged than many of its predecessors. It exhibited a strong sense of mutual accountability, reflected in the detailed sharing of numerous audits. It was clearly a test drive for the recently revised *Design*. But overriding that fact was an honest concern for what it meant to be church, the meaning of covenant, and a passion for oneness.

Despite the fine beginning of the new General Board, the constraints imposed by lack of mission funding continued. In March, Disciples Home Missions announced that, due to declining income, they could no longer afford to allocate budget support for four historic mission centers: Yakama Christian Mission in Washington; Inman Christian Center in San Antonio; Kentucky Appalachian Ministry; and All Peoples Christian Center in Los Angeles. And despite the ringing eloquence of the new "statement of identity" by the 21st Century Vision Task Force, the Council on Christian Unity in 2008 reached the end of a gradual staff reduction to a single person (a president) from a late 1980s peak of a president, vice-president, treasurer, seminary intern and two full-time support staff. Financial support for Christian Unity–the very heart of Disciples' historical mission–fell victim to multiple Disciples' mission funding systems as its allocation dropped 32% between 1999 and 2008.

The General Assembly in Fort Worth, July 2007, generated compliments from scores as an uplifting assembly. The church learned of the tremendous financial and human response it made through Week of Compassion to assist the victims of hurricanes Katrina and Rita; it learned that congregational giving for the year had increased by 4 percent—the first increase in a decade; it learned the church had 153 missionaries in forty-eight countries; it learned that its 2020 vision had passed the halfway mark on its way to 1000 new congregations, three years ahead of schedule; it learned of the positive work of pro-reconciliation/anti-racism teams across the church; it learned of lay leadership seminars conducted by regions; it learned of the expanding involvement and leadership of the church in several new Christian unity initiatives; and it learned that the church has a vision for itself as *a movement for wholeness in a fragmented world*, a vision in keeping with the Disciples' founding premise. It received a reminder that with endings come new beginnings, and that resurrection does not happen without death. The church remembered it served a God of life and promise. It was reminded again to tell the story of the good wolf—love, hope, truth, and compassion.[28]

Year Book	Membership	Congregations	Mission funding	Percent of total giving
2005	744,417	3,775	427,700,000	6.5
[participating] 480,119				
2007	698,021	3,774	$24,800,000	5.2%
[participating] 450,728				

Afterword

*This Reformation is, because of the circumstances that surround us,
an uphill business—a rowing against wind and tide. We must exhibit
among ourselves, more unity, and harmony, and holiness, honesty, truth,
kindness and charity;…we must act out our principles, and show their
superiority to all sectarian principles, promoting all that is true and
honest—pleasing to God, dignifying to man. Put our shoulders to the
wheels of Reformation and call on God, who 'will make our cause his
care.'*

ELDER JOHN ROGERS
Letter, March 27, 1832[1]

Disciples Elder John Rogers, 175 years ago, understood well the nature
of Reformation. It does not occur with the snap of the fingers, in a month,
a year, a decade, or even in a couple of centuries. It is a struggle, an uphill
struggle "against the wind and tide." So it has been for Disciples, and will
continue to be. At birth as well as in all growth that follows, there is always
struggle. It is the necessary course to growth of body and mind and spirit,
a positive dynamic within the very essence of life itself. All who are true
to their faith have struggled.

Disciples found themselves in a struggle with a changing world environment when they celebrated their centennial 100 years ago. Alva W.
Taylor (1871–1957), one of the great Disciples witnesses for social justice,
wrote a segment for the Centennial Convention Report published in 1910
entitled "The Challenge of the Opening Doors." In his report he declared,
"We are living in a world era…the universal age is upon us. All Islam is
in ferment… From every corner of the earth the call of the cross comes
unto us."[2]

Taylor's words carry a familiar sound as Disciples celebrate their
bicentennial in 2009. In today's world the term has been revised from *world
era* to *globalization,* but even yet, "Islam is in ferment." A growing body
of literature ably describes the globalization of our twenty-first–century
world—a condition that presents formidable challenges to Disciples. How do
Disciples traditions of individualism and Christian unity accommodate an
interdependent, globalized community composed of increasing diversity?
How should Disciples define and adapt their overseas mission efforts in
an age when the Christian population has shifted so dramatically? In Alva
Taylor's day Africa contained 2 percent of the Christian population, Asia
4 percent, Latin America 11 percent, America 14 percent, and Europe 69

percent; but in 2000 Africa contained 18 percent of the world's Christian population, Asia 16 percent, Latin America 24 percent, America 13 percent, and Europe 24 percent, a profound demographic shift, still in progress. With an irresolute history of witness on issues of social justice, how do Disciples respond to a globalized market that concentrates on capital and goods rather than people, that overlooks the growing divide between the haves and the have-nots, neither eliminating poverty nor bringing economic stability? What is the proper balance for Disciples focus in a globalized world–improvement of their own polity and structural machinery on which they must rely in a complex world, or education of membership for witness and proclamation among the world's marginalized and impoverished? These few are merely representative of the challenges that shape the struggle ahead.

Disciples were born of a passion for Christian unity. Through two centuries of experience and a growing depth of understanding of unity, Disciples hold an edge in today's world, and are equipped with vision and leadership toward a new global architecture. Disciples have learned that theology is not always the best path to unity. They have learned that interreligious dialogue based on the strict reading of the Word is not possible. And they have learned the practical lesson that intercultural dialogue enables a deeper understanding of basic religious ideals–such as the preservation and promotion of social justice and moral welfare. While Disciples have much to learn, they also have much to share in this new age of President Barack Obama marked by the promise of bringing people together by creating new common ground rooted in common humanity and a shared world, by putting aside our historic enmities and moving "beyond toleration."

Disciples' two most effective tools for achieving that vision are *Christian Unity* and *Covenant.* For three hundred years of Protestantism isolated voices in the Christian world spoke of unity, but not one was able to spark a lasting movement. In the early nineteenth century, however, a young frontier evangelist and a middle-aged, Scots-Irish clergyman, both unknown and far removed from the centers of culture and learning in a wilderness land, *opened* their communion tables and thereby launched a religious Reformation, the first *lasting* reformation in Christian history focused on Christian unity.

The opening of those communion tables in obscure frontier communities was an act of magnificent simplicity. Despite the several divisive shades of Presbyterianism gathered at one table, and the unimmersed gathered at the other table, Thomas Campbell and Barton Stone knew those assembled were united in faith, a personal faith in Christ. They invited *all* who had gathered to join in the sharing of communion. They little recognized the far-reaching consequences of their actions–actions born of a powerful passion for unity within Christ's Church. This passion led Thomas Campbell, within two years, to author, in simple and honest words, the *Declaration and Address*, the "prospectus for Reformation," the "charter of unity" for Disciples of Christ; and led Barton Stone a quarter century later to pen the immortal words, "Christian Unity is our Polar Star."

Although other early nineteenth-century religious figures, James O'Kelly and Elias Smith, had previously expressed the idea, it was Thomas Campbell and Barton Stone who put the concept into practice in the cultural context of their respective venues. From that long ago beginning the reformation of the Christian community toward unity has been boldly proclaimed by Disciples, giving them a unique identity and a unique mission. For a unity Movement that twice divided, and has faced daunting challenges in recent decades, "Reforming toward Unity" has been a continuous and at times a heartbreaking struggle. It is helpful to remind Disciples that without struggle, life as a church would lose its purpose and weight, becoming an "unbearable lightness of being."

Disciples should also be reminded of, and take great heart in, the fact that their ecumenical leadership is commandingly and persuasively evident in a not always ecumenical age. At this writing, Michael Kinnamon is General Secretary of the National Council of Churches; Richard Hamm is the Executive Administrator of Christian Churches Together in the USA; and Suzanne Webb is President of Churches Uniting in Christ. Despite the limited size of Disciples among Protestant denominations in the United States, the Disciples record of bilateral and conciliar involvements is difficult to match; as is Disciples long-standing lay and clerical leadership in state and local councils of churches and in ecumenical campus ministries.

Disciples have a legitimate and historic imperative as the ultimate purveyors of Christian unity, one of the noblest endeavors in the whole history of the church. This is our distinctive mission—perhaps ordained—and we dare not let it go. For a great many Disciples, there is no other reason for the continued existence of the denomination than the ecumenical imperative. It has always been a struggle; it is indeed a struggle in this age of globalized diminishing resources and Islamic reformation; it is a struggle that will continue—a struggle that *must* continue. "Having this ministry by the mercy of God, we do not lose heart" (2 Corinthians 4:1, RSV).

Campbell once noted the "foundation of the Christian Church is a Divine personage, not a mere polity." Yet, no person in all Disciples history worked harder toward or wrote more about "polity, structure and organization" than Alexander Campbell. The most significant internal accomplishment of the Christian Church (Disciples of Christ) in the last four decades was its advance in institutional structure. It was a dramatic improvement over the jerrybuilt, autonomous institutionalism of pre-restructure times. The genius of the "Provisional Design" was lodged in the concept of covenant bonding the three expressions of church. In the words of Loren Lair, covenant is the "cement that holds the three manifestations together loose enough to permit the give and take that diversity requires, yet solid enough to hold the parts of the body together."

It is crucial to the life of the Christian Church (Disciples of Christ) that covenant be understood as the fundamental nature of the church. It is through this concept that Disciples find their relationship with each other and with God, rather than through the cold legality of a structure. Maturation as a covenant people may well be Disciples' primary resource in the ongoing struggle for Reformation toward Christian unity in a global age.

The experience of living together in covenant is not free of abrasions, mistrust, competition, jealousy, problems of communication, or the routine problems with a structure that will always require revision. Critics refer to structure as a bureaucracy of specialization without heart, an outgrowth of enlightenment rationalism that organized all of life in hierarchical form without spirit, and they often cite Max Weber's famous characterization of structure as the "iron cage" of modern life. But in the long view the experience of covenant is slowly lifting the church above exclusiveness and fragmentation toward wholeness, urging the church beyond ideological and theological narrowness, and helping the church become more multicultural through embracing the gifts and diversity of a growing racial/ethnic membership–all part of the struggle that is shaping who Disciples are as a church.

At a time when it is fashionable to point out the imperfections of covenant, *The Design,* and restructure, it is important to be reminded of the multitude of advancements achieved through this new covenantal order. Through covenant Disciples have been enabled to pursue more confidently their ecumenical imperative of Christian unity through free and open discussions in representative assemblies. Through covenant Disciples were enabled to develop an order of ministry and significantly improve the means of nurture to ministers throughout the journey of their service. Through covenant Disciples were enabled to occasion a more equitable balance between some of their ageless polarities: freedom and community, unity and diversity, congregationalism and catholicity. Through covenant, the majority of congregations claim a far greater enlightenment and participation in total church ministry–regional, local, general, ecumenical–than they have known any time in their entire history; and the majority of regions and general ministries claim an enhanced colleagueship in ministry compared with pre-restructure years.. Disciples have barely entered the early years of living into covenant; and new generations of leadership will move the church beyond this nascent stage into a deeper maturity. Today, Disciples can ill-afford to turn in on themselves, limiting their horizon of hope. It is a moment for Disciples to summon forth leaders who are able to ignite the capacity for vision; who, rather than being committed to *Christian unity* and *Covenant* only by a sense of history, are consecrated by inner conviction;

who are molders of community, rather than ideologues; who are able to transcend and transform the moment; and in the words of old John Rogers, "put their shoulders to the wheels…and act out our principles."

There is a special importance to historical study of Disciples. For history is to a church much as memory is to an individual. As an individual deprived of memory becomes disoriented and lost, not knowing where he or she has been or where he or she is going, so a church lacking knowledge of its past will be disabled in dealing with its present and its future. History offers a way of coming to terms with an anxious present and an unpredictable future. "In times of change and danger," John Dos Passos wrote in *The Ground We Stand On,* "when there is a quicksand of fear under [human] reasoning, a sense of continuity with generations gone before can stretch like a lifeline across the scary present."[3]

APPENDIX A

Disciples Historic Time Line

- **Events in the Stone-Campbell movement, events in the lives of the Campbells (through 1866), and Disciples of Christ events after 1866**

- Contextual events in Europe and America

1710 • **Thomas Campbell (grandfather of Thomas) migrated from Argyle Shire, Scotland, to County Down, Ireland**

1714 • December 16: Birth of George Whitefield

1729 • John Wesley established the Methodist church at Oxford

1730 • John Glas deposed as a minister of the Church of Scotland

1735 • **Birth of James O'Kelly in Ireland**

1736 • February 5: Arrival of John and Charles Wesley as missionaries to Georgia

1738 • Evangelist George Whitefield arrived in Georgia; thirteen more voyages followed.

1745 • August 20: Birth of Frances Asbury at Staffordshire, England

1758 • March 12: Death of Jonathan Edwards at Princeton, New Jersey
     • Publication of Edwards' "Christian Doctrine of Original Sin Defended"

1759 • **September 13: While serving in the British army, Archibald Campbell (father of Thomas) fought with General James Wolfe on the Plains of Abraham during the French and Indian War**

1760 • October 25: George III became King of England
     • **James O'Kelly migrated to North Carolina, Colonial America**

1762 • June 28: Coronation of Catherine the Great, Empress of Russia
     • Publication of Rousseau's *Social Contract* and *Émile*

278

1763 • **February 1: Thomas Campbell, son of Archibald and father of Alexander, born near Newry, County Down, Ireland, and named for his grandfather, Thomas**

   • February 10: Treaty of Paris ended the French and Indian War

   • **September 1: Birth of Jane Corneigle, future wife of Thomas Campbell**

1764 • Publication of Voltaire's *Dictionary of Philosophy;* Birth of Robert Haldane

1765 • Posthumous publication of Jonathan Edwards' *The Nature of True Virtue*

1768 • Birth of James Haldane

1769 • **Birth of Elias Smith, Connecticut, Colonial America**

1770 • September 30: Death of George Whitefield, Newburyport, Massachusetts

1771 • October: Francis Asbury arrived in Philadelphia for service in America

1772 • **December 24: Birth of Barton Stone near Port Tobacco, Maryland, Colonial America**

1774 • Louis XVI became King of France

1775 • October 12: Birth of Lyman Beecher

1776 • July 4: American Declaration of Independence

   • August 25: Death of David Hume

1778 • May 10: Death of Voltaire

   • July 2: Death of Rousseau

1783 • **Thomas Campbell entered the University of Glasgow to prepare for ministry**

   • September 3: Treaty of Paris signed ending the American Revolutionary War

1784 • **October 15: Birth of "Raccoon" John Smith, in Sullivan County, Tennessee**

   • December: Francis Asbury ordained and elected general superintendent and Bishop of the Methodist church in America; beginning of Methodism as a separate denomination

1785 • September 1: Birth of Peter Cartwright

1786 • **Thomas Campbell completed his studies with honors at the University of Glasgow**

   • **Thomas Campbell entered the Anti-Burgher Seceder seminary at Whitburn to study with Archibald Bruce**

   • August 17: Death of Frederick the Great, King of Prussia

1787 • **June: Thomas Campbell married to Jane Corneigle near Ballymena, County Antrim**

   • May 25–September 17: Constitutional Convention convened in Philadelphia, Pennsylvania

1788 • **September 12: Alexander Campbell born to Thomas and Jane near Ballymena, County Antrim**

1789 • **Thomas moved his family to Sheepbridge, where he taught school**

   • April 30: George Washington became President of the United States.

   • July 14: French Revolution began; storming of the Bastille

1790 • **January: Barton Stone entered David Caldwell's Academy, Guilford Co., North Carolina**

   • April 17: Death of Benjamin Franklin

   • July 17: Death of Adam Smith

1791 • **Thomas concluded his studies at Whitburn**

   • **January 29: Birth of Margaret Brown, Lower Buffaloe, Virginia; future wife of Alexander Campbell**

   • March 2: Death of John Wesley, London, England

   • December 15: The United States Bill of Rights came into effect: separation of church and state

1792 • August 29: Birth of Charles Grandison Finney

1793 • January 21: Execution of King Louis XVI

   • **July 27: Birth of Dorthea, daughter of Thomas and Jane Campbell**

1794 • **August 4: The "James O'Kelly Secession" from the Methodist Church became the "Christian Church" near Williamsburg, Virginia**

1795 • **September 18: Birth of Nancy, daughter of Thomas and Jane Campbell**

1796 • **April 6: Barton Stone licensed to preach**

   • **October 31: Birth of Walter Scott at Moffat, Scotland**

1797 • **Thomas became a probationer; he then moved his family from Sheepbridge to Markethill in County Armagh, where he served both as minister and teacher**

1798 • **Thomas accepted appointment at the church in Ahorey, near Rich Hill where he farmed, ministered, and taught. The family actually lived in the hamlet of Hamilton's Bawn. Alexander remained in Markethill to continue his early schooling**

   • **Spring: Barton Stone called to be pastor at Cane Ridge, Kentucky**

   • **October: Thomas formed the "Evangelical Society of Ulster" using the Haldanian model**

- **October 4: Barton Stone ordained**
- 1799 • **Thomas was censured by the Synod of Northern Ireland for "fraternal attitudes"**
  - **Thomas Campbell ordained to the ministry by the Ahorey church, near Armagh**
  - December 14: Death of George Washington
  - December 24: Napoleon became Emperor of France
- 1800 • **Alexander Campbell was sent to Newry, Ireland, to study in an academy operated by his uncles Enos and Archibald**
  - **June 25: Birth of Jane, daughter of Thomas and Jane Campbell**
- 1801 • February 17: Thomas Jefferson became President of the United States
  - March 12: Alexander I became Tsar of Russia
  - **July 2: Barton Stone married to Elizabeth Campbell (no relation to Thomas)**
  - **August 7–12: Great Sacramental Occasion at Cane Ridge, Kentucky, with Barton Stone as host**
- 1802 • **May 1: Birth of Thomas, son of Thomas and Jane Campbell**
  - **November 12: Birth of Selina Bakewell in Wellsburg, Virginia; second wife of Alexander Campbell**
- 1803 • The Louisiana Purchase
  - **Fall: Formation of the Springfield Presbytery in Kentucky, led by Barton Stone**
- 1804 • **Thomas Campbell moved his family from their farm into Rich Hill where he conducted an academy in his home and was assisted by his sixteen-year-old son Alexander**
  - **April 4: Birth of Archibald, son of Thomas and Jane Campbell**
  - May 14: The Lewis & Clark Expedition across North America began
  - **June 28: Last Will and Testament of the Springfield Presbytery written; the name Christian Church adopted**
- 1805 • **July 8: Thomas Campbell named Moderator of the Associate Synod of Ireland meeting in Belfast**
  - **July 9: Thomas Campbell appointed one of the commissioners to take the union plea of Irish churches to the General Associate Synod in Glasgow, Scotland—a plea that was rejected**
- 1806 • **April: Birth of Alicia, daughter of Thomas and Jane**
  - September 26: Birth of Robert Richardson
- **1807** • **April 8: Thomas sailed to America from Londonderry, Ireland, on the ship *Brutus,* leaving his family in Rich Hill; he settled**

near Washington, Pennsylvania, and began preaching for the Presbyterians

• **December 10: Death of Archibald Campbell, father of Thomas**

1808 • **February 12: Thomas temporarily suspended by the Chartiers presbytery**

• **March 8: The suspension of Thomas declared permanent**

• **May 24: The Synod reversed the suspension, then rebuked and admonished Thomas; the suspension was lifted, but the presbytery did not give Thomas any appointments**

• **May: "Raccoon" John Smith ordained to the Baptist ministry**

• **September 1: Elias Smith published "The Last Will and Testament of the Springfield Presbytery" in *Herald of Gospel Liberty* in New England**

• **September 14: Thomas broke with the Chartiers presbytery, renouncing their authority**

• **October 1: Jane, Alexander, and the children set sail from Londonderry in the *Hibernia*. They were shipwrecked near the island of Islay**

• **November 8: Alexander Campbell enrolled at the University of Glasgow, where he studied with a famed Scottish Enlightenment faculty including George Jardine, John Young, Andrew Ure, and was much influenced as well by Glasgow luminaries Greville Ewing, and James and Robert Haldane.**

1809 • February 12: Abraham Lincoln born in Kentucky

• February 12: Charles Darwin born in Shrewsbury, England

• **April: Alexander completed his studies at Glasgow; he refused communion because he determined the strict terms of the Church of Scotland to be unbiblical**

• **May: Thomas authored the first draft of *Declaration and Address* and had his name removed from the Synod roll.**

• **Summer: Thomas gave *Address* at the home of Abraham Altars, stating, "Where the Scriptures speak, we speak; where the Scriptures are silent, we are silent"**

• **August 3: Alexander, Jane, and the children sailed from Greenock, Scotland, aboard the *Latonia* on a fifty-seven-day crossing of the Atlantic, during which Alexander passed his twenty-first birthday**

• **August 17: Thomas established the Christian Association of Washington, Pennsylvania**

- **September 7: Thomas completed the final draft of Declaration and Address of the Christian Association of Washington, Pennsylvania, and sent it to press**
- September 29-30: Alexander, Jane, and the children arrived in New York City
- **October 5: Alexander and family left New York; arrived in Philadelphia October 7**
- **October 10: Alexander and family departed Philadelphia**
- **October 20: Alexander, Thomas, Jane, and family reunited on the road near Uniontown, Pennsylvania**
- **December 1: Alexander proposed marriage to Hannah Acheson; she accepted**

1810 • **March: Alexander began writing a series of articles for the *Washington Reporter***
- **April 17: Presbytery voted to defrock Thomas Campbell**
- **May: Death of Elizabeth Stone, wife of Barton Stone**
  May 10: Birth of Tolbert Fanning
- **June: Hannah Acheson broke her engagement to Alexander Campbell**
- **July 15: Alexander preached his first sermon**
- **July 22: Alexander preached sermon on Christian Unity at Crossroads**
- **September 16: The Brush Run Congregation was organized by the Campbells**
- **October 1: Alexander wrote a critical essay about Washington College in the *Washington Reporter***
- **October 10: Denunciation of Thomas by the Synod**
- **October: Alexander Campbell met Margaret Brown**
- **November 1: Alexander responded to Synod on his father's behalf**

1811 • **March 11: Alexander Campbell was married to Margaret Brown in the Brown parlor in Lower Buffaloe, Virginia, now Bethany, West Virginia**
- **May 4: Brush Run constituted as a church and Alexander Campbell licensed to preach**
- **Fall: Alexander conducted a fall preaching tour in Virginia, Ohio, and Pennsylvania**
- **October 31: Barton Stone married Celia Bowen**

1812 • **January 1: Alexander ordained by the Brush Run Congregation; leadership of Movement passed from Thomas to Alexander**

- Winter: Alexander read and studied forty books on faith and baptism
- March 13: Birth of Jane, daughter of Alexander and Margaret
- June 12: Baptism of Alexander, Margaret, Thomas, Jane, and Dorthea by the Baptist Elder Matthias Luce; the ceremony occurred in Buffalo Creek
- June 18: Declaration of war on Great Britain; beginning of War of 1812
- Birth of Lewis L. Pinkerton
- Birth of Benjamin Franklin (the Movement member)
- Fall: Walter Scott entered the University of Edinburgh, age 16

1813 • September 13: Birth of Eliza Ann, daughter of Alexander and Margaret

1814 • Birth of Robert Milligan

1815 • January 8: Andrew Jackson defeated the British at the Battle of New Orleans

- The Brush Run Congregation accepted by the Redstone Baptist Association; the Campbells worked as reformers within the Baptist Church for fifteen years
- Thomas Campbell opened an Academy in Pittsburgh
- March: John Brown, father of Margaret, gave the use of his house and farm to Alexander Campbell to prevent a westward migration of the Alexander Campbell family to Ohio
- November 20: Birth of Maria Louisa, daughter of Alexander and Margaret
- December: Alexander Campbell traveled to Philadelphia for his naturalization ceremony to become a citizen. On this three-month trip he preached in New York City; Baltimore; and Washington, D.C.; as well as Philadelphia.

1816 • March 31: Francis Asbury died at Spotsylvania, Virginia

- September 1: Alexander Campbell delivered his famous and controversial "Sermon on the Law" at the annual meeting of the Redstone Baptist Association at Cross Creek near Wellsburg, Virginia; this same meeting rejected Thomas Campbell's application for membership on behalf of his small congregation in Pittsburgh

1817 • Alexander Campbell was faced with calls for impeachment and a heresy trial due to his "Sermon on the Law"

- Thomas moved his family to Newport, Kentucky

- **September 8: Birth of William K. Pendleton in Yanceyville, Virginia**
1818 •	**January: Alexander Campbell opened Buffalo Seminary in his home**
- **January 17: Birth of Lavinia, daughter of Alexander and Margaret Campbell**
- **July 7: Walter Scott left the University of Edinburgh and traveled to New York City**
- **October 29: Moses Lard born in Bedford County, Tennessee**
1819 •	**May: Walter Scott arrived in Pittsburgh**
- **Death of Rice Haggard**
1820 •	**January 2: Birth of Isaac Errett in New York City**
- **February 16: Birth of Hannah Corneigle, daughter of Alexander and Margaret Campbell**
- March 3: Missouri Compromise passed
- **April: Alexander began a series of articles in the *Washington Reporter* on the local moral societies; the articles ended in 1822**
- **June 19–20: Alexander Campbell engaged John Walker in a public debate on baptism, at Mt. Pleasant, Ohio, about twenty-three miles from Bethany**
- **August: Death of Hannah Corneigle, daughter of Alexander and Margaret**
1821 •	**February 12: Alexander engaged in an editorial debate with Andrew Wylie, President of Washington College, on the moral societies**
- **July 14: Birth of Clarinda, daughter of Alexander and Margaret Campbell**
1822 •	**January: Alexander Campbell met Walter Scott in Pittsburgh**
- **November 10: Birth and death of John Brown, son of Alexander and Margaret**
- **December: Alexander Campbell closed Buffalo Seminary**
1823 •	**Spring: Alexander Campbell, at age thirty-five, issued a prospectus on a new critical and satirical journal he was going to publish, entitled *Christian Baptist***
- **October 15: Alexander Campbell debated William McCalla in Washington, Kentucky**
- **Walter Scott married Sarah Whitsette**
1824 •	**Alexander Campbell made a three-month preaching tour of Kentucky; while on this tour he met Barton Stone**
- **Brush Run disfellowshipped by the Redstone Baptist Association**

1826 • **April 19: Alexander Campbell published his New Testament translation the *Living Oracles.***

• **November 25: Barton Stone began publication of *The Christian Messenger***

1827 • **October 22: Death of Margaret, wife of Alexander Campbell, from tuberculosis**

• **At Campbell's suggestion, the Mahoning Baptist Association in Ohio employed Walter Scott as a traveling evangelist**

1828 • **July 12: Alexander Campbell married Selina Bakewell**

• **Alexander Campbell published a hymnbook entitled, *Psalms, Hymns and Spiritual Songs***

• December 3: Andrew Jackson elected President of the United States

1829 • **March 1: John W. McGarvey born in Hopkinsville, Kentucky**

• **April 13: Campbell debate with Robert Owen in Cincinnati, Ohio**

• **April 23: Birth of Margaret Brown, daughter of Alexander and Selina**

• **October 4 – February 1: Alexander Campbell served as delegate to the Virginia Constitutional Convention; Campbell preached often in Richmond**

1830 • **January 4: First issue of *The Millennial Harbinger* published**

• March 26: The *Book of Mormon* published

• May 28: President Jackson signs Indian Removal Bill

• **August: The Mahoning Baptist Association in Ohio dissolved itself over a dispute on Campbell's views on baptism, creeds, and Calvinism; this marked the independence of Disciples**

1831 • **Birth of Alexander Campbell Jr., son of Alexander and Selina**

• **New Lisbon, Ohio, meeting of congregations: agreed on annual county meetings**

• **Birth of David Lipscomb in Franklin County, Tennessee**

• August 21: Nat Tuner's slave rebellion in Virginia

• **November 19: Birth of James Garfield, Cuyahoga County, Ohio**

1832 • **January 1: "Raccoon" John Smith and Barton Stone, Kentucky leaders of the Stone and Campbell movements, met at Hill Street church in Lexington, uniting the two bodies**

• **January 2: Walter Scott began publication of *The Evangelist***

1834 • **January 24: Birth of Virginia, daughter of Alexander and Selina**

• **April 12: "General Meeting of Messengers" in Brooke county: multiple counties attended; Principle of Cooperation approved**

• **September: Barton Stone retired in Jacksonville, Illinois**

1835 • **January 2: Publication of *Christianity Restored* by Alexander Campbell**

• **April 28: Death of Jane Campbell, mother of Alexander**

1836 • February 23: The Alamo siege began and lasted until March 6

• **November 10: Opening of Bacon College, Georgetown, Kentucky**

• **Walter Scott published his most important work, *The Gospel Restored***

1837 • **January 13: Alexander Campbell debated John Purcell in Cincinnati, Ohio, on Catholicism**

• February 5: Birth of Dwight L. Moody

• **June 24: Birth of Wycliffe, son of Alexander and Selina**

• **September: Campbell's controversial response to the July 8 Lunenburg letter on being a Christian without immersion**

1838 • Spring and Summer: The Trail of Tears; removal of Cherokees from Georgia

1839 • **January 16: Death of Alicia, sister of Alexander Campbell**

• **June 13: Publication of *The Christian System* by Alexander Campbell**

1840 • **March 2: Bethany College chartered in Bethany, Virginia; Alexander Campbell named first president**

• Spring: Beginning of the Overland Migration on the Oregon Trail

• **October 12: Birth of Decima, daughter of Alexander and Selina**

1842 • Death of Robert Haldane

1843 • **November 15: Alexander Campbell debated N. L. Rice in Lexington, Kentucky. The debate lasted fifteen days and was moderated by Henry Clay**

• **December 4: Forebears of National City Christian Church met in James Barclay's home in Washington, D.C.**

• **Alexander Campbell wrote a significant amount on church organization during the 1840s, including his famous metaphor entitled *Island of Guernsey* in 1843. He struggled with the tension between the needs of new congregations versus the needs of established ones, and local autonomy versus connectional accountability.**

1844 • **November 9: Death of Barton Stone at Hannibal, Missouri**

1845 • **January 27: David Burnett organized the American Christian Bible Society**

• March 1: Annexation of Texas

1846 • May 13: War declared on Mexico

- August 17: Annexation of California

1847 • **Alexander Campbell made a four-month preaching trip to the British Isles. He was imprisoned in Glasgow on the charge of being pro-slavery, but later vindicated**

- **September 4: Alexander Campbell's son, Wycliffe, drowned in a millpond on the farm**

1848 • January 24: Discovery of Gold at Sutter's Mill in California

1849 • **September 6: Birth of Archibald McLean, Prince Edward Island, Canada**

- **October 3: Kentucky Female Orphan School established at Midway, Kentucky**

- **October 23–28: Disciples hold first national convention**

- **October 24: The American Christian Missionary Society organized, headquartered in Cincinnati, Ohio, and Alexander Campbell elected president**

- **Death of Sarah Scott, wife of Walter Scott**

1850 • **January 15: Butler University chartered in Indianapolis as Northwestern Christian University**

- **March 1: Hiram College chartered in Hiram, Ohio, as Western Reserve Eclectic Institute.**

- **June 2: Alexander Campbell preached before a gathering of Congress in Washington**

- **Mary R. Williams traveled to Palestine as the first Disciples missionary**

- September 9–20: The Compromise of 1850

1851 • **January 10: Death of Clarinda, youngest child of Margaret and Alexander Campbell**

- **January 18: Columbia College chartered in Columbia, Missouri**

- **Publication of Christian Baptism**

- **James Barclay and family went to Jerusalem as first ACMS missionaries**

- Death of James Haldane

1852 • **December 30: Alexander Campbell Jr. married to Mary Ann Purvis.**

- March 20: Publication of *Uncle Tom's Cabin* by Harriet Beecher Stowe

1853 • **January 15: Culver-Stockton College chartered in Canton, Missouri, as Christian College**

- **Robert Richardson published The Principles and Objects of the Reformation, as urged by A. Campbell and Others**

- **Birth of Helen Moses**
1854 • **January 4: Death of Thomas Campbell at the Campbell home in Bethany**
1855 • **February 9: Eureka College chartered in Eureka, Illinois**
- *The Gospel Advocate* **founded by Tolbert Fanning in Nashville, Tennessee**
- **Publication of** *Campbellism Examined* **by J. B. Jeter**
- **Alexander Campbell traveled to Canada, Washington D.C., and eastern Virginia**
1856 • **Publication of Campbell's** *Christian Hymn Book*
- *The American Christian Review* **founded by Benjamin Franklin in Cincinnati, Ohio**
1857 • **Campbell traveled to New Orleans, Ohio, Illinois, Iowa, and Virginia.**
- March 4: The Dred Scott Decision
- **December 10: Bethany College main building destroyed by fire**
1858 • **Campbell tours the eastern U.S. to raise money to rebuild Bethany. In Washington he addressed a Sunday meeting of some members from both houses of Congress, and some members of the Cabinet. He was entertained at the White House by President Buchanan**
- August 21–October 15: Lincoln-Douglas debates
1859 • Publication of Charles Darwin's *On the Origin of Species*
- October 16–18: John Brown's raid on Harper's Ferry, Virginia
1860 • November 6: Abraham Lincoln elected President of the United States
- **December: Alexander, with his wife Selina, embarked on a preaching tour of Indiana**
1861 • April 12: Firing on Fort Sumter and the beginning of the Civil War
- **April 21: Death of Walter Scott**
- **December 12: Death of Dorthea, sister of Alexander Campbell**
- **Alexander Campbell wrote and published a 367-page biography of his father, Thomas**
- **Alexander Campbell published** *Popular Lectures and Addresses*
- **The American Christian Missionary Society, meeting in Cincinnati, passed resolutions supporting the Union; southern congregations were deeply offended**
1863 • January 1: Emancipation Proclamation issued
- January 10: Death of Lyman Beecher

- **April 7: Alexander's daughter Decima married to J. Judson Barclay**
- June 20: West Virginia (Campbell's home) admitted to the Union as the 35th state
- June 27: The Battle of Gettysburg began
- **October 27: Alexander's daughter Virginia married to W. R. Thompson**

1864 • **May 5: Herbert L. Willett born in Ionia County, Michigan**

1865 • April 15: Abraham Lincoln assassinated
- **August 7: Alexander Campbell consigned his *Christian Hymn Book* to the ACMS**
- **Alexander Campbell relinquished the editorship of the *Harbinger* to W. K. Pendleton.**
- **College of the Bible founded at Lexington, Kentucky**

1866 • **March 4: Alexander Campbell died at his home in Bethany**
- **April: The *Christian Standard* founded through the efforts of James A. Garfield and Thomas W. Phillips; Isaac Errett named editor**

1867 • March: First Reconstruction Act Passed
- Acquisition of Alaska
- **National Convention of Disciples (African American) founded by Rufus Conrad**
- **Milligan College Founded in Milligan, Tennessee**
- **June 3: Peter Ainslie III born in Dunnsville, Virginia**

1868 • February 24: Impeachment Trial of Andrew Johnson
- ***Lards Quarterly* ceased publication**
- **Robert Richardson published *Memoirs of Alexander Campbell***
- **Robert Milligan published *Exposition and Defense of the Scheme of Redemption***
- November 3: Ulysses S. Grant elected President of the United States
- **Death of "Raccoon" John Smith**

1869 • May 10: First Transcontinental Railroad completed at Promontory, Utah

1870 • ***The Millennial Harbinger* ceased publication**

1872 • September 25: Death of Peter Cartwright

1873 • **Add-Ran College (Texas Christian University) founded at Thorp Springs, Texas**

1874 • **October 21: Christian Woman's Board of Missions founded by Caroline Neville Pearre**

- **Birth of Winfred E. Garrison**
- **Birth of Charles Clayton Morrison**
- **Birth of Royal J. Dye**
- **Death of Tolbert Fanning**
1875 • August 16: Death of Charles Grandison Finney
- **October 22: Foreign Christian Missionary Society organized; Isaac Errett named president**
- **Southern Christian Institute founded in Edwards, Mississippi**
- **Birth of Albert L. Shelton**
- **Death of Lewis. L. Pinkerton**
- **Death of Robert Milligan**
1876 • **October 22: Death of Robert Richardson**
1877 • **Independent College of the Bible created, Lexington, Kentucky**
1878 • **October 22: Death of Benjamin Franklin**
1880 • **June 17: Death of Moses Lard**
1881 • **Young People's Society of Christian Endeavor organized**
- **Drake University founded in Des Moines, Iowa**
- July 2: Assassination attempt on President James A. Garfield, prominent Disciple (died Sept. 19)
- October 26: Gunfight at the OK Corral
1882 • *The Christian-Evangelist* **established through a merger**
1883 • **The Board of Church Extension of the ACMS established**
1887 • **The National Benevolent Association chartered**
1888 • **Death of Isaac Errett**
1889 • **Cotner University founded in Lincoln, Nebraska**
- **August 18: The "Sand Creek Address and Declaration" issued by Daniel Sommer**
- **Charles Louis Loos became president of the FCMS**
1890 • **William Woods College established in Fulton, Missouri**
- **Herbert Willett and W. E. Garrison begin their studies at Yale**
1891 • **Nashville Bible School founded in Nashville, Tennessee (later David Lipscomb College, and in 1988 it became David Lipscomb University)**
1892 • June 21: Birth of Reinhold Niebuhr
1893 • **Johnson Bible College established in Kimberlin Heights, Tennessee**
1894 • **Education Board of the ACMS established by Albertina Forrest**
- **Disciples Divinity House founded at the University of Chicago**

- September 3: Birth of H. Richard Niebuhr
1895 • **Board of Ministerial Relief (Pension Fund) established**
- **October 1: Birth of Stephen J. England in Salida, Colorado**
1896 • **The Campbell Institute founded at the University of Chicago; it began publishing *The Scroll* the same year**
1897 • **Birth of Gaines M. Cook**
- **June 28: Death of Selina Huntington Bakewell Campbell**
1898 • February 15: The sinking of the Maine
- April 20: The Spanish American War begins
- July 1: The charge up San Juan Hill
1899 • **August 30: Death of William K. Pendleton**
- **Helen Moses became president of CWBM**
- **The FCMS and CWBM send missionaries to Puerto Rico**
- **ACMS approves first Spanish-language Christian Church in San Antonio, Texas**
- December 22: Death of Dwight L. Moody
1900 • **Birth of Mae Yoho Ward in West Virginia**
- **Archibald McLean became president of the FCMS**
1901 • **Disciple Carrie Nation smashed saloons with her hatchet**
- September 6: Assassination of President William McKinley (Theodore Roosevelt became President)
- **Birth of Virgil A. Sly**
1902 • **The periodical *Christian Echo* was founded by Disciples African Americans**
- **Atlantic Christian College (Barton College) founded in Wilson, North Carolina**
1903 • **Lynchburg College founded in Lynchburg, Virginia**
1906 • **Churches of Christ recognized as a separate church body from Disciples**
- **Abilene Christian College (Abilene Christian University) established in Abilene, Texas**
- April 18: The San Francisco Earthquake
- June 29: Building of the Panama Canal authorized
- **December 17: Birth of A. Dale Fiers in Kankakee, Illinois**
1907 • **Oklahoma Christian University (Phillips University) founded in Enid, Oklahoma**
- **Disciples became charter member of the Federal Council of Churches**

1908 • **Birth of Granville Walker**

• **Death of Helen Moses; Anna Atwater became president of CWBM**

1909 • **Centennial celebration of the *Declaration and Address,* held in Pittsburgh**

• Scientific world celebrated the fiftieth anniversary of Darwin's *Origin of the Species*

1910 • **Disciples establish Commission on Christian Union (Council on Christian Unity)**

• **College of Missions opened in Indianapolis, Indiana**

1911 • **Founding of the Christian Publishing Company (Christian Board of Publication)**

• **Death of John W. McGarvey**

1912 • **Death of Thomas W. Phillips**

• November 5: Woodrow Wilson elected President of the United States

1913 • **Founding of Jarvis Christian College in Hawkins, Texas**

• **The Disciples Men and Millions Movement launched**

1914 • **Founding of Brite Divinity School**

• **Founding of the Disciples Board of Education**

• August 15: Panama Canal opened

• World War I began in Europe

1915 • May 7: The sinking of the Lusitania

1917 • April 6: American Declaration of War on Germany

• **Disciples International Convention established**

• **The Lexington College of the Bible heresy trial**

• **National Christian Missionary Convention established by Preston Taylor**

• **Birth of Ronald E. Osborn**

• **November 11: Death of David Lipscomb**

1918 • November 7: Birth of William "Billy" Graham

• November 11: The Armistice; end of World War I

1919 • **Founding of the United Christian Missionary Society; merger of FCMS, CWBM, and ACMS; Frederick W. Burnham named president—Archibald McLean and Anna Atwater named vice presidents**

• **The periodical *World Call* first published**

• January 29: The 18th Amendment ratified (Prohibition)

• May–June: Treaty of Versailles signed

1920 • **December 15: Death of Archibald McClean**

1921 • **All-Canada Committee established**
     • **December 22: Birth of Kenneth L. Teegarden in Cushing, Oklahoma**
1922 • **Death of Dr. Albert Shelton**
1925 • July: The Scopes Trial in Dayton, Tennessee (Creation vs. Evolution)
1927 • **The First North American Christian Convention convened• the beginning of the separation of Independent churches from Disciples**
     • **October 26: Birth of John O. Humbert, Kansas City, Missouri**
1929 • **June: A. Dale Fiers graduated from Bethany College**
     • October 29: The Stock Market Crash; beginning of the Great Depression
1930 • **The First World Convention of Churches of Christ**
     • **October 16: Dedication of the National City Christian Church Building**
1931 • **Death of Preston Taylor**
1932 • November 8: Election of Franklin Delano Roosevelt, President of United States
1933 • **Cotner University closed**
     • 18th Amendment repealed (Prohibition)
1934 • **February 24: Death of Peter Ainslie III**
     • **Appointment of Commission on Restudy of the Disciples of Christ**
1935 • **Disciples Peace Fellowship founded**
     • **July 1: Unified Promotion established**
     • August 14: Social Security Act passed
     • November 5: Death of William "Billy" Sunday
1938 • **Home and State Missions Planning Council established**
1939 • World War II begins in Europe
1941 • **Founding of the Disciples of Christ Historical Society**
     • December 7: Attack on Pearl Harbor
1944 • **Week of Compassion Committee established**
     • **Christian Youth Fellowship (CYF) organized**
     • **Death of Herbert Willett**
1945 • February 4: The Yalta Conference
     • February 19: The Battle of Iwo Jima
     • April 12: Death of Franklin Delano Roosevelt
     • May 7: Germany surrender: VE Day
     • August 6: Atomic Bomb dropped on Hiroshima

- August 9: Atomic Bomb dropped on Nagasaki
- September 2: Japanese surrender: VJ Day
- **Christian Men's Fellowship (CMF) organized**
1946 • **Disciples Crusade for a Christian World**
- **European Evangelistic Society organized**
1947 • **December 21: Birth of Richard L. Hamm in Crawfordsville, Indiana**
1948 • **Disciples became a charter member of the World Council of Churches**
1949 • **Christian Women's Fellowship (CWF) organized**
1950 • **Council of Agencies established**
- **Disciples became a charter member of the National Council of Churches**
- June 29: The Korean War begins
1951 • **A. Dale Fiers installed as President of the United Christian Missionary Society**
1953 • March 5: Death of Joseph Stalin
- June 26: Korean War ended
1954 • **Southern Christian Institute merged with Tougaloo College**
- **June 12: Sharon Watkins born in Wabash, Indiana**
1956 • **Panel of Scholars created and funded**
- **Committee on Brotherhood Organization and Interagency Relationships appointed**
1957 • **June 19–23: First Quadrennial Assembly of the ICWF**
- **Association of Disciples for Theological Discussion founded**
- September 24: The Little Rock Integration Crisis
1958 • **Christian Theological Seminary incorporated from Butler School of Religion**
- **Death of Edward Scribner Ames**
- **July: Williard Wickizer address, "Ideas for Brotherhood Restructure" delivered to the Council of Agencies.**
- **October: Eleven-member Study Committee on Brotherhood Structure appointed**
1959 • **August: Denver Convention approved the creation of a Commission on Brotherhood Restructure**
1960 • **October: Louisville Convention approved Commission on Brotherhood Restructure**
- November: Election of John Fitzgerald Kennedy President of the United States

1961 • **The Disciples periodical, *Midstream* on Christian Unity, founded**
- • January: Beginning of the Vietnam War
- • **Christian Church Foundation established**

1962 • **Consultation on Christian Union established**
- • July 5: Death of H. Richard Niebuhr
- • **October: Los Angeles Convention ratified appointment of 126 members to the Commission on Brotherhood Restructure; Granville Walker appointed Chair**
- • **A. Dale Fiers elected Executive Secretary of the Commission on Brotherhood Restructure**

1963 • **Panel of Scholars Reports published**
- • **A. Dale Fiers elected Executive Secretary of the International Convention**
- • August 28: "I Have a Dream" speech by Dr. Martin Luther King Jr., Washington, D.C.
- • November 22: Assassination of President John Fitzgerald Kennedy

1964 • **June: Dr. Ronald Osborn lectures on meaning of "Church" at third meeting of Commission**
- • **October: Detroit Convention approved "The Nature of the Structure Our Brotherhood Seeks"**
- • **July 1: A. Dale Fiers took office as Executive Secretary of the International Convention**

1965 • **June: Kenneth L. Teegarden became Administrative Secretary of the Restructure Commission**
- • **College of the Bible changed its name to Lexington Theological Seminary**
- • **The *American Christian Review* ceased publication**
- • August 6: Voting Rights Act Passed
- • August 15: Watts riots in Los Angeles

1966 • **October: Draft of proposed "Provisional Design" received at the Dallas convention**
- • **Death of Charles Clayton Morrison**
- • **Death of Royal J. Dye**

1967 • **October: St. Louis Convention revised and approved the "Provisional Design"**
- • **States and General Agencies approved the "Provisional Design"**

1968 • January: The Vietnam TET offensive
- • March 31: President Lyndon Johnson withdrew from 1968 presidential campaign

- April 4: The assassination of Dr. Martin Luther King Jr.
- June 4: The assassination of Senator Robert F. Kennedy
- **September 28: Adoption of the "Provisional Design" by the Kansas City Assembly**
- **A. Dale Fiers elected first General Minister and President**
- **Establishment of the Reconciliation program**
1969 • **National Christian Missionary Convention created**
- **Death of Winfred E. Garrison**
1970 • **National Convocation of the Christian Church established by African Americans**
- **April: Division of Overseas Ministries and Division of Homeland Ministries incorporated separately; formerly together in the UCMS**
1971 • **Separate listing of the Independents.**
- **Task Force on Corporate Social Responsibility appointed to develop ethically and socially responsible investment guidelines**
- June 1: Death of Reinhold Niebuhr
- **October: General Assembly approved formal "Policies and Criteria for the Order of Ministry"**
1973 • March: U.S. military participation in the Vietnam War ended
- **October 23–27: Cincinnati Assembly; A. Dale Fiers retired as General Minister and President**
- **October 27: Division of Overseas Ministries board first convened; Robert Thomas, President**
- **November 1: Kenneth L. Teegarden began ministry as General Minister and President**
1974 • **Church Finance Council replaced Unified Promotion**
- **A new periodical, *The Disciple,* launched (merger of The Christian-Evangelist and World Call)**
- August 8: Richard M. Nixon resigned as President of the United States
1975 • **The Campbell Institute and *The Scroll* dissolved**
- **General Assembly resolution on abortion approved: "affirmed the principle of individual liberty, freedom of individual conscience and the sacredness of life for all persons, and opposed attempts to legislate religious opinion"**
1976 • **June 12: Higher Education Evaluation Task Force report on development of a funding formula and a covenantal relationship with colleges and universities**
1977 • **October: The Division of Higher Education was incorporated**

- **October: Kansas City General Assembly; controversy on ordination of gays and lesbians**
- The "Focus on the Family" founded by James Dobson
- The "Moral Majority" founded by Jerry Falwell
1978 • **November 19: The Jonestown suicides**
- **Death of Virgil A. Sly**
- **"Provisional" dropped from the governing document; called simply *The Design***
1979 • **The Task Force on Ministry reported its conclusions on the ordination of gays and lesbians: "General Assembly should not legislate doctrinal or moral standards for ministers; responsibility for ordination and nurture rests with the regions; and not convinced that ordaining gays and lesbians is in accordance with God's will."**
- **AAD (American Asian Disciples) formally acknowledged as a racial-ethnic ministry**
1981 • **The Hispanic Bilingual Fellowship established**
- **Anaheim assembly approved new theological and philosophical framework for the Division of Overseas Ministries**
1982 • ***Baptism, Eucharist and Ministry* published by the World Council of Churches and affirmed by Disciples**
1983 • **Death of Mae Yoho Ward**
1984 • **The *COCU Consensus* document published; affirmed by Disciples**
1985 • **August 6: Kenneth L. Teegarden retired as General Minister and President at the Des Moines Assembly; John O. Humbert became General Minister and President**
- **Full Partnership approved with the United Church of Christ**
- **Publication of *Seeking God's Peace in a Nuclear Age* as part of the Disciples' Peace with Justice priority**
1987 • **Disciples Renewal incorporated**
- **March 8: Death of Dr. Stephen J. England**
1989 • **Disciples relationship with the United Church of Christ officially voted, "Full Communion"**
1991 • **October: Dr. Michael Kinnamon rejected as General Minister and President candidate at the Tulsa Assembly; William Nichols served a two-year interim**
- **Death of Granville Walker**
1992 • **Central Pastoral Office on Hispanic Ministries is established as an independent organization within the general church**

1993 • **July: Election of Richard L. Hamm as General Minister and President at the Pittsburgh Assembly**
  • **Process of discernment approved by the General Board of the Church**
1995 • **January 29: Closing of Missions Building**
  • **Disciples Heritage Fellowship founded as successor to Disciples Renewal**
1996 • **North American Pacific Asian Disciples (NAPAD) established**
  • **Joint Global Ministries Board with United Church of Christ established**
1997 • **Phillips Theological Seminary separately incorporated**
1998 • **April 1: Phillips University filed for bankruptcy; University closed in August**
  • **October 1: Death of Dr. Ronald E. Osborn**
2001 • **Churches Uniting in Christ (CUIC) founded; Disciples a charter member**
  • September 11: Attack on the World Trade Center in New York City and on the Pentagon in Washington, D.C.
2002 • **March: *The Disciple* ceased publication**
  • **April: The new volunteer-launched periodical *DisciplesWorld* commenced publication**
  • ***Mid-Stream* ceased publication; succeeded by *Call to Unity***
  • **September 22: Death of Kenneth L. Teegarden**
2003 • **Richard L. Hamm resigned as General Minister and President; William Hobgood served a two-year interim**
  • **Alvin O. Jackson resigned as Moderator of the Christian Church (Disciples of Christ)**
  • March 20: Invasion of Iraq
  • **September 10: Death of A. Dale Fiers**
2004 • **February 16: National Benevolent Association filed for bankruptcy**
2005 • **July 26: Dr. Sharon Watkins elected General Minister and President**
2006 • **Appointment of 21st Century Vision Team**
  • **Disciples Benevolent Services became the successor organization to the National Benevolent Association**
2007 • **Downsizing of the General Board of the Christian Church (Disciples of Christ)**

- **Church Finance Council reconstituted to become part of the Office of General Minister and President**
2009 • **Bicentennial celebration of the *Declaration and Address* in Nashville, Tennessee**

Prepared by D. Duane Cummins
Johns Hopkins University
June 4, 2008

Appendix B

The original appointed membership of the Commission on Brotherhood Restructure is cited below.

* An asterisk is used to identify members of the Central Committee of the Commission.

Adams, Hampton
New York City, N.Y.

*Austin, Spencer P.
Indianapolis, Indiana

Baird, William R.
Lexington, Kentucky

Barnes, Carnella
Los Angeles, Calif.

Barnett, Hubert L.
Wheeling, West Virginia

Bayer, Charles
Alexandria, Virginia

Beazley, George G. Jr.
Indianapolis, Indiana

Becker, Edwin L.
Des Moines, Iowa

*Blakemore, W. B.
Chicago, Illinois

Borgaard, Kent
Sioux Falls, South Dakota

Bouchard, Tommie M.
St. Joseph, Missouri

Breeland, Mrs. S.W.
Holly Hill, South Carolina

Brooks, Mrs. Wm. Orien
Winchester, Kentucky

Brown, Harold Glen
Portland, Oregon

Buhler, Arthur E.
Albuquerque, New Mexico

Burns, Benjamin F.
Oak Park, Illinois

Burns, Robert W.
Atlanta, Georgia

Cloues, Richard W.
Pittsburgh, Pennsylvania

Coil, Cullen
Jefferson City, Missouri

Cole, Mrs. O. Ivan
Cincinnati, Ohio

Cole, Myron C.
Los Angeles, California

Coleman, C. Linwood
Raleigh, North Carolina

*Cook, Gaines M.
Indianapolis, Indiana

Cramblet, Wilbur H.
St. Louis, Missouri

*Dentler, Howard
Indianapolis, Indiana

DePew, Arthur M.
St. Petersburg, Florida

Dickson, Emmett J.
Indianapolis, Indiana

Doolen, D. Wayne
Great Falls, Montana

Ely, Lawrence O.
Des Moines, Iowa

England, Stephen J.
Enid, Oklahoma

Evans, Mrs. W. K.
Austin, Minnesota

*Fiers, A. Dale
Indianapolis, Indiana

Fitzgerald, Mrs. John T.
San Francisco, Californi

Ford, Wesley P.
Pasadena, California

Gantz, Hallie G.
Enid, Oklahoma

Garrison, Carlton D.
Ponca City, Oklahoma

Gast, Mrs. Carl F.
St. Louis, Missouri

Gentry, Sloan
Tulsa, Oklahoma

Gibbs, Thomas J. Jr.
Los Angeles, California

Gray, Sidney L.
Lake Charles, Louisiana

Gresham, Perry E.
Bethany, West Virginia

Griffeth, Ross J.
Eugene, Oregon

Griffin, Thomas J.
Houston, Texas

Hooten, James L.
Savannah, Georgia

Hulan, Roy S.
Jackson, Mississippi

Jarman, William Jackson
Champaign, Illinois

Jones, Willis R.
Nashville, Tennessee

Kaufman, J. Kenneth
Murfreesboro, Tennessee

Kennedy, W. M.
St. Thomas, Ontario

Kerr, John
Austin, Minnesota

Knowles, John C.
Fort Worth, Texas

Lair, Loren
Des Moines, Iowa

Lathrop, Scott
Sacramento, Califor

*Lemmon, Clarence E.
Columbia, Missouri

Littrell, James A.
Springdale, Arkansas

Mabee, Frank C.
Enid, Oklahoma

McCully, Oliver W.
Toronto, Ontario

Miller, Raphael H. Jr.
Evansville, Indiana

Minck, Franklin H.
Akron, Ohio

*Moak, James A.
Lexington, Kentucky

Moffett, Robert
Tucson, Arizona

Monroe, Herald B.
Cleveland, Ohio

Moore, William J.
Lawrence, Kansas

*Moreland, Edward S.
Cincinnati, Ohio

Muir, Warner
Des Moines, Iowa

Munson, K. Everett
Maywood, Illinois

Murray, William Elmo
Regina, Saskatchewan

Nutting, David W.
Kent, Washington

Osborn, Ronald E.
Indianapolis, Indiana

*Owen, George Earle
Indianapolis, Indiana

Olmsted, Gilford E.
Kansas City, Kansas

Pack, John Paul
Los Angeles, California

Parry, Willbur C.
New York, New York

Pearcy, William T.
Indianapolis, Indiana

Pennybacker, Albert M.
Youngstown, Ohio

Peterson, Orval
St. Louis, Missouri

Pugh, Samuel F.
Indianapolis, Indiana

*Putnam, Mrs. Russell C.
Cleveland, Ohio

Rea, Harrell A.
Kansas City, Missou

*Richeson, Mrs. Forrest L.
Minneapolis, Minnesota

*Rickman, Lester B.
Jefferson City, Missouri

Riley, Jo M.
Decatur, Illinois

*Rogers, John
Tulsa, Oklahoma

Rowe, Mrs. F. W.
Omaha, Nebraska

Schoverling, Mrs. C.S.
Houston, Texas

Seeley, Kenneth B.
Kalamazoo, Michigan

Sharp, Paul F.
Hiram, Ohio

Short, Howard E.
St. Louis, Missouri

Sikes, Walter W.
Indianapolis, Indiana

Sly, Virgil A.
Indianapolis Indiana

Smith, Mrs. C.C.
Spray, Oregon

*Smith, Harlie L.
Indianapolis, Indiana

*Smith, Joseph M.
Indianapolis, Indiana

*Smith, Leslie R.
Lexington, Kentucky

Snedaker, Lorence W.
Colorado Springs, Color

Spaulding, Helen F.
Indianapolis, Indiana

Stauffer, Paul S.
Louisville, Kentucky

Stevenson, Archie K.
Cheyenne, Wyoming

Stover, Mrs. Howard
Bountiful, Utah

Strain, Dudly
Lubbock, Texas

*Stoner, Richard B.
Columbus, Indiana

Suggs, M. Jack
Fort Worth, Texas

Sutton, David Nelson
West Point, Virginia

Swearingen, T. T.
Fort Worth, Texas

Teegarden, Kenneth L.
Little Rock, Arkansas

Thomas, Mrs. O. G.
Birmingham, Alabama

Thomas, Robert A.
Seattle, Washington

Thompson, Rhodes Jr.
Daytona Beach, Florida

Turley, Hollis L.
Indianapolis, Indiana

Van Boskirk, Joseph J.
Washington, D.C.

*Van Doren, Earl H.
Seattle, Washington

Van Slyke, H. W.
Rupert, Idaho

*Wake, Orville W.
Lynchburg, Virginia

*Walker, Granville T.
Fort Worth, Texas

Ward, Mrs. Mae Yoho
Indianapolis, Indiana

Webb, Mrs. Charles H.
Chicago, Illinois

Welsh, W. A.
Dallas, Texas

Wenger, Arthur D.
Wilson, North Carolina

Whitley, Oliver Reed
Denver, Colorado

*Wickizer, Willard M.
Indianapolis, Indiana

Wilburn, Ralph G.
Lexington, Kentucky

Willis, Ross M.
East Orange, New Jersey

Wilson, George H.
New Orleans, Louisiana

Youngblood, Tom J.
Raleigh, North Carolina

Zimmerman, Clarence H.
Hoisington, Kansas

Notes

Preface

[1]Alexander Campbell, "The Editor's Response," *The Millennial Harbinger* 4, no. 12 (December, 1840): 556.

[2]Alexander Campbell, "Humble Beginnings," *The Millennial Harbinger* 6, no. 1 (January 1842): 4–13.

[3]Ibid., 11, 13.

[4]Ibid., 12.

[5]Ibid., 12–13.

[6]Barton W. Stone, "History of the Christian Church," *The Christian Messenger* 1, no. 4 (February 24, 1827): 74–79; (The history appeared in eight segments, one running in each issue of *The Christian Messenger,* through issue no. 12, October 25, 1827.] Barton W. Stone, *The Biography of Eld. Barton Warren Stone, written by himself ; with additions and reflections by Elder John Rogers* (Cincinnati: J.A. & U.P. James, 1847), reprint edited by Hoke Dickinson under the title *The Cane Ridge Reader* (New York: Arno Press, 1972), 50.

[7]Thomas Campbell, *The Delcaration and Address of the Christian Association of Washington,* 1809, 4 (housed in the Campbell Archives at Bethany College in West Virginia. Original copy with Campbell's notes in the margins). Alexander Campbell, "Reformation and Restoration," *The Millennial Harbinger* (1835): 24. Eva Jean Wrather, *Alexander Campbell: Adventurer in Freedom,* vol. 2 (Fort Worth, Tex.: TCU Press, 2007): 72. See Alexander Campbell, "News from the Churches," *The Millennial Harbinger* (1839): 238–39, article by Alexander Campbell to Dr. D.R. Campbell, *The Millennial Harbinger* (1858): 471.

[8]Leroy Garrett, *The Stone-Campbell Movement: The Story of the American Restoration Movement* (Joplin, Mo.: College Press, 1994), 7. James Harvey Garrison, *The Reformation of the Nineteenth Century* (St. Louis: Christian Publishing Company, 1901), Preface.

[9]W.E. Garrison and Alfred DeGroot, *The Disciples of Christ: A History* (St. Louis: Christian Board of Publication, 1948), 45. Lester McAllister and William E. Tucker, *Journey in Faith* (St. Louis: Bethany Press, 1975).

[10]Garrett, 12–13. Robert Fife, *Celebration of Heritage* (Los Angeles: Westwood Christian Foundation; Joplin, Mo.: College Press, 1992), 265–76.

[11]Clark Gilpin, "Faith on the Frontier: Historical Interpretations of the Disciples of Christ," in D. Newell Williams, *A Case Study of Mainstream Protestantism: The Disciples Relation to American Culture, 1880-1989* (Grand Rapids: Eerdmans; St. Louis: Chalice Press, 1991), 260–77. William Thomas Moore, *A Comprehensive History of the Disciples of Christ: Being an account of a century's effort to restore primitive Christianity in its Faith, Doctrine and Life* (New York: Fleming H. Revell Company, 1909), Preface.

[12]James DeForest Murch, *Christians Only: A History of the Restoration Movement* Cincinnati: Standard Publishing, 1962). James B. North, *Union in Truth: An Interpretative History of the Restoration Movement* (Cincinnati: Standard Publishing, 1994). Henry E. Webb, *In Search of Christian Unity. A History of the Restoration Movement* (Cincinnati: Standard Publishing, 1990). Richard T. Hughes, *Reviving the Ancient Faith: Story of the Churches of Christ in America* (Grand Rapids: Eerdmans, 1990).

[13]Robert Richardson, *Memoirs of Alexander Campbell: A view of the Origin, Progress and Principles of the Religious Reformation* (Cincinnati: Standard Publishing, 1890), 1: 489, 512; 2:. 168, 252, 440.

[14]John Rogers to Barton Stone, March 27, 1832, reprinted in *The Evangelist* 5, no. 1 (Monday May 7, 1832): 113. *The Millennial Harbinger* (1833): 94.

Chapter I: Roots

[1]Alexander Campbell, *Debate on the Evidences of Christianity between Robert Owen and Alexander Campbell: April 13-21, 1829,* vol. 2 (Alexander Campbell, publisher, Bethany, Virginia, 1829), 5.

[2]Diarmaid MacCulloch, *The Reformation* (New York: Viking Press, 2003), 119–28.

[3]E.J. Lowe, *Locke* (New York: Routledge, 2005), 2–14; Eva Jean Wrather, *Alexander Campbell: Adventurer in Freedom,* vol. 2 (Fort Worth, Tex.: TCU Press, 2007), 6–10; W.E. Garrison and Alfred De Groot, *The Disciples of Christ: A History* (St. Louis: Christian Board of Publication, 1948), 55; Leroy Garrett, *The Stone-Campbell Movement: The Story of the American Restoration Movement* (Joplin, Mo.: College Press, 1994), 24–29. George Beazley Jr., *The Christian Church (Disciples of Christ): An Interpretative Examination in the Cultural Context* (Toronto: Welch Co., 1973), 25.

[4]Peter Gay, *The Enlightenment,* vol. 1 (New York: W.W. Norton, 1966), 3–10, and vol. 2 (New York: W.W. Norton, 1977), 3–9.

[5]Berlin, 113; Wrather, 26; Roger Pearson, *Voltaire Almighty* (New York: Bloomsbury, 2005), 269–96; Will and Ariel Durant, *The Age of Voltaire,* vol. 9 in *The Story of Civilization* (New York: Simon & Schuster, 1965), 786.

[6]Jonathan Israel, *Radical Enlightenment* (Oxford: Oxford Univ. Press, 2001), 5–23; Edward Gibbon, *Decline and Fall of the Roman Empire* (1776; reprint, New York: Penguin Books, 1994), 446–510, 514.

[7]Berlin, 15; Durant, vii.

[8]Alan Taylor, *American Colonies* (New York: Viking Press, 2001), 344–62.

[9]Durant, 123–37; John Wesley, *The Heart of Wesley's Journal,* illustrated ed (reprint, New York: Kregel Publsihers, 1989), xiii-xxxv.

[10]George Marsden, *Jonathan Edwards: A Life* (New Haven, Conn.: Yale University Press, 2003), 202; Wesley, 9–24; and Edwin Gaustad and Leigh Schmidt, *The Religious History of America* (San Francisco: Harper SanFrancisco, 2002), 112.

[11]Marsden, 202–13; Carl Bridenbaugh, *Mitre and Sceptre* (New York: Oxford Univ. Press, 1962), 84; Frank Lambert, *Pedlar in Divinity: George Whitefield and the Transatlantic Revivals* (Princeton, N.J.: Princeton Univ. Press, 1994), 4–12, 229.

[12]Perry Miller, *Jonathan Edwards* (New York: Meridan Books, 1959), 1–5.

[13]Marsden, 45, 201–13; Garrison and DeGroot, 68–70.

[14]Frank Lambert, *Inventing the Great Awakening* (Princeton, N.J.: Princeton Univ. Press. 1999), 3; Sydney Ahlstrom, *A Religious History of the American People* (New Haven, Conn.: Yale Univ. Press, 1972), 283; Gaustad and Schmidt, 61; Daniel Boorstin, *The Americans: The Colonial Experience* (1958; reprint, New York: Vintage, 1964), 179; Alan Heimert, *Religion and the American Mind: Great Awakening to Revolution* (Cambridge, Mass.; Harvard Univ. Press, 1966), viii.

[15]See W.E. Garrison, *An American Religious Movement* (St. Louis: Christian Board of Publication, 1945), 68–70; Garrett, 48–50; Robert Calhoon, "The Evangelical Persuasion," in *Religion in a Revolutionary Age,* ed. Ronald Hoffman and Peter J. Albert (Charlottesville, Va.: Univ. Press of Virginia, 1994), 159–60. Quotes taken from Nathan O. Hatch, "In Pursuit of Religious Freedom: Church, State and People" in *The American Revolution: Its Character and Limits,* ed. Jack P. Greene (New York: New York Univ. Press, 1987), 391, and from Gordon S. Wood, "Evangelical America and Early Mormonism," *New York History* 61 (1980): 368; and Mark A. Noll, *The Rise of Evangelicalism: The Age of Edwards, Whitefield and the Wesleys* (Downers Grove, Ill.: InterVarsity Press, 2004).

[16]Peter Ainslie, *The Message of the Disciples for the Union of the Church* (New York: Fleming Revell Co., 1913), 63–72; W.E. Garrison, *Christian Unity and Disciples of Christ* (St. Louis: Bethany Press, 1955), 15–32; Charles Clayton Morrison, *The Unfinished Reformation* (New York: Harper, 31–42).

[17]Garrison and DeGroot, 38–46.

[18]Ibid., 45

[19]Garrett, 37–43.

[20]*Christian Baptist* 3 (1826): 228–29.

[21]*Christian Baptist* 5 (1827): 398–99.

[22]Ahlstrom, 422–23; Garrison and DeGroot, 59–60; Nathan Hatch, *The Democratization of American Christianity* (New Haven, Conn.: Yale Univ. Press, 1989), 3–5; Samuel Eliot

Morison, Henry Steele Commager, and William E. Leuchtenburg, *Growth of the American Republic,* vol. 1 (New York: Oxford Univ. Press, 1981), 1:331–32; Joseph Ellis, *American Creation* (New York: Alfred Knopf, 2007), 3-4; Gordon S. Wood, *The Radicalism of the American Revolution* (New York: Alfred Knopf, 1992), 230.

[23]Akhil Reed Amar, *The Bill of Rights* (New Haven, Conn.: Yale Univ. Press, 1998), 32, 309; Jon Butler, *Awash in a Sea of Faith* (Cambridge, Mass.: Harvard Univ. Press, 1990), 258; Garrison and DeGroot, 59; Lester McAllister and William E. Tucker, *Journey in Faith* (St. Louis: Bethany Press, 1975), 38; Hatch, *Democratization,* 3; George Marsden, *Understanding Fundamentalism and Evangelicalism* (Grand Rapids: Eerdmans, 1991), 81; Roger Finke, "Religious Deregulation: Origins and Consequences," *Journal of Church and State* 32 (summer 1990): 625; Steven Waldman, *Founding Faith* (New York: Random House, 2008), 200-1.

[24]Hatch, *Democratization,* 3–5, 11.

[25]Butler, 270; ibid., 5.

[26]See Garrison and DeGroot, 76–77; Morrison et al., 331–32; Henry May, *The Enlightenment in America* (Oxford, New York: Oxford Univ. Press, 1976), 307–57; Vernon Parrington, *Main Currents in American Thought,* vol. 2 (1927; reprint, New York: Harcourt Brace, 1954), 131.

[27]Elias Smith, article in first issue of *Herald of Gospel Liberty* (September 1, 1808).

[28]Wilbur E. MacClenny, *The Life of Rev. James O'Kelly and the Early History Of the Christian Church in the South* (Raleigh, N.C.: Edwards & Broughton, 1910), available through www.okelley.net/Rev_James_OKELLEY.html and www.TheRestorationMovement.com/okelley.james.htm; DCHS, 11–45; Charles Franklin Kilgore, *The James O'Kelly Schism in the Methodist Episcopal Church* (Mexico City: Casa Unida De Publicaciones, 1963); John F. Burnett, *Rev. James O'Kelly: A Champion of Religious Liberty* (Dayton, Ohio: Christian Publishing, 1921), 1–19, available through www.okelley.net/Rev_James_OKELLEY.html; Garrison and DeGroot, 84–85; Garrett, 54–59; Arthur Schlesinger Jr., "The Age of Alexander Campbell" in *The Sage of Bethany,* comp. Perry E. Gresham (St. Louis: Bethany Press, 1960), 25–31.

[29]Douglas A. Foster, Paul M. Blowers, Anthony L. Dunnavant, and D. Newell Williams, *The Encyclopedia of the Stone-Campbell Movement* (Grand Rapids: Wm. B. Eerdmans, 2005), 574. See also Burnett, ibid.; MacClenny, ibid.; Garrison and DeGroot, ibid.; and Garrett, ibid.

[30]Ibid.

[31]Colby Hall, *Rice Haggard: The American Frontier Evangelist Who Revived the Name Christian* (Fort Worth, Tex.: Stafford-Lowdon, 1957), 1–28; Rice Haggard, *An Address to the Different Religious Societies on the Sacred Import of the Christian Name* (Lexington: Charles printers, 1804), 1–31, available at http://articles.christiansunite.com/preacher354-1.shtml; Foster et al., 377; MacClenny, 121.

[32]James O'Kelly, *Plan of Christian Union,* cited in MacClenny, 248–253, also at www.okelley.net/Rev_James_OKELLEY.html.

[33]Hall, 1–28; Haggard, 1–28; Foster et al., 377; MacClenny, 121.

[34]Michael Kenny, *The Perfect law of Liberty: Elias Smith and the Providential History of America* (Washington, D.C.: Smithsonian Institution Press, 1994), 1–35; Elias Smith, *The Life, Conversion, Preaching, Travel, and Sufferings of Elias Smith* (Portsmouth, Beck & Foster, 1816), 1–25, at http://www.mun.ca/rels/restmov/people/esmith.html; Foster et al., 688; Hatch, *Democratization,* 69.

[35]Abner Jones, *Memoirs of the Life and Experiences, Travels and Preaching Of Abner Jones* (Exeter, N.H.: Norris & Sawyer, 1807 and 1842), 1–33, at http://www.mun.ca/rels/restmov/people/ajones.html. and on microfilm at the Disciples of Christ Historical Society in Nashville; Foster et al., 432; Garrison and DeGroot, 88–89; Nathan Hatch, "Elias Smith and the rise of Religious Journalism in the Early Republic," in *Printing and Society in Early America,* ed. William Joyce (Worcester, Mass.: American Antiquarian Society, 1983), 250–62; Paul Conkin, *American Originals: Homemade varieties of Christianity* (Chapel Hill: Univ. of North Carolina Press 1997), 6.

[36]Hatch, *Democratization,* 80; Schlesinger Jr., 25–35.

Chapter II: Barton Warren Stone

[1]Barton Warren Stone, article in first issue of *The Christian Messenger* (1826).

[2]Anthony Dunnavant, "From Precursor of the Movement to Icon of Christian Unity:

Barton W. Stone in Memory of the Christian Church (Disciples of Christ)" in *Cane Ridge in Context: Perspectives on Barton W. Stone and the Revival,* ed. Anthony Dunnavant (Nashville: DCHS, 1992), 1–16; G. Richard Phillips, "Barton W. Stone: His distinctive Contribution." *Discipliana* 65, no. 2 (Summer, 2005): 46; James H. Garrison, *The Story of a Century: A Brief Historical Sketch and Exposition of the Religious Movement Inaugurated by Thomas and Alexander Campbell* (St. Louis: Christian Pub., 1909), 12; Leroy Garrett, *The Stone-Campbell Movement* (Joplin, Mo.: College Press, 1994), 90–92; Lester McAllister and William E. Tucker, *Journey in Faith* (St. Louis: Bethany Press, 1975), 62; James North, *Union in Truth* (Cincinnati: Standard Publishers, 1994), 33–44.

³Charles C. Ware, *Barton Warren Stone* (St. Louis: Bethany Press, 1932), 1–17; Barton W. Stone, *The Biography of Eld. Barton Warren Stone, written by himself ; with additions and reflections by Elder John Rogers* (Cincinnati: J.A. & U.P. James, 1847), reprint edited by Hoke Dickinson under the title *The Cane Ridge Reader* (New York: Arno Press, 1972), 1–4; D. Newell Williams, *Barton Stone: A Spiritual Biography* (St. Louis: Chalice Press, 2000), 9–12; Eva Jean Wrather, *Alexander Campbell: Adventurer in Freedom,* vol. 2 (Fort Worth, Tex.: TCU Press, 2007), 143–53; William G. West, *Barton Warren Stone: Early American Advocate of Christian Unity* (Nashville: DCHS, 1954), 1–2.

⁴*Stone Autobiography,* 34; Williams, 15; Ware, 17–18.

⁵West, 4; Ware, 24; *Stone Autobiography,* 11.

⁶Barton Stone, article in *The Christian Messenger* 1, no. 4 (1827).

⁷*Stone Autobiography,* 4–5, 7–11; Williams, 18, 26–28; Ware, 28–29; West, 11; Robert Bray, *Peter Cartwright: Legendary Frontier Preacher* (Urbana: Univ. of Illinois Press, 2005), 26–30; and Peter Cartwright, *Autobiography of Peter Cartwright* (1859; reprint, Nashville: Abingdon Press, 1956), 37.

⁸West, 12–15; Williams, 29–35; Ware, 33–45; and *Stone Autobiography,* 12–16.

⁹Ware, 57–75; Williams, 40–45; West, 15–17; and *Stone Autobiography,* 25–30.

¹⁰Williams, , 57; *Stone Autobiography,* 37; Ware, 97–99; West, 31.

¹¹Leigh E. Schmidt, *Holy Fairs: Scottish Communions and American Revivals in the Early Modern Period* (Princeton, N.J.: Princeton Univ. Press, 1989), 39–53, 64–65; Paul Conkin, *Cane Ridge: America's Pentecost* (Madison: Univ. of Wisconsin Press 1990), 3, 64; Newton Fowler, "Cambuslang: The Scottish Predecessor to Cane Ridge" in *Cane Ridge in Context: Perspectives on Barton W. Stone and the Revival* (Nashville: DCHS, 1992), 111–15; Perry Miller, *The Life of the Mind in America* (New York: Harcourt-Brace, 1965), 7; Cartwright, 35.

¹²Conkin, 63, 73, 102; Schmidt, 39, 64; Williams, 49; Dunnavant, 1–16; Bray, 27.

¹³*Stone Autobiography,* 34–35; Williams, 49–51; West, 30–31; Ware, 86–88, 91, 97–98; Cartwright, 38; John Wolffe, *The Expansion of Evangelicalism* (Downers Grove, Ill.: InterVarsity Press, 2007), 58–60.

¹⁴Ware, 106; *Stone Autobiography,* 37; Williams, 59–60.

¹⁵*Stone Autobiography,* 39–42.

¹⁶"An Apology for renouncing the Jurisdiction of the Synod of Kentucky, to which is added a compendious View of the Gospel, and a few remarks on the Confession of Faith. Lexington, Ky.," 1804. The Apology is reprinted in *Stone Autobiography,* 234; West, 45–46.

¹⁷John P. MacLean, *A Sketch of the Life and Labors of Richard McNemar* (Franklin Ohio: printed for author by *Franklin Chronicle,* 1905), 2; West. 54–55; Douglas A. Foster, Paul M. Blowers, Anthony L. Dunnavant, and D. Newell Williams, *The Encyclopedia of the Stone-Campbell Movement* (Grand Rapids: Wm. B. Eerdmans, 2005), 510–12; *The Christian Messenger* 1, no. 4 (1827): 79.

¹⁸West, 58–59; *The Christian Messenger* 1, no. 5 (1827), 99; "An Apology," 232; Richard Tristano, *The Origins of the Restoration Movement: An Intellectual History* (Atlanta: Glenmary Research Center, 1988), 40–52.

¹⁹*Stone Autobiography,* 147–247; Robert Marshall and John Thompson, *A Brief Historical Account of Sundry Things in the Doctrines and State of the Christian, or as it is Commonly Called, the Newlight Church* (Cincinnati: Carpenter & Co., 1811), 21–32, cited in West, 77; Ware, 169; Williams, 97.

²⁰*Stone Autobiography,* 51–53; Garrison and DeGroot, 108; F.D. Kershner, *Declaration and Address* (St Louis: Bethany Press, 1971), 15; D. Newell Williams, "Barton Warren Stone," in Foster et al., 700–20.

²¹Stephen Stein, *The Shaker Experience in America* (New Haven, Conn.: Yale Univ. Press, 1992), 58–60; Colby Hall, *Rice Haggard: The American Frontier Evangelist Who Revived the Name*

Christian. (Fort Worth, Tex.: Stafford-Lowdon, 1957), 47.
²²*Stone Autobiography,* 20.
²³Ibid., 21, 75–76.

Chapter III: Thomas and Alexander Campbell

¹Alexander Campbell, *Memoirs of Elder Thomas Campbell, Together with a Brief Memoir of Mrs. Jane Campbell* (Cincinnati: Bosworth, 1861), 7–8; Robert Richardson, *Memoirs of Alexander Campbell, Embracing a View of the Origin, Progress and Principles of the Religious Reformation Which He Advocated,* vol. 1 (Philadelphia: Lippincott, 1868), 20–22; Lester McAllister, *Thomas Campbell: Man of the Book* (St. Louis: Bethany Press, 1954), 21; Eva Jean Wrather, *Alexander Campbell: Adventurer in Freedom,* vol. 1 (Fort Worth, Tex.: TCU Press, 2005), 4–5, 8; George Miller, Campbell Family Genealogy, Family Group Records Documentation in Historic Bethany, Bethany W.Va., September, 1996, 10th ed., 2007, 1–2; Richard Olson, Family Genealogical Records, 1–3; William Hanna, *Thomas Campbell: Seceder and Christian Union Advocate.* (Cincinnati: Standard Publishing Co., 1935), 23–24.
²McAllister, 22–23; Richardson, 21–22, 24; Wrather, 1:9–10.
³Magnus Magnusson, *Scotland: The Story of a Nation* (New York: Atlantic Monthly Press, 2000), 641–42; T.M. Devine, *The Scottish Nation: 1700-2000* (New York: Viking,1999), 65–83; John Hill Burton, *The Autobiography of the Rev. Dr. Alexander Carlyle, Minister of Inveresk* (1860; reprint, London: W. Blackwood, 1910), 93–94.
⁴McAllister, 24–30; Richardson, 25–26; Wrather, 1:13–15.
⁵McAllister, 31–32; Richardson, 20; Wrather, 1:11.
⁶Campbell, *Memoirs,* 9–10; Richardson, 39–47; McAllister, 32–44; and Henry E. Webb, *In Search of Christian Unity. A History of the Restoration Movement* (Cincinnati: Standard Publishing, 1990), 63–66.
⁷Campbell, *Memoirs,* 210–14; McAllister, 45–46, 52–55; Richardson, 53–58.
⁸Richardson, 78–82; McAllister, 56–59.
⁹McAllister, 72–95; Richardson, 222–41; Webb, 69–73.
¹⁰McAllister, 95–100; A. Campbell, *Memoirs of Elder Thomas Campbell,* 17.
¹¹Ibid.
¹²Charles L. Loos, "History of the Nineteenth Century Reformation," *Christian Evangelist* 18 (1899): 104; F. D. Kershner, *Declaration and Address* (St. Louis: Bethany Press, 1971), 10; H. E. Johnson, *The Declaration and Address for Today* (Nashville: Reed & Co., 1971), 7; Frederick Kershner, *The Christian Union Overture* (St. Louis: Bethany Press, 1923), 59–62; Thomas Campbell, *The Declaration and Address of the Christian Association of Washington. 1809* (Housed in the Campbell Archives, Bethany College: original copy with Campbell's notes in the margins.); Leroy Garrett, *The Stone-Campbell Movement* (Joplin, Mo.: College Press, 1994), 98–99; Thomas H. Olbricht and Hans Rollmann, *The Quest for Christian Unity, Peace, And Purity in Thomas Campbell's Declaration and Address* (Lanham, Md.: Scarecrow Press, 2000), 118–24; A. Campbell, *Memoirs,* 25–109, 110-140; Paul Conkin, *American Originals: Homemade Varieties of Christianity.* (Chapel Hill: Univ. of North Carolina Press, 1997), 5–6.
¹³McAllister, 107–110; Richardson, 241–46; W.E. Garrison and Alfred De Groot, *The Disciples of Christ: A History* (St. Louis: Christian Board of Publication, 1948), 145–49; Kershner, *The Christian Union Overture,* 32–33; Hiram Lester, "The Form and Function of the Declaration and Address," in Olbricht and Rollmann, 173–87.
¹⁴Garrison, 150–52; McAllister, 110–25; Richardson, 271–73, 258; Garrett, 105–8; James North, *Union in Truth* (Cincinnati: Standard Publishers, 1994), 88–94; Webb, 73–82; Kershner, 81–96; Lester, 173–87; and Perry Miller, *The Life of the Mind* (New York: Harcourt-Brace, 1965), 5, 10–11.
¹⁵T. Campbell, . *Declaration and Address* (St. Louis: Bethany Press, 1955), 35.
¹⁶A. Campbell, *Memoirs,* 353–54.
¹⁷Richardson, 30–32; W.E. Garrison and Alfred DeGroot, *The Disciples of Christ: A History* (St. Louis: Christian Board of Publication, 1948), 141.
¹⁸Richardson, 26; Wrather, 1:30.
¹⁹Richardson, 35, 48–49; Wrather, 1:43–44.
²⁰Richardson, 36–37; Wrather, 1:31; A. Campbell, *Memoirs,* 316–17, 310, 309–19.
²¹Richardson, 80.
²²Richardson, 98–107 and Wrather, 1:61–65.

[23]Ibid.

[24]Richardson, 189–90; Wrather, 1:91–93; Garrett, 119.

[25]Alexander Campbell, article in *Christian Baptist* 3 (February 1862).

[26]Richardson, 273–78, 281; Wrather, 1:131.

[27]Garrett, 124–25; Lester McAllister and William E. Tucker, *Journey in Faith* (St. Louis: Chalice Press, 1975), 116.

[28]Garrison and DeGroot, 155–57; Richardson, 365–67; McAllister and Tucker, 117; Webb, 102–6; James Haldane, *View of the Social Worship and Ordinances observed by the First Christians* (Edinburgh: n.p., 1805), 292–301.

[29]Alexander Campbell, "Humble Beginnings" *The Millennial Harbinger* 6, no. 1 (January 1842): 4–13; Richardson, 365–67.

[30]Richardson, 357–63, 392–93; Garrison and DeGroot, 158–61; and Garrett, 126–28.

[31]Ibid.; Alexander Campbell, "Anecdotes, Incidents and Facts," *The Millennial Harbinger* (1848) 283.

[32]Richardson, 402.

[33]Alexander Campbell, "Sermon on the Law," *The Millennial Harbinger* (1846): 493; Garrison and DeGroot, 163–67; Garrett, 128–31.

[34]A. Campbell, "Anecdotes, Incidents and Facts," 556.

[35]Alexander Campbell and John Walker, *A Debate on Christian Baptism between Mr. John Walker and Alexander Campbell.* (Buffaloe: Campbell & Salla, 1822); Garrison and DeGroot, 168–71; Garrett, 133–136; McAllister and Tucker, 123–25; and Wrather, 1:229–34.

[36]Alexander Campbell, *A Debate on Christian Baptism between The Rev. W. L. Maccalla and Alexander Campbell* (Buffaloe: Campbell & Salla, 1824), 41–47; Garrison and DeGroot, 171–74; Eva Jean Wrather, *Alexander Campbell: Adventurer in Freedom,* vol. 2. (Fort Worth, Tex.: TCU press, 2007), 25–35; Garrett, 133–36; McAllister and Tucker, 123–25; Alexander Campbell, *Christian Baptism, with its Antecedents and Consequents* (Bethany, Va., 1851), 215–20; and Robert Richardson, *Memoirs of Alexander Campbell: A view of the Origin, Progress and Principles of the Religious Reformation,* vol. 2 (Cincinnati: Standard Publishing, 1890), 90.

[37]Alexander Campbell, article in first issue of *Christian Baptist* in 1823.

[38]Olbricht and Rollmann, 57; Richardson, vol. 2; "Editor's Preface"; *Christian Baptist* (1835): 1.

[39]*The Millennial Harbinger* (1831): 419–20; *The Millennial Harbinger* (1830): 123; *The Millennial Harbinger* (1832): 294.

[40]*Christian Baptist* 1 no. 1 (1835): 6 (D.S.Burnett's one-volume edition); *Christian Baptist* 3, no. 1 (1838): 173; *Christian Baptist* 5, no. 1 (1840): 361.

[41]*Christian Baptist* 1, no. 2 (1835): 14 (Burnett edition); *Christian Baptist* 1, no. 1: 6–8; Richardson, vol. 2, 53–68.

[42]*Christian Baptist* 1, no. 1: 7; Richardson, vol.2, 56, 53–68.

[43]"The Ancient Order of Things," *Christian Baptist* (1835) no. 1: 126 (Burnett edition); no. 3: 133; no. 5: 165; no. 7: 180; no. 16: 214; no. 18: 322. "The Ancient Gospel," *Christian Baptist,* no. 1: 401; no. 8: 466; Alexander Campbell, "The Kingdom of Heaven," *The Millennial Harbinger* (1834, Extra): 424; Alexander Campbell, "The Ordinances," *The Millennial Harbinger* (1843) no. 1: 9; *Lectures in Honor of the Alexander Campbell Bicentennial: 1788-1988* (Nashville: DCHS, 1988); William Richardson, "Alexander Campbell as an advocate of Christian Union," in *Lectures in Honor of the Alexander Campbell Bicentennial* (1788–1988), DCHS, 1988, 110–18; Perry Gresham, *The Sage of Bethany* (St. Louis: Bethany Press, 1960), 89; Alexander Campbell, *The Christian System,* 2d ed. (Pittsburgh: Forrester and Campbell, 1840), 122.

[44]Richard Hughes, *Reviving the Ancient Faith* (Grand Rapids: Eerdmans, 1996), 21–46; North, 5–11; Earl West, *The Search for the Ancient Order,* vol. 2 (Indianapolis: Religious Book Service, 1950), 223. (Quote from W. McGarvey article in *Gospel Advocate* 27, (January 7, 1885): 7.)

[45]Wrather, *Adventurer,* vol. 2, chapters 8 and 9; Eva Jean Wrather, *Alexander Campbell and his Relevance for Today* (Nashville: DCHS, 1953), 10; Eva Jean Wrather, *Alexander Campbell: Adventurer in Freedom,* vol. 3 (Forth Worth, Tex.: TCU Press, forthcoming), in manuscript form, chapter 18, pages 5–10; *The Millenial Harbinger* 2, no. 10 (October 3, 1831): 436–37.

[46]Richard Hughes and Allen Leonard, *Illusions of Innocence* (Chicago: Univ. of Chicago Press, 1988), 170–87; Hughes, *Reviving the Ancient Faith,* 45–46.

[47] *The Millennial Harbinger* (1866): 497.

[48] Richardson, 200; Wrather, *Adventurer,* 2:143.

[49] Garrett, 82–92; Garrison, 207–12; North, 159–66.

[50] Barton Stone, "History of the Christian Church in the West," *The Christian Messenger* 1, no. 4 (February 2, 1827) [reprint, Forth Worth, Tex.: Star Bible Publications, 1978], 74. There were eight articles in the series appearing in the *Messenger* through 1, no. 12 (October 25, 1827); Barton Stone, "An Humble Address to the various Denominations of Christians In America,*" The Christian Messenger* 2, no. 1 (November, 1827): 1, 25. There were three articles in the series, appearing in the *Messenger* through vol. 2, no. 3 (January, 1828); Barton Stone, "An Address to the Churches of Christ," *The Christian Messenger* 6, no. 9 (September 1832): 263–66; Barton Stone, "Notice," *The Christian Messenger* 9, no. 12 (December): 285.

[51] Cecil Thomas, *Alexander Campbell and His New Version* (St. Louis: Bethany Press, 1958), 13-43; Garrison, 196–97; Garrett, 161–63; Wrather, *Adventuer,* vol. 2, chapter 11. (The sources used by Alexander Campbell included *Four Gospels* by George Campbell, 1789; *Family Expositor* by Philip Dodddridge, 1756; *A New Literal Translation from The Original Greek of the Apostolic Epistles* by James Macknight, 1820; *The Holy Bible Containing the Old and New Covenant* by Charles Thompson, 1808; *Greek New Testament* by J. J. Griesbach, 1775, 1806; numerous other translations were used, including ones by William Newcome, Daniel Whitby, Gilbert Wakefield, James Pierce, and John Wesley, among others.]

[52] Wrather, *Adventurer,* vol. 2, chapter 12; Richardson, 234–43; Garrett, 163–67; Garrison, 197–99; Webb, 121–24; Frances Trollope, *Domestic Manners of the Americans* (1832; reprint, New York: Alfred Knopf, 1949), 150.

[53] Wrather, *Adventurer,* vol. 2, chapter 13; Garrison, 199–200; Garrett, 167–70; Webb, 124–25; R. Richardson, 2:311; Hugh Grigsby, "The Virginia Convention of 1829-30": in *Proceedings and Debates of the Virginia State Convention of 1829-1830* (Richmond, Ind.: Ritchie & Cook Printers, 1830; DCHS et. passim).

[54] Ibid.

[55] *The Christian Messenger* 6 (1832).

[56] *Christian Baptist* (February 26, 1826): 7; *The Millennial Harbinger* (1831): 567; Garrison, 201–5.

[57] John Augustus Williams, *Life of Elder John Smith* (1870; reprint, Nashville: Gospel Advocate, 1956), 385; McAllister and Tucker, 136–46; Garrett, 156–61.

[58] Dwight Stevenson *Walter Scott: Voice of the Golden Oracle* (St. Louis: Christian Board of Publication, 1946), 18–36, 116; McAllister and Tucker, 136–46; Garrison, 201–5; Garrett, 156–61; Oliver R. Whitley, *Trumpet Call of Reformation* (St. Louis: Bethany Press, 1959), 71.

[59] Mark Toulouse, *Walter Scott: A Nineteenth-Century Evangelical* (St. Louis: Chalice Press, 1999); Mark Toulouse, "Walter Scott," in *Encyclopedia of the Stone-Campbell Movement,* ed. Douglas A. Foster, Paul M. Blowers, Anthony L. Dunnavant, and D. Newell Williams (Grand Rapids: Wm. B. Eerdmans, 2005), 673–79; Stevenson, 118; William Baxter, *Life of Walter Scott* (St. Louis: Bethany Press, 1926), 11–15.

[60] Stevenson, 118; Richardson, 1:510; *The Millennial Harbinger* (1841): 409–10; *The Millennial Harbinger* (1860): 330.

[61] *The Millennial Harbinger* 1, no. 1 (January 4, 1830): 1; Richardson, 1:511.

[62] *Christian Messenger* 5, no. 1 (1831): 22–23; no. 8: 180–85; *The Millennial Harbinger* (1831): 395; *Christian Messenger* 5, no. 11: 251.

[63] John Augustus Williams, 369–72, 374; McAllister and Tucker, 150–55; Garrison, 212–17; Garrett, 173–94; Webb, 156–58; North, 166–78; Barton W. Stone, *The Biography of Eld. Barton Warren Stone, written by himself ; with additions and reflections by Elder John Rogers* (Cincinnati: J.A. & U.P. James, 1847), reprint edited by Hoke Dickinson under the title *The Cane Ridge Reader* (New York: Arno Press, 1972), 79.

[64] Ibid.

Chapter IV: Revivalism, and Evangelicalism, and the Disciples Reform Movement

[1] *The Millennial Harbinger* (1854): 189.

[2] Paul Conkin, *American Originals: Homemade varieties of Christianity* (Chapel Hill: Univ. of North Carolina Press, 1997), 29–30; Richard Tristano, *The Origins of the Restoration Movement*

(Atlanta: Glenmary Research Center, 1988), 105–6; Robert Richardson, *The Principles and Objects of the Religious Reformation, urged by A. Campbell and Others, briefly stated and explained* (Bethany, Va.: A. Campbell, 1853), 6–44; Cloyd Goodnight and Dwight Stevenson, *Home to Bethphage* (St. Louis: CBP, 1949), 152–56; Alexander Campbell, "Synopsis of Reformation Principles and Objects," *The Millennial Harbinger* 1, no. 12 (December 1837): 530–38.

[3]Tristano, 111–12.

[4]Douglas A. Foster, Paul M. Blowers, Anthony L. Dunnavant, and D. Newell Williams, eds., *Encyclopedia of the Stone-Campbell Movement* (Grand Rapids: Wm. B. Eerdmans, 2005), 316–17; Jon Butler, *Awash in a Sea of Faith* (Cambridge, Mass.: Harvard Univ. Press, 1990), 270; W.E. Garrison and Alfred DeGroot, *The Disciples of Christ: A History* (St. Louis: Christian Board of Publication, 1948), 338; Timothy L. Smith, *Revivalism and Social Reform in Mid-19th Century America* (New York: Abingdon Press 1957), 17; Winfred E. Garrison, *Whence and Whither The Disciples of Christ* (St. Louis: Christian Board of Publication, 1948), 47.

[5]Richard Wade, *The Urban Frontier* (Chicago: Univ. of Chicago Press, 1959), 190–94; Leroy Garrett, *The Stone-Campbell Movement* (Joplin, Mo.: College Press, 1994), 231.

[6]*The Millennial Harbinger* (1854): 189; Garrison, 328–29, 218–424, 331; McAllister and Tucker, 235.

[7]David Bebbington, *The Dominance of Evangelicalism* (Downers Grove, Ill.: InterVarsity Press, 2005), 148–83; Perry Miller, *The Life of the Mind* (New York: Harcourt-Brace, 1965), 7, 14, 23.

[8]Mark Noll, *The Rise of Evangelicalism* (Downers Grove, Ill.: InterVarsity Press, 2003), 16–19; McAllister and Tucker, 159 [letter to the authors from Claude Spencer]; Bebbington, 23–40; 62.

[9]William G. McLoughlin Jr., *Modern Revivalism* (Eugene, Oreg.:Wipf & Stock, 1959), 4–15; William G. McLoughlin Jr., *Revivals, Awakenings and Reform* (Chicago: Univ. of Chicago Press, 1978), 1–23.

[10]McLoughlin. *Revivals,* 45–97.

[11]Ibid., 98–140. Robert Remini, *Andrew Jackson and the Course of American Democracy: 1833-1845* (New York: Harper & Row 1984), 337–39; John Ward, *Andrew Jackson: Symbol for an Age* (New York: Oxford Univ. Press, 1955), 49–50; Edward Pessen, *Jacksonian America* (Homewood, N.J.: Dorsey Press, 1969), 78–79; Gordon Wood, *The Creation of the American Republic* (Chapel Hill: Univ. of North Carolina Press, 1969), 6–7; Alexis De Tocqueville, *Democracy in America* (1838; Chicago: Encyclopedia Brittanica, 1990), 58; Miller, 7; McLoughlin, *Modern Revivalism,* 523; Mark Noll, *America's God* (New York: Oxford, 2002), 176.

[12]George Marsden, *Understanding Fundamentalism and Evangelicalism* (Grand Rapids: Eerdmans, 1991), 86–87; Miller, 23, 28–29, 40, 45, 48; Sidney Mead, "The Rise of the Evangelical Conception of the Ministry in America," in *The Ministry in Historical Perspectives,* ed. H. Richard Niebuhr and Daniel Williams (New York: Harper, 1956), 228; Pessen, 79; Mark Noll, *A History of Christianity in the U.S. & Canada* (Grand Rapids: Eerdmans, 1992), 176.

[13]McLoughlin, *Modern Revivalism,* 17.

[14]McLoughlin, *Revivals,* 98–140; Peter Cartwright, *Autobiography of Peter Cartwright* (Nashville: Abingdon Press, 1984), 212–25; Robert Bray, *Peter Cartwright* (Urbana: Univ. of Illinois Press, 2005), 50–75; Debby Applegate, *The Most Famous Man in America: The Biography of Henry Ward Beecher* (New York: Doubleday, 2006), 306–91; Charles Finney, *The Autobiography of Charles C. Finney* (Minneapolis: Bethany House, 1977), 53–61; Charles Hambrick-Stowe, *Charles G. Finney and the Spirit of American Evangelicalism* (Grand Rapids: Eerdmans, 1996), 228–32; Clement Eaton, *The Mind of the South* (Baton Rouge: L.S.U. Press, 1967), 200–204.

[15]McLoughlin, *Revivals,* 141–78.

[16]Ibid.; McLoughlin, *Modern Revivalism,* 452; Garrison and DeGroot, 410; Mark Noll, *The Scandal of the Evangelical Mind* (Grand Rapids: Eerdmans, 1994), 74.

[17]*The Millennial Harbinger* (1842): 59–60.

[18]Eva Jean Wrather, *Alexander Campbell on the Structure of the Church* (St. Louis: Bethany Press, 1968), 9–10.

[19]*The Millennial Harbinger* (1831): 237–38.

[20]Ibid., 446; *The Millennial Harbinger* (1835): 162–63.

[21]*The Millennial Harbinger* (1835): 163–64.

²²Ibid., 166–67.

²³*The Millennial Harbinger* (1839): 3; Garrison and DeGroot, 205, 230, 234–35, 242.

²⁴*The Millennial Harbinger* (1835): 497.

²⁵*The Millennial Harbinger* (1842): 523; *The Millennial Harbinger* (1838): 269; *The Millennial Harbinger* (1843): 82–86.

²⁶Garrison and DeGroot, 242–45; James H. Garrison, *The Reformation of the Nineteenth Century* (St. Louis: Christian Publishing Co., 1901), 103; Richardson, *Memoirs,* vol. 1, 493–94; *The Millennial Harbinger* (1849): 270.

²⁷Garrison and DeGroot, 246–47; *The Millennial Harbinger* (1849): 694; David Harrell Jr., *Quest for a Christian America* (Nashville: DCHS, 1966), 9.

²⁸*The Millennial Harbinger* (1853): 492; D. Duane Cummins, *Kenneth L. Teegarden: The Man, The Church, The Time* (Fort Worth, Tex.: TCU Press, 2007), 99–100.

²⁹*Encyclopedia of the Stone Campbell Movement,* 95, 200, 340; D. Duane Cummins, *The Disciples Colleges: A History* (St. Louis: CBP Press, 1987), 97, 99–100; Archibald McLean, "The Foreign Christian Missionary Society," *Christian Evangelist* 37 (1899): 1447; Archibald McLean, *The History of the Foreign Christian Missionary Society* (New York: Revell, 1919), 51–60.

³⁰*The Millennial Harbinger* (1853): 507.

³¹Noll, *Rise,* 37; Noll, *Scandal,* 3–27; Richard Hofstadter, *Anti-Intellectualism in American Life* (New York: Vintage, 1962), 56–57; Susan Jacoby, *The Age of American Unreason* (New York: Pantheon, 2008), 188–89; D. Newell Williams, "The Gospel as the Power of God to Salvation: Alexander Campbell and Experimental Religion," in *Lectures in Honor of the Alexander Campbell Bicentennial* (Nashville: DCHS, 1988), 129, 134, 137; William Baker, *Evangelicalism and the Stone-Campbell Movement* (Downers Grove, Ill.: InterVarsity Press, 2002), 30–49, 62–63; Richard Hughes, "Are Restorationists Evangelical?" in *Variety of Evangelicalism,* ed. Donald Dayton and Robert Johnston (Downers Grove, Ill.: InterVarsity Press, 1991), 109–34.

³²H. Richard Niebuhr, *The Social Sources of Denominationalism* (New York: Meridian, 1957), 30; Hofstadter, 56–57; David Harrell, *The Social Sources of Division within the Disciples of Christ: 1865-1900* (Atlanta: Publishing Systems, 1973), 3.

³³*Christian Baptist* 1 (1823): 52; Barbara Zikmund, "Alexander Campbell's View of Church and Ministry," in *Lectures in Honor of Alexander Campbell,* 167–81.

³⁴*The Millennial Harbinger* (1832): 497; *The Millennial Harbinger* (1834): 35; *The Millennial Harbinger* (1837): 439–41; *The Millennial Harbinger* (1839): 310–11; *The Millennial Harbinger,* (1842): 243. See also Eva Jean Wrather, *Alexander Adventurer in Freedom,* vol. 3 (Fort Worth, Tex: TCU Press, forthcoming), chapter 18.

³⁵*Christian System* (1835): 60–67, 85; *The Millennial Harbinger* (1855): 343; *The Millennial Harbinger* (1853): 507; *The Millennial Harbinger* (1850): 20.

³⁶*The Millennial Harbinger* (1850): 232; *The Millennial Harbinger,* (1841): 122, 189.

³⁷Ronald Osborn, *The Education of Ministers for the Coming Age* (St. Louis: CBP, 1987), 65–67, 84–89; McAllister and Tucker, 371; Garrison and DeGroot, 341–42; Stephen J. Corey, *Fifty Years of Attack and Controversy* (St. Louis: CBP, 1953), 18; *Christian Standard* (November 10, 1906): 1697; William E. Tucker, *J. H. Garrison and Disciples of Christ* (St. Louis: Bethany Press, 1964), 107.

³⁸D. Duane Cummins, *The Disciples Colleges: A History* (St. Louis: CBP, 1987), 25–27; Donald Tewksbury, *The Founding of American Colleges and Universities before the Civil War* (New York: Columbia Univ. Press 1932), 32–33; William T. Moore, *A Comprehensive History of the Disciples of Christ* (New York: Revell Company, 1909), 682.

³⁹Cummins, *Colleges,* 30–35; D. Duane Cummins, "Educational Philosophy of Alexander Campbell," *Discipliana* 59, no. 1 (1999): 5–15; Perry E. Gresham, *Campbell and the Colleges* (Nashville: DCHS, 1973), 21–29.

⁴⁰Cummins, *Colleges,* 35–43; Garrison, *Frontier,* 218; Garrison and DeGroot, 253, Moore, 683.

⁴¹Cummins. *Colleges,* 97–101.

⁴²Garrison and DeGroot, 534.

⁴³Osborn, 87; Garrison, *Frontier,* 210 (also cited in Tucker, 38).

⁴⁴McAllister and Tucker, 216–17; Garrett, 322–24; W.B. Blakemore, "The Sociology of Disciples Intellectual Life," in *The Renewal of Church,* ed. Ronald Osborn, vol. 1 (St. Louis: Bethany Press, 1963), 259.

[45]Garrison and DeGroot, 358; Garrett, 324–326; Tucker, 41 (from James Lamar, *Memoirs of Isaac Errett* [Cincinnati: Standard, 1893], 301); James DeForest Murch, *Christians Only: A History of the Reformation Movement* (Cincinnati: Standard, 1962), 165; Harrell. *Social History,* vol. 2, 17–19.

[46]Letter from Errett to Garrison cited in Tucker, 215, 134–40.

[47]Alexander Campbell, "American Slavery," *The Millennial Harbinger* (1845): 355; Alexander Campbell, "Our Position to American Slavery," *The Millennial Harbinger* (1845): 95; Harrell, *Quest,* 93–137l Garrett, 334–37 (provides an excellent discussion on slavery).

[48]Herman Norton, *Tennessee Christians* (Nashville: Reed, 1971), 105–8, 93; D. Duane Cummins, *Colleges,* 51–54; Garrett, 338.

[49]*The Millennial Harbinger* (1861): 175; Moses Lard, "Can We Divide?" *Lard's Quarterly* (1866): 330–32; W.K. Pendleton, "Strife and Division among the Campbellites," *The Millennial Harbinger* (1868): 152; David Lipscomb, "Christian Union," *The Gospel Advocate* (1866): 200; Garrett, 349–50.

[50]David Harrell, "The Sectinal Origins of the Churches of Christ," in *The Stone-Campbell Movement,* ed. Michael Casey and Douglas Foster (Knoxville: Univ. of Tennessee, 2002), 69–84; Harrell, *Quest,* 172–74.

[51]Garrett, 351.

[52]*Lard's Quarterly* (March 1864): 332–33; Garrison and DeGroot, 345; Richard Hughes, *Reviving the Ancient Faith* (Grand Rapids: Eerdmans, 1996), 48; Garrett, 326–29.

[53]McAllister and Tucker, 244–48.

[54]*The Gospel Advocate* (1871): 30, cited in McAllister and Tucker, 249; *American Christian Review* (June 18, 1867): 194, cited in Earl West; *The Search for the Ancient Order,* vol. 2, 60 and in McAllister and Tucker, 249.

[55]*The Millennial Harbinger* (1866): 495–505; McAllister and Tucker, 248–51; Garrison, *Frontier,* 228.

[56]D. Duane Cummins, *A Handbook for Today's Disciples* (St. Louis: Chalice Press, 2003), 8–9.

[57]Ronald Osborn, "Dogmatically Absolute, Historically Relative" in *The Reformation of Tradition* (St. Louis: Bethany Press, 1963), 279; Garrett, 329, 403.

[58]Stephen England, *We Disciples* (St. Louis: CBP, 1946), 61–76, 65.

[59]Hughes, *Reviving Ancient Faith,* 75.

[60]Garrison and DeGroot, 226–27; McAllister and Tucker, 156–58; Garrett, 384–86; *The Millennial Harbinger* (1837): 411–14, 506, 564–65.

[61]Harrell, *Quest,* 33; Hughes, *Reviving,* 70–75; Goodnight and Stevenson, 123, 171–79, 193.

[62]William Wallace, *Daniel Sommer* (n.p., 1969), 92, 254, 305; Garrett, 388–95.

[63]Arthur V. Murrrell, "The Effects of Exclusivism in the Separation of the Churches of Christ from the Christian Church," (unpublished doctoral dissertation, Vanderbilt University, 1972), 222; Garrett, 400; McAllister and Tucker, 251–52.

Chapter V: Cooperation through Mission, Christian Unity, and Cultural Expressions

[1]William R. Warren, *The Life and Labors of Archibald McLean* (St. Louis: Bethany Press, 1923), 17, 182; Archibald McLean, *The Foreign Christian Missionary Society* (New York: Revell & Co., 1919), 30; Archibald McLean, *A Circuit of the Globe* (St. Louis: Christian Publishing Co., 1897); Stephen J. Corey, "International Foreign Missionary Conference, Geneva, Switzerland," *World Call* (October, 1920): 28–30; W.E. Garrison and Alfred DeGroot, *The Disciples of Christ: A History* (St. Louis: Christian Board of Publication, 1948), 565.

[2]McLean, 30, 31; Joseph M. Smith, "A Strategy of World Mission: The Theory and Practice of Mission as seen in the Present World Enterprise of the Disciples of Christ" (Th.D dissertation, Union Theological Seminary, 1961); *The Millennial Harbinger* (1854): 547; *The Millennial Harbinger* (1852): 644; *The Millennial Harbinger* (1856):236, 298, 480, 720; William Nottingham, "Common Global Ministries Board History" DCHS' Kirkpatrick Lecture, 1998.

[3]Archibald McLean, "The Period of Foreign Missions," in *The Reformation of the Nineteenth Century,* ed. James H. Garrison (St. Louis: Christian Publishing co.,1901), 380–84.

See also Lester McAllister and William E. Tucker, *Journey in Faith* (St. Louis: CBP Press, 1975), 256–59; Leroy Garrett, *The Stone-Campbell Movement* (Joplin, Mo.: College Press, 1994), 364–71.

⁴Ida Harrison, *Forty Years of Service: A History of the Christian Woman's Board of Missions 1874- 1914* (n.p., 1920), 110; Clayton C. Smith, *The Life and Work of Jacob Kenoly* (Cincinnati: Methodist Book Concern, 1912), 2, 43; Lorraine Lollis, *The Shape of Adam's Rib* (St. Louis: Bethany Press, 1970); Fran Craddock, Nancy Heimer, Martha Faw, *In the Fullness of Time:A History Of the Women in the Christian Church (Disciples of Christ)* (St. Louis: Chalice Press, 1999), ix, 259.

⁵Eva Dye, *Bolenge: A Story of Gospel Triumphs on the Congo* (Cincinnati: Foreign Christian Missionary Society, 1910), 10, 20–21; Polly Dye and Margaret Heppe, *In His Glad Service: The Story of Royal J. and Eva Dye* (Eugene, Oreg.: Northwest Christian College, 1975), et passim; Flora Shelton, *Shelton of Tibet* (New York: Geo. Doran Co., 1923), 241–42; Douglas Wissing, *Pioneer in Tibet: The Life and Perils of Dr. Albert Shelton* (New York: Macmillan, 2004); McLean, *FCMS*, 42–50.

⁶Grant K. Lewis, *American Christian Missionary Society and the Disciples of Christ* (St. Louis: Christian Board of Publication, 1937); Harold Watkins, *Continuity, Conservation and Cutting Edge* (Indianapolis: BCE, 2005), 3–11.

⁷Hiram Lester and Marge Lester, *The Saga of NBA* (St. Louis: NBA, 1987), 21, 27–29.

⁸Interview with Jim Hamlett by D. Duane Cummins, July 17, 2007.

⁹McLean, *FCMS*, 40–41; Mark Toulouse, *Joined in Discipleship* (St. Louis: Chalice Press, 1997), 189–214; Mark Toulouse, "The United Christian Missionary Society," in Douglas A. Foster, Paul M. Blowers, Anthony L. Dunnavant, and D. Newell Williams, *The Encyclopedia of the Stone-Campbell Movement* (Grand Rapids: Wm. B. Eerdmans, 2005), 750–53; Toulouse, *Joined in Discipleship*, 193–205; McAllister and Tucker, 344–51; William R. Warren, ed., *Survey of Service* (St. Louis: Christian Board of Publication, 1928), 13–15.

¹⁰Mark Chaves, "The Changing Career Tracks of Elite Disciples Professionals" in *A Case Study of Mainstream Protestantism,* ed. Newell Williams (Grand Rapids: Eerdmans, 1991), 343–44.

¹¹Toulouse, *Joined in Discipleship,* 200-8.

¹²D. Duane Cummins, *Dale Fiers: Twentieth Century Disciple* (Fort Worth, Tex.: TCU press, 2003), 89–131, 107; A. Dale Fiers, "United Society Revises Plan of Operation," *World Call* (1956); A. Dale Fiers, *This is Missions* (St. Louis: Bethany Press, 1953), 165–90.

¹³McAllister and Tucker, 388–97, 400.

¹⁴Ibid., 398; Garrison and DeGroot, 509; Foster et al., *Encyclopedia,* 749; Spencer Austin, "Unified Devotion: A Fifty Year Struggle," *Discipliana* 45, no. 1 (1985): 3–6.

¹⁵Garrison and DeGroot, 452–57; McAllister and Tucker, 303–7; Foster et al., *Encyclopedia,* 151–62.

¹⁶*The Millennial Harbinger* (1843): 376.

¹⁷Reuben Butchart, *The Disciples of Christ in Canada Since 1830* (Toronto: Canadian Headquarters Publications, 1949), 175–77.

¹⁸Peter Ainslie III, *The Message of the Disciples for the Union of the Church* (New York, 1913), 18.

¹⁹Kenneth Teegarden, *We Call Ourselves Disciples* (St. Louis: Bethany Press, 1975), 36.

²⁰Paul Crow Jr., *Christian Unity: Matrix for Mission* (New York: Friendship Press, 1982), 12–18; Sidney Mead, *The Lively Experiment* (New York: Harper and Row, 1963), 103–33; H. Richard Niebuhr, *The Social Sources of Denominationalism* (New York: Henry Holt, 1929), 6; W.E. Garrison, *The Quest and Character of a United Church* (New York: Abingdon Press, 1957), 167–93; Charles C. Morrison, *The Unfinished Reformation* (New York: Harper, 1953), 28–47.

²¹Garrison and DeGroot, 550–57; McAllister and Tucker, 422–25; Teegarden, 38–40; W.E. Garrison, *Christian Unity and Disciples of Christ* (St. Louis: Bethany Press, 1955), 107–38.

²²Finis S. Idleman, *Peter Ainslie, Ambassador of Good Will* (New York: Willett, Clark & Co., 1941), 8–22; Paul Crow Jr., "Peter Ainslie (1867-1934)," in Foster et al., *Encyclopedia,* 21–23.

²³McAllister and Tucker, 422–25; Garrison and DeGroot, 550–57; Garrison, *Christian Unity,* 107–38; D. Duane Cummins, *Kenneth L. Teegarden: The Man, the Church, the Times* (Fort Worth, Tex.; TCU Press, 2007), 104.

[24]Thomas Best, *The Vision of Christian Unity: Essays in Honor of Paul A. Crow Jr.* (Indianapolis: Oikoumene Publications, 1997), et passim.

[25]William Tabbernee, "Sailing the Ecumenical Boat in the Twenty-First Century" *Call to Unity* (July 2005): 1–12; Michael Kinnamon, *The Vision of the Ecumenical Movement and How It Has Been Impoverished by Its Friends* (St. Louis: Chalice Press, 2002), 51.

[26]Rosa Page Welch, Crossing That Deep River," in *The Untold Story: A Short History of Black Disciples* (St. Louis: CBP Press, 1976), 52.

[27]*The Millennial Harbinger* 1, no. 1 (January 4, 1830): 44–46.

[28]Stephen J. England, *Oklahoma Christians* (St. Louis: Bethany Press, . 1975), 34–47; J. Edward Moseley, *Disciples of Christ in Georgia* (St. Louis: Bethany Press, 1954),. 123–31; *The Gospel Advocate* (March 1856): 110–12; *Christian Standard* (May 25, 1878): 169, (Nov. 2, 1878): 353, (May 23, 1874): 162f.

[29]*The Millennial Harbinger (*1860): 505–7; Orval Peterson, *Washington-Northern Idaho Disciples* (St. Louis: Bethany Press, 1945), 115–19.

[30]Herbert Bolton, *The Spanish Borderlands* (New Haven, Conn.: Yale Univ. Press, 1921); Herbert Bolton, *Rim of Christendom* (New York: Macmillan, 1936), 3–14; David Weber, *The Spanish Frontier in North America* (New Haven, Conn.: Yale Univ. Press, 239, 310; W. Eugene Hollon, *The Southwest Old and New* (New York: Knopf, 1961), 443; John Francis Bannon, *The Spanish Borderlands Frontier 1513-1821* (New York: Holt Rinehart, 1970), 55–71, 149–54; Harry W. Crosby, *Antigua California* (Albuquerque: Univ. of New Mexico Press, 1994), 6–8.

[31]Bolton. *Rim of Christendom,* 584–92.

[32]Crosby, 372–73.

[33]Daisy L. Machado, *Of Borders and Margins* (New York: Oxford Univ. Press, 2003), 88–93.

[34]Pablo Jiménez, "Hispanics in the Movement," in Foster et al., *Encyclopedia,* 395–99; Machado, 58–61, 88–93; David Weber, *Myth and the History of the Hispanic Southwest* (Albuquerque: Univ. of New Mexico Press, 1988), 135 (cited in Machado, 80).

[35]Colby Hall, *Texas Disciples* (Fort Worth, Tex.: TCU Press, 1953), 221; William Castleman, *On This Foundation: A Historical Literary Biography of the Early Life of Samuel Guy Inman 1877-1904* (St. Louis: Bethany Press, 1966), 15–25.

[36]Jiménez, 395–99, and Machado, 58–61, 88–93.

[37]Byron Spice, *Discípulos Americanos: Sixty-five Years of Christian Churches' Ministry to Spanish-Speaking Persons* (Indianapolis: UCMS), 84, 30, 74–76, 23–26, 34.

[38]Marcelo Suarez-Orozco and Mariela Paez, *Latinos* (Berkeley: Univ. of California Press and the Rockefeller Center for Latin American Studies, Harvard University, 2002), 3, 13–15, 293.

[39]D. Duane Cummins, *A Handbook for Today's Disciples,* 3d ed. (St. Louis: Chalice Press, 2003), 13–14.

[40]Archibald McLean, *Circuit of the Globe,* 15.

[41]Geunhee Yu, "Asian American Disciples," in Foster et al., *Encyclopedia,* 40–41; Janet Casey-Allen, "Disciples of Asian Origin Vie for Their Place," *The Disciple* (May 1994): 8–10.

[42]Clifford Cole, *The Christian Churches of Southern California* (St. Louis: Christian Board of Publication, 1959), 143–45.

[43]Yu, 40–41; Casey-Allen, 8–10; Cole, 140–42; Cummins, *Handbook,* 14; interview with Harold R. Johnson, September 12, 2007.

[44]Robert Jordan, *Two Races in One Fellowship* (Detroit: United Christian Church, 1944), 24; Hap Lyda, *A History of Black Christian Churches (Disciples of Christ) in the United States through 1899* (Ann Arbor: University microfilms), 10–57, 162–65; Hap Lyda, "Black Disciples in the Nineteenth Century," in *The Untold Story,* 9–19; William K. Fox Jr., *Effective Discipleship for Blacks in the Christian Church (Disciples of Christ)*(Indianapolis: Central Publishing, 1982), 10–14.

[45]*The Millennial Harbinger* (1845): 3–8, 49–53, 67–71, 108–12, 145–49, 193–96, 232–40, 257–64, 355–58, 418–19; Robert Tibbs Maxey, *Alexander Campbell and the Peculiar Institution* (El Paso, Tex.:Spanish American Evangelism, 1986), xiii; Selina Campbell, *Home Life and Reminiscences of Alexander Campbell,* (St. Louis: Burns Publisher, 1882), 454; Garrison and DeGroot, 330–33; McAllister and Tucker, 190–95; Roy Basler, *The Collected Works of Abraham Lincoln* (New Brunswick, N.J.: Rutgers Univ. Press, 1953), 74–75, 388–89; Ronald White Jr., *A. Lincoln* (New York: Random House, 2009), 75–76, 504–5.

⁴⁶McAllister and Tucker, 190–95; William K. Fox Jr., "African Americans in the Movement," in Foster et al., *Encyclopedia,* 11–15; Garrison, 474–80.

⁴⁷Fox, 11–15; Garrison, 474; McAllister and Tucker, 294, 300–304; Jordan, 29; Clayton Smith, 2, 8, 10.

⁴⁸James L. Blair, "Preston Taylor: A Doer of the Word," in *The Untold Story,* 30–34; Booker T. Washington, *The Negro in Business* (Chicago: Afro-American Press, (1969), 99–103 (originally published in 1907 by Hertel and Jenkins).

⁴⁹Brenda Cardwell and William K. Fox Jr., *Journey Toward Wholeness: A History of Black Disciples of Christ in the Mission of the Christian Church,* vol. 1, *From Convention to Convocation* (Indianapolis: National Convocation, 1990), 14–22.

⁵⁰Fox, "African Americans in the Movement," 11–15; Cardwell and Fox, 175–83.

⁵¹Leon Litwack, *How Free Is Free?: The Long Death of Jim Crow* (Cambridge, Mass.: Harvard Univ. Press, 2009), 4–6, 90–94.

⁵²*2007 Year Book of the Christian Church (Disciples of Christ).*

⁵³Ann E. Dickerson, "Another View of What is Needed," in *The Untold Story,* 59–60.

Chapter VI: Division and Restructure

¹Henry Webb, "Christian Churches-Churches of Christ" in Douglas A. Foster, Paul M. Blowers, Anthony L. Dunnavant, and D. Newell Williams, *The Encyclopedia of the Stone-Campbell Movement* (Grand Rapids: Wm. B. Eerdmans, 2005), 180–85; Leroy Garrett, *The Stone-Campbell Movement* (Joplin, Mo.: College Press, 1994), 407–9; James DeForest Murch, *Christians Only* (Cincinnati: Standard, 1962), 277.

²M. Eugene Boring, *Disciples and the Bible* (St. Louis: Chalice Press, 1997), 221–53, 224; M. Eugene Boring, "John W. McGarvey" in Foster et al., *Encyclopedia,* 506–7; W. C.Morro, "Brother McGarvey" in *The Life of President J. W. McGarvey of the College of the Bible. Lexington* (St. Louis: Bethany Press, 1940); Dwight and DeLoris Stevenson, "The Autobiography of J. W. McGarvey," *College of the Bible Quarterly,* no. 37 (1960).

³Boring, *Disciples and the Bible,* 221–53; Larry Bouchard, "Herbert Lockwood Willett," in Foster et al., *Encyclopedia,* 774.

⁴Boring, *Disciples and the Bible,* 221–253, 231.

⁵Ibid.; Stephen J. Corey, "International Foreign Missionary Conference, Geneva, Switzerland," *World Call* (October, 1920): 46–56.

⁶Corey, 46–56; George G. Beazley, ed., *The Christian Church (Disciples of Christ) An Interpretative Examination in the Cultural Context* (St. Louis: Bethany Press, 1973), 29; Dwight E. Stevenson, *Lexington Theological Seminary* (St. Louis: Bethany Press, 1964), 165–207; Lester McAllister and William E. Tucker, *Journey in Faith* (St. Louis: CBP Press, 1975), 364–71.

⁷Ronald E. Osborn, "Theology among the Disciples" in *The Christian Church (Disciples of Christ): An Interpretative Examination in the Cultural Context,* ed. George B. Beazley Jr. (St. Louis: Bethany Press, 1973), 104; D. Duane Cummins, *Handbook of the Christian Church (Disciples of Christ),* 3d ed. (St. Louis: Chalice Press, 2003), 9.

⁸Corey, 184; Alfred T. DeGroot, *The Grounds of Division Among the Disciples Of Christ* (Chicago: DeGroot, 1940), 220; W.E. Garrison and Alfred DeGroot, *The Disciples of Christ: A History* (St. Louis: Christian Board of Publication, 1948), 553.

⁹Edwin V. Hayden, *50 years of Digression and Disturbances* (Joplin, Mo.: Hayden, 1955), 6; A. T. DeGroot, *New Possibilities for Disciples and Independents* (St. Louis: Bethany Press, 1963), 33; Garrett, 413–16.

¹⁰Corey, 60–70; William R. Warren, *The Life and Labors of Archibald McLean* (St. Louis: Bethany Press, 1923), 273; *Christian Standard* (June 7 thru July 12, 1919); *Christian Standard* (July 5): 972; *Christian Standard* (October 4):5.

¹¹Quoted in Corey, 82–83

¹²Ibid., 85–91.

¹³Mark Toulouse, "Practical Concern and Theological Neglect: The UCMS and the Open Membership Controversy" in *A Case Study in Mainstream Protestantism,* ed. D. Newell Williams (Grand Rapids: Eerdmans, 1991), 194–235; Warren, *Survey,* et passim; Mark Toulouse, *Joined in Discipleship* (St. Louis: Chalice Press, 1997), 200-208.

¹⁴Corey, 102–36.

¹⁵*Report of the Commission on Restudy of the Disciples of Christ,* 1948, 11–15.

[16]*Arkansas Gazette* (April 1, 1965), 10a; Granville Walker, Installation Charge to Kenneth Teegarden in Installation Program for Kenneth Teegarden, June 21, 1965, DCHS, Restructure, Box 1; Cummins, *Teegarden.* Much of this section on "The Process," and the section on "Reflections" benefits from my extensive research for and writing of the biography of Kenneth Teegarden.

[17]Kenneth Teegarden, Installation Address, June 21, 1965, 1-2, DCHS, Restructure, Box 1.

[18]D. Duane Cummins, *Dale Fiers: Twentieth Century Disciple* (Fort Worth, Tex.: TCU press, 2003), 148–49.

[19]Ibid., xvii-xviii.

[20]McAllister and Tucker, 415–21.

[21]Willard Wickizer, "Ideas for Brotherhood Restructure" (unpublished, July 1958), 1–9, DCHS, Restructure, Box 1; Robert L. Friedly and D. Duane Cummins, *Search for Identity* (St. Louis: CBP Press, 1987), 29–30.

[22]Sydney Ahlstrom, *A Religious History of the American People* (New Haven, Conn.: Yale Univ. Press, 1972), 1015; Cummins, *Dale Fiers,* 139 (this is an updated rewrite, with new research of four paragraphs originally appearing in the biography of Fiers.); T. J. Ligget, DCHS interview, November 29, 1990, 1.

[23]Granville Walker, DCHS interview, March 10, 1990, 1; Ronald Osborn, DCHS interview, May 20, 1990, 1; Kenneth Teegarden, DCHS Interview, March 9, 1990, 1; Howard Dentler, DCHS interview, November 19, 1993, 1; James Moak, DCHS interview, December 12, 1989, 1.

[24]Teegarden and Osborn interviews; Robert Thomas, DCHS interview, May 26, 1990, 1; Paul Stauffer, DCHS interview, May 8, 1992, 1; Charles Bayer, DCHS interview, April 3, 1990, 1; Howard Short, DCHS interview, July 23, 1990.

[25]Thomas and Bayer interviews, DCHS.

[26]Spencer Austin, DCHS interview, November 14, 1989, 1; Jean Woolfolk, DCHS interview, March 14, 1990, 1.

[27]Commission on Brotherhood Restructure Minutes, July 6–7, 1962 meeting in Fort Worth, Texas. Attachment: "An Apologetic for Restructure," by A. Dale Fiers, 1–4, DCHS, Restructure, Box 1.

[28]Anthony L. Dunnavant, *Restructure* (New York: Peter Lang, Publishing, 1993), 191–95, 186–87.

[29]Commission on Brotherhood Restructure Budget Reports, DCHS, Restructure, Box 1, File 2.

[30]Dunnavant, 213; "The Nature of the Structure Our Brotherhood Seeks," *Mid-Stream* (Fall 1964): 24–27.

[31]Kenneth Teegarden, "Report of the Administrative Secretary," November 3, 1965, 1–5 DCHS, Restructure, Box 1, Teegarden File; Kenneth Teegarden, Report of the Administrative Secretary, March 24, 1966, 1-4, DCHS, Restructure, Box 1, Teegarden File; *The Christian* (January 30, 1966), DCHS, Restructure, Box 1; The Direction in Brotherhood Restructure Report, 1966, DCHS, Restructure, Box 1; Kenneth Teegarden, Administrative Secretary Reports, 1965–1966, DCHS, Restructure, Box 1, Teegarden File.

[32]Commission on Brotherhood Restructure Minutes, June 21–25, 1965, 2–7, DCHS, Restructure, Box 1.

[33]Kenneth Teegarden, Report of the Administrative Secretary, March 24, 1966, 1–4, DCHS, Restructure, Box 1, Teegarden File; Central Committee Minutes, March 24–25, 1966, 3, DCHS, Restructure, Box 1; *A Possible Constitution,* working paper with Kenneth Teegarden's notes, March 24, 1966, 1–22, DCHS, Restructure, Box 1, Teegarden File.

[34]Commission on Brotherhood Restructure Minutes, July 58, 1966, meeting in Cincinnati, Ohio, 1–3. DCHS, Restructure, Box 1; Central Committee Minutes, January 11–12, 1967, 5, DCHS, Restructure, Box 1; George Earle Owen, DCHS interview, January 21, 1992, 2.

[35]Kenneth Teegarden, Report of the Administrative Secretary, July 5–8, 3, DCHS, Restructure, Box 1, Teegarden File; Commission on Brotherhood Restructure Minutes, September 29, 1966, meeting in Dallas, Texas, 1, DCHS, Restructure, Box 1.

[36]Ibid., 2–4. Central Committee Minutes, November 2–3, 1966, 7, DCHS, Restructure, Box 1; Lillian Moir, "Portrait of a Nominee," *World Call* (October, 1973): 13.

[37]Kenneth Teegarden, Report of the Administrative Secretary, January 11, 1967, 1–2, DCHS, Restructure, Box 1, Teegarden File.

[38]Commission on Brotherhood Restructure Minutes, June 21–25, 1965. 2–3, DCHS, Restructure, Box 1; Charles Bayer, DCHS interview, April 3, 1990, 3; Cummins, *Dale Fiers,* 152 (updated writing with new research of three paragraphs originally appearing in biography of Dale Fiers); Kenneth Teegarden, DCHS interview, March 9, 1990, 4–5; Dunnavant, 211.

[39]Cummins, *Dale Fiers,* 152; Restructure Report, September 1965 and September 1966, DCHS, Restructure, Box 2, Comm. on Pres. of Brotherhood File; "Freedom or Restructure?" pamphlet, DCHS, Restructure, Box 2; DCHS, Restructure, Box 2, CBP file; Granville Walker to Lesley L. Walker, November 9, 1967, 3, DCHS, Restructure, Box 3, black binder of correspondence.

[40]Cummins, *Dale Fiers,* 153; Robert Burns, DCHS interview, November 18, 1989, 1–6; Kenneth Teegarden, Report of the Administrative Secretary, March 8, 1967, 3, DCHS, Restructure, Box 1, Teegarden File.

[41]Atlanta Declaration Group Meeting Minutes by Robert Burns, Aug. 3, 1967, 7–10, DCHS, Restructure, Box 2, Atlanta Declaration File; Kenneth Teegarden to Commission on Brotherhood Restructure, August 9, 1967, 1, DCHS, Restructure, Box 1, Teegarden File; Robert Burns to Kenneth Teegarden and Commission on Brotherhood Restructure, August 23, 1967, DCHS, Restructure, Box 2, Atlanta Declaration File; Bob Friedly to D. Duane Cummins, November 2005, 4; Friedly and Cummins, 63.

[42]Kenneth Teegarden to W. J. Sneed, January 16, 1968, 1, Restructure, DCHS, Box 3, black binder of correspondence; Howard Dentler, Report to the Central Committee, February 1968, 1; Dunnavant, 212.

[43]Commission on Brotherhood Restructure Minutes, November 1–2, 1967, Howard Dentler Report, 1, DCHS, Restructure, Box 1; Friedly and Cummins, 9; Kenneth Teegarden to Commission on Brotherhood Restructure, April 10, 1968, 1; Kenneth Teegarden, Report of Administrative Secretary, February 1968, 1–2, DCHS, Restructure, Box 1, Teegarden File; Dale Fiers to Commission on Brotherhood Restructure, October 29, 1967.

[44]"Provisional Design," 1968, 6, 7–17: *The Design,* 2005, 1; Dunnavant, 178–205.

[45]"Provisional Design," 16.

[46]"Provisional Design," 11; Friedly and Cummins, 13.

[47]"Provisional Design," 14, *The Design,* 2005, 6.

[48]Dunnavant, 183–252.

[49]A. Dale Fiers, "The State of the Church–1968," DCHS, Fiers papers, 10; Friedly and Cummins, 9–10.

[50]A. Dale Fiers to T.J. Liggett, August 17, 1999. Subject of letter was "Reflections on Restructure," DCHS, Fiers papers.

[51]Kenneth Teegarden, DCHS interview, March 9, 1990, 1; Central Committee Minutes, January 1962, 3, DCHS, Box 1; Commission on Brotherhood Restructure Minutes, July 6–7, 1962, Attachment. "An Apologetic for Restructure" by Dale Fiers; Ronald Osborn, "The Calling of the Church," June 29, 1964, DCHS, Restructure, Box 2; Ronald Osborn, "The Nature of the Church," June 30, 1964, DCHS, Restructure, Box 2; Ronald Osborn, "The Building of the Church," July 1, 1964, DCHS, Restructure, Box 2; Ronald Osborn, *Toward the Christian Church* (St. Louis: CBP, 1964), 11, 26, 54. DCHS, Restructure, Box 2.

[52]Kenneth Teegarden, DCHS interview, March 9, 1990, 3.

[53]Ibid., 9; Teegarden interview with David Roozen, n.d., 311; Howard Dentler interview with D. Duane Cummins, February 26, 2005; Ronald Osborn, *The Faith We Affirm* (St. Louis: Bethany Press, 1979), 57–66.

[54]Dentler interview; Kenneth Teegarden to Howard C. Cole, March 18, 1975,1, DCHS, GMP files, Box 1, Correspondence C.

[55]Dentler interview; Teegarden interview with Roozen, 319.

Chapter VII: A Community in Covenant

[1]Henry Shaw, *Buckeye Disciples* (St. Louis: CBP, 1952), 396; Lester McAllister and William E. Tucker, *Journey in Faith* (St. Louis: CBP Press, 1975), 413–14.

[2]McAllister and Tucker, 412; "International Convention of Christian Churches (Disciples of Christ)," unpublished description and history, DCHS, n.d., 1; Gaines Cook, "It's Convention Time," *Unified Promotion: Minister's Bulletin* 8, no. 1 (September 1956), 1.

[3]D. Duane Cummins, *Kenneth L. Teegarden: The Man, The Church, The Time* (Fort Worth, Tex.: TCU press, 2007), 96–98; McAllister and Tucker, 411–22; Gaines Cook,

"Our Brotherhood," International Convention Address in Miami Beach, October 15, 1963, DCHS, Cook papers, 4–5.

[4]A. Dale Fiers, Installation Address as Executive Secretary at International Convention in Detroit on October 2, 1964.

[5]D. Duane Cummins, *Dale Fiers: Twentiety Century Disciple* (Fort Worth, Tex.: TCU Press, 2003), 107 (this section is drawn from my research for and writing of the Fiers biography).

[6]Ibid., 178–79.

[7]Cummins interview with T.J. Liggett, September 10, 2000 (cited in Cummins, *Dale Fiers*, 133–35); Cummins interview with Kenneth Teegarden, May 12, 2000 (cited in Cummins, *Dale Fiers*, 133–35); Joseph Smith interview by DCHS, October 17, 1990, 1; Cummins interview with A. Dale Fiers, November 25, 2002 (cited in Cummins, *Dale Fiers*, 133–135); Herald Monroe, "Now he is our Man," *World Call* (June 28, 1964), 5.

[8]Cummins interview with Kenneth Teegarden, May 12, 2000.

[9]Robert L. Friedly and D. Duane Cummins, *Search for Identity* (St. Louis: CBP Press, 1987), 103–7; Mark Toulouse, *Joined in Discipleship* (St. Louis: Chalice Press, 1997), 163–85; "Policies and Criteria for the Order of Ministry in the Christian Church (Disciples of Christ)," (Indianapolis, DHM, 1971); D. Newell Williams, *Ministry Among Disciples: Past, Present and Future* (St. Louis: CBP, 1985), 11–15; Anthony Dunnavant, "Abstract," *Lexington Theological Quarterly* 37 (Spring-Summer 2002): 6.

[10]*Indianapolis Star,* June 3, 1970, 8.

[11]*Indianapolis News,* October 16, 1971, 24.

[12]Kenneth L. Teegarden, "State of the Church Address" to the Kansas City General Assembly, October 22, 1977.

[13]Cummins, *Teegarden* (this section is drawn from the research for and writing of the Teegarden biography).

[14]Roozen interview with Kenneth Teegarden, 311.

[15]Committee on Structure and Function Minutes, September 5–6, 1972, 1, DCHS, Teegarden GMP files, Box 5, Structure File: "The Provisional Design," June 1972, Paragraph 43, 11 (Membership of the Committee on Structure and Function included: Spencer Austin, William Howland, James Moak, Robert Thomas, Albert Pennybacker, Kenneth Teegarden, Robert Stewart, Orville Wake, W. A. Welsh, Art Wenger, Charles Dietze, Dale Fiers T. J. Liggett, Sam Hylton, Jay Calhoun, John Wolfersburger and Gertrude Dimke.)

[16]"Provisional Design," June 1972, Paragraph 44, 11; Committee on Structure and Function, Progress Report, October 1973, 1–14. DCHS, GMP, Box 5, Structure File; D. Duane Cummins, "The First Decade of D.H.E.," *Disciples Theological Digest* 9, no. 1 (1994): 35–51; *The Design,* July 2005, Paragraph 68, 14.

[17]Spencer Austin and Albert Pennybacker, Report of the Sub-Committee on the Function of General Units, January 8, 1973, 7, DCHS, GMP, Box 5, Structure File.

[18]Committee on Structure & Function Minutes, May 9–11, 1972, 1–7, DCHS, Teegarden GMP files, Box 5, Structure File; Committee on Structure & Function Minutes, Sept. 5–6, 1972, 1–5, DCHS, Teegarden GMP files, Box 2, Structure File; Committee on Structure & Function, Progress Report, October 1973, 1–14, DCHS, GMP, Box 5, Structure File; Committee on Structure & Function, Guiding Principles for use in Further Development of the General Manifestation, May 30, 2–5, DCHS, GMP, Box 5, Structure File. Committee on Structure & Function Minutes, February 5–7, 1976, 2, DCHS, Teegarden GMP files, Box 5, Structure File.

[19]Committee on Structure & Function, Progress Report, October 1973, 1–14, DCHS, DCHS, GMP, Box 5, Structure File.

[20]The "Provisional Design," June 1972, Paragraph 75, 14.

[21]Jean Woolfolk to Regional Ministers, October 17, 1972, 2, DCHS, Teegarden GMP files, Box 5, Structure File.

[22]John D. Wolfersberger, Toward Regionalization of the Christian Church, Committee on S & F, May 1, 1973, 1–15, DCHS, Teegarden GMP files, Box 5, Structure File.

[23]Kenneth Teegarden, A review of the Area Concept with Fewer and Comparable Regions, Committee on S & F, October 2, 1973, DCHS, Teegarden GMP files, Box 5, Structure File.

[24]Robert Stewart, An Evaluation of Fewer and Comparable Regions, October 1976, DCHS, Teegarden GMP files, Box 5, Structure File; *The Design,* July 2005, Paragraph 29, 6.

[25]Higher Education Evaluation Task Force Report, June 12–15, 1976, 1–22 of 150 pages. In possession of the author. (Membership: C.C. Nolen, Duane Cummins, Ann Dickerson, Jim Spainhower, Bill Howland, Kenneth Teegarden, Robbie Chisholm).

[26]Business Dockets of the General Board: 1973, 1975, 1977, 1979, 1983 and 1985, DCHS, General Board Dockets; Howard Dentler to William Howland, December 11, 1975, 1–4, DCHS, Teegarden GMP files, Box 5, Structure File; Kenneth Teegarden, "State of the Church," October 22, 1977, Kansas City General Assembly, Wanda Teegarden Collection.

[27]*The Cleveland Press,* January 31, 1978, 7; *The New York Times,* January 23, 1978, 12.

[28]Business Docket of the General Board, 1977, Resolution 7760, 211; Resolution 7747, 188; Resolution 7750, 191.

[29]Kenneth Teegarden to James A. Noe, January 30, 1978, 1, DCHS, Teegarden GMP files, Box 3, Homosexuality File.

[30]Kenneth Teegarden to Eli McRorey, November 21, 1977, 1–2; Kenneth Teegarden to Maxine Miller, June 7, 1979, 1, DCHS, Teegarden GMP files, Box 4, File M; *1978 Year Book and Directory,* Pastoral Letter, 288; Teegarden, 1977 State of the Church.

[31]Packet of Regional Ministers' letters to Kenneth Teegarden, April 1978 responding to seven questions. Kenneth summarized the results in a letter to Jack Naff, March 19, 1979, DCHS, Teegarden GMP files, Box 3, Task Force on Ministry.

[32]Religious News Service, July 10, 1978, and Christian Church News, July 18, 1978, DCHS, GMP files, Box 3, Task Force on Ministry; Christian Church News, March 1, 1978, Study Packet.

[33]*1980 Year Book and Directory,* 296–98. (Membership of the Task Force on Ministry included: Lester Palmer-Chair, Fred Craddock, Duane Cummins, David Darnell, Claudia Grant, William Fox, Gilford Olmsted, Harry Smith, Keith Watkins, and Tom Wood; It was staffed by Kenneth Teegarden and Bill Howland).

[34]Kenneth Teegarden, "Statement of the General Minister and President," Adm. Com, March 12, 1979, 1–4, DCHS, Jonestown File.

[35]Ibid.

[36]Ray Ruppert, "Church President wary of politics," *The Seattle Times,* October 18, 1980, A-10 [Interview with Kenneth Teegarden]; George Beazley, "Conversations toward Union," General Board Business Docket, 1973, 133–36, DCHS; Paul Crow, "Report of Joint Working Group," General Board Business Docket, 1979, 207–9, DCHS; Report of Steering Committee, General Board Business Docket, 1983, 186–88, DCHS.

[37]Kenneth Teegarden to J. S. McKenney, March 5, 1979; J. S. McKenney to Kenneth Teegarden, February 26, 1979, DCHS, Teegarden GMP files, Box 4, File M.

[38]Kenneth Teegarden, "Verdict Before Trial," *The Disciple* (August 1976): 15.

[39]Business Docket of the General Board, 1977, 165–67, 204–07; *1976 Year Book and Directory,* 204, 207, 215, 225, 241, 243.

[40]Business Docket of the General Board, 1979, 226, 227, 215; Business Docket of the General Board, 1983, 192–97, 202–5.

[41]Kenneth Teegarden, "Disciples Witness to Ethics in a Nuclear Age," *The Disciple* (May 1985): 52 (membership of the panel: Gene Brice, Duane Cummins, Newton Fowler, Kenneth Henry, Jane Hopkins, JoAnne Kagiwada, T. J. Liggett-chair, Ronald Osborn, Kenneth L. Teegarden); T.J. Liggett et al., *Seeking God's Peace in a Nuclear Age* (St. Louis: CBP Press, 1985), 6, 85; D. Duane Cummins, *A Handbook for Today's Disciples,* 3d ed. (St. Louis: Chalice Press, 2003), 53; Ronald Osborn to Kenneth Teegarden, June 26, 1985; T.J. Liggett to Kenneth Teegarden, June 25, 1985.

[42]Business Docket of the General Board, 1981, "General Principles and Policies–DOM," 165–76, DCHS. Friedly and Cummins, 153–60.

[43]Kenneth Teegarden, "State of the Church–1985," Des Moines General Assembly, August 3, 1985, 5

Chapter VIII: Into the Twenty-First Century

[1]Richard L. Hamm, *From Mainline to Frontline: An Invitation to Dialogue with the General Minister and President* (Lexington: Lexington Theological Quarterly, 1996), v.

[2]Bruce Schulman, *The Seventies* (New York: Free Press, 2001), 102–17; Robert Bezilla, *Religion in America*: 1992-1993 (Princeton, N.J.: The Gallup Poll, 1993), 40; Sydney Ahlstrom

The Religious History of the American People (New Haven, Conn.: Yale Univ. Press, 1972), 1093; Mark Toulouse, *Joined in Discipleship* (St. Louis: Chalice Press, 1997), 245–69 (Bezilla cited in Toulouse).

³Russell Chandler, *Racing Toward 2001: The Forces Shaping America's Religious Future* (Grand Rapids, Zondervan; Harper SanFrancisco: San Francisco, 1992), 191, 240–44; Toulouse, 245–69 (Chandler cited in Toulouse); Robert Wuthnow and John Evans, *The Quiet Hand of God* (Berkeley: Univ. of Calif. Press, 2002), 159–66; Edwin Gaustad and Leigh Schmidt, *The Religious History of America* (San Francisco: Harper, 2002), 398–404, 420–21 Charles Taylor, *A Secular Age* (Cambridge, Mass.: Harvard Univ. Press, 2007), 504–35; Wade Roof and William McKinney, *American Mainline Religion* (New Brunswick, N.J.: Rutgers Univ. Press, 1967), 11–39.

⁴Ibid.

⁵Ibid.

⁶Ibid. Robert Cueni, "Facing the Disciples Leadership Challenge on the Front Edge of the Twenty First Century," *Lexington Theological Quarterly* (June, 2007): 223–32.

⁷John O. Humbert, "Proposed New Church Priority," *The Disciple* (May 1987).

⁸Cummins interview with John Humbert, July 17, 2007; John O. Humbert, "Notes for an Autobiography" (unpublished, 2007), 1–12; Robert Richardson, *Memoirs of Alexander Campbell,* 2 vols. (Philadelphia: Lippincott, 1868, 1870), 81–82; Lillian Moir, "Bridge to the Future," *The Disciple* (May 1985): 8–9.

⁹Ibid.

¹⁰Ibid.

¹¹John Humbert, Installation Address, August 6, 1985, 3; Leroy Garrett, *The Stone-Campbell Movement* (Joplin, Mo.: College Press, 1994), 511–15.

¹²D. Newell Williams, "Disciples and the Liberal Conservative Divide," *Disciples Theological Digest* 7, no. 2 (1992): 5–22; George Cornell, "Father to Son Line Continues," *The Oregonian,* February 16, 1985, D6.

¹³John Humbert, "From the General Minister and President," *The Disciple* (May 1987): 30–31; John Humbert, "From the General Minister and President," *The Disciple* (March 1988): 30; John Humbert, "From the General Minister and President," *The Disciple* (November 1989): 30; "Resolution 8949–Implementing the Priority," *1990 Year Book and Directory,* 304–7.

¹⁴Ibid.

¹⁵*1990 Year Book and Directory;* Garrett, 517; Cornell, D6.

¹⁶Humbert, "Autobiography," 49–51.

¹⁷Cornell; *Disciples News Service,* November 25, 1987. 1–2; Resolution 8530, *1986 Year Book and Directory,* 260; John Humbert, "From the General Minister and President," *The Disciple,* (June 1987): 30; William Nottingham, "John O. Humbert," Appreciation Dinner Address, General Cabinet, Sept. 4, 1991, 2–3.

¹⁸James B. North, *Union in Truth* (Cincinnati: Standard Publishing, 1994), 349.

¹⁹Richard L. Hamm, *2020 Vision for the Christian Church (Disciples of Christ)* (St. Louis: Chalice Press, 2001), 125.

²⁰Cummins interview with Richard Hamm, Sept. 10, 2007.

²¹Hamm, *2020 Vision,* 114–16.

²²Ibid., 119–25.

²³News Release by Houlihan, Lokey, Howard, and Zukin, St. Louis, April 15, 2005.

²⁴Cummins interview with Richard Hamm, Sept. 10, 2007.

²⁵Sharon Watkins, "State of the Church Address," at the Fort Worth General Assembly in 2007.

²⁶Cummins interview with Sharon Watkins, Sept. 15, 2007.

²⁷Ibid.; Verity Jones, "Sharon E. Watkins interprets the future of the church," *DisciplesWorld* 4, no. 9 (November 2005): 8–9; Sheri Emmons, "GMP candidate Sharon E. Watkins," *DisciplesWorld* 4, no. 5 (June 2005): 8–9, 15–16; Verity Jones, "What a difference three years can make," *DisciplesWorld* 7, no. 5 (June 2008): 1; Verity Jones, "Mission Alignment Coordinating Council begins its work," *DisciplesWorld* 7 (July 2008): 41.

²⁸D. Duane Cummins, "Observations" on the January 2007 meeting of the General Board, in possession of the author; Sharon Watkins, "State of the Church Address" Fort Worth General Assembly, July 2007; Business Docket & Program, General Assembly in Fort Worth, Texas, July 21-25, 2007.

Afterword

[1]John Rogers, Letter dated March 27, 1832, in *The Evangelist* (May 7, 1832).

[2]Available at: http://www.mun.ca/rels/restmov/texts/wwarren/ccr/CCRO7R.HTM.

[3]John Dos Passos, *The Ground We Stand On* (New York: Harcourt Brace, 1941), 3; Gordon Wood, *The Purpose of the Past* (New York: Penguin Books, 2008), 14.

BIBLIOGRAPHY

Supportive Sources Consulted for *The Disciples*

History of Religion in the United States

Ahlstrom, Sydney E. *A Religious History of the American People.* New Haven, Conn.: Yale Univ. Press, 1972.

Butler, Jon, and Harry S. Stout, eds. *Religion in American History.* New York: Oxford, 1998.

Forbes, David, and Jeffrey H. Mahan, *Religion and Popular Culture in America.* Berkeley: Univ. of California, 2000.

Gaustad, Edwin S. *A Religious History of America.* New York: Harper and Row, 1966.

Gaustad, Edwin, and Leigh Schmidt. *The Religious History of America.* San Francisco: Harper, 2002.

Hackett, David G., ed. *Religion and American Culture.* New York: Routledge, 1995.

Hart, D. G., and Harry S. Stout, eds. *New Directions in American Religious History.* New York: Oxford, 1997.

Latourette, Kenneth Scott. *A History of Christianity.* New York: Harper & Bro., 1953.

Marty, Martin. *Righteous Empire: The Protestant Experience in America.* New York: Dial Press, 1970.

_____. *Modern American Religion.* Volumes I, II, and III. Chicago: University of Chicago Press, 1986; 1991; 1996.

Noll, Mark A. *A History of Christianity in the United States and Canada.* Grand Rapids: Eerdmans, 1992.

Olmstead, Clifton E. *History of Religion in the United States.* Englewood Cliffs: Prentice-Hall, 1960.

Sweet, William W. *The Story of Religion in America.* New York: Harper and Row, 1950.

Walker, Williston. *A History of the Christian Church.* New York: Scribners and Sons, 1959.

Religious Life in Early America

Boorstin, Daniel. *The Americans: The Colonial Experience.* New York: Vintage, 1958.

Bridenbaugh, Carl. *Mitre and Sceptre.* New York: Oxford, 1962.

Butler, Jon. *Awash in a Sea of Faith.* Cambridge, Mass.: Harvard Univ. Press. 1990.

Gaustad, Edwin. *Faith of the Founders.* Waco, Tex.: Baylor Univ. Press, 2004.

Hatch, Nathan. *The Democratization of American Christianity.* New Haven, Conn.: Yale Univ. Press, 1989.

Heimert, Alan. *Religion and the American Mind: From the Great Awakening to the Revolution.* Cambridge, Mass.: Harvard Univ. Press, 1966.

Holmes, David. *The Faiths of the Founding Fathers.* Oxford: Oxford Univ. Press, 2006.

Lambert, Frank. *The Founding Fathers and the Place of Religion in America.* Princeton, N.J.: Princeton Univ. Press, 2003.

Parrington, Vernon. *Main Currents in American Thought.* Vol. II. New York: Harcourt Brace, 1954.

Taylor, Alan. *American Colonies.* New York: Viking Press, 2001.

Waldman, Steven. *Founding Faith.* New York: Random House, 2008.

Wood, Gordon. *The Radicalism of the American Revolution.* New York: Knopf, 1992.

Religion in Contemporary America

Bezilla, Robert. *Religion in America: 1992–1993.* Princeton, N.J.: Princeton Univ. Press. 1993.

Chaves, Mark. *Congregations in America.* Cambridge, Mass.: Harvard Univ. Press, 2004.

Marty, Martin E. *Modern American Religion.* Vol. I–III. Chicago: Univ. of Chicago Press, 1986; 1991; 1996.

Niebuhr, H. Richard. *The Social Sources of Denominationalism.* New York: Meridian, 1957.

Roof, Wade, and William McKinney. *American Mainline Religion.* New Brunswick, N.J.: Rutgers Univ. Press, 1967.

Wuthnow, Robert. *The Restructuring of American Religion.* Princeton, N.J.: Princeton Univ. Press., 1988.

Wuthnow, Robert, and John Evans. *The Quiet Hand of God.* Berekeley: Univ. of California Press 2002.

The First Great Awakening

Lambert, Frank. *Inventing the Great Awakening.* Princeton, N.J.: Princeton Univ. Press, 1999.

_____. *Pedlar in Divinity: George Whitefield and the Transatlantic Revivals.* Princeton, N.J.: Princeton Univ. Press, 1994.

Marsden, George. *Understanding Fundamentalism and Evangelicalism.* Grand Rapids: Eerdmans, 1991.

Marsden, George. *Jonathan Edwards: A Life.* New Haven, Conn.: Yale Univ. Press, 2003.

Miller, Perry. *Jonathan Edwards.* New York: Meridian, 1959.

Noll, Mark. *The Rise of Evangelicalism: The Age of Edwards, Whitefield and the Wesleys.* Downers Grove, Ill.: InterVarsity Press, 2004.
Wesley, John. *The Heart of Wesley's Journal.* Grand Rapids: Kregel, 1989.

The Second Great Awakening

Applegate, Debby. *The Most Famous Man in America: The Biography of Henry Ward Beecher.* New York: Doubleday, 2006.
Bebbington, David. *The Dominance of Evangelicalism.* Downers Grove, Ill.: InterVarsity Press, 2005.
Bray, Robert. *Peter Cartwright: Legendary Frontier Preacher.* Urbana: Univ. of Illinois Press, 2005.
Cartwright, Peter. *Autobiography of Peter Cartwright.* Nashville: Abingdon Press, 1956.
Finney, Charles. *The Autobiography of Charles G. Finney.* Minneapolis: Bethany, 1977.
Hambrick-Stowe, Charles. *Charles G. Finney and the Spirit of American Evangelicalism.* Grand Rapids: Eerdmans, 1996.
Marsden, George. *Understanding Fundamentalism and Evangelicalism.* Grand Rapids: Eerdmans, 1991.
McLoughlin, William G., Jr. *Modern Revivalism.* Eugene, Oreg.: Wipf & Stock, 1959.
_____. *Revivals, Awakenings and Reform.* Chicago: Univ. of Chicago Press, 1978.
Noll, Mark. *America's God.* New York: Oxford Univ. Press, 2002.
_____. *The Scandal of the Evangelical Mind.* Grand Rapids: Eerdmans, 1994.
Schmidt, Leigh E. *Holy Fairs: Scottish Communions and American Revivals in the Early Modern Period.* Princeton, N.J.: Princeton Univ. Press, 1989.
Stein, Stephen. *The Shaker Experience in America.* New Haven, Conn.: Yale Univ. Press, 1991.
Wolfe, John. *The Expansion of Evangelicalism.* Downers Grove, Ill.: InterVarsity Press, 2007.

The Reformation

Hillerbrand, Hans. *Oxford Encyclopedia of the Reformation.* 4 vol. Oxford: Oxford Univ. Press, 1996.
McCulloch, Diarmaid. *The Reformation.* New York, Viking, 2003.
Spitz, Lewis. *The Protestant Reformation.* New York: Harper & Row, 1985.

John Calvin

Battles, Ford Lewis. *Interpreting John Calvin.* Grand Rapids: Baker Book House, 1996
Cottret, Bernard J. *Calvin: A Biography.* Grand Rapids: Eerdmans, 2000.
Parker, T.H.L. *John Calvin: A Biography.* Louisville: Westminster John Knox Press, 2007.

Martin Luther

Bainton, Roland. *Here I Stand: A Life of Martin Luther.* New York: Abingdon Press, 1950.
Brecht, Martin. *Martin Luther.* 3 vol. Minneapolis: Fortress Press, 1985; 1990; 1995.

Kittelson, James M. *Luther the Reformer: The Story of the Man and His Career.* Minneapolis: Augsburg, 1986.

The Enlightenment

Berlin, Isaiah. *The Age of Enlightenment.* New York: Mentor Books, 1956.

Damrosch, Leo. *Jean-Jacques Rousseau.* New York: Houghton Mifflin, 2005.

Gay, Peter. *The Enlightenment.* Volumes I & II. New York: W.W. Norton, 1966–1977.

Israel, Jonathan. *Radical Enlightenment.* Oxford: Oxford Univ. Press, 2001.

Lowe, E.J. *Locke.* New York: Routledge, 2005.

May, Henry. *The Enlightenment in America.* New York: Oxford, 1976.

Pearson, Roger. *Voltaire Almighty.* New York: Bloomsbury, 2005.

Hispanic Cultural Context

Bannon, John Francis. *The Spanish Borderlands Frontier 1513–1821.* New York: Holt Rinehart, 1970.

Bolton, Herbert. *Rim of Christendom.* New York: Macmillan, 1936.

Crosby, Harry. *Antigua California.* Univ. of New Mexico Press., Albuquerque. 1994.

Fox, Geoffrey. *Hispanic Nation: Culture, Politics and the Constructing of Identity.* Phoenix: Univ. of Arizona Press, 1997.

González, Juan. *Harvest of Empire: A History of Latinos in America.* New York: Viking, 2000.

Hollon, W. Eugene. *The Southwest Old and New.* Lincoln: Univ. of Nebraska, 1961.

Suárez-Orozco, Marcelo, and Mariela M. Paez. *Latinos: Remaking America.* San Francisco: Univ. of California Press, 2002.

Weber, David. *The Spanish Frontier in North America.* New Haven, Conn.: Yale Univ. Press, 1992.

Asian American Cultural Context

Chan, Sucheng. *Asian Americans: An Interpretive History.* Boston: Twayne Publishers. 1991.

Min, Gap Pyong, ed. *Asian Americans: Contemporary Trends and Issues.* Thousand Oaks, Calif: Pine Forge, 2005.

Zhou, Min. *Contemporary Asian America.* New York: NYU Press, 2007.

Zia, Helen. *Asian American Dreams: The Emergence of an American People.* New York: Farrar, Straus, and Giroux, 2001.

African American Cultural Context

Blackmon, Douglas. *Slavery by Another Name: Re-Enslavement of Black Americans From the Civil War to World War II.* New York: Doubleday, 2008.

Branch, Taylor. *America in the King Years.* Vol. I–III. New York: Simon & Schuster, 1988; 1998; 2006.

Davis, David Brion. *In Human Bondage.* New York: Oxford, 2006.

Elkins, Stanley. *Slavery: A Problem in American Institutional and Intellectual Life.* New York: Grosset & Dunlap, 1963.

Franklin, John Hope. *From Slavery to Freedom: A History of Negro Americans.* New York: Alfred Knopf, 1967.

Litwack, Leon. *How Free Is Free? The Long Death of Jim Crow.* Cambridge, Mass.: Harvard Univ. Press, 2009.

Mayer, Henry. *All on Fire: William Lloyd Garrison and the Abolition of Slavery.* New York: St. Martin's Press, 1998.

Richardson, Joe. *Christian Reconstruction: The American Missionary Association and Southern Blacks 1861-1890.* Birmingham: Univ. of Alabama Press, 2009.

General Sources

Burton, John Hill. *The Autobiography of Dr. Alexander Carlyle of Inveresk: 1722–1805.* Edinburgh, London: W. Blackwood, 1860.

Cash, W. J. *The Mind of the South.* New York: Vintage, 1941.

De Tocqueville, Alexis. *Democracy in America.* 1838; Chicago: Encyclopedia Brittanica, 1990.

Devine, T. M. *The Scottish Nation: 1700–2000.* New York: Viking, 1999.

Dos Passos, John. *The Ground We Stand On.* New York: Harcourt & Brace, 1941.

Eaton, Clement. *The Mind of the South.* Baton Rouge: L.S.U. Press. 1967.

Hofstadter, Richard. *Anti-Intellectualism in American Life.* New York: Vintage, 1962.

Howe, Daniel Walker. *What Hath God Wrought: The Transformation of America 1815–1848.* New York: Oxford, 2007.

Huntington, Samuel. *The Clash of Civilizations & the Remaking of World Order.* New York: Simon and Schuster, 1996.

Jacoby, Susan. *The Age of American Unreason.* New York: Pantheon Books, 2008.

Magnusson, Magnus. *Scotland: The Story of a Nation.* New York: A.N. Press, 2000.

Miller, Perry. *The Life of the Mind in America.* New York: Harcourt-Brace, 1965.

Pessen, Edward. *Jacksonian America.* Homewood, Ill.: Dorsey Press, 1969.

Remini, Robert. *Andrew Jackson and the Course of American Democracy: 1833–1845.* New York: Harper & Row, 1984.

Rudolph, Frederick. *The American College and University.* New York: Knopf, 1962.

Schulman, Bruce. *The Seventies.* New York: Free Press, 2001.

Stiglitz, Joseph. *Globalization and Its Discontents.* New York: Norton, 2002.

_____. *Making Globalization Work.* New York: Norton, 2007.

Taylor, Charles. *A Secular Age.* Cambridge: Harvard, 2007.

Tewksbury, Donald. *The Founding of American Colleges and Universities before the Civil War.* New York: Columbia, 1932.

Wade, Richard. *The Urban Frontier.* Chicago: Univ. of Chicago, 1959.

Ward, John. *Andrew Jackson: Symbol for an Age.* New York: Oxford, 1955.

White Ronald Jr. *A. Lincoln.* New York: Random House, 2009.

Winik, Jay. *The Great Upheaval: America and the Birth of the Modern World, 1788–1800.* New York: Harper-Collins, 2007.

Wood, Gordon. *The Creation of the American Republic.* Chapel Hill: Univ. of North Carolina, 1969.

Zakaria, Fareed. *The Post-American World.* New York: Norton, 2008.

Select Bibliography Christian Church (Disciples of Christ)

Bibliographies of and Indexes to Disciples of Christ Literature

Garrison, Winfred E. "The Literature of the Disciples of Christ," *Bulletin of the Disciples Divinity House.* Chicago. April 1923.

McAllister, Lester, and William Tucker. "A Guide to the Literature of the Christian Church (Disciples of Christ)," in *Journey in Faith.* St. Louis: Bethany Press, 1975.

Monser, John W. *The Literature of the Disciples, a Study.* St. Louis: Christian Publishing Co., 1906.

Pierson, Roscoe M. "The Literature of the Disciples of Christ and Closely Related Groups." *The College of the Bible Quarterly.* Lexington. July 1957.

Short, Howard. "The Literature of the Christian Church," in George Beazley Jr., *The Christian Church (Disciples of Christ): An Interpretative Examination in the Cultural Context.* St. Louis: Bethany Press, 1973.

Smith, Joseph M. *A Guide to Materials related to the United Christian Missionary Society.* Nashville: DCHS, 1987.

Spencer, Claude E. *An Author Catalog of Disciples of Christ and Related Religious Groups.* Canton, Mo.: DCHS, 1946.

_____. *Periodicals of the Disciples of Christ.* Canton, Mo.: DCHS, 1943.

_____. *Theses Concerning Disciples of Christ and Related Religious Groups.* Nashville: DCHS, 1964.

Williams, Marvin D. *Preliminary Guide to Black Materials in the Disciples of Christ Historical Society.* Nashville: DCHS, 1971.

General References

Foster, Douglas, Paul Blowers, Anthony Dunnavant, and D. Newell Williams. *The Encyclopedia of the Stone-Campbell Movement.* Grand Rapids: Eerdmans, 2004.

Survey of Service. St. Louis: Christian Board of Publication, 1928.

Year Book and Directory of the Christian Church (Disciples of Christ). Published annually: 1897 through 2007.

Periodical Literature

Pre-Civil War

Christian Baptist 1823–1830
The Millennial Harbinger 1830–1870
The Christian Messenger 1826–1845
The Evangelist 1832–1844

Post-Civil War

The American Christian Review 1856–1887
The Gospel Advocate 1855– continuing
Christian Standard 1866– continuing
The Christian-Evangelist 1863–1919

Twentieth Century
The Christian/World Call 1919–1973
The Disciple 1974–2002
DisciplesWorld 2002–continuing

Other Useful Periodicals
Christian Century 1884–continuing
College of the Bible Quarterly (Lexington Theological Quarterly) since *1910*
Lard's Quarterly 1863–1868
Encounter since *1955*
Mid-Stream (Call to Unity) since *1961*
Disciples Theological Digest 1986–1994

General Histories of the Disciples of Christ

Cummins, D. Duane. *The Disciples: A Struggle for Reformation.* St. Louis: Chalice Press, 2009.

Garrett, Leroy. *The Stone-Campbell Movement.* Joplin: College Press, 1994.

Garrison, James H. *The Story of a Century.* St. Louis: Christian Publishing Company, 1909.

Garrison, Winfred E. *An American Religious Movement: A Brief History of the Disciples of Christ.* St. Louis: Christian Board of Publication, 1945.

_____. *Religion Follows the Frontier: A History of the Disciples of Christ.* New York: Harper and Bro., 1931.

Garrison, Winfred E., and Alfred DeGroot. *The Disciples of Christ: A History.* St. Louis: Christian Board of Publication, 1948.

Hughes, Richard T. *Reviving the Ancient Faith: The Story of the Churches of Christ in America.* Grand Rapids: Eerdmans, 1996.

Jennings, Walter W. *Origin and Early History of the Disciples of Christ.* Cincinnati: Standard, 1919.

McAllister, Lester G., and William E. Tucker. *Journey in Faith.* St. Louis: Bethany Press, 1975.

Moore, William T. *A Comprehensive History of The Disciples of Christ.* New York: Revell Co., 1909.

Murch, James DeForest. *Christians Only: A History of the Restoration Movement.* Cincinnati: Standard, 1962.

North, James B. *Union in Truth: An Interpretive History of the Restoration Movement.* Cincinnati: Standard, 1994.

Tyler, Benjamin B. *A History of the Disciples of Christ.* New York: Christian Literature Company, 1894.

Webb, Henry E. *In Search of Christian Unity: A History of the Restoration Movement.* Abilene: ACU Press, 2003.

West, Earl I. *The Search for the Ancient Order: A History of the Restoration Movement.* Vol. I. Nashville: Gospel Advocate Co., 1949; Vol. II. Indianapolis: Religious Book Service, 1950.

Sociocultural and Theological Interpretations of Disciples

Abbott, Byrdine A. *The Disciples: An Interpretation.* St. Louis: Christian Board of Publication, 1924.

Beazley, George G. Jr. *The Christian Church (Disciples of Christ): An Interpretative Examination in the Cultural Context.* St. Louis: Bethany Press, 1973.

Blakemore, W. B., general ed. *The Renewal of the Church: Panel of Scholars Reports.* Vol. I, *The Reformation of Tradition*; Vol. II, *The Revival of the Churches*; Vol. III, *The Reconstruction of Theology.* St. Louis: Bethany Press, 1963.

Boring, M. Eugene. *Disciples and the Bible: A History of Disciples Biblical Interpretation in North America.* St. Louis: Chalice Press, 1997.

Casey, Michael W., and Douglas A. Foster. *The Stone-Campbell Movement.* Knoxville: Univ. of Tennessee, 2002.

Crain, James A. *The Development of Social Ideas Among the Disciples of Christ.* St. Louis: Bethany Press, 1969.

DeGroot, Alfred T. *The Restoration Principle.* St. Louis: Bethany Press, 1960.

Dunnavant, Anthony L., and Richard L. Harrison Jr. *Explorations in the Stone-Campbell Traditions.* Nashville: DCHS, 1995.

England, Stephen J. *We Disciples: A Brief View of History and Doctrine.* St. Louis: Christian Board of Publication, 1946.

Fife, Robert O. *Celebration of Heritage.* Joplin: College Press, 1992.

Garrison, James H. *The Reformation of the Nineteenth Century.* St. Louis: Christian Publishing Co., 1901.

Harrell, David E. Jr. *Quest for a Christian America: The Disciples of Christ and American Society to 1866.* Nashville: DCHS, 1966.

_____. *The Social Sources of Division in the Disciples of Christ: A Social History of the Disciples of Christ.* Atlanta: Publishing Systems, 1973.

Heltzel, Peter. *Chalice Introduction to Disciples Theology.* St. Louis: Chalice Press, 2008.

Jorgenson, Dale A. *Theological and Aesthetic Roots in the Stone-Campbell Movement.* Kirksville, Mo.: Thomas Jefferson University, 1989.

Lair, Loren E. *The Christian Church (Disciples of Christ) and Its Future.* St. Louis: Bethany Press, 1971.

Lawrence, Kenneth. *Classic Themes of Disciples Theology.* Fort Worth: TCU Press, 1986.

Milligan, Robert. *An Exposition and Defense of the Scheme of Redemption as It Is Taught in the Holy Scriptures.* Cincinnati: R. W. Carroll, 1869.

Osborn, Ronald E. *Experiment in Liberty: The Ideal of Freedom in the Experience of the Disciples of Christ.* St. Louis: Bethany Press, 1978.

_____. *The Faith We Affirm: Basic Beliefs of Disciples of Christ.* St. Louis: Bethany Press, 1979.

Richardson, Robert. *The Principles and Objects of the Religious Reformation urged by A. Campbell and Others, Briefly Stated and Explained.* Bethany, Va.: A. Campbell, 1853.

Richesin, L. Dale, and Larry D. Bouchard. *Interpreting Disciples: Practical Theology in the Disciples of Christ.* Fort Worth: TCU Press, 1987.

Short, Howard E. *Doctrine and Thought of the Disciples of Christ.* St. Louis: Christian Board of Publication, 1951.

Toulouse, Mark G. *Joined in Discipleship: The Shaping of Contemporary Disciples Identity.* St. Louis: Chalice Press, 1997.

Tristano, Richard M. *The Origins of the Restoration Movement: An Intellectual History.* Atlanta: Glenmary Research Center, 1988.

Whitley, Oliver Read. *Trumpet Call of Reformation.* St. Louis: Bethany Press, 1959.

Williams, D. Newell, ed. *A Case Study of Mainstream Protestantism: The Disciples' Relation to American Culture 1880–1989.* Grand Rapids: Eerdmans, 1991.

Regional Histories of the Disciples of Christ

Badger, Bryant D. *History of the Christian Church (Disciples of Christ) in Wyoming.* Casper: Mountain States Lithographing, 1996.

Burlingam, Merrill G., and Harvey C. Hartling. *Big Sky Disciples: A History of the Christian Church (Disciples of Christ) in Montana.* Great Falls, Mont.: Christian Church (Disciples of Christ) in Montana, 1984.

Butchart, Reuben. *The Disciples of Christ in Canada since 1830.* Toronto: Canadian Headquarters, 1949.

Cauble, Commodore W. *Disciples of Christ in Indiana: Achievements of a Century.* Indianapolis: Meigs Publishing, 1930.

Cole, Clifford A. *The Christian Churches (Disciples of Christ) of Southern California.* St. Louis: Christian Board of Publication, 1959.

Cramblet, Wilbur H. *The Christian Church (Disciples of Christ) in West Virginia.* St. Louis: Bethany Press, 1971.

Darst, H. Jackson. *Ante-Bellum Virginia Disciples.* Richmond: VCMS, 1959.

England, Stephen J. *Oklahoma Christians.* St. Louis: Bethany Press, 1975.

Fortune, Alonzo W. *The Disciples in Kentucky.* Louisville: Convention of Christian Churches in Kentucky, 1932.

Hall, Colby D. *Texas Disciples.* Fort Worth: TCU Press, 1953.

Hamlin, Griffith A. *Remember, Renew, Rejoice: 150 years of Disciples In Mid-America 1837–1987.* Fulton, Mo.: Ovid Bell Press, 1986.

Harmon, Marion F. *A History of the Christian Churches (Disciples of Christ) in Mississippi.* Aberdeen, Miss., 1929.

Harrison, Richard L. *From Camp Meeting to Church: A History of the Christian Church (Disciples of Christ) in Kentucky.* St. Louis: Christian Board of Publication, 1992.

Hayden, A. S. *Early History of the Disciples in the Western Reserve, Ohio.* Cincinnati: Chase and Hall Publishers, 1875.

Haynes, Nathaniel S. *History of the Disciples of Christ in Illinois 1819–1914.* Cincinnati: Standard Publishing Co., 1915.

Lair, Loren E. *From Restoration to Reformation: Development of the Christian Church in Iowa.* Iowa, 1970.

Marvel, P. O. *A Century of Cooperation in Nebraska.* 1963.

McAllister, Lester G. *Arkansas Disciples.* Christian Church (Disciples of Christ), 1984.

Moseley, J. Edward. *Disciples of Christ in Georgia.* St. Louis: Bethany Press, 1954.

Norton, Herman A. *Tennessee Christians: A History of the Christian Church (Disciples of Christ) in Tennessee.* Nashville: Reed & Co., 1971.

Peters, George L. *The Disciples of Christ in Missouri.* Centennial Commission. 1937.

Peterson, Orval D. *Washington-Northern Idaho Disciples.* St. Louis: Bethany Press, 1945.

Shaw, Henry K. *Buckeye Disciples: A History of the Disciples of Christ in Ohio.* St. Louis: Christian Board of Publication, 1952.

_____. *Hoosier Disciples: A Comprehensive History of the Christian Churches (Disciples of Christ) in Indiana.* St. Louis: Bethany Press, 1966.

Stanger, Allen B. *The Virginia Christian Missionary Society: One Hundred Years 1875–1975.* Richmond: Christian Church in Virginia, 975.

Swander, C. F. *Making Disciples in Oregon.* OCMC, 1928.

Updegraff, John C. *The Christian Church (Disciples of Christ) in Florida.* Winter Park: Anna Publishing, 1981.

Ware, Charles C. *North Carolina Disciples of Christ.* St. Louis: Christian Board of Publication, 1927.

_____. *South Carolina Disciples of Christ.* Charleston: Christian Churches of South Carolina, 1967.

Watson, George H. & Mildred B. *History of the Christian Churches in the Alabama Area.* St. Louis: Bethany Press, 1965.

Eighteenth Century

Burnett, John F. *Rev. James O'Kelly: A Champion of Religious Liberty.* Dayton: Christian Publishing, 1921.

Haggard, Rice. *An Address to the Different Religious Societies on the Sacred Import of the Christian Name.* Lexington: Charles Printers, 1804.

Hall, Colby. *Rice Haggard: The American Frontier Evangelist Who Revived the Name Christian.* Fort Worth: Stafford-Lowdon, 1957.

Jones, Abner. *Memoirs of the Life and Experiences, Travels and Preaching of Abner Jones.* Exeter: Norris & Sawyer, 1807; 1842.

Kenny, Michael. *The Perfect Law of Liberty: Elias Smith and the Providential History of America.* Washington, D.C.: Smithsonian, 1994.

Kilgore, Charles F. *The James O'Kelly Schism in the Methodist Episcopal Church.* Mexico City: Casa Unida De Publicaciones, 1963.

MacClenny Wilbur E. *The Life of Rev. James O'Kelly and the Early History of the Christian Church in the South.* Raleigh: Edwards & Broughton, 1910.

Smith, Elias. *The Life, Conversion, Preaching, Travel, and Sufferings of Elias Smith.* Portsmouth: Beck and Foster, 1816.

Barton Warren Stone

Conkin, Paul K. *Cane Ridge: America's Pentecost.* Madison: Univ. of Wisconsin, 1990.

Dunnavant, Anthony L. *Cane Ridge in Context: Perspectives on Barton W. Stone and the Revival.* Nashville: DCHS, 1992.

Schmidt, Leigh E. *Holy Fairs: Scottish Communions and American Revivals in the Early Modern Period.* Princeton, N.J.: Princeton University Press, 1989.

Stone, Barton W. *The Biography of Eld. Barton Warren Stone with Additions and Reflections by Eld. John Rogers.* Cincinnati: James Publishers, 1847. (reprinted in *The Cane Ridge Reader,* edited by Hoke S. Dickinson, 1972.)

_____. *The Christian Messenger,* Vol. I, 1826, through Vol. XIV, 1844.

Thompson, Rhodes. *Voices from Cane Ridge.* St. Louis: Bethany Press, 1954.

Ware, Charles C. *Barton Warren Stone: Pathfinder of Christian Union.* St. Louis: Bethany Press, 1932.

West, William G. *Barton Warren Stone: Early American Advocate of Christian Unity.* Nashville: DCHS, 1954.

Williams, D. Newell. *Barton Stone: A Spiritual Biography.* St. Louis: Chalice Press, 2000.

_____. "Barton Warren Stone," in *Encyclopedia of the Stone-Campbell Movement.* 2004.

Thomas Campbell

Campbell, Alexander. *Memoirs of Elder Thomas Campbell, Together with a Brief Memoir of Mrs. Jane Campbell.* Cincinnati: Bosworth, 1861.

Hanna, William. *Thomas Campbell: Seceder and Christian Union Advocate.* Cincinnati: Standard, 1935.

McAllister, Lester. *Thomas Campbell: Man of the Book.* St. Louis: Bethany Press, 1954.

Miller, George. *Campbell Family Genealogy.* Family Group Records. Bethany, Va.: Historic Bethany, 1996.

[Declaration and Address]

Campbell, Thomas. *The Declaration and Address of the Christian Association of Washington.* 1809. (Housed in the Campbell Archives, Bethany College: Original copy with Campbell's notes in the margins.)

Johnson, H. E. *The Declaration and Address for Today.* Nashville: Reed & Co., 1971.

Kershner, Frederick. *The Christian Union Overture.* St. Louis: Bethany Press, 1923.

_____. *Declaration and Address.* St. Louis: Bethany Press, 1971.

Olbricht, Thomas H., and Hans Rollmann. *The Quest for Christian Unity, Peace, and Purity in Thomas Campbell's Declaration and Address.* Lanham, Md.: Scarecrow Press, 2000.

Alexander Campbell

Athearn, Clarence. *The Religious Education of Alexander Campbell: Morning Star of the Coming Reformation.* St. Louis: Christian Board of Publication, 1928.

Campbell, Selina. *Home Life & Reminiscences of Alexander Campbell.* St. Louis: John Burns Publisher, 1882.

Cochran, Louis. *Fool of God.* New York: Duell, Sloan & Pearce, 1958.

Cochran, Louis, and Leroy Garrett. *Alexander Campbell: The Man and his Mission.* Dallas: Wilkinson Publishers, 1965.

Fitch, Alger. *Alexander Campbell: Preacher of Reform, Reformer of Preaching.* Austin: Sweet Publishing, 1970.

Garrett, Leroy. "Alexander Campbell," in *Encyclopedia of the Stone-Campbell Movement.* 2004.

Garrison, Winfred E. *Alexander Campbell's Theology: Its Sources & Historical Setting.* St. Louis: Christian Publishing Co., 1900.

Grafton, Thomas W. *Alexander Campbell: Leader of the Great Reformation of the Nineteenth Century.* St. Louis: Christian Publishing Co., 1897.

Gresham, Perry E. *The Sage of Bethany: Pioneer in Broadcloth.* St. Louis: Bethany Press, 1960.

Humbert, Royal. *Compend of Alexander Campbell's Theology.* St. Louis: Bethany Press, 1961.

Kellems, Jesse. *Alexander Campbell and the Disciples.* New York: R. R. Smith, 1930.

Lindley, D. Ray. *Apostle of Freedom.* St. Louis: Bethany Press, 1957.

Long, Loretta. *The Life of Selina Campbell.* Tuscaloosa: Univ. of Alabama, 2001.
Lunger, Harold. *Political Ethics of Alexander Campbell.* St. Louis: Bethany Press, 1954.
Maxey, Robert T. *Alexander Campbell and The Peculiar Institution.* El Paso: Spanish American Evangelism, 1986.
Richardson, Robert. *Memoirs of Alexander Campbell.* 2 vols. Philadelphia: Lippincott, 1868; 1870.
Seale, James. *Lectures in Honor of Alexander Campbell.* Nashville: DCHS, 1988.
Thomas, Cecil K. *Alexander Campbell and His New Version.* St. Louis: Bethany Press, 1958.
Walker, Granville. *Preaching in the Thought of Alexander Campbell.* St. Louis: Bethany Press, 1954.
Wrather, Eva Jean. *Alexander Campbell: Adventurer in Freedom.* Vol. I. Fort Worth: TCU Press, 2004.
_____. *Alexander Campbell: Adventurer in Freedom.* Vol. II. Fort Worth: TCU Press, 2007.
_____. *Alexander Campbell: Adventurer in Freedom.* Vol. III. Fort Worth: TCU Press, 2009.
_____. *Alexander Campbell and His Relevance for Today.* Nashville: DCHS, 1953.
_____. *Creative Freedom in Action: Alexander Campbell on The Structure of the Church.* St. Louis: Bethany Press, 1968.

Publications by Alexander Campbell

Campbell, Alexander. *Christian Baptism with Its Antecedents and Consequences.* Cincinnati: Standard, 1851.
_____. *Christian Baptist.* Volumes 1 through 7. 1823–1830.
_____. *The Christian System.* Pittsburgh: Forrester & Campbell, 1839.
_____. *A Debate on Christian Baptism: N. L. Rice.* Lexington: Skillman & Son, 1844.
_____. *A Debate on Christian Baptism: W. L. Maccalla.* Buffaloe: Campbell & Salla, 1824.
_____. *Debate on the Evidences of Christianity: Robert Owen.* Buffaloe: Campbell Printer, 1829.
_____. *Debate on Roman Catholic Religion: J. Purcell.* Cincinnati: J. A. James & Co., 1837.
_____. *Living Oracles.* Buffaloe: Campbell Printer, 1826.
_____. *Memoirs of Elder Thomas Campbell together with a brief memoir of Mrs. Jane Campbell.* Cincinnati: Bosworth, 1861.
_____. *The Millennial Harbinger.* Volumes 1 through 36. 1830–1866.
_____. *Popular Lectures and Addresses.* Cincinnati: Standard, 1863.

Walter Scott

Baxter, William. *The Life of Walter Scott.* Bosworth, Cincinnati: Chase & Hall, 1874.
Gerrard, William A. III. *A Biographical Study of Walter Scott: American Frontier Evangelist.* Joplin: College Press, 1992.

Scott, Walter. *The Evangelist.* Periodical published 1833 to 1842.
_____.*The Gospel Restored.* Cincinnati: Donogh, 1836.
Stevenson, Dwight E. *Walter Scott: Voice of the Golden Oracle.* St. Louis: Christian Board of Publication, 1946.
Toulouse, Mark. *Walter Scott: A Nineteenth-Century Evangelical.* St. Louis: Chalice Press, 1999.
_____."Walter Scott," in *Encyclopedia of the Stone-Campbell Movement.* 2004.

Other Biographies of Nineteenth-Century Leaders

Baxter, William. *Life of Knowles Shaw, The Singing Evangelist.* Cincinnati: Central Book Concern, 1879.
Cochran, Louis. *Raccoon John Smith.* St. Louis: Bethany Press, 1963.
Goodnight, Cloyd, and Dwight Stevenson. *Home to Bethphage: A Biography of Robert Richardson.* St. Louis: Christian Board of Publication, 1949.
Grafton, Thomas W. *Men of Yesterday: A Series of Character Sketches of Prominent Men Among the Disciples of Christ.* St. Louis: Christian Publishing Co., 1899.
Haley, J. J. *Makers and Molders of the Reformation Movement: A Study of Leading Men among the Disciples of Christ.* St. Louis: Christian Board of Publication, 1914.
Keith, Noel L. *The Story of D.S. Burnet: Undeserved Obscurity.* St. Louis: Bethany Press, 1954.
Lamar, James S. *Memoirs of Isaac Errett.* 2 vols. Cincinnati: Standard, 1893.
Morro, William C. *Brother McGarvey: The Life of President J. W. McGarvey of the College of the Bible.* St. Louis: Bethany Press, 1940.
Power, Frederick D. *Life of William Kimbrough Pendleton, President of Bethany College.* St. Louis: Christian Publishing Co., 1902.
_____.*Sketches of Our Pioneers.* St. Louis: Christian Publishing Company, 1898.
Rogers, John. *Biography of Elder J. T. Johnson.* Cincinnati: Standard, 1861.
Rogers, John I. *An Autobiography of Elder Samuel Rogers.* Cincinnati: Standard, 1880.
Shackelford, John Jr. *Life, Letters and Addresses of Dr. Lewis L. Pinkerton.* Cincinnati: Chase and Hall, 1871.
Tucker, William E. *J. H. Garrison and Disciples of Christ.* St. Louis: Bethany Press, 1964.
West, Earl L. *The Life and Times of David Lipscomb.* Henderson: Religious Book Service, 1954.
Wilburn, James R. *The Hazard of the Die: Tolbert Fanning and the Restoration Movement.* Austin: Sweet Publishing, 1969.
Williams, John A. *Life of Elder John Smith with Some Account of the Rise and Progress of the Current Reformation.* Cincinnati: Carroll & Co., 1870.

Missionary Work of the Disciples of Christ

Burnham, Frederick W. *Unification; The How, What and Why of The United Christian Missionary Society.* St. Louis: UCMS, 1927.
Castleman, William J. *On This Foundation: A Biography of Samuel Guy Inman.* St. Louis: Bethany Press, 1966.

Corey, Stephen J. *Re-Thinking Missions: A Laymen's Inquiry After One Hundred Years.* New York: Harpers, 1932.

Craddock, Fran, Nancy Heimer, and Martha Faw. *In the Fullness of Time: A History of the Women in the Christian Church (Disciples of Christ).* St. Louis: Chalice Press, 1999.

Dye, Eva. *Bolenge: A Story of Gospel Triumphs on the Congo.* Cincinnati: FCMS, 1910.

Fiers, Dale. *This Is Missions: Our Christian Witness.* St. Louis: Bethany Press, 1954.

Harrison, Ida. *Forty Years of Service: A History of the Christian Woman's Board of Missions 1874–1914.* 1920.

Lewis, Grant K. *American Christian Missionary Society and the Disciples of Christ.* St. Louis: Christian Board of Publication, 1937.

Lollis, Lorraine. *The Shape of Adam's Rib: A Lively History of Women's Work in the Christian Church.* St. Louis: Bethany Press, 1970.

Maeda, Itoko. *Jessie Trout.*

McLean, Archibald. *A Circuit of the Globe.* St. Louis: Christian Publishing Co. 1897.

_____.*The Foreign Christian Missionary Society.* New York: Revell & Co., 1919.

_____. *Missionary Addresses.* 1895.

Moses, Jasper T. *Helen E. Moses of the Christian Woman's Board of Missions.* New York: Revell, 1909.

Shelton, Flora. *Shelton of Tibet.* New York: Geo. Doran Co., 1923.

Warren, William R. *The Life and Labors of Archibald McLean.* St. Louis: Bethany Press, 1923.

Wissing, Douglas. *Pioneer in Tibet: The Life and Perils of Dr. Albert Shelton.* New York: Macmillan, 2004.

Christian Unity

Ainslie, Peter III. *If Not a United Church—What?* New York: Revell Co., 1920.

_____. *The Message of the Disciples for the Union of the Church.* New York: Revell Co., 1913.

Baptism, Eucharist and Ministry: Faith and Order Paper, No. 111. Geneva: World Council of Churches, 1982.

Best, Thomas F., and Theodore J. Nottingham. *The Vision of Christian Unity: Essays in Honor of Paul A Crow Jr.* Indianapolis: Oikoumene Publications, 1997.

Blakemore, W. B. *The Challenge of Christian Unity.* St. Louis: Bethany Press, 1963.

Churches in Covenant Communion: The Church of Christ Uniting. New Orleans: COCU, 1989.

Crow, Paul Jr. "The Christian Church (Disciples of Christ) in the Ecumenical Movement," in George Beazley Jr., *The Christian Church (Disciples of Christ): An Interpretive Examination in the Cultural Context.* St. Louis: Bethany Press, 1973.

_____.*Christian Unity: Matrix for Mission.* New York: Friendship Press, 1982.

Garrison, Winfred E. *Christian Unity and Disciples of Christ.* St. Louis: Bethany Press, 1955.

_____.*The Quest and Character of a United Church.* New York: Abingdon Press, 1957.

Idleman, Finis S. *Peter Ainslie: Ambassador of Good Will.* New York: Willett, Clark and Co., 1941.

Kinnamon, Michael. "A Special Calling: Christian Unity and the Disciples of Christ," in L. Dale Richesin and Larry D. Bouchard, *Interpreting Disciples: Practical Theology in the Disciples of Christ.* Fort Worth: TCU Press, 1987.

_____. *The Vision of the Ecumenical Movement and How It Has Been Impoverished by Its Friends.* St. Louis: Chalice Press, 2003.

Kinnamon, Michael, and Brian E. Cope. *The Ecumenical Movement: An Anthology of Key Texts and Voices.* Grand Rapids: Eerdmans, 1997.

Morrison, Charles C. *The Unfinished Reformation.* Harper & Bro., New York. 1953.

Short, Howard E. *Christian Unity Is Our Business: Disciples of Christ Within the Ecumenical Fellowship.* St. Louis: Bethany Press, 1953.

Higher Education

Adams, Harold. *The History of Eureka College: 1855–1982.* Henry, Ill.: M.D. Printing, 1982.

Cummins, D. Duane. *The Disciples Colleges: A History.* St. Louis: Chalice Press, 1987.

____. "Educational Philosophy of Alexander Campbell." *Discipliana,* Vol. 59, No. 1, Spring 1999: 5–16. Nashville: DCHS.

____. "The First Decade of DHE." *Disciples Theological Digest,* Vol. 9, No. 1., 1994: 35–51. St. Louis: DHE.

____. "Higher Education in the Movement." In *Encyclopedia of the Stone-Campbell Movement,* 390–94. Grand Rapids: Eerdmans, 2004.

Cummins, Dickerson,Howland, Nolen, Spainhower, Chisholm. Higher Education Evaluation Task Force Report. Indianapolis: CC-DOC, 1976.

England, George. *In a Tall Shadow* (Biography of Stephen J. England). Privately published. 1990.

Giovannoli, Harry. *Kentucky Female Orphan School.* Midway, Ky.: Self-published, 1930.

Gresham, Perry E. *Campbell and the Colleges.* Nashville: DCHS, 1973.

Hale, Allean L. *Petticoat Pioneer: The Christian College Story 1851–1951.* Columbia: Artcraft Press, 1956.

Hall, Colby D. *History of Texas Christian University.* Fort Worth: TCU Press, 1947.

Hamlin, Griffith A. *In Faith and History: The Story of William Woods College.* St. Louis: Bethany Press, 1965.

Lee, George R. *Culver-Stockton College: The First 130 Years.* Canton: Culver-Stockton, 1984.

MacLean, William J. *Barton College: Our Century.* Wilson, N.C.: Barton College, 2002.

Marshall, Frank H. *Phillips University's First Fifty Years.* Vol I., 1957; Vol. II, 1960; Vol. III, 1967. Enid, Okla.: Phillips Univ. Press.

McAllister, Lester G. *Bethany: The first 150 Years.* Bethany: Bethany College Press, 1991.

McCormick, Thomas R. *Campus Ministry in the Coming Age.* St. Louis: CBP Press, 1987.

Myers, Oma Lou. *This One Thing I Do: A Biography of Frank Hamilton Marshall, Pioneer Christian Educator.* Portland: Binfords and Mort Publishers, 1942.

Osborn, Ronald E. *Ely Vaughn Zollars: Teacher of Preachers, Builder of Colleges.* St. Louis: Christian Board of Publication, 1947.

Reeves, Floyd, and John Russell. *College Organization and Administration.* Indianapolis: Disciples Board of Higher Education, 1929.

Short, Howard. "A Centennial History of the Division of Higher Education." *Disciples Theological Digest.* 1994, Vol. 9, No. 1.

Ware, Charles C. *A History of Atlantic Christian College.* St. Louis: Bethany Press, 1956.

Wright, John D. *Transylvania: Tutor to the West.* Lexington: Transylvania , 1975.

African American Disciples

Blair, James L. "Preston Taylor: A Doer of the Word," in *The Untold Story: A Short History of Black Disciples.* St. Louis: Christian Board of Publication, 1976.

Cardwell, Brenda, and William K. Fox Jr. *Journey Toward Wholeness: A History of Black Disciples of Christ in the Mission of The Christian Church: Vol. I, From Convention to Convocation.* Indianapolis: National Convocation, 1990.

Fox, William K. Jr. *Effective Discipleship for Blacks in the Christian Church (Disciples of Christ).* Indianapolis: Central Publishing, 1982.

Fuller, Bertha. *Sarah Lue Bostick, Minister and Missionary.* Little Rock: Private Printing, 1949.

Jordan, Robert L. *Two Races in One Fellowship.* Detroit: United Christian Church, 1944.

Liverett, Alice. *Biographical Sketches of Leaders of Negro Work of The Disciples of Christ.* 1936.

Lyda, Hap. "Black Disciples in the Nineteenth Century," in *The Untold Story: A Short History of Black Disciples.* St. Louis: Christian Board of Publication, 1976.

_____.*A History of Black Christian Churches (Disciples of Christ) In the United States through 1899.* Ann Arbor, Mich.: University Microfilms, 1973.

Myers, Oma Lou. *Rosa's Song: The Life and Ministry of Rosa Page Welch.* St. Louis: CBP Press, 1984.

Smith, Clayton C. *The Life and Work of Jacob Kenoly.* Cincinnati: Methodist Book Concern, 1912.

Widner, Gregory. "The Interethnic Black Preaching Style of Cynthia Hale." PhD. Dissertation, Univ. of Ky. 1998.

Hispanic Disciples of Christ

De La Torre, Miguel A. *Handbook of Latina/o Theologies.* St. Louis: Chalice Press, 2006.

Hall, Colby. *Texas Disciples.* Fort Worth: TCU Press, 1953.

Jiménez, Pablo. "Hispanics in the Movement" in *Encyclopedia of the Stone Campbell Movement.* Grand Rapids: Eerdmans, 2004.

____.*Somos Uno.* St. Louis: Chalice Press, 2005.

Machado, Daisy L. *Of Borders and Margins.* New York: Oxford, 2003.

Rodriguez, Domingo F. *Vivencias y Memorias de un Pastor.* 1999; 2005.

Spice, Byron. *Discipulos Americanos: Sixty-five Years of Christian Churches Ministry to Spanish-Speaking Persons.* Indianapolis: UCMS, 1964.

Vargas, David. *Somos Uno. Trasfondo Historico de la Confraternidad Hispana y Bilingüe.* n.d.

Asian American Disciples of Christ

Casey-Allen, Janet. "Disciples of Asian Origin Vie for Their Place," *The Disciple.* May 1994.

Cole, Clifford. *The Christian Churches of Southern California.* St. Louis: CBP, 1959.

Lee, Timothy. "NAPAD History," *NAPAD Newsletter.* Winter 1998–99.

Yu, Geunhee. "Asian American Disciples." in *Encyclopedia of the Stone Campbell Movement.* Grand Rapids: Eerdmans, 2004.

The Twentieth Century and Restructure

Ames, Van Meter. *Beyond Theology: The Autobiography of Edward Scribner Ames.* Chicago: Univ. of Chicago, 1959.

Beazley, George G. Jr. *The Christian Church (Disciples of Christ): An Interpretative Examination in the Cultural Context.* St. Louis: Bethany Press, 1973.

Blakemore, W.B. *The Panel of Scholars Reports.* 3 vols. St. Louis: Bethany Press, 1963.

Corey, Stephen J. *Fifty Years of Attack and Controversy.* St. Louis: Christian Board of Publication, 1953.

Cummins, D. Duane. *Dale Fiers: Twentieth Century Disciple.* Fort Worth: TCU Press, 2003.

_____.*A Handbook for Today's Disciples.* St. Louis: CBP Press, 1981; 2d ed. Chalice Press, 1991; 3d. ed. Chalice Press, 2003.

_____.*Kenneth L. Teegarden: The Man, The Church, The Time.* Fort Worth: TCU Press, 2007.

DeGroot, Alfred T. *Church of Christ Number Two.* Privately Published. 1956.

Design, The, with 2005 revisions, available on www.disciples.org.

Dunnavant, Anthony L. *Restructure.* New York: Lang Publishers, 1993.

Friedly, Robert L., and D. Duane Cummins. *The Search for Identity: Disciples of Christ–the Restructure Years.* St. Louis: CBP Press, 1987.

Hamm, Richard. *2020 Vision for the Christian Church (Disciples of Christ).* St. Louis: Chalice Press, 2001.

Kinnamon, Michael. *Disciples of Christ in the 21st Century.* St. Louis: CBP Press, 1988.

Murrell, Arthur V. *The Effects of Exclusivism in the Separation of the Churches of Christ from the Christian Church.* Ann Arbor, Mich.: Univ. Microfilms, 1972.

Osborn, Edwin G. *Christian Worship: A Service Book.* St. Louis: Christian Board of Publication, 1953.

Osborn, Ronald E. *Toward the Christian Church.* St. Louis: Christian Board of Publication, 1964.

Paulsell, William O. "The Disciples of Christ and the Great Depression." Unpublished Ph.D. dissertation, Vanderbilt University. 1965.

Shelton, Orman L. *The Church Functioning Effectively.* St. Louis: Christian Board of Publication, 1946.

Teegarden, Kenneth L. *Seeking God's Peace in a Nuclear Age: A Call to Disciples of Christ.* St. Louis: CBP Press, 1985.

Toulouse, Mark G. *Joined in Discipleship: The Shaping of Contemporary Disciples Identity.* St. Louis: Chalice Press, 1997.

Williams, D. Newell, ed. *A Case Study of Mainstream Protestantism: The Disciples' Relation to American Culture 1880–1989.* Grand Rapids: Eerdmans, 1991.

Williams, Newell. *Ministry Among Disciples: Past, Present and Future.* Indianapolis: Council of Christian Unity, 1985.

Repository Summary of Primary Source Materials

Researched for This Writing

(Detailed bibliographical citations on extensive primary source materials referenced for the writing of this volume, including thirty-eight interviews, unpublished sources, and correspondence, are fully noted in the multi-page bibliographies of *Dale Fiers: Twentieth Century Disciple* and *Kenneth L. Teegarden: The Man, The Church, The Time,* both authored by the author and therefore repeated here only in summary. Primary sources are also detailed in the footnotes.)

Disciples of Christ Historical Society

United Christian Missionary Society papers   Boxes and Files
(See Joseph Smith Guide to UCMS Materials)
Fiers, Dale; General Minister and President papers   Folders 1-12
Restructure, File Boxes 1-2
Teegarden, Kenneth; General Minister & President papers, File Boxes 1-7

Wanda Teegarden

Teegarden personal files in Fort Worth residence   Cabinets 1-5

John O. Humbert

Humbert papers and autobiography in possession of John O. Humbert

Disciples Headquarters Indianapolis

Fiers correspondence and photograph folders
Teegarden correspondence and photograph folders
Humbert correspondence and photograph folders

Bethany College Library

Campbell Archives
Bethany Archives

Index

Berlin, Isaiah (1909–1997), 4, 5, 85
Bethany College, 106, 107, 113,
121, 169, 196
Bible chair movement, 157
Bill of Rights, 15
Bingham, Walter D. (1921–2006),
192, 245
bishop, 102
Blakemore, W. Barnett
(1911–1975), 171
Board of Church Extension, 159,
161–63
Board of Higher Education, 107,
164
Boggess, E. F. (1869–1931), 159
Bolenge, Belgian Congo, 158
Boring, M. Eugene (b.1937),
196–98
Bostick, Mancil M. (1864–1928),
190
Bostick, Sarah Lue (1868–1948),
190
Brown, John (1761–1835), 55, 57
Bruce, Archibald (d.1816), 40
Brush Run Church, ix, 53–59, 186
Brutus, 42
Bucer, Martin (1491–1551), 11
Buckner, George Walker Jr.
(1893–1981), 170
Buckner, Samuel (1820–1904), 189
Buffalo Seminary, 100
Burnet, David Staats (1808–1867),
96
Burnham, Frederick D.
(1891–1960), 161, 177
Burns, Robert W. (1904–1991), 214
Butler, Ovid (1801–1881), 190
Butler University, 107, 113, 255,
262, 269

C

Caldwell, David (1725–1821), 10, 25
Calixtus, George (1586–1656), 11
Calvin, John (1509–1564);

Calvinism,   2, 11, 14, 17, 167
Campbell, Alexander (1788–1866),
ix, x, xii, xiii, 2,3,4, 13, 19,
22, 23, 37, 48, 83, 104, 108,
109, 118, 156, 187; baptism, 55;
Campbell & Stone compared,
67–70; church organization,
92–98; early education, 49–50;
educational philosophy, 105;
genealogy & childhood, 38–39;
Glasgow education, 51–52;
joining with Stone's Christians,
74–78, 80–81; leadership of
Movement, 56; marriages, 55,
70; ordination, 55; shipwreck,
51; slavery, 187–89
Campbell, Archibald (1719–1807),
38–39
Campbell, Jane [Corneigle],
(1763–1835), 40–41, 50
Campbell, Joan Brown, 171
Campbell, Margaret [Brown]
(1791–1827), 55, 57, 70
Campbell, Selina [Bakewell]
(1802–1897), 70–71, 156
Campbell-Maccalla debate, 58–59
Campbell-Owen debate, 71–72
Campbell-Purcell debate, 59
Campbell-Rice debate, 59
Campbell-Walker debate, 57–58
Campbell's New Translation,
Living Oracles, 70
Campbell, Thomas (1680–1787),
38–39
Campbell, Thomas (1763–1854),
x, 2,3, 13, 14, 48, 50, 51, 53, 54,
101, 104, 108, 118, 187; Ahorey
ministry, 41–42; children, 41;
Declaration and Address, 44–48;
education, 40; genealogy &
childhood, 38–39; marriage,
40–41; Washington Association
ministry, 43–48
Canada, 165–67

Other Disciples Books from
D. Duane Cummins

Kenneth L. Teegarden: The Man, The Church, The Time. Fort Worth: TCU press, 2007.
A. Dale Fiers: A Biography. Forth Worth: TCU Press, 2002.
A Handbook for Today's Disciples in the Christian Church (Disciples of Christ), third edition.
    St. Louis: Chalice Press, 2003.
Un Manual para los Discípulos de Hoy en la Iglesia Cristiana (Discípulos de Cristo), revised
    edition. St. Louis: Chalice Press, 1995.
The Disciples Colleges: A History. St. Louis: Christian Board of Publication, 1987.

Edited by D. Duane Cummins

Alexander Campbell: Adventurer in Freedom, A Literary Biography. Three volumes written
    by Eva Jean Wrather. Fort Worth: TCU Press, 2005–2009.